Additional Praise for *H..... .....* *of Mattl....*

"Wilson brings an impressive battery of methodological approaches to bear on the Matthean miracle stories, especially those collected in chapters 8 and 9. His exegesis of these chapters is perceptive and ever sensitive to Matthew's narrative techniques. Not least, this book represents a valuable contribution both to the discussion of *why* Matthew arranged the miracle stories in these two chapters as he did and to our understanding of the Evangelist's use of miracle stories."

Eric Eve, Harris Manchester College

"Historical, literary, and archaeological concerns dominate Wilson's close and careful reading of Matthew 8–9 and the healings encountered therein. Clearly written, this will be important reading for those working on Matthew's Gospel in general and ancient views on disability, disease and healing in particular."

Louise Lawrence, University of Exeter

Healing in the Gospel of Matthew

Healing in the Gospel of Matthew

Reflections on Method and Ministry

Walter T. Wilson

Fortress Press
Minneapolis

HEALING IN THE GOSPEL OF MATTHEW

Reflections on Method and Ministry

Cover design: Alisha Lofgren

Cover image: Gianni Dagli Orti / The Art Archive at Art Resource, NY

Library of Congress Cataloging-in-Publication Data is available

Print ISBN: 978-1-4514-7037-6

eBook ISBN: 978-1-4514-8977-4

The paper used in this publication meets the minimum requirements of American National Standard for Information Sciences — Permanence of Paper for Printed Library Materials, ANSI Z329.48-1984.

Manufactured in the U.S.A.

This book was produced using PressBooks.com, and PDF rendering was done by PrinceXML.

Contents

Abbreviations

Old Testament Pseudepigrapha

Apocr. Ezek.	*Apocryphon of Ezekiel*
2 Bar.	*2 Baruch*
1–3 En.	*1–3 Enoch*
Jub.	*Jubilees*
Ps.-Philo, L.A.B.	*Liber antiquitatum biblicarum*
Pss. Sol.	*Psalms of Solomon*
T. Levi	*Testament of Levi*
T. Sol.	*Testament of Solomon*

Dead Sea Scrolls

CD	Cairo Genizah copy of the *Damascus Document*
1QH	*Thanksgiving Hymns*
1QM	*War Scroll*
1QSa	*Rule of the Congregation*
4QD^a	*Damascus Document^a*
4QMMT	*Halakhic Letter*
4QPrNab	*Prayer of Nabonidus*
11QMelch	*Melchizedek*

Mishnah (*m.*), Talmud (*b.*), and Tosefta (*t.*)

Ber.	*Berakot*
B. Mes.	*Baba Mesi'a*
B. Qam.	*Baba Qamma*
Hag.	*Hagigah*
Ketub.	*Ketubbot*
Ned.	*Nedarim*
Neg.	*Nega'im*
Ohal.	*Ohalot*
Pesah.	*Pesahim*
Qidd.	*Qiddushin*
Sabb.	*Shabbat*
Sanh.	*Sanhedrin*
Sukk.	*Sukkah*
Ta'an.	*Ta'anit.*
Tehar.	*Teharot*

Other Primary Sources

Did.	*Didache*
Gos. Thom.	*Gospel of Thomas*
IG	*Inscriptiones graecae*
LXX	Septuagint
PGM	*Papyri graecae magicae*
P.Oxy.	Papyrus Oxyrhynchus

Secondary Sources

AB	Anchor Bible
ABD	*Anchor Bible Dictionary*
ABR	*Australian Biblical Review*
ANRW	*Aufstieg und Niedergang der römischen Welt*

BAR	*Biblical Archaeology Review*
Bib	*Biblica*
BibInt	*Biblical Interpretation*
BZNW	Beihefte zur Zeitschrift für die neutestamentliche Wissenschaft
CBQ	*Catholic Biblical Quarterly*
FLRANT	Forschungen zur Religion und Literatur des Alten und Neuen Testaments
GRBS	*Greek, Roman, and Byzantine Studies*
HTR	*Harvard Theological Review*
HUCA	*Hebrew Union College Annual*
ICC	International Critical Commentary
JBL	*Journal of Biblical Literature*
JFSR	*Journal of Feminist Studies in Religion*
JJS	*Journal of Jewish Studies*
JSJ	*Journal for the Study of Judaism*
JSJSup	Journal for the Study of Judaism: Supplement Series
JSNTSup	Journal for the Study of the New Testament: Supplement Series
JSOTSup	Journal for the Study of the Old Testament: Supplement Series
JSP	*Journal for the Study of the Pseudepigrapha*
JSS	*Journal of Semitic Studies*
LCL	Loeb Classical Library
NeoT	*Neotestamentica*
NICNT	New International Commentary on the New Testament
NIGTC	New International Greek Testament Commentary
NovT	*Novum Testamentum*
NovTSup	Novum Testamentum Supplements
NTOA	Novum Testamentum et Orbis Antiquus
NTS	*New Testament Studies*
SBLDS	Society of Biblical Literature Dissertation Series
SBLSP	*Society of Biblical Literature Seminar Papers*
SBLTT	Society of Biblical Literature Texts and Translations

ScrB	*Scripture Bulletin*
SJLA	Studies in Judaism in Late Antiquity
SNTSMS	Society for New Testament Studies Monograph Series
STDJ	Studies on the Texts of the Desert of Judah
TDNT	*Theological Dictionary of the New Testament*
TSAJ	Texte und Studien zum antiken Judentum
WBC	Word Biblical Commentary
WUNT	Wissenschaftliche Untersuchungen zum Neuen Testament

Preface

As an aspect of human experience, healing is as multifaceted as it is universal. In biblical traditions, healing appears as a prominent theme, a social practice, and a form of storytelling. Its study attracts scholars from various disciplines, including not only historical and literary studies but also feminist studies, disability studies, and medical anthropology. Within the realm of Christian theology, healing is very much a "meaning-making" endeavor, impinging upon such topics as Christology, soteriology, discipleship, mission, and eschatology.[1] What is perhaps most intriguing about the healing traditions of Scripture is the insistent manner in which they draw our attention to individual human bodies, the limitations of these bodies, and the possibilities for reimagining the significance of such limitations. Since living in finite bodies is something all people must do, it is no wonder that we continue to find the Bible's accounts of healing to be so compelling, sometimes on a very personal level. At the same time, there is no denying that people continue to find these accounts to be very challenging as well.

---

1. For an illuminating example of how the theme of healing can be developed in support of constructive theological reflection, see Karen Baker-Fletcher, "More than Suffering: The Healing and Resurrecting Spirit of God," in *Womanist Theological Ethics: A Reader*, eds. Katie Geneva Cannon, Emilie M. Townes, and Angela D. Sims (Louisville: Westminster John Knox, 2011), 155–79.

This book investigates the topic of healing in the Gospel of Matthew, with a focus on chapters 8–9, a discrete composition that the evangelist has created by reworking a group of healing (and other) stories gathered from different sources. While a range of specific issues will be addressed along the way, the overarching aim is to explore what new meanings attach to these stories in their new setting, not only the setting provided by chapters 8–9 but also the setting provided by the First Gospel as a whole.[2] In his classic study of the Matthean miracle tradition, Heinz Joachim Held observed that while the Second Gospel has two collections of miracle stories and the Third Gospel has three, in the First Gospel we find only one such collection.[3] Chapters 8–9, then, are a unique composition, one of singular importance for understanding both Matthew's distinctive activity as an editor and his distinctive interpretation of Jesus' healing ministry.

The material for this book originates from a course I teach at Candler School of Theology entitled "Healing in the New Testament." Because it is offered in support of the school's Contextual Education program, participants in the course are all second-year MDiv students working a prescribed number of hours per week in an approved ecclesial setting under the supervision of a site mentor. Predictably, our conversations in class tend to gravitate towards questions of a practical nature, especially questions concerning the implications of the biblical text for congregational ministry.[4] Second-

2. In what follows I refer to the Gospel of Matthew as the "First" Gospel, referring to the text's priority not as the first New Testament Gospel to be written but as the first Gospel of the New Testament canon. For the theory of Markan priority, see the discussion of source and redaction criticisms in Chapter One.

3. Heinz Joachim Held, "Matthew as Interpreter of Miracle Stories," in *Tradition and Interpretation in Matthew*, eds. Günther Bornkamm, Gerhard Barth, and Heinz Joachim Held (Philadelphia: Westminster, 1963), 246.

4. For examples of a practical approach to the theme, see Abigail Evans, *The Healing Church: Practical Programs for Health Ministries* (Cleveland, OH: United Church Press, 1999), 191–231;

year MDiv students at Candler are also required to take a yearlong introduction to the New Testament, which includes a survey of different critical methods and hermeneutical perspectives for biblical study. Accordingly, one of my goals for the healing course is to show students how these methods and perspectives might be germane to the kinds of practical questions they bring to the text. This pedagogical priority is reflected in the organization of the book, which begins with a discussion of method (Chapter One). Like the phenomenon of healing itself, my approach is multifaceted, utilizing categories of analysis that interface with various disciplines. After laying out the perspectives and assumptions guiding my investigation, Chapters Two through Thirteen then analyze the text itself, working through the material in Matthew 8–9 pericope by pericope. The Conclusion, finally, summarizes the principal findings, especially with respect to the "emplotted" structure and "inclusive" logic of the text.

As we shall see, the First Gospel is best approached as an emerging narrative. For the evangelist, the stories about healing in his source materials constitute a living tradition, and as such are subject to new patterns of storytelling, contextualization, and symbolic world building. It is apparent that the evangelist has been busy not only revising received stories but also rearranging them, a fact that raises a number of interpretive questions: What reasons might Matthew have had for assembling this particular set of healing stories? What difference does it make when we read these stories together and in the particular order that the evangelist has chosen for them? Why has he incorporated non-healing stories into the unit and what impact does their presence have on the overall message? How do the diverse materials in chapters 8–9 combine to create a coherent "statement" on

Susan J. Dunlap, *Caring Cultures: How Congregations Respond to the Sick* (Waco, TX: Baylor University Press, 2009), 1–15.

healing, and what does this statement contribute to the development of the Gospel narrative as a whole?

In formulating a response to these questions, it will be helpful to keep the following tasks in mind as we examine the individual stories of the unit:

- Detecting *generic transformations* in the stories themselves. When Matthew revises a story, he often alters its literary genre or "form," adapting and recombining different narrative structures, themes, and motifs. This has the effect of altering the sort of context within which the story's characters find themselves, which in turn has implications for understanding the significance of the healing event for both the healer and the person being healed.

- Tracking *narrative developments* in the means of storytelling. This includes especially changes from one story to the next in the types of settings, characters, and activities being recounted, including changes in the style of narration. In coming to terms with such developments, it is important to remember that with his storytelling Matthew is not just rethinking the past but also constructing an unfolding social drama, one in which the readers themselves are implicated.

- Identifying *thematic connections* that ground the story of Jesus the healer in the story of Israel. In some cases these connections will be explicit, as when Matthew claims that what Jesus does represents the fulfillment of a prophetic oracle (e.g., 8:17), while in other cases the connections will be more subtle. However they are communicated, it is incumbent upon the interpreter to appreciate how such connections contribute to the author's underlying social and rhetorical agenda.

- Recognizing the *programmatic transgressiveness* of Jesus' healing ministry. The narratives of chapters 8–9 present Jesus traversing and transcending boundaries of many different kinds. Appreciating this fact entails paying special attention both to the representational character of the individuals whom Jesus encounters in these stories and to what their healings signify within the worldview projected by the text. As we shall see, in their interactions with each other, healers and those in need of healing often appear as actors within a complex cultural performance, one infused with symbolic roles, actions, and interpretations.

★ ★ ★

Material for some of the chapters in this book has been published previously. Portions of chapters 4 and 5 originally appeared in "The Uninvited Healer: Houses, Healing and Prophets in Matthew 8.1-22," *Journal for the Study of the New Testament* 36 (2013): 1–20, while portions of chapters 10 and 11 originally appeared in "The Crucified Bridegroom and His Bleeding Daughter: Reflections on the Narrative Logic of Matt 9,9-26," *Ephemerides Theologicae Lovanienses* 89 (2013): 323–43.

Many people have helped with my work on this project. I am grateful to Professor Vernon Robbins for introducing me to the scholarship of Elaine Wainwright, especially her book on the genderization of healing in early Christianity. Another one of my Emory colleagues, Professor Tom Long, gave a thoughtful response to a presentation I gave on the story of the two blind men to the Candler faculty on November 18, 2013. The research assistant for the entire project was Meredyth Fleisher, who was also a student in my New Testament and Healing course. Two of our graduate students, David Carr and Jennifer Wyant, also helped review the final proofs. Finally, it would be remiss of me not to mention the staff at Fortress

Press, especially Neil Elliott, Carolyn Halvorson, and Marissa Wold. To one and all my sincere thanks.

1

Methodology

As recent scholarship has made abundantly clear, the First Gospel is a complex document and healing is a complex topic. In order to appreciate the nuances of both, it is necessary to adopt an approach that is interdisciplinary in nature. The survey that follows sketches the basic methods and assumptions that will inform the analysis of Matthew 8–9, the target text for this study.[1] No attempt is made to be comprehensive, either in terms of the methodological procedures themselves or in terms of their impact on the history of biblical scholarship. Instead, my approach is selective and strategic, integrating perspectives and insights culled from a number of different "criticisms," namely, historical criticism, form criticism, source and redaction criticisms, narrative criticism, reader-response criticism, feminist criticism, disability studies, and medical anthropology. My focus throughout is on the relevance of these methods for the study of the First Gospel in general and for the

---

1. Unless indicated otherwise, translations of biblical texts are my own.

theme of healing in particular. In what follows, I review each of the methods in turn, beginning with those that are more traditional and continuing with those whose impact on the field of biblical studies is more recent.[2]

Historical Criticism

In many respects, historical criticism constitutes an umbrella method for our study, insofar as everything that follows endeavors to understand the First Gospel as an ancient form of communication. In keeping with recent trends in scholarship, the reflections that follow are aided especially by sociological insights and models.[3]

While certainty is impossible, many scholars have suggested for the First Gospel a likely date of 80–90 CE, and Syria, the city of Antioch in particular, as a likely place of origin (cf. 4:24).[4] In addition, it is widely agreed that this text preserves the witness of a Jewish-Christian community, that is, a Christian community that originated in the synagogue, an institutional home that would have been of fundamental significance in shaping the group's religious and social commitments.[5] It is obvious from the text itself, however, that the community's most recent history is one of separation from and

---

2. For more comprehensive reviews of these and other methods, see Joel B. Green, ed., *Hearing the New Testament: Strategies for Interpretation*, 2nd ed. (Grand Rapids: Eerdmans, 2010); Mark Allan Powell, ed., *Methods for Matthew* (Cambridge: Cambridge University Press, 2009).

3. In addition to the sources cited below, see J. Andrew Overman, *Matthew's Gospel and Formative Judaism: The Social World of the Matthean Community* (Minneapolis: Fortress Press, 1990), 150–61; Ever-Jan Vledder, *Conflict in the Miracle Stories: A Socio-Exegetical Study of Matthew 8 and 9*, JSNTSup 152 (Sheffield: Sheffield Academic Press, 1997), 117–67; David C. Sim, *The Gospel of Matthew and Christian Judaism: The History and Social Setting of the Matthean Community*, Studies of the New Testament and Its World (Edinburgh: T&T Clark, 1998), 109–63.

4. W. D. Davies and Dale C. Allison, *The Gospel According to Saint Matthew*, ICC (London: T&T Clark, 1988), 1:127–47.

5. Davies and Allison, *Saint Matthew*, 3:692–704; Paul Foster, *Community, Law and Mission in Matthew's Gospel*, WUNT 2.177 (Tübingen: Mohr Siebeck, 2004), 22–79; Donald A. Hagner, *Matthew*, WBC 33 (Dallas: Word Books, 1993), 1:lxiv–lxxiii; Ulrich Luz, *Matthew: A Commentary*, Hermeneia (Minneapolis: Fortress Press, 2001), 1:45–56; Boris Repschinski, *The*

antagonism with Judaism, especially its leadership. This disaffection appears to have been fueled in part by the increasing prominence of the nascent rabbinic movement, sometimes referred to as "formative" Judaism.[6] The evangelist's perspective on these developments is often described as evidencing "sectarian" or "factional" tendencies insofar as strategies of both *differentiation* and *legitimation* inform his discourse.

To begin with the former: it is evident from various features of his Gospel that Matthew is endeavoring to differentiate his fledgling group from the "parent body" and the influence that it represents. Accordingly, matters of self-definition are cast in a contested mode, that is, as a struggle over which group embodies a more valid interpretation of texts and traditions deemed essential to Jewish identity. Matthew discredits oppositional leaders by caricaturing them as corrupt, obstinate, and malicious, while Jesus and his followers are portrayed as a beleaguered, dissident minority. This feature comes to expression most vividly in the author's intense polemic against the Pharisees (e.g., 23:1-39), who seem to function as ciphers for the Jewish leaders of his own day, just as the followers of Jesus whom they condemn function as stand-ins for the members of his own community.[7] By means of this and related tactics the First Gospel establishes what one scholar refers to as "a stabilized deviant identity":

Controversy Stories in the Gospel of Matthew, FRLANT 189 (Göttingen: Vandenhoeck & Ruprecht, 2000), 13–61.

6. This term refers to the reorganization of Jewish thought and practice in the decades after the destruction of the temple in 70 CE. No doubt this was a complex and gradual process, one subject to regional variations. How such consolidation would have impacted the development of synagogues in Matthew's particular milieu remains a matter of conjecture. See Shaye J. D. Cohen, "The Significance of Yavneh: Pharisees, Rabbis, and the End of Jewish Sectarianism," *HUCA* 55 (1984): 27–53.

7. Davies and Allison, *Saint Matthew*, 3:261.

Because of the conflict, polemics, and resultant differentiation, the members of Matthew's group find their core identity and their "master status" in being believers-in-Jesus. All other aspects of their Jewish life and world view are filtered through this central commitment, which has alienated them from many fellow Jews and colored all their activities and relationships.[8]

It is important to remember that such strategies of communal self-definition (including the acrimonious forms of rhetoric that often attend them) are not unique to Matthew's Gospel but can be found in other sectarian writings of the era as well, especially the Dead Sea Scrolls.[9]

In conjunction with this, Matthew also endeavors to legitimize the existence of his dissenting group in terms of both its distinctive theological commitments and its alternative social arrangements. Toward this end, he appropriates a range of traditional symbols, norms, and idioms so as to amplify the Jewish character of Jesus and his ministry. As one would imagine, of critical importance in this task of legitimation is the appropriation of sacred scripture. Indeed, it is not an overstatement to say that for Matthew's community, "[w]hat is at stake is its own standing within the traditions of the Bible."[10] So, like most Jewish Christians, Matthew takes the authority of the Mosaic law for granted (5:17-19): not the law as the Pharisees practice it, however (5:20; 23:2-3), but as it is realized in the teaching of Jesus (e.g., 5:21-48), allegiance to which would have not only fostered group cohesion but also served as a marker of group identity. Similarly illustrative are Matthew's distinctive "fulfillment" quotations (e.g., 8:17), according to which Jesus' ministry is properly understood

8. Anthony J. Saldarini, *Matthew's Christian-Jewish Community* (Chicago: University of Chicago Press, 1994), 112–13.
9. Graham N. Stanton, *A Gospel for a New People: Studies in Matthew* (Edinburgh: T&T Clark, 1992), 85–107.
10. John K. Riches, *Conflicting Mythologies: Identity Formation in the Gospels of Mark and Matthew,* Studies of the New Testament and Its World (Edinburgh: T&T Clark, 2000), 181.

as the culmination of God's purposes as set forth in Scripture.[11] Expanding on this assertion is all manner of intertextual allusions, comparisons, and typologies, which together represent a major and growing area of scholarly interest. The evangelist's underlying point seems clear enough: the Old Testament provides a lens through which to understand the meaning of Jesus, just as the life and teachings of Jesus provide a lens through which to interpret the Old Testament.[12] To cite just one pertinent example: it is sometimes argued that the ten miracles attributed to Jesus in chapters 8–9 are meant to recall the ten wonders performed by Moses in Exodus 7–12, a parallel whose likelihood is increased by the fact that Moses is mentioned by name in conjunction with the first of those miracles (8:4).[13] If such an allusion is indeed at work here, it contributes to a broader narrative priority for Matthew, namely, to draw typological associations between Jesus and Moses.[14]

Form Criticism

The reference to fulfillment quotations in the preceding paragraph serves as a reminder that in coming to terms with Matthew's sectarian agenda it behooves us to recognize the various literary forms through which this agenda is articulated. In chapters 8–9, the reader in fact encounters a number of different forms—not only a fulfillment

---

11. See the discussion of Matt. 8:17 below (Chapter Five).
12. For overviews, see Richard Beaton, *Isaiah's Christ in Matthew's Gospel*, SNTSMS 123 (Cambridge: Cambridge University Press, 2002), 14–43; Brandon D. Crowe, *The Obedient Son: Deuteronomy and Christology in the Gospel of Matthew*, BZNW 188 (Berlin: Walter de Gruyter, 2012), 6–38.
13. Of course, the wonders performed by Moses in Exodus are very different in nature than the (mostly healing) miracles attributed to Jesus in the Gospel. Note, too, that while there may be ten miracles recounted in Matthew 8–9, there are (as we shall see) only nine miracle *stories*, the seventh of these (9:18-26) combining the accounts of two miracles. For discussion, see Dale C. Allison, *The New Moses: A Matthean Typology* (Minneapolis: Fortress Press, 1993), 207–13; Michael Theophilos, *Jesus as New Moses in Matthew 8–9: Jewish Typology in First Century Greek Literature* (Piscataway, NJ: Gorgias, 2011), 159–65.
14. Allison, *The New Moses*, 271–90. Cf. Theophilos, *Jesus as New Moses*, 1–19.

quotation (8:17), but also two summary statements (8:16; 9:35), a pair of pronouncement stories (8:19-20, 21-22), a nature miracle (8:23-27), a call narrative (9:9), and two controversy stories (9:10-13, 14-17). The most common type of form in chapters 8–9, of course, is the healing story, of which there are eight examples, including five healing stories proper (8:1-4, 5-13, 14-15; 9:1-8, 27-31), a revivification story into which a healing story has been inserted (9:18-26), and two examples of a closely related form, the exorcism story (8:28-34; 9:32-34). Given its prominence, a word is in order regarding the basic characteristics of the healing story form.[15]

First of all, in conveying their narrative depictions, healing stories draw on a field of typical characters. At a minimum, there is the healer (Jesus) and the person in need of healing, whose affliction will vary. In some cases (e.g., 8:14-15), these two are the only characters in the story. More often, one or more other character types are included in the action: crowds (e.g., 9:8), disciples (e.g., 9:19), opponents (e.g., 9:3), companions of the person in need of healing (e.g., 9:2), or petitioners advocating on behalf of the person (e.g., 8:5). In exorcism stories, demons also sometimes function as a character type (e.g., 8:31).

Healing stories also draw on a field of typical motifs, which can be combined in various ways depending on the aims of the storyteller. To begin with, there is the appearance of the healer. Usually (e.g., 8:5), but not always (e.g., 9:18), this involves reporting some sort of movement on Jesus' part. Matching this we have the appearance of the person in need of healing. Sometimes the person approaches Jesus (e.g., 8:2), sometimes the person is brought to Jesus by companions (e.g., 9:2), and sometimes the person is simply "there" waiting for

---

15. For what follows, see Gerd Theissen, *The Miracle Stories of the Early Christian Tradition* (Philadelphia: Fortress Press, 1983), 47–72. Cf. E. P. Sanders and Margaret Davies, *Studying the Synoptic Gospels* (London: SCM; Philadelphia: Trinity Press International, 1989), 163–73.

help (e.g., 8:14). Alternatively, it is not the person in need of healing who approaches Jesus but the petitioner advocating on his or her behalf (e.g., 9:18). Regardless of how the need is brought to Jesus' attention, its report will include some identification (e.g., 8:2) or description (e.g., 8:28) of the person's condition.

Once the afflicted person (or petitioner) is brought into contact with the healer, there is usually a request for help, which is usually (e.g., 9:18), but not always (e.g., 9:20), expressed verbally. Accompanying the request there may be some word (e.g., 8:6) or combination of word and act (e.g., 8:2) expressing respect for the healer, thereby indicating that the individual making the request is assuming the role of supplicant. The word of respect will sometimes include a title of christological significance (e.g., 9:27), thereby indicating that the individual making the request recognizes some deeper meaning regarding the person of Jesus. The word of respect may even be enhanced by an affirmation of some kind (e.g., 9:28). Contrasting with this, there may be an expression of skepticism from the crowds (e.g., 9:24).

In response to the request, the healer may offer a word of encouragement (e.g., 9:22) in addition to the healing itself, which may occur through word (e.g., 8:32), through touch (e.g., 8:15), or through a combination of the two (e.g., 8:3), though in some cases the means of healing is left unstated (e.g., 9:33). When the healing occurs through a word, it may also be accomplished at a distance (e.g., 8:13). In some situations, the healer takes steps to ensure the privacy of the healing (e.g., 9:24-25) or instructs the persons healed to keep the matter secret (e.g., 9:30), though other kinds of post-healing instructions are also possible (e.g., 8:4), especially the instruction to depart (e.g., 8:13). In some cases a report is made regarding the activity of the healed person (e.g., 8:15), thereby demonstrating the effectiveness of the cure.

The healing, given that it is a miraculous event, will often elicit reactions from onlookers. For instance, the disciples (e.g., 8:27) or the crowds (e.g., 9:8) may express amazement, including perhaps some verbal acclamation (e.g., 9:33). Alternatively, the crowds (e.g., 8:34) or the opponents (e.g., 9:3) may reject the healer, and in some cases (e.g., 9:33-34), the response is divided. In other cases, there is simply a report that the miracle-worker's reputation is expanding (e.g., 9:26).

We can conclude this brief overview by noting that while the healing story incorporates a number of conventional features, which together create certain expectations for the reader, there is abundant evidence that the evangelist did not see it as a fixed or stagnant genre. Indeed, as we shall see, one of the more important ways in which Matthew communicates his narrative theology is by blending healing stories with elements of other forms, thereby disrupting such expectations through the development of distinctive literary creations.

Source and Redaction Criticisms

There is a consensus in scholarship that for the material of chapters 8–9 Matthew relies on stories adapted from two sources, the Gospel of Mark and the Q source.[16] In utilizing these sources, Matthew has altered both the content of the stories, a process that usually entails abbreviating their overall length, as well as the order of the stories, rearranging them into a substantially new composition. In the chart below, parallels printed in **bold** represent material based on a sequence of events that occurs fairly early in the Second Gospel, namely, Mark 1:29—2:22 (cf. Luke 4:38—5:39), while parallels that are underlined represent material based on a sequence of events that occurs somewhat later in the Second Gospel, namely, Mark

---

16. Davies and Allison, *Saint Matthew*, 1:97–127.

4:35—5:43 (cf. Luke 8:22-56).[17] Parallels printed in *italics*, finally, represent material drawn from the Q source.[18]

Matthew	Mark	Luke
8:1-4	**1:40-45**	
8:5-10+13		*7:1-10*
8:11-12		*13:28-29*
8:14-16	**1:29-34**	
8:17		
<u>8:18+23-27</u>	<u>4:35-41</u>	
8:19-22		*9:57-60*
<u>8:28-34</u>	<u>5:1-20</u>	
9:1-8	**2:1-12**	
9:9-13	**2:14-17**	
9:14-17	**2:18-22**	
<u>9:18-26</u>	<u>5:21-43</u>	
9:27-31 (cf. 20:29-34)	10:46-52	
9:32-34 (cf. 12:22-24)	(3:22)	*11:14-15*
9:35-36	6:34	
9:37-38		*10:2*

Matthew has integrated the two Markan sequences into a larger unit, interweaving stories from the two sequences and occasionally inserting Q material both between and into the stories. Except for the transposition of Mark 1:29-34 and 1:40-45, it appears that Matthew has been careful to follow the *relative* order of stories in the Markan sequences. The only place where Matthew presents stories in the same *consecutive* order as either of the Markan sequences, however,

17. Matthean parallels for the material *between* these two sequences (i.e., for Mark 2:23–4:34) are to be found largely in Matt. 12:1–13:35.
18. Cf. R. T. France, *The Gospel of Matthew*, NICNT (Grand Rapids: Eerdmans, 2007), 300–301.

is Matthew 9:1-8 + 9-13 + 14-17 (= Mark 2:1-12 + 14-17 + 18-22), though even here the narrative context provided for the material differs dramatically.[19] The last two miracle stories in the unit, Matthew 9:27-31 and 9:32-34, represent special cases, insofar as both are examples of literary "doublets" and, as such, are based only indirectly on material from the evangelist's source material. An item that stands out in the chart, the only Matthean element that does not have a parallel in either Mark or the Q source, is the fulfillment quotation in 8:17.[20] The transitional segment in 9:35-38, finally, cobbles together elements from Mark and the Q source.

A major task for the interpreter (and thus for the Chapters that follow) involves identifying the implications of all this redactional activity for the interpretation of both the individual stories within chapters 8–9 and the contribution that they make collectively to the portrayal of Jesus and his healing ministry.

Narrative Criticism

One obvious result of all this redactional activity is that we are left with a very different kind of "story" about Jesus, one that would have presented Matthew's original readers with a combination of the familiar (assuming they were acquainted with the sorts of traditions preserved in Mark and Q) and the innovative. The contents of this story can be outlined as follows:

19. The material in Matthew 9:1-17 is immediately preceded by the story of the Gadarene demoniacs (Matt. 8:28-34) and immediately followed by the story of the official's daughter and the woman with the flow of blood (Matt. 9:18-26). The parallel material in Mark 2:1-22, on the other hand, is immediately preceded by the cleansing of the leper (Mark 1:40-45) and immediately followed by a controversy story about the Sabbath (Mark 2:23-28).
20. Note that the quotation of Hosea 6:6 in Matthew 9:13 is absent from the parallel passage in Mark 2:17. Such explicit scriptural grounding, then, represents a special Matthean interest.

1. First miracle story: the cleansing of the "leper" (8:1-4)
2. Second miracle story: the healing of the centurion's servant (8:5-13)
3. Third miracle story: the healing of Peter's mother-in-law (8:14-15), plus a summary statement (8:16) and fulfillment quotation (8:17)
4. A pair of pronouncement stories about "following" Jesus (8:19-22), prefaced by a narrative statement that helps set the scene (8:18)
5. Fourth miracle story: a sea rescue story (8:23-27)
6. Fifth miracle story: the exorcism of the Gadarene demoniacs (8:28-34)
7. Sixth miracle story: the healing of the paralytic (9:1-8)
8. A pair of controversy stories about food (9:10-17), prefaced by a call narrative that helps set the scene (9:9)
9. Seventh miracle story: the revivification of the official's daughter (9:18-19 + 23-26), into which has been inserted the healing of the hemorrhaging woman (9:20-22)
10. Eighth miracle story: the healing of two blind men (9:27-31)
11. Ninth miracle story: the exorcism of a mute demoniac (9:32-34)
12. Transitional segment (9:35-38), including a summary statement (9:35) and instructions for the disciples (9:37-38)

A narrative approach to the analysis of this material can be divided into two related tasks. The first task is to ascertain how these dozen different elements fit or "flow" together to create a larger and more complex unit. In this case, the work of the narrative critic focuses on questions of literary structure. A survey of recent scholarship reveals a number of different options in this regard, several of which can be mentioned here.

To begin with, there is W. D. Davies and Dale Allison, who divide the contents of the unit into three sections: 8:1-22, 8:23—9:17, and 9:18-38. In their view, the three sections "are near relatives in that each recounts first three miracle stories and then tacks on teaching material."[21] As they correctly observe, the alternation of miracle stories (8:1-15; 8:23—9:8; 9:18-34) and non-miracle story elements (8:18-22; 9:9-17; 9:35-38) supports a basic narrative pattern, separating the nine miracle stories into three triads: (1) 8:1-4, 5-13, 14-15; (2) 8:23-27, 28-34, 9:1-8; and (3) 9:18-26, 27-31, 32-34. Their understanding of how the "tacked on" material (i.e., 8:16-22; 9:9-17, 35-38) relates to these triads, however, raises some concerns. The structural break that Davies and Allison posit between 8:22 and 8:23 is especially problematic, even contradictory, insofar as their own interpretation acknowledges the narrative continuity between 8:18-22 (where Jesus gives orders to depart and has conversations with individuals about "following" him) and 8:23-27 (where Jesus proceeds to depart, with his disciples "following" him).[22]

John Nolland also organizes the unit into three sections, though his divisions fall at different places in the narrative: 8:2-17, 8:18—9:13, and 9:14-32.[23] While the break after 8:17 is logical enough, the break after 9:13 is not, separating as it does two passages (9:10-13 and 9:14-17) that have the same literary form (controversy story), setting (Jesus dining with tax collectors and sinners), and basic topic (food). Note, too, that the events recounted in 9:1-17 evidence a certain narrative coherence insofar as Jesus is presented interacting with representatives from a series of three different religious groups: first the scribes (9:1-8), then the Pharisees (9:10-13), then the disciples of John the Baptist (9:14-17).

---

21. Davies and Allison, *Saint Matthew*, 1:67, cf. 1:101–102.
22. Ibid., 2:39, 68, 71.
23. John Nolland, *The Gospel of Matthew*, NIGTC (Grand Rapids: Eerdmans, 2005), 347–404.

Yet another attempt to divide the unit into three parts is set forth by Heinz Joachim Held, who argues that the contents of the unit should be arranged as follows: 8:2-17, 8:18—9:17, and 9:18-31, with 9:32-34 serving as a conclusion to the whole composition.[24] While positing a break after 9:17 makes more sense than positing one after 9:13, it should be observed that no change in setting takes place in the transition from 9:14-17 to 9:18-19, and, furthermore, Matthean redaction actually has the effect of creating an overlap between the two passages. Even more questionable is Held's idea that 9:18-31 constitutes a triad matching those of 8:2-17 and 8:18—9:17. While 9:18-31 may recount three miracles, it contains only two miracle stories, the two accounts in 9:18-26 being correlated in such a way (both formally and thematically) as to form an indissoluble unity.

A different approach is represented by Ulrich Luz, who suggests that chapters 8–9 be divided into not three, but four sections (8:1-17; 8:18—9:1; 9:2-17; 9:18-34), each of which he describes as "a self-contained unit."[25] The virtue of this proposal is that it recognizes the narrative coherence of both 8:18—9:1 (which begins with Jesus giving orders to depart and concludes with him returning from the journey) and 9:2-17 (whose coherence was noted above). The proposal's weakness is that it ignores the chapters' most obvious literary pattern, namely, the separation of the nine miracle stories into three triads, resulting in a structural imbalance: the first (8:1-17) and fourth (9:18-34) sections in Luz's proposal have three miracle stories each, while the second (8:18—9:1) has two, and the third (9:2-17) has only one.

---

24. Heinz Joachim Held, "Matthew as Interpreter of the Miracle Stories," in *Tradition and Interpretation in Matthew*, eds. Günther Bornkamm, Gerhard Barth, and Heinz Joachim Held (Philadelphia: Westminster, 1963), 246–49. A similar proposal is made by William G. Thompson, "Reflections on the Composition of Mt 8:1–9:34," *CBQ* 33 (1971): 365–88.

25. Luz, *Matthew*, 2:1. Similar is Jack D. Kingsbury, "Observations on the 'Miracle Chapters' of Matthew 8–9," *CBQ* 40 (1978): 562.

These disagreements among the experts (not to mention the mixed success of their proposals) present the interpreter with significant challenges when it comes to discerning the narrative structure(s) at work in Matthew 8–9. Given that the most persuasive arguments about the composition of a story will be based on a close reading of the text, the analysis that follows in Chapters Two through Thirteen is not organized according to any particular scheme but rather approaches the Gospel as a running narrative, deferring further discussion of the matter until the Conclusion.

With this overview in mind, we can now turn to the second task of the narrative critic, which is to ascertain the function of chapters 8–9 within the context of the Gospel story as a whole. Given the complexities attending this question, at this point a handful of preliminary observations will have to suffice.

There is little doubt that the most distinctive literary feature of the First Gospel as a whole is its five major discourses (chapters 5–7, 10, 13, 18, and 23–25), segments whose placement within the narrative has the effect of creating an alternating pattern of action and speech. Of special interest for the study of chapters 8–9 are the discourses located on either side of the unit. On one hand, chapters 8–9 are connected to chapters 5–7, a connection reinforced by similarly worded summary statements in 4:23 and 9:35, which together form a narrative frame around the intervening material.[26] The Sermon on the Mount and the cycle of miracle stories, then, are not functionally unrelated but are meant to complement one another, the former presenting "the Messiah of the Word," the latter "the Messiah of Deed."[27]

---

26. "He went about in all Galilee teaching in their synagogues and proclaiming the good news of the kingdom and healing every disease and every sickness among the people" (Matt. 4:23). "Jesus went about all the cities and the villages teaching in their synagogues and proclaiming the good news of the kingdom and healing every disease and every sickness" (Matt. 9:35).

The connection between chapters 8–9 and chapter 10, on the other hand, is signaled more specifically by the theme of healing. The latter, in fact, begins with Jesus authorizing the twelve disciples to carry out a ministry of healing (10:1).[28] Specifically, in 10:8 they are instructed to heal the sick (cf. 8:14-17), raise the dead (cf. 9:18-19 + 23-26), cleanse lepers (cf. 8:1-4), and cast out demons (cf. 8:28-34; 9:32-34), miracles that they had just witnessed Jesus himself perform.[29] The healing ministry of Jesus as recounted in chapters 8–9, then, provides a model for the disciples to follow in their own ministry.

The significance of chapters 8–9 for the broader narrative does not end there, however. Having given instructions to his own disciples, Jesus fields a question from the disciples of John the Baptist (11:3; cf. 9:14). In his response (11:5), Jesus enumerates some of "the works of the Messiah" (11:2), namely, that the blind receive sight (cf. 9:27-31), the lame walk (cf. 9:1-8), the lepers are cleansed (cf. 8:1-4), the deaf hear (cf. 9:32-34), and the dead are raised up (cf. 9:18-19 + 23-26). As with 10:8, Jesus refers back to specific events recounted in chapters 8–9, though here they serve as proofs of Jesus' messianic status.

Moving on, yet another kind of narrative contribution for chapters 8–9 can be observed when we include chapter 12 in the discussion. Specifically, the exorcism story in 9:32-34 has a close parallel in 12:22-24, both stories concluding with the Pharisees accusing Jesus of collusion with Satan. While the former is situated within a set of miracle stories, however, the latter is situated within a set of controversy stories that dramatizes Jesus' recurring dispute with the

---

27. Held, "Matthew as Interpreter," 246. Note also the correspondence of 7:28-29 and 9:33-34 (cf. J. R. C. Cousland, *The Crowds in the Gospel of Matthew*, NovTSup 102 [Leiden: Brill, 2002], 140–41).

28. Note how Matthew's statement (10:1) is more expansive than its counterparts in Mark 6:7 and Luke 9:1. Also note how it corresponds with the summary statement in Matt. 9:35.

29. Again, Matthew's statement (10:8) is more expansive than its counterparts. Cf. Mark 6:13; Luke 9:2; 10:9; Cousland, *The Crowds in the Gospel of Matthew*, 112; John K. Ridgway, *"Let Your Peace Come Upon It": Healing and Peace in Matthew 10:1-15*, Studies in Biblical Literature 2 (New York: Peter Lang, 1999), 224–37.

Pharisees (12:1-45). The duplication created by 9:32-34 + 12:22-24, then, is not mere repetition but has the effect of showing how the Pharisees' opposition to Jesus intensifies over time.

The contents of chapters 8–9, then, when examined within their broader narrative context, can be seen serving a number of different functions. Connections with chapter 10 are suggestive of contributions these chapters make to the theme of *discipleship*, connections with chapter 11 are suggestive of contributions they make to the theme of *Christology*, and connections with chapter 12 are suggestive of contributions they make to the theme of *Israel's response* to Jesus. The relationship with chapters 5–7, finally, establishes a motif of both structural and theological significance to Matthew, namely, the relationship of words and deeds, a motif that has a bearing on all three of these themes.

Reader-Response Criticism

Simply put, reader-response theory attends to the different ways in which a story invites its readers to enter into the narrative world created by its author as well as the different ways in which readers appropriate and involve themselves in this world.[30] An important task for the reader-response critic involves explicating how the "inclusive" or "transparent" nature of the narrative contributes to this process, a task that has been addressed in the case of our text by David Howell in his book *Matthew's Inclusive Story: A Study in the Narrative Rhetoric of the First Gospel*. According to Howell, the evangelist's rhetoric projects a narrative world in which a "double horizon" is visible, with the different dimensions of this horizon corresponding

---

30. For general discussion, see Anthony C. Thiselton, *Hermeneutics: An Introduction* (Grand Rapids: Eerdmans, 2009), 306–26; Kevin J. Vanhoozer, "The Reader in New Testament Interpretation," in *Hearing the New Testament: Strategies for Interpretation*, ed. Joel B. Green (Grand Rapids: Eerdmans, 1995), 301–28.

to different historical vantage points.[31] Typical of this phenomenon, he says, is the so-called mission discourse in chapter 10. On one hand, within the narrative world projected by the text, Jesus' instructions were directed to the twelve disciples on an occasion that, from the vantage point of Matthew's readers, belonged to the historical past. On the other hand, it is apparent that some of these instructions are principally directed not to the past but to the situation of the post-Easter church (e.g., 10:17-23).[32] Jesus' instructions, then, are not only for the twelve but "include" Matthew's readers as well, being "transparent" of experiences specific to their situation. Similarly, the disciples in the story appear not only as historical individuals, that is, as followers of the earthly Jesus, but, when viewed from a different vantage point, are also "transparent" for members of Matthew's community, who, when reading the narrative, come to identify with what the disciples represent.[33] Jesus himself, finally, is depicted not only as addressing the twelve at some point in the past but also, in a way, as available in the present, speaking directly to Matthew's audience, a point that would have been especially meaningful to the evangelist given his distinctive commitment to the theological concept that Jesus is "with" his people (1:23; 18:20; 28:20).[34]

Of special interest for our study is Howell's application of this reader-response approach to the interpretation of Matthew 8–9. In his interpretation, the material of this unit is properly described as

---

31. David B. Howell, *Matthew's Inclusive Story: A Study in the Narrative Rhetoric of the First Gospel*, JSNTSup 42 (Sheffield: JSOT, 1990), 14–15.
32. In this regard it is also significant that, having received their instructions, the disciples are not actually sent out (Matt. 11:1; cf. Mark 6:7; Luke 9:2; 10:1), the mission authorized at this point in the story apparently being postponed until *after* the resurrection (cf. Matt. 28:16-20).
33. Riches, *Conflicting Mythologies*, 181–86; Jeannine K. Brown, *The Disciples in Narrative Perspective: The Portrayal and Function of the Matthean Disciples*, Society of Biblical Literature Academia Biblica 9 (Leiden: Brill, 2002), 25–29; Ben Cooper, *Incorporated Servanthood: Commitment and Discipleship in the Gospel of Matthew*, Library of New Testament Studies (London: Bloomsbury, 2013), 48–65.
34. Cf. David D. Kupp, *Matthew's Emmanuel: Divine Presence and God's People in the First Gospel*, SNTSMS 90 (Cambridge: Cambridge University Press, 1996), 41–44.

transparent as well, though the manner in which it does so differs from Matthew 10. Specifically, according to Howell, the stories in this unit are transparent of the community's experience insofar as they present the readers with a decision to accept or reject Jesus.[35] Indeed, he goes so far as to contend that the dual themes of acceptance and rejection "control the plotting of events in the two chapters."[36] However, while it is certainly true that in these stories people are shown responding to Jesus in all sorts of different ways, such an interpretation does little to illuminate the topic of healing itself, that is, the topic that holds the contents of these chapters together. Similarly, it is telling that in Howell's discussion of Matthew 8–9 little attention is paid to how the depiction of people in need of healing *as people in need of healing* might also be "transparent" for Matthew's audience.[37]

Nevertheless, a case can be made that such depictions in fact play a critical role in making the evangelist's narrative theology relevant for his readers. The story of the paralytic, for instance, can be interpreted as an "inclusive" story insofar as it not only recounts an event of the past but also becomes expressive of the readers' experience of being forgiven (9:1-8), just as the story of the woman with the flow of blood, to cite another example, becomes expressive of their experience of being "saved" (9:20-22). Such stories are transparent in a more direct sense as well, insofar as they would have spoken both to experiences of physical healing within the Matthean community as well as to the different forms of healing ministry observed by the community's members.[38] Indeed, consideration for the inclusive

---

35. Howell, *Matthew's Inclusive Story*, 133–35, cf. 102–103, 113; Alistair Stewart-Sykes, "Matthew's 'Miracle Chapters': From Composition to Narrative, and Back Again," *ScrB* 25 (1995): 55–65.
36. Howell, *Matthew's Inclusive Story*, 134.
37. Cf. ibid., 218–43.
38. In addition to the healing stories themselves, passages like 7:22; 10:1, 8; 17:19-20; 25:36 suggest the observance of healing ministries within the Matthean community.

nature of these stories draws our attention to the various ways in which what Ulrich Luz calls the "symbolic" and "corporeal" aspects of their relevance for the audience inform one another:

> To view miracle stories symbolically does not mean, according to Matthew, to transport them from the realm of the corporeal to a realm of the spirit. Rather, it means that the corporeal realm recounted in the miracle stories goes above and beyond itself. The corporeal miracle is, as it were, the hub of meaning for an event that affects men and women as a whole, including their spirit.[39]

In support of this "hub" or nexus of meaning, it is essential for the evangelist to maintain the historical dimension of the narrative's double horizon. For Matthew, a healing story does more than illustrate a theological theme: it reports an actual event in salvation "history," that is, an event in which Jesus alleviated the suffering of a particular person at a particular place and time, changing that person's life through an act of divine power and grace. In communicating this personalized, embodied dimension of meaning, it is safe to assume that the Gospel would have had the effect of both reflecting and shaping the readers' experiences of Jesus. In their encounter with the Gospel, they would have been able to recognize their own "stories" in the text as well as the continuity of these stories with the story of the earthly Jesus.

Feminist Criticism

Embodiment is also a theme of some consequence for the next theory to be discussed, namely, feminist criticism, an approach that, for our purposes, is best represented by Elaine Wainwright's groundbreaking book, *Women Healing/Healing Women: The Genderization of Healing*

---

39. Ulrich Luz, *The Theology of the Gospel of Matthew* (Cambridge: Cambridge University Press, 1995), 69–70.

in Early Christianity.[40] In expounding her methodology, Wainwright takes it for granted that ancient healing narratives, like the practices and events of healing that they recount, were subject to forces of "genderization." By this she means that, in any given circumstance, men and women engage and interpret the processes associated with healing differently, depending in part on how constructions of gender and construals of gendered bodies inform the dominant paradigms or "systems" of healing within a particular society. It is therefore incumbent upon the reader of such narratives to adopt an approach to their interpretation that is *socio-rhetorical* in nature, that is, an approach that takes seriously the manner in which such narratives function as venues for the interplay of the (often implicit) ideologies underpinning these constructions and construals.[41] As Wainwright shows, when the reader's attention turns to depictions of ancient women in healing narratives, what one encounters most often are silences, both in the texts themselves and in the world behind the texts.[42] In response, her project endeavors to give greater voice to the diverse subjectivities of healing women in antiquity and to provide richer contextuality to the gendering in which such subjectivities were embedded. By its very nature, this is a reading strategy that aligns itself with alternative healing practices and perspectives, including spaces and gestures of creative resistance to prevailing paradigms. Ultimately, then, Wainwright is interested not only in how women experienced healing but also in the cultural construction of healing itself, especially in how its potential for

40. See also Elaine M. Wainwright, *Towards A Feminist Critical Reading of the Gospel According to Matthew*, BZNW 60 (Berlin: Walter de Gruyter, 1991), 25–55.
41. Vernon K. Robbins, *Exploring the Texture of Texts: A Guide to Socio-Rhetorical Interpretation* (Harrisburg, PA: Trinity Press International, 1996), 1–6.
42. As we shall learn, the theme of silence is of particular relevance for analyzing the stories in chapters 8–9; see 8:14-15 (Chapter Four) and 9:20-22 (Chapter Eleven).

meaning would have been subject to reconstruction through female agency.

In order to uncover the multidimensionality of such agency, Wainwright incorporates a *postcolonial* perspective as well as an *ecological* perspective into her hermeneutic. While the former is useful in showing how issues of gender intersect with other variables of difference (race, class, political status, etc.), the latter emphasizes how health encompasses all aspects of life, including the relationships that human communities establish with their natural environments.[43] Building on such insights, Wainwright's interpretation of early Christian narratives seeks to expose and deconstruct the network of dualities that underpinned prevailing ideologies of healing in Mediterranean antiquity: not only male/female but also self/other, master/slave, Jew/Gentile, public/private, and culture/nature. The resulting conceptuality of health care is therefore comprehensive in scope, taking into account not only physical wounds but also the wounds of oppression and alienation as well. As indicated above, an interpretive priority in the articulation of this conceptuality is the theme of embodiment, a priority that comes to expression in various ways. This is expressed, for example, through attention to matters of materiality: the material world of human bodies, including the material contexts and resources with which such bodies interact.

Another way in which this priority comes to expression is through attention to the body as a site and signifier of power, specifically, the kinds of transformative power manifested in the processes of healing. Accordingly, in the analysis of specific stories, Wainwright is highly attuned to the potency of the body as a symbol (or "marker") and to the pivotal role that representations of bodies often have in sustaining the symbolic worlds projected by ancient healing narratives.[44] As she

43. Cf. Val Plumwood, *Feminism and the Mastery of Nature* (London: Routledge, 1993), 19–40.
44. See Chapter Eleven.

demonstrates, the symbolism of the body within a particular tradition does not remain inert but is subject to ongoing reconfiguration in rhetorically charged, often contested arenas, a point of relevance when considering the symbolic world of an author like Matthew, that is, an author whose choice and depiction of core symbols are governed (as we have seen) by sectarian priorities. Very often, such reconfigured or contested bodies find themselves in what Wainwright (borrowing a term from postcolonial studies) calls "borderland" spaces, an appropriate metaphor for conceptualizing the rhetorical and theological space occupied by the First Gospel itself.[45]

Disability Studies

One variable of difference that does not figure appreciably in Wainwright's method is disability, this despite the fact that the Gospels are populated with disabled bodies (e.g., Matt. 9:27-34) and recent years have witnessed a growing body of scholarship dealing with representations of disability in Scripture.[46] In fact, a major aim of this scholarship is to problematize such representations and the perceptions they engender, according to which disability is associated with punishment, dependency, and brokenness, and disabled bodies are seen as deficient, flawed, and aberrant, that is, as deviations from normative perceptions of health, productivity, self-sufficiency, and rationality.[47] Paradoxically, in biblical stories of both testaments, people with disabilities are simultaneously overrepresented and under-appreciated, a reflection of the fact that "disability has been

---

45. See Chapter Four.
46. For an example of an approach that integrates feminist criticism with disability perspectives, see Carole R. Fontaine, "Disabilities and Illness in the Bible: A Feminist Perspective," in *A Feminist Companion to the Hebrew Bible in the New Testament*, ed. Athalya Brenner (Sheffield: Sheffield Academic Press, 1996), 286–300.
47. Cf. Thomas E. Reynolds, *Vulnerable Communion: A Theology of Disability and Hospitality* (Grand Rapids: Brazos, 2008), 73–101.

used throughout history as a crutch upon which literary narratives lean for their representational power, disruptive potentiality, and analytical insight."[48] For its part, Scripture often metaphorizes disability in order to make abstract points or offer social commentary, reducing individuals with disabilities to stereotypes, ciphers, or passive objects upon which more powerful characters act, the implication in many cases being that humanity's final redemption involves the elimination of such individuals and what they represent.[49]

In response, disability scholarship embraces what can be summarized as a fourfold hermeneutical strategy, the basic goals of which are: (1) to recover the lived experiences, counter-narratives, and distinctive forms of agency represented by biblical characters with disabilities; (2) to dismantle traditional explanations and representations of disability; (3) to retrieve biblical and other theological resources that support an inclusive understanding of disability and the role of people with disabilities in the economy of salvation; and (4) to explore the repercussions of the first three steps for rethinking biblically based understandings of discipleship and community.[50] Viewed as a whole, this strategy involves "developing a redemptive theology of disabilities."[51] At the heart of this project is the idea that as both a descriptive and analytical category the meaning of disability is never fixed or transparent but represents a

---

48. David T. Mitchell and Sharon L. Snyder, *Narrative Prosthesis: Disability and the Dependencies of Discourse* (Ann Arbor: University of Michigan Press, 2000), 49. They go on to write that disabled bodies "show up in stories as dynamic entities that resist or refuse the cultural scripts assigned to them."
49. Jeremy Schipper, "Disabling Israelite Leadership: 2 Samuel 6:23 and Other Images of Disability in the Deuteronomistic History," in *This Abled Body: Rethinking Disabilities in Biblical Studies*, eds. Hector Avalos, Sarah J. Melcher, and Jeremy Schipper (Atlanta: Society of Biblical Literature, 2007), 103–13.
50. Amos Yong, *The Bible, Disability, and the Church: A New Vision of the People of God* (Grand Rapids: Eerdmans, 2011), 49–50.
51. Ibid., 58.

complex mode for understanding human difference. This affirmation is reflected in the fact that in its implementation the fourfold strategy is supported by not one but three different interpretive models, each of which brings different aspects of disability into relief.[52]

According to the *medical* model, to begin with, disability is understood in terms of an individual's physical, cognitive, or psychological condition. Specifically, there is some part, sense, or capacity of the person that fails to perform in accord with prescribed standards for what constitutes "normal" human functioning, thereby restricting his or her participation in certain basic activities. An advantage of this model is that it draws attention to the embodied experience of disability, including the personal challenges that accompany it. On the other hand, this model has a tendency to reduce persons with disabilities to their impairments, essentially defining them in terms of their dependence on others (healers, caregivers, etc.) to diagnose, treat, and (if possible) correct the deficiencies or incapacities in question and restore proper functioning.

For most people with disabilities, however, it is possible to distinguish the difficulties associated directly with one's medical condition from the various obstacles compounding the condition in any given instance by discriminatory perceptions and practices. The reality of disability, then, is not something located entirely within the individual. Hence the need for a *minority* or social group model,

---

52. For what follows, see Reynolds, *Vulnerable Communion*, 25–27; Deborah Beth Creamer, *Disability and Christian Theology: Embodied Limits and Constructive Possibilities* (Oxford: Oxford University Press, 2009), 22–33; Molly C. Haslam, *A Constructive Theology of Intellectual Disability: Human Being as Mutuality and Response* (New York: Fordham University Press, 2012), 1–18; Roy McCloughry and Wayne Morris, *Making a World of Difference: Christian Reflections on Disability* (London: SPCK, 2002), 8–24; Hans S. Reinders, *Receiving the Gift of Friendship: Profound Disability, Theological Anthropology, and Ethics* (Grand Rapids: Eerdmans, 2008), 54–62, 167–79; John Swinton, *Resurrecting the Person: Friendship and the Care of People with Mental Health Problems* (Nashville: Abingdon, 2000), 31–52; Jeremy Schipper, *Disability and Isaiah's Suffering Servant* (Oxford: Oxford University Press, 2011), 14–20.

according to which disability is defined not by clinical criteria but by shared experiences of stigmatization and exclusion. From this perspective, disability is seen principally as a social construction and a cultural product, that is, as a form of human difference to which (negative) social and cultural meanings have been attached.[53] Impairment becomes disability only when a society responds to it in a devaluing manner by imposing obstacles to full inclusion upon groups of people because they fail to meet certain somatic or agential norms. The meaning of disability will vary, therefore, depending on what sort of socially inscribed discourse one uses to explain it, while the underlying "problem" to be addressed for those with disabilities involves dismantling oppressive rhetorics, attitudes, and structures.

In its basic approach, the second model, not unlike the first, typifies the propensity to divide groups of people into social binaries, in this case, into those with disabilities and those without disabilities. It also tends to have a flattening effect with respect to the former group, lumping all individuals with disabilities into a single category, without much space left for degrees or kinds of difference. It is undoubtedly the case, however, that disability encompasses many forms of physical and cognitive impairment, as well as many different kinds of experience, which is just another way of saying that humanity as such exhibits a wide range of physiological, psychological, and functional variety. Hence the need for a third model, the *limits* model, according to which ability and disability relate to one another not as polarities but as fluid descriptors on a continuum. Fundamental to this model is the assumption that the experience of limits is an inherent aspect of the human condition. Indeed, it is even possible to speak of how "limits constitute our self-understandings and relationality with others."[54] From this

---

53. Saul M. Olyan, *Disability in the Hebrew Bible: Interpreting Mental and Physical Differences* (Cambridge: Cambridge University Press, 2008), 2.

perspective, disability is not understood in absolute terms or judged as something "other," but rather represents a specific instantiation of the sorts of fundamental realities with which all human beings in their creatureliness must contend. Just as there are manifold forms of embodiment, then, there are manifold forms of limits and ways that people engage them. Limits in this sense are not seen as a "problem" to be overcome but a reality that shapes who we are and our relationships with others, including our relationship with God. The study of disability provides an opportunity to reflect on what the reality of limits reveals about human nature and how we as human beings live with limits, that is, how we as finite beings live within a finite world. As I will try to show in the Conclusion, such reflection is applicable to the study of disability (and other topics) in the First Gospel as well.

Medical Anthropology

Another relatively new discipline that will be of use to our study of Matthew is medical anthropology, a major aim of which is to disentangle "the closely interwoven natural-environmental, human-biological, and socio-cultural threads forming the behavioral and conceptual network of human responses to the experience of illness."[55] Toward this end, practitioners in this field have developed various conceptual models for conducting cross-cultural analyses of different healing regimens and the ideologies that support them. For the purposes of our study, two of these models are worth mentioning at this point.[56]

---

54. Creamer, *Disability and Christian Theology*, 95. Cf. Reynolds, *Vulnerable Communion*, 177–88.
55. Paul U. Unschuld, "Culture and Pharmaceutics: Some Epistemological Observations on Pharmacological Systems in Ancient Europe and Medieval China," in *The Context of Medicines in Developing Countries: Studies in Pharmaceutical Anthropology*, eds. Sjaak van der Geest and Susan Reynolds Whyte (Dordrecht: Kluwer Academic, 1988), 179.

The first model involves differentiating two concepts: "disease" and "illness," a dichotomy whose basic contours are familiar from the first two models of disability discussed above. According to medical anthropologists, *disease* refers to a biomedical disorder of an organ or organ system that disrupts the performance of an individual's vital functions. *Illness*, on the other hand, designates the socially recognizable meanings imputed to disease by a given culture. Corresponding to the distinction between disease and illness is a distinction between "cure" and "heal," the former referring to the treatment of disease, the latter to the process by which disease is made into illness, the significance of which is then addressed so that the afflicted person can return to purposeful living. "Healing," then, is properly understood as a social event or exchange, one laden with symbolic meaning.

This leads to the second model, namely, that of healthcare systems, a concept to which reference has already been made. In the parlance of medical anthropology, a healthcare "system" refers to the collective view within a given society on matters of illness and health, a view whose internal structures encompass an array of variously interlocking elements, including specific beliefs, values, symbols, myths, rules, and relationships. The system is of importance to individual members of the society insofar as it situates the healing processes (or options) available to them within a coherent explanation of reality, thereby creating a sense of order and purpose for the specific roles, practices, and institutions that support those processes.

56. For what follows, see Allan Young, "The Anthropologies of Illness and Sickness," *Annual Review of Anthropology* 11 (1982): 257–85; John J. Pilch, *Healing in the New Testament: Insights from Medical and Mediterranean Anthropology* (Minneapolis: Fortress Press, 2000), 1–36; Hector Avalos, *Health Care and the Rise of Christianity* (Peabody, MA: Hendrickson, 1999), 19–30; Elaine M. Wainwright, *Women Healing/Healing Women: The Genderization of Healing in Early Christianity* (London: Equinox, 2006), 26–30; Eric Eve, *The Jewish Context of Jesus' Miracles*, JSNTSup 231 (London: Sheffield, 2002), 350–76; Eric Eve, *The Healer from Nazareth: Jesus' Miracles in Historical Context* (London: SPCK, 2009), 51–69.

Insofar as the healthcare system constitutes both a social construct and a semantic network, it is correct to say that, in their interactions with the sick, healers mediate culture: "it is the whole system that heals, not just the healer."[57] The sick, meanwhile, must undergo a process of "socialization" into the healthcare system's explanatory framework if they are to draw meaningful connections between their personal views and the collective view the framework represents.

Any particular healing event, then, needs to be evaluated within the total ecology of the healthcare system available to its participants, including especially the various "sectors" into which the system is divided, bearing in mind that in any given scenario of healing two or more sectors may be interacting or even competing with one another. It is therefore conceivable that participants in the same healing event may evaluate the meaning of the event differently, depending on the sector with which they are operating (e.g., 9:32-34), thus making it necessary in the analysis of any given instance to speak of a "hermeneutic" of healing.

For the purposes of this study, I have identified a total of four such healthcare sectors, which can be laid out schematically as follows:[58]

---

57. Pilch, *Healing in the New Testament*, 61.
58. Pilch (*Healing in the New Testament*, 25–27, 77–86) postulates three sectors: the professional, the popular, and the folk. When applied to the ancient Mediterranean world, however, this taxonomy fails to take into account the healing that takes place in temples. In addition, what Pilch labels the folk sector is more accurately described as the charismatic sector, while what he labels the popular sector is more accurately described as the folk sector, insofar as it corresponds with what in most societies is described as "folk medicine," for which see the references in n. 68.

	supernatural	natural
official	cultic	professional
unofficial	charismatic	folk

For the labels across the top of the chart, I rely on the analysis of Hector Avalos, who describes "secular" healing as referring to "approaches that emphasized natural, not supernatural, assumptions in illness's etiology and therapy," while acknowledging that "we cannot assume that emphasis on the natural meant absolute exclusion of the supernatural. The predominant pattern was for natural and supernatural etiologies and therapies to interact in the life of the average patient."[59] The term "official," on the other hand, applies to sectors in which greater emphasis is placed on healing traditions that are transmitted and authorized through formalized or institutionalized channels than in the sectors designated "unofficial." Below I give a basic description and one or more examples for each of the four sectors.

The **cultic sector**, to begin with, refers to that part of the healthcare system that is institutionalized in sacred places of worship

59. Avalos, *Health Care*, 55. Wainwright (*Women Healing*, 35) employs the term "secular" in her descriptions of ancient healthcare sectors as well.

and formalized in traditions, personnel (especially priesthoods), and rituals supporting the veneration of healing deities in these settings. In Greco-Roman society, the most popular of such deities was Asclepius, whose temple complexes were scattered throughout the Mediterranean basin.[60] Pilgrims of both genders, various ages, and all social classes flocked to such sanctuaries in search of cures for a wide range of ailments. After participating in the necessary sacrifices and purificatory rites, the sick would sleep (or "incubate") in a sacred hall (or *abaton*), hoping to encounter the god in a dream wherein he would either effect a cure or advise a treatment. Successful healings might be subsequently commemorated with thanksgiving offerings, inscriptional testimonies, or votive dedications.[61] Like other major deities of the era, Asclepius enjoyed both official public recognition and the support of wealthy patrons.[62] Other healing deities included the Egyptian goddess Isis, whose temple at Canopus evidently supported the practice of incubation as well.[63] There also appears to have been a well-established cult of Isis in the city of Antioch, which (as we have seen) is the likely setting of the First Gospel.[64]

---

60. See especially Emma J. Edelstein and Ludwig Edelstein, *Asclepius: Collection and Interpretation of the Testimonies* (Baltimore: Johns Hopkins University Press, 1945), 2:145–58, 181–213, 232–57. Cf. H. S. Versnel, *Coping with the Gods: Wayward Readings in Greek Theology*, Religions in the Graeco-Roman World 173 (Leiden: Brill, 2011), 400–21; Avalos, *Health Care*, 49–51; Wainwright, *Women Healing*, 83–92.

61. For an example of an inscriptional testimony, see the Conclusion.

62. For example, the Athenians recognized him as one of their official gods in the fifth century BCE, the same century in which he was honored with a sacred precinct at Delphi. See Edelstein and Edelstein, *Asclepius*, 2:120–21. For an example of patronage, see Bronwen L. Wickkiser, "Asklepios in Greek and Roman Corinth," in *Corinth in Context: Comparative Studies on Religion and Society*, NovTSup 134, eds. Steven J. Friesen, David N. Schowalter, and James C. Walters (Leiden: Brill, 2010), 57.

63. Jane Draycott, *Approaches to Healing in Roman Egypt*, BAR International Series 2416 (Oxford: Archaeopress, 2012), 34–35.

64. Frederick W. Norris, "Isis, Sarapis and Demeter in Antioch of Syria," *HTR* 75 (1982): 189–207. See further R. E. Witt, *Isis in the Graeco-Roman World* (Ithaca, NY: Cornell University Press, 1971), 185–97; Howard Clark Kee, *Medicine, Miracle and Magic in New Testament Times*, SNTSMS 55 (Cambridge: Cambridge University Press, 1986), 67–68, 90–91, 95–99, 112–13; Avalos, *Health Care*, 51–53.

The **professional** sector refers to healing institutionalized in fields of medical "science" and formalized in the structured acquisition of specialized therapeutic methods and a systematized body of therapeutic knowledge. In Greco-Roman society, this sort of education-based tradition was represented especially by the "schools" of Hippocratic physicians and the extensive corpus of Hippocratic writings in accordance with which they were credentialed.[65] Like other ancient arts, this is a tradition that relies extensively on technical jargon, distinctive forms of logic, and theory-driven constructs (e.g., the doctrine of the humors).[66] Socially, this was the smallest and most elite of the four sectors, with some of its participants serving as "civic" doctors, enjoying public patronage and carrying out officially recognized roles.[67] Participants in this sector also would have been more likely to seek out the "natural" causes of disease. For example, a Hippocratic treatise on the "sacred" disease (i.e., epilepsy) begins by explaining that it is "not any more divine or more sacred than other diseases but has a natural cause, and its supposed divine origin is due to men's inexperience" (*The Sacred Disease* 1.2-6). The author goes on to differentiate his own "empirical" approach from that of "magicians, purifiers, charlatans, and quacks" who have "sheltered themselves behind superstition" (2.1-10).

For the large majority of people living in Mediterranean antiquity, the household would have served as the primary locus for administering healing therapies as well as transmitting healing

---

65. Vivian Nutton, *Ancient Medicine* (London: Routledge, 2004), 53–103; Vivian Nutton, "Healers in the Medical Market Place: Towards a Social History of Graeco-Roman Medicine," in *Medicine in Society: Historical Essays*, ed. Andrew Wear (Cambridge: Cambridge University Press, 1992), 15–58; Kee, *Medicine, Miracle and Magic*, 27–66; Wainwright, *Women Healing*, 33–70.

66. For the doctrine of the humors, see Avalos, *Health Care*, 65–66.

67. For example, Wainwright (*Women Healing*, 51) discusses a first century BCE or CE inscription in which the healing art (*technē*) of a certain Antiochis is recognized by the citizens and council of the city of Tlos in Asia Minor. Cf. Draycott, *Healing in Roman Egypt*, 22–23.

knowledge. Accordingly, the **folk** sector, representing the non-professional, non-specialist traditions of healing, was the most prevalent and most generalized of the four sectors.[68] In contrast to the theory-driven criteria of traditions associated with the professional sector, here the orientation is more fully practical in nature, with many of the sector's therapeutic strategies falling under the category of self-help. Representative here is the sort of pharmacological lore preserved by Pliny in his compendium *Natural History* and in the Roman farming manuals written by Cato the Elder, Varro, and Columella.[69] W. H. S. Jones notes "the rarity of religious means of healing in these works,"[70] though occasionally a ritual or incantation (apparently preserving a lost superstition of some kind) accompanies the preparation or administration of the remedy. A cure for stomach worms prescribed by Cato, for instance, "based on pomegranate blossoms, fennel, frankincense, honey, wild marjoram, and wine, ends with the injunction that the patient must climb up a square pillar and jump down from it ten times, before going for a walk."[71] The use of such herbal remedies, drawing on resources from the local "natural" environment, does not presuppose any special gifts or training, thereby making the sector's strategies accessible to all social classes, even the poor and slaves. This represents another departure from Hippocratic physicians, who typically expected remuneration for their services.[72]

---

68. Wainwright, *Women Healing*, 71–83; W. H. S. Jones, "Ancient Roman Folk Medicine," *Journal of the History of Medicine* 12 (1957): 459–72; Draycott, *Healing in Roman Egypt*, 40–60; Pieter F. Craffert, *Illness, Health and Healing in the New Testament World: Perspectives on Health Care* (Pretoria: Biblia, 1999), 67–87; Joan E. Taylor, *The Essenes, The Scrolls, and the Dead Sea* (Oxford: Oxford University Press, 2012), 304–40.

69. For the former, see H. Rackham, *Pliny: Natural History*, LCL (Cambridge, MA: Harvard University Press, 1938), 1:vi–xiv. For the latter, see William D. Hooper, *Cato: On Agriculture; Varro: On Agriculture*, LCL (Cambridge, MA: Harvard University Press, 1935), ix–xviii.

70. Jones, "Ancient Roman Folk Medicine," 461.

71. Nutton, *Ancient Medicine*, 162 (referring to Cato, *On Agriculture* 127.1–3).

The **charismatic** sector, finally, refers to healing conducted by non-credentialed specialists, individuals whose authority stems from unusual powers, personal inspiration, and the acquisition of esoteric techniques, formulas, and rituals through which such powers and inspiration are channeled.[73] The forms of legitimation supporting this sort of healthcare are accordingly more ad hoc and individualized than what we find in the other sectors, its strategies depending on the "manipulation of various (often impersonal) supernatural forces or the coercion of a deity in order to obtain a desired concrete benefit."[74] Typical in this regard is Apollonius of Tyana, an itinerant sage, seer, and ascetic of the late first century CE, who, according to a third century CE biography, performed healings and exorcisms in addition to numerous other wonders.[75] Here, as in many ancient sources, the ability of malevolent spirits to harm and even invade human bodies is taken for granted. Mention may also be made in this context of the Greek Magical Papyri, an anthology of spells, incantations, and related materials deriving from Hellenistic and Roman Egypt, in which we find such things as cures for fevers and instructions for performing an exorcism.[76] The engagement with supernatural forces projected by these texts is more eclectic and syncretistic than

72. As Kee (*Medicine, Miracle and Magic,* 5–8) points out, Pliny sometimes contrasts his folk remedies with those offered by medical professionals.
73. The designation "charismatic" for such individuals is derived from Theissen, *Miracle Stories,* 231–46.
74. John P. Meier, *A Marginal Jew: Rethinking the Historical Jesus* (New York: Doubleday, 1994), 2:549.
75. E.g., Philostratus, *Life of Apollonius* 3.38–39; 4.20, 45; 6.43. As Meier (*A Marginal Jew,* 2:578) notes, within the worldview projected by this text, "the supernatural atmosphere is all-pervading." He also notes the seer's attraction to "various mystical and esoteric traditions" (*A Marginal Jew,* 2:576). See further Ewen Bowie, "Apollonius of Tyana: Tradition and Reality," *ANRW* II.16.2 (1978): 1652–99.
76. For the former, see *PGM* VII.211–21. For the latter, see *PGM* IV.1227–64, 3007–86; V.96–172 (with Graham H. Twelftree, *In the Name of Jesus: Exorcism Among Early Christians* [Grand Rapids: Baker Academic, 2007], 39–40). See further Hans Dieter Betz, ed., *The Greek Magical Papyri in Translation: Including the Demotic Spells,* 2nd ed. (Chicago: University of Chicago Press, 1992), xli–lviii.

that evidenced by the other sectors, reflecting both the pragmatic orientation and social marginalization of its practitioners.[77] Charismatic healers, of course, were not restricted to Greco-Roman society.[78] Josephus, for example, claims to have witnessed exorcisms performed by a certain Eleazar using a ring embedded with roots prescribed by Solomon for casting out demons together with incantations that the king had composed for the same purpose.[79] As we shall see, traditions regarding Solomon are relevant for understanding the person and ministry of Jesus as a healer as well.[80]

It should be emphasized that while the differentiation of these four categories may be helpful for heuristic purposes, in reality the lines separating the sectors in the chart above were often blurred. Some of the treatments advised by Asclepius, for example, are similar to those recommended by Hippocratic physicians,[81] who, for their part, sometimes venerated Asclepius as a patron deity.[82] There is

77. For more on ancient magic, see Jack N. Lightstone, *The Commerce of the Sacred: Mediation of the Divine Among Jews in the Graeco-Roman Diaspora* (Chico, CA: Scholars, 1984), 17–56; Meier, *A Marginal Jew*, 2:537–52; Eve, *Jewish Context*, 361–76; Susan R. Garrett, *The Demise of the Devil: Magic and the Demonic in Luke's Writings* (Minneapolis: Fortress Press, 1989), 11–36; P. S. Alexander, "Incantations and Books of Magic," in *The History of the Jewish People in the Age of Jesus Christ*, eds. Emil Schürer, Geza Vermes, Fergus Millar, and Martin Goodman, rev. ed. (Edinburgh: T&T Clark, 1986), 3:342–79 .

78. Under the category of "Charismatic Judaism," Geza Vermes (*Jesus the Jew: A Historian's Reading of the Gospels* [Philadelphia: Fortress Press, 1981], 58–82) includes the wonder-worker Hanina ben Dosa. For more on Hanina ben Dosa, see also my discussion in the Conclusion.

79. Josephus, *Antiquities* 8.45–49. The evidence for ancient exorcists is surveyed by Eve, *Jewish Context*, 197–214, 326–49; Eve, *Healer from Nazareth*, 27–37; Meier, *A Marginal Jew*, 2:404–23; Gideon Bohak, "Jewish Exorcism Before and After the Destruction of the Second Temple," in *Was 70 CE a Watershed in Jewish History? On Jews and Judaism Before and After the Destruction of the Second Temple*, Ancient Judaism and Early Christianity 78, eds. Daniel R. Schwartz and Zeev Weiss (Leiden: Brill, 2012), 277–300; Twelftree, *In the Name of Jesus*, 35–54; Amanda Witmer, *Jesus, The Galilean Exorcist: His Exorcisms in Social and Political Context*, Library of Historical Jesus Studies 10 (London: T&T Clark, 2012), 22–60; Larry P. Hogan, *Healing in the Second Temple Period*, NTOA 21 (Göttingen: Vandenhoeck & Ruprecht, 1992), 139–40, 148, 225–28, 236–39, 253–54.

80. See Chapter Twelve.

81. Wickkiser, "Asklepios," 45–46; Versnel, *Coping with the Gods*, 400–401. For more on the relation between medicine and religion, see Nutton, *Ancient Medicine*, 104–15, 280–98.

82. Edelstein and Edelstein, *Asclepius*, 2:139–40.

also evidence for the incorporation of "folk" remedies into the Hippocratic treatises,[83] as well as a certain amount of overlap between "medical" and "magical" approaches to treating disease.[84] Wainwright, finally, notes how the services offered by midwives often would have traversed the boundaries separating the professional and folk sectors.[85] Such boundary-crossing activity is worth bearing in mind when investigating the distinctive healthcare "system" represented by the First Gospel, a task to which we now turn.

83. John Scarborough, "Adaptation of Folk Medicines in the Formal Materia Medica of Classical Antiquity," in Folklore and Folk Medicines, ed. John Scarborough (Madison, WI: American Institute of the History of Pharmacy, 1987), 21–32.
84. Nutton, "Healers in the Medical Market Place," 32–33.
85. Wainwright, Women Healing, 72–73.

2

The Living Temple: Matthew 8:1-4

In the first triad of miracle stories, Jesus encounters people who in Jewish society would have experienced different kinds of social marginalization: a leper (8:1-4), a Gentile (8:5-13), and a sick woman (8:14-15). For a sense of the isolation endured by the first of these individuals, we can turn to the *Against Apion* of Josephus, a text written around the same time as the Gospel of Matthew:[1]

> He [Moses] prohibited lepers from staying in a city or living in a village, requiring that they travel about alone, with their clothes torn; and he regards as unclean anyone who touches them or lives under the same roof.

It is worth noting that the exclusionary practices laid out here are more rigorous than what is actually prescribed by the Mosaic law. The ban against touch, for example, is derived not from the legislation on leprosy in Leviticus 13–14 but from a set of parallel

---

1. Josephus, *Against Apion* 1.281. Translation from John M. G. Barclay, *Against Apion: Translation and Commentary* (Leiden: Brill, 2007), 151.

purity rules about bodily emissions in Leviticus 15:1-15, 19-24. The ban against cohabitation, meanwhile, is not derived from Scripture at all, even if Leviticus 14:33-53 does mention houses as potential infection sites. The heightened measure of repulsion implicit in Josephus's comments reflects the fact that in antiquity leprosy was not simply a "social" disease but also a disease that imposed upon its victims a kind of social "exile," that is, an exile from the sources of one's personal, social, and religious identity.[2]

As we have seen, in constructing this first triad of stories, Matthew draws twice on Mark and once on the synoptic sayings source, though in doing so he exhibits his typical freedom as a redactor:

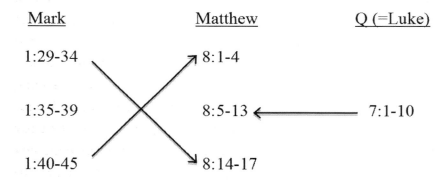

In the Second Gospel, the healing of Peter's mother-in-law comes first (Mark 1:29-34), followed by a scene in which Jesus departs from Capernaum (Mark 1:35-39) and then the healing of a man with leprosy (Mark 1:40-45). In the First Gospel, meanwhile, the order of the two healing episodes has been reversed, and the intervening material (Mark 1:35-39)[3] has been replaced with a text derived from the Q source, the story of the centurion and his slave (cf. Luke 7:1-10).[4] Among other things, this means that the story of Jesus

2. Susan R. Holman, "Healing the Social Leper in Gregory of Nyssa's and Greogory Nazianzus's *peri philoptōchias*," *HTR* 92 (1999): 285.
3. A vestige of Mark 1:39 can be detected in Matthew 4:23.

and the leper has been shifted to a more prominent, introductory position in the narrative. Coming to terms with the implications of this change represents an important issue for the interpreter.

While the Greek word *lepra* could refer to what we today call leprosy (or Hansen's disease), more often the term was used to designate a variety of exfoliative skin conditions, such as psoriasis or vitiligo.[5] In contrast to most of the other ailments that Jesus will encounter in Matthew 8–9, this disease carried with it a stigma of ritual uncleanness (Lev. 13:1-44).[6] Because of this stigma, "lepers" were systematically ostracized by the community (Lev. 13:45-46; Num. 5:1-4), the impurity attached to them being so severe that touching an afflicted person meant contracting the same sort of defilement as touching a corpse.[7] Accordingly, such individuals were treated as though they were socially dead (Num. 12:12; 2 Kgs. 5:7; Job 18:13), while their recovery could be likened to a resurrection.[8]

In order to better understand Israelite society's seeming preoccupation with skin disease, it is necessary to enlist the assistance of cultural anthropologist Mary Douglas and her work on the book of Leviticus. Douglas begins by looking at the various, often implicit ways in which the individual human body can function as a model or symbol of a society's "bounded system," referring to the particular configuration of social rules, roles, and institutions that define and distinguish one society over against others.[9] Of course, both human

---

4. In Q, this appears to have been the pericope that immediately followed the inaugural sermon (elements of which are preserved in the Sermon on the Mount and the Sermon on the Plain). Luke apparently preserves this order, while Matthew instead has the story in 8:1-4. Cf. John S. Kloppenborg, *Q Parallels: Synopsis, Critical Notes and Concordance* (Sonoma, CA: Polebridge, 1988), 48–51.

5. David P. Wright and Richard N. Jones, "Leprosy," *ABD* 4 (1992): 277–82.

6. Matters of ritual impurity will also be of some importance to the interpretation of Matthew 9:18-26, for which see Chapter Eleven.

7. Jacob Milgrom, *Leviticus*, AB 3 (New York: Doubleday, 1991), 1:819.

8. A rabbinic text (*b. Sanh.* 47a) interprets Elisha's healing of Naaman in such terms (cf. 2 Kgs. 5:7). A text from Qumran uses the term "death" in a diagnosis of scale-disease while attributing its cure to "the spirit of life" (4QD[a] 4–5, 10–12).

bodies and human societies are subject to change, and, of course, change is often accompanied by anxiety. Douglas argues that one of the ways in which members of a society process their collective anxieties is by projecting them onto the human body, turning it into a symbolic focal point of common social concern. In the case of ancient Israelite society, it is evident that the people's anxieties revolved especially around a need to protect their community from a variety of perceived threats to its social boundaries. Within what was perceived to be a menacing environment, "[t]he threatened boundaries of their body politic would be well mirrored in their care for the integrity, unity, and purity of the physical body."[10] Hence the preoccupation with skin disease: concerns about social boundaries (boundaries separating insiders from outsiders) are expressed as concerns about bodily boundaries (boundaries separating the inside of a person from the outside). In order to make such concerns culturally meaningful, they are mapped onto a ritual dichotomy of pure versus impure, the surface of the "leprous" body becoming the object of intense ritual scrutiny and elaborate purificatory practice, as the lengthy prescriptions of Leviticus 13–14 attest.[11]

Against such a social and cultural background, the story of Jesus and the "leper" in Matthew 8:1-4 takes on special meaning. Remember that Matthew has chosen this incident to serve not only as the introduction to chapters 8–9, but also as the first healing story of the entire Gospel (cf. 4:23-25). The incident is appropriate as a foundation for what follows in that it announces a theme that we will encounter repeatedly in our analysis of Matthew's healing stories, namely, the willingness of Jesus to confront and transcend

9. Mary Douglas, *Purity and Danger: An Analysis of the Concepts of Pollution and Taboo* (New York: Praeger, 1966), 115–29.

10. Ibid., 113.

11. The prescriptions regarding clothes (Lev. 13:47-59) and walls (Lev. 14:34-42) are consistent with the general focus on boundaries.

social boundaries of various kinds, especially boundaries that exclude individuals from participating in the community of God's holy people. As a demonstration of his ability to grant new life to one who is socially dead, the story illustrates the authority over all boundaries and limits that has been bestowed on Jesus, the one who will overcome the power of death itself (Matt. 9:18).

Matthew's account of the incident is based on Mark 1:40–45 (cf. Luke 5:12–16):

	(1) When he came down from the mountain, large crowds followed him.
(40) And a man with a scale-disease came up to him pleading with him, and kneeling he said to him, "If you are willing, you can cleanse me."	(2) And coming up to him, a man with a scale-disease bowed down before him, saying, "Lord, if you are willing, you can cleanse me."
(41) And moved with compassion, he stretched out his hand and touched him and said to him, "I am willing; be cleansed!" (42) And at once the scale-disease left him and he was cleansed.	(3) And stretching out his hand he touched him, saying, "I am willing; be cleansed!" And at once his scale-disease was cleansed.
(43) and strictly charging him, he at once cast him out,	
(44) and he said to him, "See that you tell no one anything; but go, show yourself to the priest and offer for your cleansing what Moses commanded, as a testimony to them."	(4) And Jesus said to him, "See that you tell no one; but go, show yourself to the priest and offer the gift that Moses commanded, as a testimony to them." (Matt. 8:1-4)
(45) But he went out and began to proclaim it freely and to spread the word, so that he was no longer able to enter a city openly, but stayed out in deserted places; and they were coming to him from everywhere. (Mark 1:40-45)	

The first thing we note when comparing the two versions is that Matthew has added an introduction to the story (Matt. 8:1) that connects it with the preceding narrative. As commentators sometimes note, the first half of this transitional sentence ("When he came down from the mountain . . .") is reminiscent of Exodus 34:29, where Moses descends from Mount Sinai after receiving the law, while the sentence's second half (". . . large crowds followed him") is reminiscent of Matthew 4:25 ("Large crowds followed him . . ."), which together with Matthew 8:1 creates a literary frame around the Sermon on the Mount, a text that interacts with the law of Moses at some length.[12] Indeed, near the beginning of that sermon (Matt. 5:17), Jesus had identified himself as the one who was sent to fulfill the law, an assertion for which narrative proof is provided here in Matthew 8:4: Jesus obeys the law of Moses and instructs others to do likewise (cf. 5:19).[13] In that same passage near the beginning of the sermon (5:17), Jesus had also identified himself as the one who was sent to fulfill "the prophets" as well, an assertion for which narrative proof will be forthcoming (see Chapters Four and Five).

Characteristically, when it comes to redacting the incident itself (Matt. 8:2-4), the evangelist busies himself more with deleting material than with adding it. As for the former, it is possible to identify significant deletions at two points: one when we compare Matthew 8:2-3 with Mark 1:40-43, and the other when we compare Matthew 8:4 with Mark 1:44-45.

Take Matthew 8:2-3 first. Even as he retains the verbal exchange between Jesus and the man, Matthew drops two (rather vivid)

12. See Paul Foster, *Community, Law and Mission in Matthew's Gospel*, WUNT 2.177 (Tübingen: Mohr Siebeck, 2004), 94–143.

13. Note that Matthew 8:4 refers to Moses by name and that Numbers 12:1-16 preserves a story in which Moses pleads for the healing of a leper. Also, perhaps the phrase "stretched out his hand" (Matt. 8:3) is meant to recall texts where Moses employs the same gesture in the context of a miracle story (e.g., Exod. 14:16, 21, 26-27).

narrative elements that contribute to the depiction of the former's procedure: "strictly charging him" and "cast him out" (Mark 1:43).[14] What makes this redaction noteworthy is that elsewhere in ancient literature (including elsewhere in the Gospels) these same sorts of depictions are sometimes associated with the practice of exorcism.[15] While Matthew will have occasion to present Jesus as an exorcist later (Matt. 8:28-34 and 9:32-34), his version of the story here shifts attention away from the possibility of Jesus' exorcistic comportment and toward the content of his dialogue with the man.[16]

This editorial contraction also has implications for understanding the story's literary *structure*. Most important, the account of the healing now presents the reader with a more streamlined narration. The man: (1) approaches Jesus, (2) bows down before him (note that the Greek verb here can also be translated as "worships"),[17] (3) makes a petition after addressing Jesus as "Lord" (a title missing from Mark's version of the story), and (4) has his petition granted. In its combination of words and actions, this sequence of events outlines the same basic procedure according to which ancient supplicants would have worshipped at cultic centers, including cultic centers of healing.[18] From a structural perspective, then, it seems that Jesus functions for the man very much like a temple (cf. Matt. 2:11; Luke 17:15-16). The healer has become, in essence, the living embodiment of a cultic center of healing, emanating the sort of purifying power

14. Matthew also drops "pleading with" (Mark 1:40) and "left him" (Mark 1:42).

15. Marcus, *Mark*, 1:209 (note that he translates *embrimēsamenos* in Mark 1:43 as "growling at" rather than "strictly charging"). For more on the First Gospel's tendency to minimize Jesus' profile as an exorcist, see the discussion in Chapter Thirteen.

16. Cf. Heinz Joachim Held, "Matthew as Interpreter of the Miracle Stories," in *Tradition and Interpretation in Matthew*, eds. Günther Bornkamm, Gerhard Barth, and Heinz Joachim Held (Philadelphia: Westminster, 1963), 214–15.

17. In the First Gospel, the NASB usually renders the verb (*proskuneō*) as "worship," as in 2:2, 8, 11; 4:9-10; 14:33; 28:9, 17. In our section, the word will occur again in Matthew 9:18.

18. W. D. Davies and Dale C. Allison, *The Gospel According to Saint Matthew*, ICC (London: T&T Clark, 1991), 2:10.

often associated with such sites.[19] The relevance of such a narrative strategy for conceptualizing the person of Jesus becomes especially apparent when we take into account how Matthew concludes the story. This occurs in v. 4, where Jesus instructs the man to show himself to the priest and offer the necessary sacrifice, a reference to the rituals of reincorporation prescribed for "lepers" in Leviticus 14:1-32 (cf. Luke 17:14).[20] The parallelism between vv. 2-3 and v. 4 is hard to miss: having approached Jesus the living temple for cleansing, the man must now approach the temple in Jerusalem for confirmation of the cleansing.

Here we come to Matthew's second and more substantial deletion of Markan material. Mark 1:44-45 is a good example of what modern interpreters call the "messianic secret," a term that refers to the occasions on which Jesus forbids the disciples (e.g., Mark 8:30), demons (e.g., Mark 3:12), and people whom he has healed (e.g., Mark 7:36) from speaking publically about his deeds and identity.[21] Whatever theological significance such silencing may have had for Mark and his original readers, it is apparent from his redactional activity that Matthew found the concept to be problematic, at least in certain contexts.[22] Evidence of this can be found in the fact that even as he retains the command to secrecy itself ("See that you tell no one anything"), Matthew drops Mark 1:45 in its entirety from the narrative here, relocating some of its content to a later point in the Gospel (Matt. 9:31).[23] Thus any hint that the man

---

19. For temples as venues of not only purity but also healing, see the discussion of the "cultic" sector of the ancient Mediterranean healthcare system in Chapter One.

20. Thus the demonstration of the cure, a regular form-critical element of healing stories, is projected into events that occur beyond the narrative itself. Note that among the evangelists, Matthew is alone in using the expression "to offer a gift" (*prospherōdōron*), a construction familiar from Leviticus (e.g., 1:2, 14; 2:1, 4, 12, 13; 4:23, 32). Cf. Matt. 2:11; 5:23-24; Heb. 5:1; 8:3.

21. Heikki Räisänen, *The 'Messianic Secret' in Mark* (Edinburgh: T&T Clark, 1990), 242–58.

22. See the discussion of Matt. 8:17 (in Chapter Five) and 9:30 (in Chapter Twelve). Also see Matt. 13:34-35 (cf. Mark 4:33-34); 15:15 (cf. Mark 7:17), 21 (cf. Mark 7:24), 30-31 (cf. Mark 7:36-37).

23. See Chapter Twelve.

disobeyed Jesus or that Jesus' intention for him remained unfulfilled has been omitted, producing a significant shift in the meaning of Jesus' command for secrecy. In Mark, the purpose of the command had been to prevent "word" of the healing from becoming public (Mark 1:45). In Matthew, such a purpose for the command makes little sense, given the presence of a witnessing crowd (Matt. 8:1). Instead, Jesus' command for secrecy is meant to convey a sense of urgency regarding the command that immediately follows: the man must not talk to anyone about what has happened until he sees the priest, since only the priest can declare him ritually clean.[24] This procedure is indeed urgent, since the priest's declaration is necessary for the sort of "healing" described by medical anthropologists to be completed.[25] Jesus may have "cured" the man's physical ailment, but given the cultural stigma associated with this particular disease, only the priest can ensure the man's reincorporation into society.

These comments have implications for how we interpret not only the function of Matthew 8:1-4 within the broader narrative but also the basic character of the story itself. In order to understand these implications, it is helpful to look at an incident that occurs later in the Gospel:

> (9) The crowds that were going ahead of him and those who were following were shouting, saying, "Hosanna to the Son of David!" ...
> (12) Then Jesus entered the temple and drove out all those who were selling and buying in the temple, and he overturned the tables of the money changers and the seats of those who were selling the doves. (13) And he said to them, "It is written, 'My house shall be called a house of prayer'; but you are making it a den of robbers." (14) *And the blind and the lame came to him in the temple, and he healed them.* (15) But when the chief priests and the scribes saw the wonders he performed and the

---

24. So *m. Neg.* 3:1; cf. Ps.-Philo, *L.A.B.* 13.3.
25. See Chapter One. See also John J. Pilch, *Healing in the New Testament: Insights from Medical and Mediterranean Anthropology* (Minneapolis: Fortress Press, 2000), 39–54.

children who were shouting in the temple, "Hosanna to the Son of David," they became indignant. (Matt. 21:9-15)

The italicized sentence in this quotation, which is found only in Matthew's Gospel (cf. Mark 11:15-19; Luke 19:45-48; John 2:13-22), is best understood as an allusion to 2 Samuel 5:6-8:

> (6) The king and his men marched to Jerusalem against the Jebusites, the inhabitants of the land, who said to David, "You will not come in here, even the blind and the lame will turn you back"—thinking, "David cannot come in here."(7) Nevertheless David took the stronghold of Zion, which is now the city of David. (8) David had said on that day, "Whoever would strike down the Jebusites, let him get up the water shaft to attack the lame and the blind, those whom David hates." Therefore it is said, "The blind and the lame shall not come into the house." (NRSV)

The actions of King David, who barred the blind and the lame from entering the temple,[26] are now reversed by the messianic Son of David, a title that represents an important identity marker for Jesus in Matthew's Gospel, not only in the passage just cited (Matt. 21:15), but throughout the text (e.g., Matt. 1:1), especially in the healing stories (see Chapter Twelve).[27] In this role, Jesus appears as an agent of accessibility for those living with disease and disability, welcoming society's outcasts into the holy place and center of communal worship. This is an important and distinctive aspect to Matthew's understanding of Jesus' action in the temple.[28] Meanwhile, the man, for his part, now appears as Jesus' emissary, charged by Jesus to "go" ahead of him to the temple in Jerusalem and give "testimony" (Matt. 8:4): not only testimony that he has been made whole and is ready to re-enter society but also testimony about the one who has made him

---

26. Cf. Lev. 21:16-21; *m. Hag.* 1:1; 4QMMT 52–57.
27. Note that 21:15 (like 21:14) is found only in Matthew's Gospel.
28. Cf. Boris Repschinski, "Re-Imagining the Presence of God: The Temple and the Messiah in the Gospel of Matthew," *ABR* 54 (2006): 37–49.

whole, the one who will eventually arrive in Jerusalem himself and make the people whole by overcoming barriers of social exclusion.[29] In this capacity, the man can be likened to one of Jesus' disciples, who similarly receive a commission from their Lord to "go" (Matt. 10:6) and give "testimony" (Matt. 10:18; cf. 24:14) on his behalf.[30] While the disciples are empowered to heal others (Matt. 10:1, 8), however, this man bears the effects of Jesus' healing power on his own body, a body whose cleansing here foreshadows the "cleansing" of the temple later in the Gospel.

In evaluating this correlation between the man's healed or "cleansed" body and the healed or "cleansed" space of the temple, we can invoke another anthropological insight from the work of Mary Douglas. As we learned earlier, she observed that in the book of Leviticus the individual human body often functions as a model of Israelite society. In this capacity, she further observed that the body can also function as a model of a particular institution within Israelite society, namely, the temple and the temple mount.[31] Let me raise the possibility that a similar sort of "modeling" might be relevant for thinking about the relationship between the healing stories in Matthew 8:1-4 and 21:9-15. While the body-temple analogy in Leviticus is mapped onto a ritual dichotomy of pure versus impure, however, in Matthew it is reconfigured in accordance with Jesus' agenda of inclusion.

At this point, the results of the analysis of Matthew 8:1-4 so far can be expressed in terms of an identification of the episode's literary *form*: in his redaction of the text, Matthew has taken what was originally a healing story with elements of an exorcism story (Mark 1:40-45) and

---

29. For the dismissal formula ("Go!") in miracle stories (e.g., 8:4, 13, 32; 9:6), see Gerd Theissen, *The Miracle Stories of the Early Christian Tradition* (Philadelphia: Fortress Press, 1983), 67–68.

30. In stretching out his hand toward the man (Matt. 8:3), Jesus interacts with him much as he will interact later in the Gospel with his disciples (Matt. 12:49; 14:31).

31. Mary Douglas, *Leviticus as Literature* (Oxford: Oxford University Press, 2000), 66–86.

transformed it into a healing story with elements of a commissioning story. Moreover, it is appropriate to think of what transpires here as a "sacred" commission, sacred in the sense that both its basis and its outcome manifest the power of Jesus to render the unclean clean.

The dimensions of this literary transformation are more fully appreciated when we compare Matthew 8:1-4 with its principal biblical antecedent, 2 Kings 5:1-27.[32] The miraculous healing of Naaman there serves as a sign for participants in the story that Elisha is indeed God's prophet (2 Kgs. 5:8), a designation that is relevant for understanding the identity of Jesus as well.[33] Much like Jesus, the prophet tells Naaman to "be cleansed" (2 Kgs. 5:13) and then to "go" (2 Kgs. 5:19). Much like the man in our story, Naaman the "leper" will provide evidence of his healing by offering a sacrifice to the God of Israel (2 Kgs. 5:17). Additional points of comparison can be found in 2 Kings 5:11, where Naaman expresses prevailing expectations regarding how a prophetic healing would take place:

> He will surely come out to me and stand and call on the name of the Lord his God, and wave his hand over the place and cure the leper. (NASB)

Here it is assumed that in order to accomplish a deed of power the prophet must call on the name of the Lord (cf. 1 Kgs. 18:24). In our story, by contrast, Jesus does not call on the name of the Lord. Rather, he *is* the Lord, a point that Matthew (unlike Mark) makes explicit by having the man address Jesus as such (Matt. 8:2), using a title that is found frequently on the lips of those seeking his help.[34] As for the significance of the title, no doubt Matthew expected his

---

32. Davies and Allison, *Saint Matthew*, 2:11.
33. Matt. 10:41; 13:57; 14:5; 16:14; 21:11, 46; 23:34, 37; cf. Luke 4:27.
34. Matt. 8:6, 8; 9:28; 15:22, 25, 27; 17:15; 20:30-31, 33.

readers to recall the warning that Jesus had just issued regarding those who speak to him this way:

> Not everyone who says to me, "Lord, Lord," will enter the kingdom of heaven, but only the one who does the will of my Father in heaven. (Matt. 7:21; cf. 12:50)

Here, the designation of Jesus as "Lord" refers to his role as agent of God's eschatological kingdom. In conjunction with this role, he is identified specifically as the agent of his heavenly Father's "will" (*thelēma*), a concept that plays an important role in our passage as well: "if you are willing (*thelēs*) . . . I am willing (*thelō*) . . ." (Matt. 8:2-3). As noted above, Matthew's redactional activity has the effect of drawing attention to the dynamics of this verbal exchange: the question upon which everything in the story depends is not Jesus' *ability* to heal (which is taken for granted) but his *willingness* to heal. In communicating such willingness, Jesus reveals something of the divine power and sovereignty working through him.[35] It is not just that Jesus knows (Matt. 11:27) and obeys (Matt. 26:39, 42) the will of his Father. As the "Lord," he actually embodies this will. Matthew's readers would understand that Jesus their Lord "wills" the healing of all those who call on him for help, and in this he expresses the will of God's very self (cf. Matt. 18:14). It is from this perspective that we can comprehend the nature of Jesus' divine agency: the same authority that was evident in his teaching (Matt. 7:28-29) has now become evident in his actions.

Another difference between Jesus and Elisha concerns their respective techniques of healing. In 2 Kings 5:11, the prophet is envisioned as waving his hand over the afflicted area.[36] In Matthew 8:3, by contrast, Jesus actually touches the afflicted person, a gesture

---

35. Cf. Theissen, *Miracle Stories*, 77–78.
36. The version of this sentence in the LXX has "lay his hand" instead of "wave his hand."

that he will employ elsewhere.[37] While physical contact with a "leper" would not have entailed a violation of the law, it ordinarily would have entailed the contraction of ritual impurity.[38] Through his seeming indifference to such defilement, yet another signal is provided regarding the nature of Jesus' divine power and sovereignty: the "Lord" does not contract ritual impurity; he conquers it. More than this, Jesus' healing touch symbolically anticipates the man's acceptance back into the community.[39] This does not mean, however, that the rituals of reincorporation prescribed by Leviticus 14:1-32 are no longer necessary. Quite the contrary: Jesus recognizes that in order for the man's reintegration into the community to take place, it must be acknowledged in the community's place of worship. The traditional roles, rules, and institutions of the liturgy still have their place, so long as they provide an opportunity for offering the right kind of "testimony."

37. The miracles in Matthew 8:15 and 9:25 occur by touch alone. In Matthew 9:29, touch is combined with a word of power, while in Matthew 9:20 it is the person seeking a cure who initiates the touch. Note that Matthew 9:20 and 25 also involve individuals who would have been thought to be ritually impure.
38. Marcus, *Mark*, 1:210; John Nolland, *The Gospel of Matthew*, NIGTC (Grand Rapids: Eerdmans, 2005), 350.
39. The reference to Simon "the leper" in Matthew 26:6 (hosting Jesus in his home) suggests that people known to have had scale-diseases were welcomed into the movement.

3

From East and West: Matthew 8:5-13

In the Gospel of Mark, the story of Jesus and the man with a scale-disease (Mark 1:40-45) is immediately followed by a story that takes place in Capernaum, the healing of the paralytic (Mark 2:1-12). The author of the First Gospel postpones the account of this healing to Matthew 9:1-8 (see Chapter Eight) and in its place inserts a story that also occurs in Capernaum, though for this he draws not on the Second Gospel but on the Q source.[1] This is the healing of the centurion's servant, which in its prior literary setting immediately followed the so-called inaugural sermon (i.e., Q/Luke 6:20-49).[2] This incident has the distinction of being the only healing story preserved in the Q source, a document that generally focuses more on Jesus' words than on his actions.[3] Matthew's distinctive pairing of the story

---

1. It looks as though a trace of the paralytic's story has been left on the story here, which introduces the afflicted man not as "ill and close to death" (Luke 7:2), but as "paralyzed, in terrible distress" (Matt. 8:6; cf. 9:2).
2. John S. Kloppenborg, *Q Parallels: Synopsis, Critical Notes and Concordance* (Sonoma, CA: Polebridge, 1988), 22–47. The narrative in John 4:46-54 (which has the sick son in Capernaum, but the encounter with Jesus in Cana) appears to be an independent account of the same incident.

of the "leper" with the story of the centurion is reinforced by the distinctive manner in which he introduces the two narratives:[4]

> And *coming up to him*, a man with a scale-disease bowed down before him, *saying*, "*Lord* . . ." (Matt. 8:2)

> . . . a centurion *came up to him* imploring him [6]and *saying*, "*Lord* . . ." (Matt. 8:5-6)

There appear to be at least two reasons for Matthew's particular way of pairing these stories. The first is that the ordering of the stories conveys a certain cultural and religious hierarchy. In Matthew 8:1-4, we have not only the healing of a Jewish man but also a healing accomplished in accordance with the Jewish law. It is only *after* such priorities have been established for the healing ministry of Jesus that we hear of his interaction with a Gentile, someone who lives outside the law.

Another reason why Matthew may have considered it appropriate to create this pairing is that both stories exhibit analogies with the account of Naaman's cleansing in 2 Kings 5. While the analogy in Matthew 8:1-4 is based on Naaman's ailment, however, the analogy in Matthew 8:5-13 is based on his status as a Gentile military officer, "a captain in the army of the king of Aram" (2 Kgs. 5:1). As commentators observe, the centurion of Matthew 8:5 was most likely a commander in the army of the tetrarch Herod Antipas, who was popularly known as a king (e.g., Mark 6:14).[5] It is noteworthy that in 2 Kings 5 when Naaman first approaches Elisha for help, the prophet

---

3. John S. Kloppenborg, Q, *The Earliest Gospel: An Introduction to the Original Stories and Sayings of Jesus* (Louisville: Westminster John Knox, 2008), 69–72.

4. Note that all of the italicized items are the result of Matthean redaction except "saying" in 8:2. Both stories also end with Jesus telling the healed person to "Go!" (8:4, 13), the latter command being redactional (cf. 8:32; 9:6).

5. For example, Ulrich Luz, *Matthew: A Commentary*, Hermeneia (Minneapolis: Fortress Press, 2005), 2:9–10. It is historically unlikely that the centurion was Roman, though in the absence of any specific indication some of Matthew's original readers may have come to such a

does not meet with him personally but instead sends a messenger to speak with him (5:10). Messengers play a role in the centurion's story as well, though only in one of the story's two versions:

(1) When he finished all his sayings in the hearing of the people, he went to Capernaum. (2) And a centurion had a slave whom he valued highly, who was sick and about to die.	(5) When he entered Capernaum, a centurion came up to him imploring him (6) and saying, "Lord, my servant is lying at home paralyzed, in terrible distress."
(3) When he heard about Jesus, he sent to him elders of the Jews, asking him to come and save his slave. (4) When they came to Jesus they pleaded with him earnestly, saying, "He is worthy for you to grant this to him. (5) For he loves our nation and it was he who built the synagogue for us."	
(6) And Jesus went with them. But when he was not far from the house, the centurion sent friends, saying to him, "Lord, do not trouble yourself, for I am not worthy for you to come under my roof; (7) therefore I did not consider myself worthy to come to you; but speak the word, and my servant will be cured.	(7) And he said to him, "Will I come and heal him?" (8) And in answer the centurion said, "Lord, I am not worthy for you to come under my roof, but only speak the word, and my servant will be cured.
(8) For I am also someone set under authority, with soldiers under me; and I say to this one, 'Go!' and he goes, and to another, 'Come!' and he comes, and to my slave, 'Do this!' and he does it."	(9) For I am also a person under authority, with soldiers under me; and I say to this one, 'Go!' and he goes, and to another, 'Come!' and he comes, and to my slave, 'Do this!' and he does it."
(9) When he heard these things Jesus was amazed at him, and turning to the crowd following him, he said, "I say to you, not even in Israel have I found such faith."	(10) When he heard this, Jesus was amazed and said to those who were following, "Truly I say to you, with no one in Israel have I found such faith.

conclusion. See Jonathan Reed, *Archaeology and the Galilean Jesus: A Re-examination of the Evidence* (Harrisburg, PA: Trinity Press International, 2000), 161–62.

(11) I say to you that many will come from east and west and dine with Abraham and Isaac and Jacob in the kingdom of heaven, (12) but the sons of the kingdom will be cast out into the outer darkness, where there will be weeping and gnashing of teeth."

(10) When those who had been sent returned to the house, they found the slave in good health. (Luke 7:1-10)

(13) And Jesus said to the centurion, "Go, let it be done for you according to your faith." And the servant was cured in that hour. (Matt. 8:5-13)

In contrast to Luke 7:1-10, the version of events recorded in the First Gospel lacks any reference to the Jewish elders (Luke 7:3) or the friends (Luke 7:6) whom the centurion sends to speak with Jesus on his behalf. As Matthew envisions the incident, the centurion eschews such intermediaries, instead making his appeal directly to Jesus, twice addressing him as "Lord" (8:6, 8). The absence of the elders' endorsement, however, creates a certain tension in the narrative. Knowing nothing about the man, Jesus' initial response to his implied request (Matt. 8:6) is one of implied reluctance (Matt. 8:7).[6] Given the cultural context, such a reply would not have been unexpected, since Jews often expressed reservations about entering Gentile domiciles (cf. John 18:28; Acts 10:28).[7] On a more personal level, the centurion's request also seems to represent a misunderstanding regarding the individual to whom he is speaking.[8] As Jesus explains in a parallel incident (responding to a Gentile's

6. Some translators treat Jesus' question as a statement: "I will come and heal him." See W. D. Davies and Dale C. Allison, *The Gospel According to Saint Matthew*, ICC (London: T&T Clark, 1991), 2:21–22 for discussion.

7. According to the Mishnah (*m. Ohal.* 18:7), Gentile houses are unclean. If this view applies to the scenario here, then the theme of impurity represents another feature linking the story of the centurion with the story of the "leper." See further Christine E. Hayes, *Gentile Impurities and Jewish Identities: Intermarriage and Conversion from the Bible to the Talmud* (Oxford: Oxford University Press, 2002), 45–67, 107–44.

8. The grammatical construction of the question in Matthew 8:7 draws attention to the personal pronoun: "Will *I* come and heal him?"

request for healing), he "was sent only to the lost sheep of the house of Israel" (Matt. 15:24). Ministry to non-Jews like the centurion, then, does not fall within the purview of either his own mission or the mission of his followers (Matt. 10:5-6).

Matthew's way of setting up the story, then, draws attention to the social barriers separating its two main characters. If the man with a scale-disease was excluded from the community of God's people on account of his ritual impurity, the centurion, being a Gentile, is not considered a member of the community to begin with. Moreover, the one on whose behalf he pleads for healing is not only a Gentile as well, but also a slave, the ultimate "nobody" in the eyes of ancient Mediterranean society.[9] Given such circumstances, the answer that the centurion gives to Jesus' question (Matt. 8:8-9) is truly amazing, even to Jesus himself (Matt. 8:10). Even the initial words that this non-Jew uses in his reply are rather remarkable, entailing an apparent allusion to the Jewish Scriptures:

> And in answer the centurion said, "*Lord*, I am not worthy for you to come under my roof, but only speak the *word*, and my servant will be *cured*." (Matt. 8:8)

> Then they cried to the *Lord* in their affliction and from their troubles he saved them; [20]he sent out his *word* and *cured* them, and delivered them from their destruction. (Ps. 107:19-20)

These lines are taken from a psalm of thanksgiving uttered by Diaspora Jews who have returned to their homeland, a theme to which Jesus will allude in his response (Matt. 8:11; cf. Ps. 107:3). In appealing to this form of discourse, then, the centurion not only enters into the vernacular of biblical healing but also implicitly invites Jesus to do the same.

---

9. The Greek word *pais* can also mean "son" (cf. John 4:46), though in the Septuagint the term usually refers to a servant (cf. Matt. 12:18; 14:2).

This is not the centurion's only rhetorical stratagem, however. In Matthew 8:9, he continues his response to Jesus' question, drawing now on his own experience and understanding of authority. On one level, the scenario of a Gentile military commander openly assuming the role of supplicant to a Jewish holy man strikes the observer as odd, but as his statement demonstrates, the centurion's particular profession actually provides him with a vantage point from which to make an apt observation regarding the nature of Jesus' power and status. Because he operates within an established chain of command, the centurion does not need to carry out tasks directly himself but can dictate to his subordinates what must be done. He infers that what applies to the sphere of human affairs applies to the sphere of spiritual affairs as well. As one "under authority" (Matt. 8:9), that is, as one who operates with authority conferred by God (cf. Matt. 11:27; 28:18), Jesus does not need to carry out the healing himself but only has to "speak the word" (Matt. 8:8) and it will be accomplished.[10] The spiritual "subordinates" subject to this word—presumably the forces responsible for the slave's paralysis—are left unidentified, though perhaps they should be understood as demonic spirits, which, according to Matthew 8:16, Jesus similarly casts out "with a word."[11]

The idea that such forces could be controlled from a distance was something that the centurion may have encountered in other cultural contexts. The philosopher Apollonius of Tyana, for example, was credited with a miracle that amounted to performing an exorcism through the mail. Upon hearing the appeal of a woman to help her possessed son, he produced a threatening letter, instructing her to

---

10. The centurion addresses Jesus as though he were a "broker" of divine power. See David B. Gowler, "Text, Culture, and Ideology in Luke 7:1-10: A Dialogic Reading," in *Fabrics of Discourse: Essays in Honor of Vernon K. Robbins*, eds. David B. Gowler, L. Gregory Bloomquist, and Duane F. Watson (Harrisburg, PA: Trinity Press International, 2003), 119–20.

11. Note the parallel between the centurion's command in Matthew 8:9 ("Go!") and the command that Jesus issues when casting out demons in Matthew 8:32 ("Go!"). The healing from a distance in Matthew 15:21-28 also involves a demon.

deliver it to the demon in question.[12] In terms of basic procedure, what the centurion requests here is similar, though its potential implications are far more profound. While the miracle performed by Apollonius overcame physical distance alone, the one performed by Jesus (like the one performed by his forerunner Elisha) overcomes both physical and social distance, and it is in this that the centurion's faith resides, a faith that persists even in the face of the healer's disinclination to help him. Rather than surrendering to this potential obstacle, he articulates a vision of Jesus' power, a power that has no limits, that is, a power that can efface boundaries, even the boundaries that separate people of different ethnic origins. And it is precisely through the act of healing that this manifestation of power occurs. Healing provides the venue in which people can palpably experience the authority of Jesus to re-envision and remake the family of God.

By now, readers familiar with the story of the Canaanite woman (Matt. 15:21-28) will have noted more than a few parallels between that incident and the one narrated here.[13] In each story a Gentile seeks help for a member of his or her household, only to encounter initial reluctance from Jesus. In each story the healing not only occurs from a distance but also is described using metaphors associated with food and table fellowship (8:11; 15:26-27). And in each story the Gentile petitioner both acknowledges his or her unworthiness and demonstrates remarkable faith. For all these similarities, however, it is possible to detect at least one important difference. This is to be found in Matthew 8:11-12, an element that distinguishes the centurion's story not only from the story of the Canaanite woman but also from the story of Elisha and Naaman. If the centurion has just said something "amazing" (Matt. 8:10), then Jesus has something amazing

---

12. Philostratus, *Life of Apollonius* 3.38.

13. For Matthew 15:21-28, see Elaine M. Wainwright, *Women Healing/Healing Women: The Genderization of Healing in Early Christianity* (London: Equinox, 2006), 153–55.

to say in return, a statement that announces the symbolic significance of what is transpiring for the course of salvation history. Comparison with Luke 7:1-10 indicates that the saying in Matthew 8:11-12 was not original to the story of the centurion but rather derives from a separate, later tradition in the Q source:

> (28) There will be weeping and gnashing of teeth when you see Abraham and Isaac and Jacob and all the prophets in the kingdom of God, but you yourselves are thrown out. (29) And they will come from east and west and north and south and dine in the kingdom of God. (Luke 13:28-29)

> (11) I say to you that many will come from east and west and dine with Abraham and Isaac and Jacob in the kingdom of heaven, (12) but the sons of the kingdom will be cast out into the outer darkness, where there will be weeping and gnashing of teeth. (Matt. 8:11-12)

The insertion of the saying here, then, reflects the evangelist's priorities in reformulating the narrative, which now takes on the features of a pronouncement story.[14] The healing itself is no longer the sole focus, but now provides an occasion for Jesus to turn from his conversation with the centurion and address "those who followed him" (Matt. 8:10), teaching this ready-made audience about the kingdom of God.[15] As in Luke's version of the story, Jesus begins by observing that he has found faith such as the centurion's nowhere in Israel. Only Matthew's Jesus goes on, however, to interpret this

14. For a similar redactional transformation, compare Matthew 12:9-14 with Mark 3:1-6. Cf. Heinz Joachim Held, "Matthew as Interpreter of the Miracle Stories," in *Tradition and Interpretation in Matthew*, eds. Günther Bornkamm, Gerhard Barth, and Heinz Joachim Held (Philadelphia: Westminster, 1963), 176, 180, 234–37, 241–46. In Matthew 8–9 generally, Jesus' words are not words of power (as in, say, Mark 5:41 or 7:34) but words of instruction, the acceptance of which can be characterized as a kind of healing (Matt. 9:12-13; 13:15).

15. "[I]n his redaction of miracle-stories Matthew has enhanced the element of direct speech to the point where the dialogue, or conversation, between Jesus and the suppliant(s) has become the focus of attention" (Jack D. Kingsbury, "Observations on the 'Miracle Chapters' of Matthew 8–9," *CBQ* 40 [1978]: 569). Further evidence that Matthew wants to turn this event into a "teaching moment" can be found in the more formal introductions he provides for the sayings: "Truly I say to you" (8:10) . . . "I say to you" (8:11). Cf. Luke 7:9.

demonstration of faith as a sign of eschatological reversal. Surprisingly, he takes it as a sign not only that many of those currently outside the family of faith will be included, but also that many of those currently inside the family of faith will be excluded.

While Matthew's reconfiguration of Q material may evidence a bold theological vision, with this surprise announcement he also runs the risk of disorienting his readers. Here two comments are in order.

First, as scholars note, the severe tone of Jesus' declaration regarding insiders is not especially well-suited to its narrative context.[16] Indeed, up to this point in the Gospel the reception accorded Jesus' ministry by the Jewish people has been generally positive (e.g., Matt. 8:1-4). Readers familiar with the Gospel narrative as a whole recognize that these words of judgment do not look back in the story, however, but forward, functioning as a prophetic anticipation of the rejection that Jesus will later experience (Matt. 8:34; 9:3, 34).[17] He will have occasion to utter another prophetic pronouncement on the subject in Matthew 11:23-24:

> (23) And you, Capernaum, will you be exalted to heaven? No, you will be brought down to Hades. For if the deeds of power had occurred in Sodom that occurred in you, it would have remained until this day. (24) But I say to you that it will be more tolerable for the land of Sodom on the day of judgment than for you.

Ironically, the residents of Capernaum, the very place where Jesus made his home (Matt. 4:13; 9:1) and performed many wonders, including acts of healing like the one recorded here in Matthew 8:5-13, face the terrible prospect of eschatological indictment.[18] Presupposed by this statement is the idea that those who witness such

---

16. For example, John P. Meier, *A Marginal Jew: Rethinking the Historical Jesus* (New York: Doubleday, 1994), 2:309–17. Cf. E. P. Sanders, *Jesus and Judaism* (Philadelphia: Fortress Press, 1985), 212–21.

17. Luz, *Matthew*, 2:10–11.

wonders are called upon to make a decision. The eruption of Jesus' healing power into human lives creates division and conflict (cf. Matt. 10:5-15), testing people's ability to perceive the meaning of what they see and hear in Jesus and respond with a change of heart, the sort of change through which one experiences true "healing" from God (Matt. 13:14-15). Note that in chapters 8–9 both Jews (Matt. 9:34) and Gentiles (Matt. 8:34) are represented as rejecting Jesus the healer, just as later both Jews (Matt. 23:34) and Gentiles (Matt. 24:9) will be represented as persecuting the church. What Matthew 8:11-12 signals to the reader, then, is that the potential for controversy is intrinsic to any act of Christian healing, a point to bear in mind as we examine the rest of chapters 8–9.

Second, Matthew's readers may also sense a certain tension regarding the *subjects* of Jesus' pronouncement. Note that Jesus nowhere explicitly mentions "the Jews" or "the Gentiles" here, resorting instead to more descriptive categories. Nevertheless, modern interpreters sometimes take "sons of the kingdom" (Matt. 8:12) as a reference to the former and thus as an indication that the Jews as a people are being rejected.[19] However, as comparison with Matthew 19:28 indicates, Jesus envisioned the reconstituted twelve tribes of Israel participating in the kingdom of God, while comparison with Matthew 13:38 shows that the expression "sons of the kingdom" could be applied to Christians as well as to Jews. Bearing in mind the broader context of the evangelist's eschatological vision, then, the word of judgment in 8:12 appears to have a twofold meaning, serving as a warning not only to Jesus' Jewish listeners but

18. For the imagery of Matthew 8:12, see R. T. France, *The Gospel of Matthew*, NICNT (Grand Rapids: Eerdmans, 2007), 319. In Matthew 22:13, the imagery is similarly applied to a banqueting scene.

19. For example, Donald A. Hagner, *Matthew*, WBC 33 (Dallas: Word Books, 1993), 1:206. Note that the reference to "sons of the kingdom" in Matthew 8:12 (cf. Luke 13:28) is redactional; cf. Davies and Allison, *Saint Matthew*, 2:26; Kloppenborg, *Q Parallels*, 156–57.

also to Matthew's Christian readers.[20] In the case of the latter, the verse serves as a reminder that they too must respond to the healing power of Jesus in their lives with boundary-effacing faith.[21] This function is consistent with warnings of judgment that Jesus issues to members of the church elsewhere in the Gospel (e.g. Matt. 5:20; 22:13; 24:51; 25:30). The cumulative effect of these warnings is clear: no one should presume to have a place in the kingdom.

Similar nuancing is in order when it comes to identifying the "many" who "will come from east and west" (Matt. 8:11). Comparable expressions are found in the Old Testament, though always with reference not to Gentiles but to Jews living in the Diaspora.[22] Jesus promises that this "many" will eat with the patriarchs in the kingdom, an allusion to the coming messianic banquet.[23] In Matthew's distinctive reconfiguration of Q material, healings like the one performed for the centurion's servant are now seen as a foretaste of this meal, prefiguring the sort of eschatological joy, fellowship, and bounty it was believed to represent.[24] An inspection of the Gospels shows that the meal was a symbol of wide-ranging importance to Jesus, both in his preaching and in his practice.[25] As an example of the latter we can turn to Matthew 9:10-13, where Jesus is presented as dining with "many tax collectors and sinners," groups that would

20. Recall the discussion of reader-response criticism in Chapter One.
21. Held, "Matthew as Interpreter," 196–97.
22. E.g., Ps. 107:3; Isa. 43:5; Zech. 8:7; Bar. 4:37; 5:5.
23. For the imagery of the messianic banquet, see Isa. 25:6-8; 55:1-2; 65:13-14; Zeph. 1:7; Matt. 22:1-14; 25:1-13; Luke 14:15; 22:28-30; Rev. 19:9; *1 En.* 62:14; *3 En.* 48A:10; *2 Bar.* 29:4-7; 1QSa 2:14-22; J. Priest, "A Note on the Messianic Banquet," in *The Messiah: Developments in Earliest Judaism and Christianity*, ed. James H. Charlesworth et al. (Minneapolis: Fortress Press, 1992), 222–38; Peter-Ben Smit, *Fellowship and Food in the Kingdom: Eschatological Meals and Scenes of Utopian Abundance in the New Testament*, WUNT 2.234 (Tübingen: Mohr Siebeck, 2008), 19–34; Dennis E. Smith, *From Symposium to Eucharist: The Banquet in the Early Christian World* (Minneapolis: Fortress Press, 2003), 166–71.
24. Similarly, in the story of the Canaanite woman, the gift of healing is likened to the gift of food (Matt. 15:26-27).
25. Cf. Matt. 5:6; 14:13-21; 15:29-39; 22:1-14 (note the similarity between 8:12 and 22:13); 25:1-13; 26:29-29; Smit, *Fellowship and Food*, 201–58.

have been representative of Jewish society's most despised outcasts. There is little doubt that Jesus intended his association with such "sick" people (Matt. 9:12) to be interpreted as a symbolic act, one that prophetically anticipated the inclusivity of the coming messianic banquet and the healing it would bring.[26]

Reading Matthew 8:11 within the broader context of Matthew's eschatological vision suggests that those living "east and west," then, are not only the Gentiles but all those who have been displaced from the fellowship of God's people, all those who find themselves outside the boundaries of the kingdom. Accordingly, the centurion can be interpreted as a forerunner not only of Gentile faith but also of the faith that overcomes such displacement, a faith that can even overcome the restriction of Jesus' mission to the people of Israel. For his part, Jesus responds to such faith—regardless of its source—with a gesture of healing, reconciling power. In contrast to Luke, Matthew has Jesus remark on the centurion's faith not just once but twice, underscoring the significance of the concept (Matt. 8:10, 13; cf. Luke 7:9). In addition, Matthew 8:10 is the first time in the Gospel that the evangelist employs the term for faith (*pistis*), indicating perhaps that he sees the particular way in which it is demonstrated here as setting a precedent for subsequent demonstrations. As he also states in 8:10, this is a kind of faith that Jesus has yet to encounter in his ministry, even (presumably) among his disciples. While they may have enough faith in Jesus to follow him (Matt. 4:18-22), this does not necessarily translate into a faith in his power to save, as we will soon learn (see Chapter Six on Matt. 8:25-26). Instead, the faith that the centurion shows in Jesus will be manifested by other people who come to him for help (Matt. 9:22, 28-29; cf. 15:28).

---

26. Note once again the metaphorical connection between healing and eating.

One final point can be made regarding the individual who is actually healed in our story, the centurion's slave. Note that while Matthew gives no indication as to his ethnic status, he does make a particular point regarding the nature of his affliction. While the Third Gospel describes him as "ill and close to death" (Luke 7:2), the First Gospel tells us that he was "paralyzed, in terrible distress" (Matt. 8:6; cf. 9:2). The slave's status as someone with a disability may be relevant for interpreting the theme of eschatological ingathering discussed above. In an essay entitled, "With Whom Do the Disabled Associate? Metaphorical Interplay in the Latter Prophets," Sarah Melcher identifies two passages in which physically impaired persons are explicitly mentioned among those returning from exile in the Diaspora to the promised land:

> (8) See, I am going to bring them from the land of the north,
>   and gather them from the farthest parts of the earth,
> among them the blind and the lame,
>   those with child and those in labor, together;
>   a great company, they shall return here.
> . . .
> (12) They shall come and sing aloud on the height of Zion,
>   and they shall be radiant over the goodness of the LORD,
> over the grain, the wine, and the oil,
>   and over the young of the flock and the herd;
> their life shall become like a watered garden,
>   and they shall never languish again. (Jer. 31:8, 12 NRSV)

> (19) I will deal with all your oppressors at that time.
> And I will save the lame and gather the outcast,
> and I will change their shame into praise and renown in all the earth.
> (20) At that time I will bring you home, at the time when I gather you;
> for I will make you renowned and praised among all the peoples of
>   the earth,
> when I restore your fortunes before your eyes, says the LORD.
> (Zeph. 3:19-20 NRSV)

Note that in Jeremiah 31:8-12, the blind and the lame not only return to the land; they also enjoy its bounty, feasting in a manner reminiscent of Matthew 8:11. The ingathering of God's people is so inclusive, the restorative power that guides it so effective, that "even those who are physically weakened will make the trip to Israel."[27] In Zephaniah 3:19, meanwhile, the lame are paired with the outcast, indicating "some sort of social equivalence."[28] Returning to our story in Matthew 8:5-13, let me suggest that just as Jesus includes the centurion in the fellowship of God's people through his prophetic word, he does the same for the centurion's slave through his healing action. Just as the centurion serves as a forerunner of the faith that overcomes displacement, the paralyzed slave serves as a symbol of society's outcasts, people whom God will gather even "from the farthest parts of the earth" into the eschatological kingdom, where "they shall be radiant over the goodness of the Lord."

27. Sarah J. Melcher, "With Whom Do the Disabled Associate? Metaphorical Interplay in the Latter Prophets," in *This Abled Body: Rethinking Disabilities in Biblical Studies*, eds. Hector Avalos, Sarah J. Melcher, and Jeremy Schipper (Atlanta: Society of Biblical Literature, 2007), 121. Cf. Saul M. Olyan, *Disability in the Hebrew Bible: Interpreting Mental and Physical Differences* (Cambridge: Cambridge University Press, 2008), 81–85.
28. Melcher, "With Whom Do the Disabled Associate?" 121.

4

The Uninvited Healer: Matthew 8:14-15

For the third miracle story of the first triad in chapters 8–9, the author of the First Gospel returns to Mark:

(29) As soon as they left the synagogue, they entered the house of Simon and Andrew, with James and John. (30) Now Simon's mother-in-law was in bed with a fever, and they told him about her at once. (31) He came and took her by the hand and raised her up. Then the fever left her, and she began to serve them. (Mark 1:29-31)	(14) When Jesus entered Peter's house, he saw his mother-in-law lying in bed with a fever; (15) he touched her hand, and the fever left her, and she rose up and began to serve him. (Matt. 8:14-15)

It is best to begin an analysis of this passage by looking back and seeing how the evangelist has situated the story within the context of Matthew 8:1-15. This is critical since, as noted earlier, he has exercised considerable freedom in editing not only the content but also the order of the material in this section:

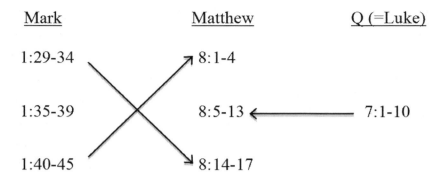

In contrast to Mark, in Matthew the story of Peter's mother-in-law now comes after the story of the man with a scale-disease. In addition, the story of the centurion and his slave has been inserted between these two stories, creating an entirely new narrative sequence. In evaluating the results of this work, it is important to recognize that Matthew has altered not only the narrative's structure but also the narrative's *scope*. Specifically, as they transition from the first two stories of the unit to the third, the readers encounter various forms of what we might call "narrowing" or "contraction" in terms of how the narrative is conveyed. This progression in the means of storytelling can be detected in four areas.

The first form of narrowing concerns the narrative's mix of action and dialogue. As we have seen, in the first two stories of the triad, Matthean redaction has the result of amplifying the role of verbal exchange in the flow of the narrative. In the case of Matthew 8:5-13, the dialogue has been expanded to such an extent that it is possible to categorize the episode formally as a hybrid of healing story and pronouncement story.[1] In Matthew 8:14-15, by contrast, there are no pronouncements. In fact, this is the only healing story in the First Gospel in which no dialogue of any kind occurs. Even Mark's

---

1. See Chapter Three.

report that the disciples informed Jesus "at once" about the woman's condition has been dropped. The form of narration has contracted to sheer action. As a consequence, Matthew 8:14–15 is the only healing story in the Gospel where the initiative for the healing comes from Jesus rather than from the person in need of healing or from some third-party character.[2] In the absence of dialogue, there is no supplication, even from the sick woman herself. In the first two stories of the unit, the supplicants had initiated their conversations with Jesus by addressing him as "Lord" (Matt. 8:2, 5). Here, by contrast, no such indication is given as to the woman's attitude toward Jesus as a healer. Evidently, Jesus does not need to be informed regarding either her condition or her beliefs. He simply knows and acts.

Second, contraction also takes place in the number of characters appearing in the story. In the first two stories of the unit, the presence of the crowds is explicitly mentioned (Matt. 8:1, 10). Indeed, up to this point in the Gospel, Jesus' healing (like his teaching) has been very much a "public" practice, with large numbers of people having been present either to be healed or to witness healing (cf. Matt. 4:23–24). Here not only are the crowds gone, but the disciples—even Peter—have been written out of the story as well. In fact, there are no third-party characters at all: no advocates to petition on behalf of the afflicted, no opponents to contest what Jesus is doing, no onlookers to marvel and spread the news.[3] Even the fever is envisioned as "leaving" the house (cf. Luke 4:39). If we were to imagine a stage production of

2. Heinz Joachim Held, "Matthew as Interpreter of the Miracle Stories," in *Tradition and Interpretation in Matthew*, eds. Günther Bornkamm, Gerhard Barth, and Heinz Joachim Held (Philadelphia: Westminster, 1963), 169–70. The summary statement in Matthew 14:14 indicates that Jesus takes the initiative, though what he "sees" there is specified not as those in need of healing but as the crowds. Other summary statements (e.g., Matt. 9:35) seem to leave the question open. It is interesting that the two Lukan stories in which Jesus "sees" someone in need of healing (7:11–17 and 13:10–17) also involve women.
3. Cf. Birger Gerhardsson, *The Mighty Acts of Jesus According to Matthew* (Lund: CWK Gleerup, 1979), 42–45.

the scene, it would be carried out with only two actors and entirely in silence, all attention being focused on the actions of the healer and the one healed.

Third, with each successive story in our unit the reader is presented with an increased level of specificity with regard to the location of Jesus' healing activity. The action moves from an unspecified area outside of Capernaum (Matt. 8:1), to somewhere in Capernaum (Matt. 8:5), to a specific place within the city, the home of Peter (Matt. 8:14). This narrowing appears to be significant with regard not only to the particular place but also to the particular kind of place, the enclosed space of the house. While in the story of the centurion it was Jesus' healing power that entered into this space (Matt. 8:6), here—for the first time in the Gospel—it is the healer himself who enters into this space (Matt. 8:14). The sequence of events, then, creates a spatial contraction in the venue of Jesus' activity as well as a focusing in the direction of Jesus' movements, so that the house, this particular house, takes on added significance.

Fourth, a similar dynamic of increasing specificity can be observed with regard to the principal individuals with whom Jesus interacts as healer. The first petitioner is an anonymous person known only by his ailment (Matt. 8:2); the second is an anonymous person known by his profession, his status as a slave-owner, and by his (likely) place of residence (8:5-6); while the beneficiary of Jesus' healing in the third story is a specific individual linked to a specific, named character. This narrowing appears to be significant with regard not only to the particular person but also to the particular kind of person. Corresponding with the healer's first entry into a house is the first healing story in the Gospel that involves a woman (cf. Matt. 9:18-26; 15:21-28).

Even as it is critical to recognize the nexus of silence, gender, and domestic space in our healing story, it is also important not to overstate its significance. After all, in Matthew's Gospel neither the space of the house nor the receipt of healing is gendered. Both men (9:28-30) and women (9:23-25) are reported as receiving healing inside of a house, just as both men (9:32-33) and women (9:20-22) can receive healing outside of a house. This parity applies to the technique of healing as well, with Jesus healing both men (20:34) and women (9:25) by means of mere touch, just as he heals both men (8:13) and women (15:28) with just a word. In assessing the significance of this evidence, we can turn for guidance to Elaine Wainwright's work on the "genderization" of healing in the New Testament, discussed above in Chapter One. Wainwright begins her analysis of the episode in Mark 1:29-31/Matthew 8:14-15 by eschewing the sort of model-driven approaches (endorsed by medical anthropologists like John Pilch) that presuppose a strict alignment between gender and "the cultural code of the public/private."[4] Rather than operating according to rigid dichotomies, she suggests that in the Gospels the gendering of both healing spaces and healing practices is subject to constant negotiation through the artful reconfiguration of authoritative narratives.

Such is the case, she says, with our story, where the mutability of explanatory categories like "public" and "private" is signaled in part by the specific actions associated with Peter's mother-in-law in Matthew 8:15. The first of these actions is indicated by the verb "to rise up" (*egeirō*), which elsewhere is used in Jesus' passion predictions (Matt. 16:21; 17:23; 20:19; cf. 17:9; 28:6-7). The same eschatological power by which God will raise Jesus from the dead is, by implication, at work in this woman's healed body, just as it will be at work in the raising of the official's daughter in Matthew 9:25 (cf. 10:8; 11:5). Healing, then, both brings new life and anticipates the new

4. Elaine Wainwright, *Women Healing/Healing Women: The Genderization of Healing in Early Christianity* (London: Equinox, 2006), 106.

life in Christ that transcends death. The second of these actions is indicated by the verb "to serve" (*diakoneō*), which elsewhere describes the service rendered to Jesus not only by women but also by men and even angels (Matt. 4:11; 25:44; 27:55), as well as the "service" that Christ himself renders to humanity through his life and death (Matt. 20:28). The woman's response, then, can be understood not only as referring to an act of domestic service, but also as intimating a connection between healing and discipleship.[5] Thus, as Wainwright puts it, the fact that Peter's mother-in-law resumes her domestic duties in Matthew 8:15 "is not an affirmation of fixed gender and spatial categories," but indicates that her domestic space has been "transformed" so as to "encompass male and female activities of both a public and private nature."[6]

As for the physical configuration of the domestic space in which this transformation occurs, Wainwright suggests that the evangelists probably had in mind the sort of courtyard house that was typical of urban areas in Syro-Palestine at the time.[7] A visitor to such a dwelling would have to pass through a single entranceway and then through a central courtyard in order to gain access to the rooms surrounding it, rooms that, like the courtyard itself, served multiple functions.[8] In some cases, the complex would have been large enough to accommodate as many as three or four (presumably related) families.[9] Imagining such a setting, Wainwright surmises that it

5. Donald A. Hagner, *Matthew*, WBC 33 (Dallas: Word Books, 1993), 1:208–209: in contrast to the Markan account, the woman's service in Matthew 8:15 takes on "a distinct christological aspect" thereby displaying "a fundamental aspect of discipleship" that "becomes a model for the Christian reader."

6. Wainwright, *Women Healing*, 111.

7. Ibid., 107.

8. Eric M. Meyers, "The Problems of Gendered Space in Syro-Palestinian Domestic Architecture: The Case of Roman-Period Galilee," in *From Antioch to Alexandria: Recent Studies in Domestic Architecture*, eds. Katharina Galor and Tomasz Waliszewski (Warsaw: University of Warsaw Press, 2007), 118: the interior of a typical courtyard house "does not represent private space as distinct from work space . . . The public/private dichotomy simply cannot characterize this space wherein every manner of household, family, and everyday activities was conducted."

would have been necessary for Jesus to traverse not just one, but a number of social and spatial "boundaries" in order to reach Peter's mother-in-law lying in one of the rooms of the house.[10] Such a reconstruction certainly seems to be applicable in the case of Mark's version of the story, since there Jesus does not proceed immediately to the woman upon entering the house but does so only after being informed of her condition by the disciples accompanying him. Whether the reconstruction applies to Matthew's version of the story is more difficult to say, though we can infer from Matthew 26:3, 58, and 69 that the evangelist was familiar with courtyards, while Matthew 6:6 and 24:26 project an organization of domestic space that includes not only "inner" rooms, but also rooms separated from the rest of the house by doors.[11] If we were to envisage Jesus entering the sort of "pastas-style" houses found throughout the Greco-Roman world, then it would have been necessary for him to traverse even more symbolic boundaries, since domiciles of this type would have included a "transverse hall" adjacent to the courtyard and facing a suite of two or more inner rooms, thereby functioning as an "intramural zone" mediating "between the semipublic space of the courtyard and the fully private sanctum."[12]

However we are to envision the space, Wainwright is probably correct in assuming that the movement depicted in Matthew 8:14

9. Santiago Guijarro, "The Family in First-Century Galilee," in *Constructing Early Christian Families: Family as Social Reality and Metaphor*, ed. Halvor Moxnes (London: Routledge, 1997), 42–65. The so-called House of Peter excavated in Capernaum may have been of this type. James F. Strange and Hershel Shanks, "Has the House Where Jesus Stayed in Capernaum Been Found?" *BAR* 8, no. 6 (1982): 26–37.

10. Wainwright, *Woman Healing*, 144 (cf. 107–109). Ordinarily, neither the courtyard nor the rooms surrounding it would have been visible from the street (see Jonathan Reed, *Archaeology and the Galilean Jesus: A Re-examination of the Evidence* [Harrisburg, PA: Trinity Press International, 2000], 125).

11. Cf. Marianne Sawicki, *Crossing Galilee: Architectures of Contact in the Occupied Land of Jesus* (Harrisburg, PA: Trinity Press International, 2000), s.v. "doors."

12. Bradley A. Ault, *The Excavations at Ancient Halieis*, vol. 2, *The Houses: The Organization and Use of Domestic Space* (Bloomington: Indiana University Press, 2005), 66–67.

involved "stages of entry into the house."[13] What remains uncertain, however, is how best to assess the meaning of this entry in light of the various forms of narrative "contraction" identified above. Regardless of how many social and spatial boundaries the Matthean Jesus may be envisioned as traversing in order to reach the woman, in the absence of third-party characters or a request for healing, he does so not only unaccompanied, but also uninvited. Mark's version of the story may have Jesus entering a cultural "borderland" where a "public" healer performs in a "private" venue, but in Matthew's retelling of the story, "the entry of Jesus alone into the very presence of a woman lying sick seems a breach of even the most carefully nuanced construction of public and private space in first-century imaginations."[14] The Roman architect Vitruvius (first century BCE), for example, would have been expressing a common sentiment of the time when he wrote, "into the private rooms no one can come uninvited" (*On Architecture* 6.5.1). Rabbinic delineations of social and symbolic space similarly generated "a domestic world of women to which men had limited access."[15] With regard to the women's quarters of a Greek home, meanwhile, "no male is allowed entrance unless he is a relative" (Cornelius Nepos, *Lives of Eminent Men*, pref. 7).

Even as it acknowledges the seriousness of Jesus' social "breach," however, Wainwright's investigation does little to explain the significance of this unusual act for understanding either the distinctive character of our story or its contribution to the literary and thematic profile of chapters 8–9. In order to address these issues, it is necessary to expand the scope of analysis beyond Matthew's redaction of Mark 1:29-31 to include the manner in which the evangelist has

13. Wainwright, *Woman Healing*, 144.
14. Ibid.
15. Judith R. Baskin, *Midrashic Women: Formations of the Feminine in Rabbinic Literature* (Hanover, NH: Brandeis University Press, 2002), 141.

situated the episode both within its immediate literary context and with relation to possible biblical precedents.

As we learned in Chapter One, Matthew 8:1-17 constitutes a literary unity. Further unifying this material are thematic features that ground its story of Jesus in the story of Israel. For example, each of the three major segments of 8:1-17 refers by name to one or more great figures from salvation history: Moses in Matthew 8:4, Abraham, Isaac, and Jacob in Matthew 8:11, and Isaiah "the prophet" in Matthew 8:17. As we have seen, the first two of these episodes recall the exploits of another great figure from Israelite history, the prophet Elisha, specifically, his healing or "cleansing" of Naaman the Aramite. The former episode, Matthew 8:1-4, parallels 2 Kings 5:1-14 in that both of the supplicants in question suffer from a similar affliction ("leprosy," i.e., a scale-disease), while the latter, Matthew 8:5-13, parallels 2 Kings 5:1-14 in that both of the supplicants in question have a similar status and profession (Gentile military officer). Matthew's redactional activity in constructing this three-part section, then, has the result of drawing together two healing stories that evoke the prophet Elisha. Given this feature, as well as the fact that Matthew interprets what transpires in the unit as the fulfillment of a prophetic oracle (Matt. 8:17), it is worth asking if the same can be said of the third. After all, as Raymond Brown has observed, it "is in respect to miracles that we find the closest similarities between Jesus and Elisha."[16] As he further observes, these similarities are based not so much on specific verbal parallels as on "general similarities in the *type* of miracles," a point worth bearing in mind as we proceed.[17]

16. Raymond E. Brown, "Jesus and Elisha," *Perspective* 12 (1971): 89. For example, compare Matthew 14:13-21 with 2 Kings 4:42-44. Just as Elijah was succeeded by Elisha, the Elijah-like John (Matt. 11:14; 17:10-13) is succeeded by the Elisha-like Jesus (Joel Marcus, *Mark*, AB 27 [New Haven, CT: Yale University Press, 2000], 1:416).
17. Brown, "Jesus and Elisha," 92 (emphasis original).

An inspection of the commentary literature, unfortunately, is of little assistance in addressing this question. In fact, most commentaries do not posit much of an Old Testament background for Matthew 8:14-15 at all. An exception in this regard is W. D. Davies and Dale Allison, who suggest that "perhaps we should recall the OT texts in which the prophets Elisha (2 Kgs 5.9; 6.1-2, 32) and Ezekiel (3.24) stay in houses."[18] A somewhat better parallel, one that also occurs in a house, comes from the story of Elisha's raising of the Shunammite woman's son (2 Kgs. 4:18-37). Of particular interest are the following texts:

> (29) As soon as they left the synagogue, they entered the house of Simon and Andrew, with James and John. (30) Now Simon's mother-in-law was in bed with a fever, and they told him about her at once. (Mark 1:29-30 NRSV)

> When Jesus entered Peter's house, he saw his mother-in-law lying in bed with a fever. (Matt. 8:14 NRSV)

> When Elisha came into the house, he saw the child lying dead on his bed. (2 Kgs. 4:32 NRSV)

Matthean redaction produces a statement, one unique to his Gospel, that parallels 2 Kings 4:32. Note that the incident described there occurs in an upper room of the house (2 Kgs. 4:10, 21; cf. 1 Kgs. 17:19), the door of which Elisha closes in order to ensure privacy (4:33), and that the healing technique he subsequently employs also involves physical contact (4:34-35). Note further that at one point the Shunammite woman is identified as the prophet's "servant" (2 Kgs. 4:16), with which we can compare the "service" offered Jesus by Peter's mother-in-law after he has healed her. If Matthew drew on this prophetic story for inspiration in reshaping his own story, it

18. W. D. Davies and Dale C. Allison, *The Gospel According to Saint Matthew*, ICC (London: T&T Clark, 1991), 2:34.

would help to explain why his account seems to be more "private" than the one provided by Mark. It is probably also significant that the miracle Elisha performs involves bringing someone back from the dead (cf. 1 Kgs. 17:17-24). Readers who recognized similarities between the two episodes would be more likely to appreciate not only the prophetic character of Jesus' person and actions but also the symbolic undercurrents of the woman's "rising up" in Matthew 8:15. A similar "privatization" of healing can be detected in the redaction of Matthew 9:18-19, 23-26, the story of the raising of the official's daughter. In contrast to the report in Mark 5:40 (which has him accompanied by a group of witnesses), the First Gospel has Jesus enter her room alone (Matt. 9:25), just as Elijah (1 Kgs. 17:19) and Elisha (2 Kgs. 4:33) had done when they raised dead youths to life.[19]

While such comparisons help bring the biblical character of our story into relief, they do not exhaust the intertextual possibilities that it presents. In order to clarify these possibilities, however, we need to proceed by comparing our passage not with another Old Testament text, but with two pericopes found elsewhere in Matthew:

> (18) As he walked by the Sea of Galilee, he saw (*eiden*) two brothers, Simon, who is called Peter, and Andrew his brother, casting a net into the sea—for they were fishermen. (19) And he said to them, "Follow me, and I will make you fish for people." (20) Immediately they left their nets and followed him. (Matt. 4:18-20; cf. 4:21-22)

> As Jesus was walking along, he saw (*eiden*) a man called Matthew sitting at the tax booth; and he said to him, "Follow me." And he got up and followed him. (Matt. 9:9)

Both of these pericopes (as well as 4:21-22) belong to the literary genre of the "call" or vocation story.[20] The structural elements of the

---

19. For the privacy motif, see also Mark 7:33; Acts 9:40; Gerd Theissen, *The Miracle Stories of the Early Christian Tradition* (Philadelphia: Fortress Press, 1983), 60–61, 154–58.

20. A. J. Droge, "Call Stories," *ABD* 1 (1992): 821–23.

form can be outlined as follows: (1) appearance of Jesus, (2) Jesus sees the prospective disciple(s), (3) observation on the location and activity of the one(s) called, (4) the call to discipleship, (5) positive response to the call. A re-examination of Matthew 8:14-15 indicates that its contents correspond with this basic structure, except for element 4, where in lieu of a call to discipleship we have a healing. It is worth noting, however, that the association between calling and healing is one that figures in the analysis of healing stories elsewhere in the Gospel.[21]

> (1) When Jesus entered Peter's house, (2) he saw his mother-in-law (3) lying in bed with a fever; (4) he touched her hand, and the fever left her, (5) and she got up and began to serve him.

Note further how the particular word that Matthew uses for "saw" in 8:14 (*eiden*), a word unique to his version of the narrative, is also used in element 2 of all three of the call stories (Matt. 4:18, 21; 9:9). Commenting on such stories, Joel Marcus suggests that the sort of vision being attributed to Jesus should be interpreted not as passive observation, but as an active "possessive gaze" and, as such, an expression of the viewer's prophetic acuity.[22] The parallels identified above suggest that the same can be applied to the interpretation of our passage as well.[23]

On both the formal and verbal levels, then, it appears that Matthean redaction has transformed Mark's rather standard healing story into a healing story with features of a call story. This development would

---

21. The "healing as call" motif is probably best represented elsewhere by Matthew 20:29-34, where the evangelist (following Mark 10:52) has the cured individuals "follow" Jesus. His other story about two blind men (Matt. 9:30-31) presents a more ambiguous scenario (see Chapter Twelve). Cf. Luke 8:1-3; Acts 9:17-19.
22. Marcus, *Mark*, 1:183.
23. Comparison can also be made with Matthew 9:2. By dropping the action of Mark 2:4, Matthew renders Jesus' ability to "see" others in the context of a healing story more impressive. Also cf. Matthew 9:22.

help to account not only for the absence of third-party characters in Matthew 8:14-15 but also for the fact that here, in contrast to the other healing stories in the Gospel, Jesus is the one who initiates the narrative action, in a manner consistent with the general pattern of the New Testament "call" genre.[24] Readers who recognized similarities between our story and this genre would also be more likely to understand "she served him" in Matthew 8:15 as an anticipation of Matthew 27:55:

> Many women were also there, looking on from a distance; they had followed Jesus from Galilee and served him.

Healing calls Peter's mother-in-law to a form of service that is appropriate to one who follows the Lord.

As commentators often note, the basic form of the call story did not originate with the evangelists themselves, but has its roots in Old Testament prophetic narratives, especially the story of Elijah's call of Elisha.[25] Comparison with 1 Kings 19:19-21 is appropriate for the analysis of Matthew 8:14-15 as well, especially when we take into account the way in which the two stories conclude:

> . . . and he set out and followed Elijah and became his servant. (1 Kgs. 19:21 NRSV)

> . . . and she got up and began to serve him. (Matt. 8:15 NRSV)

Elisha's positive response to Elijah's call has two components, following and serving. In Matthew, we have the former in 4:20, 22, and 9:9, the latter in 8:15, and both (interestingly enough) only in 27:55. Looking at our story, given the nature of the "call" genre, it is

24. In Matthew 8:14-15, as in the call stories (and in contrast to most healing stories), the encounter with Jesus is not a matter of human volition. Another regular feature of the call narrative is the instantaneous nature of the "conversion" experience, a feature present in the experience of healing as well.
25. See John Nolland, *The Gospel of Matthew*, NIGTC (Grand Rapids: Eerdmans, 2005), 177–81.

not surprising that the First Gospel has Peter's mother-in-law serving "him" and not "them" as in the Markan version (Mark 1:31). For Matthew, all that matters is her response to Christ.

As commentators also note, the story of Elijah's call of Elisha has influenced the shape not only of the pericopes cited above, but also of two pronouncement stories on discipleship in the New Testament, stories that Matthew appears to have repositioned from their original context in the synoptic sayings source to a location immediately following the material in Matthew 8:14-17.[26]

> (18) Seeing the crowd around him, Jesus gave orders to depart to the other side. (19) Then a certain scribe approached and said to him, "Teacher, I will follow you wherever you go." (20) And Jesus said to him, "The foxes have holes, and the birds of the air nests, but the Son of Man has nowhere to lay his head." (21) But another, one of the disciples, said to him, "Lord, permit me first to go and bury my father." (22) But Jesus said to him, "Follow me, and let the dead bury their own dead." (Matt. 8:18-22)

There is a consensus that Matthew 8:21-22 in particular entails a clear allusion to 1 Kings 19:20, where Elisha requests permission to take leave of his father and mother:[27]

> He left the oxen, ran after Elijah, and said, "Let me kiss my father and my mother, and then I will follow you." Then Elijah said to him, "Go back again; for what have I done to you?" (NRSV)

Indeed, it is comparison with the Elijah-Elisha typology that makes Jesus' response to the would-be disciple in Matthew 8:22 seem so

26. Cf. Luke 9:57-60. In their original Q setting, it appears that these pronouncement stories on discipleship came immediately after the material preserved in Matthew 11:2-19/Luke 7:18-35. Cf. John S. Kloppenborg, Q Parallels: Synopsis, Critical Notes and Concordance (Sonoma, CA: Polebridge, 1988), 52–65.
27. For example, Martin Hengel, The Charismatic Leader and His Followers (New York: Crossroad, 1981), 16–18; Davies and Allison, Saint Matthew, 2:54–56; Hagner, Matthew, 1:218; Ulrich Luz, Matthew: A Commentary, Hermeneia (Minneapolis: Fortress Press, 2005), 2:18.

shocking. Like the story of Peter's mother-in-law, this pair of discipleship apothegms has no third-party characters, Matthew's redaction of 8:14-15 having the effect of creating formal alignment with 8:18-22 in this regard.

It appears, then, that the different ways in which Matthew 8:14-15 alludes to the figure of Elisha correspond to the different ways in which the passage relates to its literary context. Specifically, the passage serves both as the third of three stories (Matt. 8:1-4, 5-13, 14-15) that evoke the prophet's healings as well as the first of three stories (Matt. 8:14-15, 19-20, 21-22) that evoke the prophet's call.[28] Similarities between Matthew 8:14-15 and 2 Kings 4:18-37 help to align the former with the stories in Matthew 8:1-13, which recall 2 Kings 5:1-14, while similarities between Matthew 8:14-15 and 1 Kings 19:19-21 suggest that the former can be interpreted as a transition to Matthew 8:18-22, which, as we have seen, is also rooted in 1 Kings 19:19-21.[29] Matthew 8:18-22, in turn, segues to Matthew 8:23-27 and the second triad of miracle stories. An appreciation for these intertextual features provides a perspective from which to explicate more fully the results of the evangelist's literary activity in Matthew 8:1-17, contributing as they do not only to the section's thematic unity, but also to the revelation of Jesus' prophetic identity, one that extends to his disciples as well, who in their ministry of healing (Matt. 10:1, 8) are sent out as prophets in the name of a prophet (Matt. 10:41).[30]

---

28. The Third Gospel contains an Elisha "cycle" of sorts as well, namely, Luke 7:1-10 + 11-17, for which see Brown, "Jesus and Elisha," 93; Joel B. Green, *The Gospel of Luke*, NICNT (Grand Rapids: Eerdmans, 1997), 282, 290, 292.

29. Within the trio of stories in Matthew 8:14-22, Peter's mother-in-law compares favorably with the scribe and the disciple, since she is the only one actually reported as responding positively to Jesus.

30. The saying in 10:41 is unique to Matthew. Cf. Matt. 5:12; 12:39; 13:57; 14:5; 16:14; 21:11, 46; 23:34, 37; Luke 4:27; Lidija Novakovic, *Messiah, the Healer of the Sick: A Study of Jesus as the Son of David in the Gospel of Matthew*, WUNT 2.170 (Tübingen: Mohr Siebeck, 2003), 109–18; Paul Foster, "Prophets and Prophetism in Matthew," in *Prophets and Prophecy in Jewish and Early*

Christian Literature, WUNT 2.286, eds. Joseph Verheyden, Korinna Zamfir, and Tobias Nicklas (Tübingen: Mohr Siebeck, 2010), 117–38.

5

Houses, Healing, and Prophets:
Matthew 8:16-17

As we have seen, the various forms of narrative "contraction" evident in Matthew's manner of rewriting and recontextualizing the story of Peter's mother-in-law draw attention both to the private nature of her encounter with Jesus and to the domestic setting in which this encounter occurs. The seeming breach of cultural norms attending the evangelist's re-envisioning of the scene lends the story a distinctive character. In concert with this, the previous chapter showed how Matthew 8:14-15 can be understood to function as a kind of narrative hinge, serving both as the third of three stories (Matt. 8:1-4, 5-13, 14-15) that evoke healings performed by Elisha (2 Kgs. 4:18-37; 5:1-14) and as the first of three stories (Matt. 8:14-15, 19-20, 21-22) that evoke his call by Elijah (1 Kgs. 19:19-21). By aligning the action of 8:1-22 with such biblical narratives, Matthew dramatizes the prophetic nature of Jesus' person, reinforcing the place of his ministry in salvation history, and legitimating the house as the venue of such ministry. It is important to note, however, that Matthew 8:14-15 is accompanied by a segment (8:16-17) that not only extends the healing narrative but also further explicates the "prophecy" theme.

This segment consists of two elements: a summary statement (Matt. 8:16) followed by a Scripture verse attributed to Isaiah "the prophet" (Matt. 8:17). While Matthew 8:14-15 was based on Mark 1:29-31, Matthew 8:16-17 is based on Mark 1:32-34:

(32) When evening came, when the sun had set, they brought to him all who were sick or possessed with demons. (33) And the whole city had gathered at the door. (34) And he healed many who were sick with various diseases, and cast out many demons; and he did not allow the demons to speak, because they knew him. (Mark 1:32-34)	(16) When evening came, they brought to him many who were possessed with demons; and he cast out the spirits with a word, and healed all who were sick. (17) This was to fulfill what had been spoken through Isaiah the prophet, "He himself took our infirmities and bore our diseases." (Matt. 8:16-17)

With this passage we have our first reference in chapters 8–9 to Jesus' interaction with "demons" and "spirits," a reference upon which the exorcism stories in 8:28-34 and 9:32-34 will expand.[1] An inspection of Matthew's redaction of the passage reveals two literary inversions. First, the evangelist inverts the order of references to healings and exorcisms in his source. While Mark mentions the sick first and then those possessed by demons, Matthew has the possessed first and then the sick, thus creating a more effective transition from 8:16 to 8:17. Second, the evangelist inverts the order of "all" and "many" in his source. While Mark has "all" the sick people of Capernaum being brought to him and Jesus healing "many" of them, Matthew has "many" people being brought and Jesus healing "all" of them.

---

1. For other references to demons and spirits in the Gospel, see Matthew 4:24; 7:22; 10:1, 8; 11:18; 12:22-29, 43-45; 15:22; 17:18; cf. Clinton Wahlen, *Jesus and the Impurity of Spirits in the Synoptic Gospels*, WUNT 2.185 (Tübingen: Mohr Siebeck, 2004), 117–39; Amanda Witmer, *Jesus, The Galilean Exorcist: His Exorcisms in Social and Political Context*, Library of Historical Jesus Studies 10 (London: T&T Clark, 2012), 33–35.

This redaction is consistent with an editorial tendency in the First Gospel to emphasize the comprehensiveness of Jesus' healing activity, evident, for example, in Matthew 4:23 (cf. Mark 1:39), 12:15 (cf. Mark 3:10), and 14:35 (cf. Mark 6:55).[2]

Beyond these minor changes, the summary statement in Matthew 8:16 is of particular interest for the various shifts that it ushers into the narrative.[3] To begin with, we see that here Jesus resumes his usual, more reactive role as healer, with the afflicted being "brought to him" (cf. Matt. 4:24; 9:2, 32; 12:22; 14:35). In addition, the silence of Matthew 8:14-15 is broken, with Jesus now casting out spirits "with a word," an expression that links this episode with the healing described in Matthew 8:8 and the exorcism described in Matthew 8:32. Most important, the house, which had been the space of private healing, now opens up as a space for public healing.[4] Note that while Matthew 8:16 indicates a change in time, it does not indicate a change in setting. It is therefore not just the state of Peter's mother-in-law that is transformed but also the state of Peter's house. W. D. Davies and Dale Allison imagine the crowds of 8:16 as gathering "around" the house, but this reading seems to reflect Mark's version of the story (Mark 1:33) more than Matthew's.[5] As Eric Meyers points out, in a typical courtyard house, the space created by the courtyard itself was not "a convenient barrier between public and

2. John J. Pilch (*Healing in the New Testament: Insights from Medical and Mediterranean Anthropology* [Minneapolis: Fortress Press, 2000], 107–10) proposes that the healing ministry of Jesus pertains to three "symbolic body zones" (heart-eyes, mouth-ears, hands-feet), noting how each is represented in Matthew 8–9 (8:6; 9:2, 27, 32). However, in order to capture the comprehensiveness of Jesus' activity, it is necessary to add at least two more "zones": the skin (8:2) and the reproductive system (9:20).

3. For other summary statements in the Gospel, see Matthew 4:23-25; 9:35; 12:15-16; 14:13-14, 35–36; 15:29-31; 19:1-2. Cf. Birger Gerhardsson, *The Mighty Acts of Jesus According to Matthew* (Lund: CWK Gleerup, 1979), 20–37.

4. As we will see, a similar movement from private to public occurs in Matthew 9:25-26 and 9:28-31.

5. W. D. Davies and Dale C. Allison, *The Gospel According to Saint Matthew*, ICC (London: T&T Clark, 1991), 2:40.

private domains," but rather permitted "multiple connections with neighbors and multiple relationships among people residing within the domicile."[6] This fact raises the possibility that the courtyard (or perhaps also the transverse hall) of Peter's house was the place in Matthew 8:16 where people were being brought to Jesus.[7]

A domestic setting for the action of Matthew 8:16 would also accord with subsequent texts in the Gospel that draw attention to the house as a venue of healing.[8] To effect the cures in Matthew 9:27-31, for example, Jesus is presented as entering a house with the supplicants, an item not found in the story's Markan counterparts (Mark 8:22-26; 10:46-52), while Matthew 9:10-12 presents Jesus "the physician" teaching "in the house" (cf. Matt. 13:36; 17:25). Houses also figure prominently as physical and social centers for the disciples' missionary work (Matt. 10:11-14), which includes healing the sick (Matt. 10:1, 8). The narrative connection between houses and healing may be based in part on the experience of Matthew's original readers, for whom the house-church would have served as a place of ritual healing, an institutional role reflected in other early Christian texts as well.[9] In the evangelist's narrative world, this space can be seen to contrast symbolically both with the "house" of the Jerusalem temple (Matt. 12:4; 21:13; 23:38), which can serve as a venue of ritual healing only after Jesus has "cleansed" it (Matt. 21:14), as well as with the

---

6. Eric M. Meyers, "The Problems of Gendered Space in Syro-Palestinian Domestic Architecture: The Case of Roman-Period Galilee," in *From Antioch to Alexandria: Recent Studies in Domestic Architecture*, eds. Katharina Galor and Tomasz Waliszewski (Warsaw: University of Warsaw Press, 2007), 118. Cf. Matt. 26:3, 58, 69.

7. See the discussion of domestic architecture in Chapter Four.

8. Matthew follows Mark in having the healing of the official's daughter take place in his house (Matt. 9:23-25; cf. Mark 5:38-42). In Matthew 9:2, on the other hand, he drops Mark's reference to the house (Mark 2:1). Similarly, compare Matthew 15:21 with Mark 7:24. A more complicated scenario is presented by Matthew 17:19 (cf. Mark 9:28). See further Matt. 12:22; 15:15; 19:7.

9. For example, Mark 2:1; Acts 9:17-19, 39-40; 28:7-9; *Acts of John* 19-25; *Acts of Andrew* 22, 29; *Acts of Xanthippe and Polyxenia* 10; cf. 1 Cor. 12:9, 28, 30; James 5:14-15.

"house" of the "strong man" (Matt. 12:29), which Jesus "plunders" by healing those possessed of demons (Matt. 12:22-28).[10]

In evaluating the import of such texts for Matthew's original readers, it is worth remembering that early Christianity was not the first or only movement to situate healing practices within domestic spaces. In Tobit 3:10-17, for example, an agent of divine healing is said to enter such a space while one supplicant is in an upper room and another is in the house's courtyard. Hippocratic physicians sometimes operated out of their own homes, carrying out "public" work in the "private" realm,[11] while charismatic healers were not unknown to operate in domestic settings as well.[12] There is also evidence that devotees of the Asclepius cult would sometimes consecrate their homes to the god's service.[13] A household could even serve as the location for the sort of "healing as call" experience described earlier (Chapter Four). The author of a second century CE papyrus, for example, recounts how, in response to his prayers, Asclepius appeared to him one night while he was sleeping in his home: after curing the man of his fever, the god demanded that he fulfill his previous pledge to translate a sacred book into Greek.[14]

Against such a backdrop, narratives like Matthew 8:14-17 can be interpreted as providing needed legitimation for the Christian "house" as a center of ritual healing, a need that would have taken on added urgency if the "house" of prayer (i.e., the synagogue)

---

10. Cf. Elizabeth Struthers Malbon, *Narrative Space and Mythic Meaning in Mark* (San Francisco: Harper & Row, 1986), 106–40.

11. Vivian Nutton, "Healers in the Medical Market Place: Towards a Social History of Graeco-Roman Medicine," in *Medicine in Society: Historical Essays*, ed. Andrew Wear (Cambridge: Cambridge University Press, 1992), 49; Jane Draycott, *Approaches to Healing in Roman Egypt*, BAR International Series 2416 (Oxford: Archaeopress, 2012), 27.

12. See, for example, Hippolytus, *Refutation of All Heresies* 4.32 (from Emma J. Edelstein and Ludwig Edelstein, *Asclepius: Collection and Interpretation of the Testimonies* [Baltimore: Johns Hopkins University Press, 1945], 1:167–68); *b. Ber.* 34b; Philostratus, *Life of Apollonius* 3.39.

13. For example, IG^2, no. 4969 (from Edelstein and Edelstein, *Asclepius*, 1:377–78).

14. P.Oxy. XI, 1381 (from Edelstein and Edelstein, *Asclepius*, 1:169–75).

in Matthew's milieu was also seeking recognition as a center of healing in its own right.[15] For Matthew's readers, who themselves worshipped in house-churches, such descriptions of Jesus' activity would have had both spiritual and social relevance. The same power manifested in houses during his earthly ministry is now manifested in house-churches through his continued presence "with" the community (Matt. 1:23; 18:20; 28:20). The healing narratives are not just illustrating theological themes like discipleship or resurrection, then, but also authorizing and eliciting the personal experiences that believers have of Christ in their time of need, including the role of such experiences in establishing and sustaining the life of faith. In support of this, stories like ours project the "house" as both the social and the symbolic space in which such experiences are given expression. With regard to the latter, an instructive connection can perhaps be drawn between Matthew 8:14-17 and a passage that similarly combines imagery of vision with imagery of domestic space, Matthew 6:6. It is not just that the heavenly Father "sees" the faithful when they pray in "the inner room," that is, in the private, quiet places of life, but that Jesus "sees" them there as well (8:14) and, moreover, enters into this space to transform the believer with a healing touch (8:15).[16]

We can conclude our analysis of both Matthew 8:16-17 and Matthew 8:1-17 as a whole with a discussion of what is perhaps the unit's most distinctive feature: the citation of Isaiah 53:4 in Matthew 8:17. As he does elsewhere, Matthew drops Mark's reference to Jesus silencing the demons he has cast out (Mark 1:34).[17] In its place, we have the sixth of ten so-called fulfillment quotations that Matthew has

---

15. For the evidence that ancient synagogues served as centers of healing, see Gideon Bohak, *Ancient Jewish Magic: A History* (Cambridge: Cambridge University Press, 2008), 314–18.

16. Cf. Walter T. Wilson, "Seen in Secret: Inconspicuous Piety and Alternative Subjectivity in Matthew 6:1-6, 16-18," *CBQ* 72 (2010): 475–97.

17. See also Mark 1:25 and 3:12 (cf. Matt. 12:16).

inserted into his Gospel.[18] What makes the substitution interesting is that both statements have something to do with Jesus' identity, though they reflect contrary approaches to the topic: in Mark 1:34, Jesus silences the demons because they know who he is, while in Matthew 8:17 the evangelist reveals something important regarding Jesus' role as a healer. As with the other examples of this form, Matthew reminds his readers that the acts of Jesus are not self-interpreting, that is, they do not by themselves provide sufficient evidence of his true identity and mission. As one modern author puts it: "It is not the miracles that attest, rather they themselves must first be attested."[19] The citation here in Matthew 8:17, situated near the beginning of the cycle of miracle stories in chapters 8–9, also corresponds with a statement made by Jesus in Matthew 5:17, which occurs near the beginning of the Sermon on the Mount: "Do not think that I came to abolish the Law or the Prophets; I did not come to abolish but to fulfill." On one level, the point that Matthew is making here is clear enough: Jesus' ministry of deeds is just as much a fulfillment of Scripture as his ministry of word. As we shall see, however, there is more to the citation than this.

The Greek translation of the Scripture text that Matthew cites here, Isaiah 53:4, is not taken from the Septuagint, but appears to be Matthew's own rendering of the Hebrew.[20] Presumably, he had reasons for presenting the citation in this particular way. In this

---

18. On the fulfillment quotations, see Krister Stendahl, *The School of St. Matthew and its Use of the Old Testament* (Philadelphia: Fortress Press, 1968), 97–127; Davies and Allison, *Saint Matthew*, 3:573–77; Richard Beaton, *Isaiah's Christ in Matthew's Gospel*, SNTSMS 123 (Cambridge: Cambridge University Press, 2002), 22–34; John K. Riches, *Conflicting Mythologies: Identity Formation in the Gospels of Mark and Matthew*, Studies of the New Testament and Its World (Edinburgh: T&T Clark, 2000), 232–40.

19. Heinz Joachim Held, "Matthew as Interpreter of the Miracle Stories," in *Tradition and Interpretation in Matthew*, eds. Günther Bornkamm, Gerhard Barth, and Heinz Joachim Held (Philadelphia: Westminster, 1963), 255.

20. Maarten J. J. Menken, "The Source of the Quotation From Isaiah 53:4 in Matthew 8:17," *NovT* 39 (1997): 314–16; Stendahl, *School of St. Matthew*, 106–107. Cf. 1 Pet. 2:24.

regard it is noteworthy that the particular terms he has chosen for infirmity (*astheneia*) and disease (*nosos*) in making the translation are used to describe Jesus' healings elsewhere in the Gospel (4:23-24; 9:35; 25:36, 39; cf. 10:1, 8). This suggests that what is being claimed in Matthew 8:17 is not just a commentary on Matthew 8:16 or even Matthew 8:1-16, but a statement that applies to the entirety of his healing ministry. As is usually the case, it is worthwhile to examine the cited text within the context of its original literary setting, namely, Isaiah 53:4-5:

> (4) Surely he has borne our infirmities and carried our diseases;
> yet we accounted him stricken, struck down by God, and afflicted.
> (5) But he was wounded for our transgressions, crushed for our
> iniquities;
> upon him was the punishment that made us whole, and by his bruises
> we are healed. (NRSV)

Assuming that Matthew and his community were familiar with this passage, a perusal of its contents raises some intriguing questions regarding the presentation of Jesus as a healer in the First Gospel. It is important to note that the words of Matthew 8:17 are neither spoken nor heard by any of the characters in the story. Rather, here Matthew steps outside of his usual role as storyteller and speaks directly to the readers, providing them with guidance as to the proper interpretation of what they are hearing.[21] This fact reveals something important about the nature and function of the quotation itself: since only the readers know the full Gospel narrative, only the readers can grasp the full significance of the quotation for interpreting that narrative.

The text that Matthew quotes belongs to the last of four so-called Servant Songs preserved in the book of Isaiah. In his original context, the servant is an anonymous and innocent figure who meekly

---

21. Cf. David B. Howell, *Mathew's Inclusive Story: A Study in the Narrative Rhetoric of the First Gospel*, JSNTSup 42 (Sheffield: JSOT, 1990), 213–14.

endures pain, disability, and humiliation.[22] As Isaiah 53:5 indicates, the suffering borne by the servant is not arbitrary but has a particular purpose: he suffers "for our iniquities," that is, he suffers on behalf of others in order to redeem or "heal" their sins. Readers familiar with this passage would recognize in the quotation of Matthew 8:17 not only a claim that Jesus' healings represent the fulfillment of Scripture but also the application of the imagery of Isaiah's servant to the person of Jesus as he is presented in the Gospel. For example, within the immediate context of Matthew 8–9, the imagery of "healing" transgressions anticipates 9:1-8, which draws an analogy between healing and the forgiveness of sins, as well as 9:9-13, where Jesus is identified as the "physician" of sinners, that is, the one sent by God to "save his people from their sins" (Matt. 1:21). The Isaianic imagery of "wounds" and "punishment," meanwhile, points forward to Jesus' suffering on the cross, the moment when his blood "is poured out for many for the forgiveness of sins" (Matt. 26:28; cf. Isa. 53:12). In Matthew 20:28, Jesus interprets this suffering not only as an act of redemption but also as the act of a *servant*: "the Son of Man came not to be served but to serve, and to give his life as a ransom for many" (cf. Isa. 53:10-11).

At this point it is important to be clear about how the evangelist both does and does not apply the imagery of Isaiah's servant to Jesus in Matthew 8:16-17. What Matthew does *not* state is that Jesus heals those with disease and disability by taking their suffering upon himself: the text simply states that he "takes" or "bears" their infirmities away. What Matthew *does* issue is an implicit invitation to ponder the significance of Jesus' ministry to those who suffer in the light of his status as God's servant. Those who accept this invitation

---

22. Jeremy Schipper (*Disability and Isaiah's Suffering Servant* [Oxford: Oxford University Press, 2011], 31–59) has argued that Isaiah 53 describes the servant using language associated elsewhere in the Hebrew Bible with disability, an interpretation that sees the biblical figure as an image not so much of individual tragedy as of social experience.

are led to a deeper appreciation for the nuances of what we might call Matthew's Christology of healing, the elements of which can be outlined as follows.[23]

In his passion, Christ is seen as embracing not only human mortality but also human pain and suffering, his body on the cross manifesting his solidarity with all broken, disabled, and disfigured bodies. This is very much the Christ who is "with" the community of the faithful (Matt. 28:20), since this is the Christ who joins with them in covenant, redeeming them of their sins (Matt. 26:28). Moreover, in his passion, Christ knows what it is like to feel hopeless and abandoned, to feel abandoned even by God (Matt. 27:46). Of course Christ was not abandoned by God, and this fact rewrites the narrative of human suffering. Christ's death does not remove suffering, to be sure, but the divine power manifested in his resurrection does transform its meaning (Matt. 28:18).

Viewed in the shadow of the cross, Jesus' ministry of healing can be seen as an extension of his solidarity with human suffering, especially the suffering of those who have been "abandoned" by society. The bodies of those healed, meanwhile, are marked by the power of the divine to create new life out of hopelessness, their stories representing new chapters in the rewritten narrative of human suffering. As Matthew 8:17 reminds us, however, the one who wields this power is not only the Son of God (e.g., Matt. 8:29) but also the servant of God, the one whose body will be broken in service to others. Accordingly, the bodies of the healed are marked not only by Christ's power but also by Christ's weakness. They are transformed not only into images of abundant life but also, like Peter's mother-in-

---

23. Cf. Frederick J. Gaiser, *Healing in the Bible: Theological Insight for Christian Ministry* (Grand Rapids: Baker, 2010), 226–38; Jürgen Moltmann, "Liberate Yourselves by Accepting One Another," in *Human Disability and the Service of God: Reassessing Religious Practice*, eds. Nancy L. Eiesland and Don E. Saliers (Nashville: Abingdon, 1998), 115–16; Thomas Reynolds, *Vulnerable Communion: A Theology of Disability and Hospitality* (Grand Rapids: Brazos, 2008), 175–213.

law, into agents of service (Matt. 8:15). If solidarity with the infirmed is an expression of Christ's status as the servant of God, the same applies to those who would become servants of Christ (e.g., Matt. 10:1, 8). The faithful participate in the brokenness of Christ, then, not only through the Eucharist (Matt. 26:28) but also by ministering to the sick and the needy, those with whom Christ is ever present (Matt. 25:35-40).

A more explicit identification of Jesus as the servant can be found in Matthew 12:15-21, which, like Matthew 8:14-17, contains a summary statement followed by a fulfillment quotation:

Many crowds followed him, and he healed them all, (16) and ordered them not to make him known, (17) in order to fulfill what was spoken through Isaiah the prophet:

(18) "Behold, my servant whom I have chosen, my beloved,
in whom my soul is well pleased.
I will put my Spirit upon him,
and he will proclaim justice to the Gentiles.
(19) He will not quarrel, nor cry out;
neither will anyone hear his voice in the streets.
(20) A bruised reed he will not break,
and a smoldering wick he will not quench,
until he leads justice to victory.
(21) And in his name the Gentiles will hope."

It is more than happenstance that once again we have a citation from Isaiah, this time Isaiah 42:1-4 (cf. Matt. 3:17; 17:5), that applies a description of the servant to Jesus' ministry of healing.[24] Here the citation is used to explain why Jesus commands those healed not to speak about him (cf. Matt. 8:4; 9:30): such reluctance to broadcast his miraculous accomplishments is a fulfillment of Scripture. In addition, there are several elements of the quotation that reflect Matthew's

---

24. The citation from Isaiah represents a complex blending of elements familiar from different traditions, for which see Stendahl, *School of St. Matthew*, 107–15.

broader priorities in depicting Jesus as a healer, adding depth to the Christology sketched above.[25] To begin with, like the servant, who does not "wrangle or cry aloud," Jesus is depicted as someone who is "gentle and humble in heart" (Matt. 11:29).[26] This connects with repeated notices in the Gospel that Jesus heals people out of compassion for them (Matt. 9:35-36; 14:14; 20:34). Such concern is directed especially toward the "bruised reed" and the "smoldering wick" of Isaiah 42:3, likely symbols for society's weak and forgotten members. Such concern also comes to expression in Jesus' passion for justice (cf. Matt. 5:6, 10, 20; 6:33), which he proclaims and enacts on behalf of all people, even the Gentiles (cf. Matt. 8:5-13; 15:21-28). Finally, there is the reminder that Jesus' power to perform healings and exorcisms is an outworking of the Spirit that God has bestowed upon him (Matt. 3:16-17; 12:28). In sum, the reader sees that Jesus' ministry of healing is not something that he carries out under his own authority but only in his capacity as God's servant and out of obedience to God's will (cf. Matt. 4:10; 26:39).

In conclusion, it can be noted that there are several passages in the Old Testament outside of the book of Isaiah where God refers to a messianic figure as "my servant" (e.g., Zech. 3:8). Probably the most important of these for our study of Matthew is Ezekiel 34:23:[27]

> I will set up over them one shepherd, my servant David, and he shall feed them: he shall feed them and be their shepherd. (NRSV)

As commentators often observe, the author of the First Gospel is particularly fond of referring to Jesus as the Son of David (Matt.

---

25. For further analysis, see Beaton, *Isaiah's Christ*, 122–73; Lidija Novakovic, *Messiah, the Healer of the Sick: A Study of Jesus as the Son of David in the Gospel of Matthew*, WUNT 2.170 (Tübingen: Mohr Siebeck, 2003), 133–51; Leroy A. Huizenga, *The New Isaac: Tradition and Intertextuality in the Gospel of Matthew*, NovTSup 131 (Leiden: Brill, 2009), 201–8.

26. Cf. Num. 12:3; Matt. 5:5; 18:4; 21:5; 23:12.

27. For more on Ezekiel 34, see Chapter Thirteen.

1:1; 9:27; 12:23; 15:22; 20:30-31; 21:9, 15).[28] Like David, Jesus is the shepherd of his people (Matt. 2:6; 9:36; 25:32; 26:31), who are likened to lost sheep (Matt. 9:36; 10:6; 15:24; cf. 18:12). Of particular interest here are Matthew 9:36 and 15:24, which associate Jesus' role as shepherd with his ministry of healing.[29] Evidently, Matthew understood this ministry as contributing to Jesus' role not only as God's servant but also as the Son of David. The practice of healing, then, functions as something of a christological linchpin for the Gospel, linking Jesus' identity as the expected Davidic shepherd-king with his identity as the suffering servant of God.

---

28. For example, Davies and Allison, *Saint Matthew*, 1:156–57. Cf. Wayne Baxter, "Healing and the Son of David: Matthew's Warrant," *NovT* 48 (2006): 36–50.
29. For discussion of Matthew 9:36, see Chapter Thirteen.

6

The Other Side: Matthew 8:18-27

With this passage we encounter the first miracle story in the second triad of miracle stories preserved in Matthew 8–9. From a form-critical perspective, this is the most varied of the triads, consisting of a nature miracle (8:23-27), an exorcism (8:28-34), and a healing story with elements of a controversy story (9:1-8). For the contents of the triad, Matthew relies on Mark, though his order of the miracles differs from that of his source material, with the story of the paralytic (Matt. 9:1-8; cf. Mark 2:1-12) now coming immediately after rather than well before the parallel material in Mark 4:35-41 (the stilling of the storm) and 5:1-20 (the Gerasene demoniac):

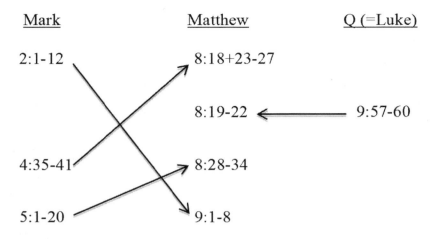

In addition, Matthew has inserted into Mark 4:35-41 some non-miracle material on the theme of discipleship derived from the Q source (Matt. 8:19-22; cf. Luke 9:57-60). This material anticipates the episode in Matthew 8:23-27, the only miracle story in chapters 8–9 in which the disciples have a speaking role.

According to Matthew 5:1, when Jesus saw crowds gathering around him, he led his followers "up on the mountain," that is, to a symbolic place of divine revelation. According to Matthew 8:18, when Jesus saw crowds gathering around him, he led his followers to "the other side," a place to which symbolic meaning can also be attached. These two episodes are also similar in that each is reminiscent of a defining moment from the life of Moses, the former recalling his ascent of Mount Sinai in order to give the people the law, the latter recalling his parting of the Red Sea in order to lead the people to safety. Despite these similarities, however, it is also possible to discern differences between the two Matthean episodes—differences not only in terms of their content and length but also in terms of the kind of revelation that they convey. This is signaled in part by the different audiences to which the respective revelations are made: while both the crowds and the disciples are recipients of the revelation conferred by the Sermon on the Mount (7:28), for Matthew the revelation that takes place in 8:23-27 is one in which the crowds do not participate.

Having healed "all" their sick (8:16), Jesus now decides, rather abruptly, that the time has come for him to leave Capernaum (8:18). No reason is given for the decision, a fact that raises certain questions for the reader: where exactly is "the other side" and why is Jesus' designation for this place so vague? What does Jesus hope to accomplish with this journey? Why does he take others with him and what does he expect of them?

Much like the story of the centurion and his slave, Matthew 8:18-27 is a unified narrative that the evangelist has created by combining a story from Mark (cf. Luke 8:22-25) with material from the synoptic sayings source.

(34) ... he was explaining everything in private to his own disciples. (35) And he said to them on that day, when evening came, "Let us go across to the other side."	(18) Seeing the crowd around him, Jesus gave orders to depart to the other side.	
	(19) Then a certain scribe approached and said to him, "Teacher, I will follow you wherever you go."	(57) And as they were traveling on the road, someone said to him, "I will follow you wherever you go."
	(20) And Jesus said to him, "The foxes have holes, and the birds of the air nests, but the Son of Man has nowhere to lay his head."	(58) And Jesus said to him, "The foxes have holes, and the birds of the air nests, but the Son of Man has nowhere to lay his head."

(21) But another, one of the disciples, said to him, "Lord, permit me first to go and bury my father."

(59) To another he said, "Follow me." But he said, "Lord, permit me first to go and bury my father."

(22) But Jesus said to him, "Follow me, and let the dead bury their own dead."

(60) But he said to him, "Let the dead bury their own dead; but as for you, go and proclaim the kingdom of God." (Luke 9:57-60)

(36) And leaving the crowd, they took him as he was in the boat; and other boats were with him.

(23) And when he got into the boat, his disciples followed him.

(37) And there was a great windstorm and the waves beat against the boat, so that the boat was already filling up. (38) But he was in the stern, sleeping on the cushion. And they woke him up and said to him, "Teacher, doesn't it matter to you that we are perishing?"

(24) And behold, there was a great earthquake in the sea, so that the boat was swamped by the waves; but he was asleep. (25) And they went and woke him, saying, "Lord, save us! We are perishing!"

(39) And he got up and rebuked the wind and said to the sea, "Peace! Be still!" And the wind ceased and there was a great calm. (40) And he said to them, "Why are you afraid? Do you still have no faith?"

(26) And he said to them, "Why are you afraid, you of little faith?" Then he got up and rebuked the winds and the sea; and there was a great calm.

(41) And they were filled with great fear and said to one another, "Who then is this, that even the wind and the sea obey him?" (Mark 4:34-41)

(27) And the men were amazed, saying, "What sort of man is this, that even the winds and the sea obey him?" (Matt. 8:18-27)

Up to this point in chapters 8–9, no mention has been made of the disciples (cf. Matt. 5:1). Now the nature of their relationship with Jesus takes center stage. In contrast to Mark 4:34-35 (which has Jesus speaking to "his own disciples"), the recipient of the order in Matthew 8:18 is left unstated. The fact that the first person to approach him afterwards is a scribe (8:19) leaves the impression that Jesus' order to "depart" was a general call, that is, a call that included the crowds gathering around him (8:18).[1] It is significant, then, that in 8:23 it is only the disciples who actually climb into the boat with Jesus. It seems that the symbolism of space and movement plays a critical role in conveying the author's narrative theology: being a disciple means "following" Jesus, and following Jesus means separating from the crowds, ultimately finding oneself on "the other side" of the people. This symbolic act of departure anticipates subsequent episodes in the Gospel in which Jesus and his followers withdraw from a venue in order to minister elsewhere (12:15; 14:13; 15:21; 16:4).[2] As J. R. C. Cousland notes, in the First Gospel the crowds often "follow" Jesus for healing (4:24-25; 12:15; 14:13-14; 19:2; cf. 20:29), while the disciples "follow" him in response to his call (4:18-22; 8:22-23; 9:9).[3] In other words, the crowds follow Jesus because *they* want something from *him*, while the disciples follow Jesus because *he* wants something from *them*.

This focus on discipleship is signaled in several other ways by our passage, but especially by two major redactional features. First, Matthew 8:23 offers us a carefully reworked version of Mark 4:36. While the Second Gospel reports how "they took him with them

---

1. Stephen C. Barton, *Discipleship and Family Ties in Mark and Matthew*, SNTSMS 80 (Cambridge: Cambridge University Press, 1994), 142–43; Ulrich Luz, *Studies in Matthew* (Grand Rapids: Eerdmans, 2005), 229–31. Different is Jack D. Kingsbury, "On Following Jesus: The 'Eager' Scribe and the 'Reluctant' Disciple (Matthew 8.18-22)," *NTS* 34 (1988): 46–47.

2. Luz, *Studies in Matthew*, 230–31.

3. J. R. C. Cousland, *The Crowds in the Gospel of Matthew*, NovTSup 102 (Leiden: Brill, 2002), 164–68.

in the boat," the First Gospel explicitly refers both to the disciples and to their doing something characteristic of discipleship, namely, following Jesus (cf. Matt. 4:18-22; 9:9; 10:38; 16:24; 19:21). This has the effect of highlighting Jesus' role as the catalyst of events, a point also reinforced by Matthew 8:18, where, in contrast to Mark 4:35, Matthew refers to Jesus by name and to the "orders" that he issues (cf. Matt. 14:22).[4] Note also that Matthew drops the reference in Mark 4:36 to people in "other boats" accompanying the group on its journey. Apparently, in this version of the story, the only witnesses that matter are the disciples.

Second, Matthew inserts into the narrative framework that he has borrowed from Mark 4:35-41 two pronouncement stories on discipleship derived from the Q source (cf. Luke 9:57-60). Matthew's reworking of the inserted material has the effect of enhancing the structural parallelism between 8:19-20 and 8:21-22.[5] The two stories are clearly meant to be read in tandem, with the former exemplifying an improper response to Jesus' orders and the latter exemplifying a proper response. Matthew underscores the negative character of the first respondent by identifying him as one of the scribes, a group that usually opposes Jesus (e.g., Matt. 9:3), and by having him address Jesus as "teacher," a term that usually indicates a deficient understanding of Jesus' identity.[6] The second respondent, by contrast, is identified as one of the disciples, addresses Jesus as "Lord" (cf. Matt. 8:2, 6, 8), and receives from the Lord a call to "follow me," the same

---

4. Cf. Harry T. Fleddermann, "The Demands of Discipleship: Matt 8,19-22 par. Luke 9,57-62," in *The Four Gospels: Festschrift Frans Neirynck*, ed. F. Van Segbroek (Leuven: Leuven University Press, 1992), 555–56.

5. The enhanced symmetry of Matthew 8:19-22 (in comparison with Luke 9:57-60) is accomplished in two ways: (1) by adding the opening address, "Teacher," in 8:19 (matching the opening address, "Lord," in 8:21), and (2) by placing Jesus' command, "Follow me," *after* the disciple's request (8:21-22).

6. See especially Matthew 12:38, where a group of unbelieving scribes refers to Jesus this way. Cf. 9:11; 17:24; 22:15-16, 23-24. In contrast to passages like Mark 4:38; 9:38; 10:35; 13:1, Matthew avoids having the disciples refer to Jesus as "teacher."

summons that Peter and Andrew received in 4:19 and that Matthew the tax collector will receive in 9:9.[7]

In concert with this, it is also evident that Matthew has made an effort not only to integrate the two pronouncement stories with one another but also to integrate them with the sea rescue story that immediately follows. One of the ways in which he does so is through the literary device of catchword. Note in particular the use of "follow" in verses 19, 22, and 23, "disciple" in verses 21, 23, and "Lord" in verses 21 and 25. It is interesting that both episodes also contain allusions to the teaching on anxiety that Jesus had imparted in the Sermon on the Mount, the reference to "birds of the air" in 8:20 recalling 6:26, while the address, "you of little faith," in 8:26 recalls 6:30.[8] As we shall see, the participants in the story will have good reason to feel anxious! Moreover, the literary integration just described has the effect of heightening the overall sense of uncertainty and suspense: while the order to depart is given in 8:18, the actual departure does not occur until 8:23, and the actual arrival does not occur until 8:28. In the meantime, obstacles posed by both the social world (family ties) and the natural world (the storm at sea) must be overcome.

Examining Matthew 8:18-27 from the perspective of *narrative criticism*, then, we can see that this editorial activity has the effect of achieving a double clarification. The first clarification has to do with the nature of the "following" presented in the two pronouncement stories.[9] In its original setting (i.e., the setting provided by the Q source), it appears that the destination and purpose of this following were left unspecified. In its new Matthean setting, this following

7. See the discussion in Chapter Nine.
8. Thus both passages address the theme of trust, though they do so in different ways.
9. Heinz Joachim Held, "Matthew as Interpreter of the Miracle Stories," in *Tradition and Interpretation in Matthew*, eds. Günther Bornkamm, Gerhard Barth, and Heinz Joachim Held (Philadelphia: Westminster, 1963), 202.

entails joining Jesus on a journey to "the other side" (8:18). As we eventually learn, this other side is "the country of the Gadarenes" (8:28), a reference to the environs of Gadara, a city belonging to a predominantly Gentile region known as the Decapolis.[10] Following Jesus, then, means leaving home and encountering the ethnic, political, and religious "other," an encounter that Matthew will narrate shortly, in 8:28-34 (cf. 15:21-28).

The second clarification has to do with the meaning of the sea storm from which the disciples must be saved in order to reach this "other." The sayings derived from the Q source in 8:20 and 22 had indicated the sort of demands placed upon those who follow Jesus on his journey.[11] Unlike the people whom Jesus heals, who either return home (e.g., 9:6-7) or remain at home (e.g., 8:14-15), the disciples must not only leave home but also embrace a life of homelessness, the commitment to Jesus outweighing even the commitment to one's own family.[12] Discipleship, then, entails more than an initial decision to follow Jesus: it also entails a willingness to follow him specifically in his role as the Son of Man (8:20; cf. 20:28). Seen in this light, the stilling of the storm can be read as a dramatic illustration of what it means to accept this call and follow Jesus. Having stated that he has "nowhere" to lay his head, Jesus now leads his followers into a "nowhere" place, the Sea of Galilee constituting not only a geographical barrier between two sociopolitical entities but also a liminal zone symbolic of the uncertainty and danger that the disciples will experience as Jesus' followers.[13] Separated from home and family,

---

10. Cousland, *The Crowds in the Gospel of Matthew*, 58–61; Jean-Paul Rey-Coquais, "Decapolis," *ABD* 2 (1992): 116–21.

11. The harsh saying in 8:22 is better taken as an oxymoron than as a reference to the spiritually dead. See Ulrich Luz, *Matthew: A Commentary*, Hermeneia (Minneapolis: Fortress Press, 2005), 2:18–20 for discussion. According to *m. Ber.* 3:1, burying one's relatives takes precedence over fundamental obligations like reciting the Shema.

12. Jesus may have taken up residence in Capernaum (4:12-13) but his ministry is clearly itinerant in nature.

they now face fear, stress, and even the forces of death itself. The crowds may "follow" Jesus (8:1) because they are impressed by his teaching (7:28-29), but it is the disciples who must "follow" him in the full sense, that is, they must heed his orders to "depart" and follow him into the storm.[14]

As subsequent sayings in the Gospel will demonstrate, the sort of domestic disruption suggested by Matthew 8:20 and 22 is not simply a social reality with which the disciples must cope. It also names a deeper, theological reality about the person of Jesus and the ministry of those who would align themselves with him:

> (34) Do not think that I came to bring peace to the earth; I came not to bring peace but a sword. (35) For I came to set a man against his father, and a daughter against her mother, and a daughter-in-law against her mother-in-law; (36) and one's enemies will be members of one's own household. (Matt. 10:34-36)

The scenario depicted here is one predicated upon what Ulrich Luz has referred to as "the deep opposition" separating the kingdom of God from "the world," an opposition that the disciples are called upon to embody as a sign to those who would choose the former over the latter (cf. 12:46-50; 19:27-30).[15] Against this background, the sea rescue story can be seen as dramatizing not simply the nature of discipleship in general but also the testing to which the disciples will be subjected as they live out this call.

Even as he reveals the nature of this testing, however, Matthew also injects an element of uncertainty as to whether the disciples are up to the task. Unlike Mark, Matthew is careful to state that Jesus'

---

13. Indeed, as the ensuing narrative will show, Jesus has nowhere to rest his head except in a storm-tossed boat, and even then without a cushion (cf. Mark 4:38)!

14. As Cousland (*The Crowds in the Gospel of Matthew*, 164–68) notes, the crowds often follow Jesus in search of healing (4:24-25; 12:15; 14:13-14; 19:2; cf. 20:29), while the disciples do so in response to his call (4:18-22; 8:18-22; 9:9).

15. Luz, *Matthew*, 2:19. Recall that in 4:21-22 James and John had left their father to follow Jesus.

disciples "followed him" into the boat (8:23; cf. Mark 4:36). At the same time, Matthew is also careful to include indications that the disciples have yet to comprehend what such following entails. The request made by one of the disciples in 8:21, for instance, suggests that even within Jesus' inner circle there are still some for whom obligations to "the world" outweigh obligations to the Lord. Equally revealing is 8:26, where Jesus responds to the disciples' manifestation of fear by characterizing them as persons "of little faith," an expression unique to Matthew's version of the story. Once again, attention to editorial differences between the First and Second Gospels is in order:

> (38) But he was in the stern, sleeping on the cushion. And they woke him up and said to him, "Teacher, doesn't it matter to you that we are perishing?" (39) And he got up and rebuked the wind and said to the sea, "Peace! Be still!" And the wind ceased and there was a great calm. (Mark 4:38-39)

> (25) And they went and woke him, saying, "Lord, save us! We are perishing!" (26) And he said to them, "Why are you afraid, you of little faith?" Then he got up and rebuked the winds and the sea; and there was a great calm. (Matt. 8:25-26)

In the Markan account, the first thing that Jesus does after waking up is to rebuke the sea. In the Matthean account, the first thing that Jesus does after waking up is to rebuke the disciples. This redactional alteration draws attention not only to the theme of discipleship but also to the element of verbal exchange in the narrative.[16] As we have seen, the latter is a feature of the Matthean healing stories as well (e.g., 8:11-12), though the nature of the verbal exchange in 8:25-26 is different from what we find elsewhere. On one level, it is apparent that the disciples' plea for help in 8:25 (including the address to

---

16. For the possibility of a ring composition in 8:23-27, see Birger Gerhardsson, *The Mighty Acts of Jesus According to Matthew* (Lund: CWK Gleerup, 1979), 53; W. D. Davies and Dale C. Allison, *The Gospel According to Saint Matthew*, ICC (London: T&T Clark, 1991), 2:68.

Jesus as "Lord") parallels the pleas for help uttered by supplicants in passages like 8:2, 6, and 15:25.[17] However, while in the healing stories Jesus is generous in his appraisal of the supplicants, commending them for their abundant faith (8:10, 13; 9:22, 29; 15:28), here Jesus castigates the disciples for their deficient faith, that is, for their failure to understand that so long as their Lord is with them they have nothing to fear.

In coming to terms with the different responses that Jesus gives to what are basically similar pleas for help, it is important to recognize that what the sea rescue story illustrates is a different *aspect* or *type* of faith.[18] What is being illustrated by the healing stories is the faith of the one seeking help, the faith that asks for a miracle. What is being illustrated in the sea rescue story, by contrast, is the faith of the one called upon to give help, the faith of the one who performs miracles (cf. 10:1, 8). This is the reason why in Matthew's rendition of the story the crowds are not—indeed cannot—be present to participate in the events of 8:23-27.

These observations are borne out when we examine subsequent episodes in the Gospel. In 14:31, for example, Jesus castigates Peter as a person "of little faith" when his fear prevents him from walking on water, that is, when it prevents him from imitating Jesus' miracle.[19] Similarly, in 17:20, Jesus castigates the "little faith" of the disciples when it prevents them from casting out a demon, that is, when it prevents them from performing the sort of miraculous ministry that he has been modeling for them. In Matthew, then, the descriptor

---

17. For example, compare 8:25 ("Lord, save us!") with 15:25 ("Lord, help me."). See also Matt. 17:15; 20:30. Note that in 8:25 Matthew has the disciples address Jesus as "Lord," while Mark has them address him as "Teacher." Indeed, the address in Mark 4:38 looks more like a reproach than a plea.

18. Gerhardsson, *Mighty Acts of Jesus*, 60–65.

19. Matthew 14:22-33 is a second sea rescue story that, as such, exhibits numerous parallels with 8:23-27. See Luz, *Matthew*, 2:16; Patrick J. Madden, *Jesus' Walking on the Sea: An Investigation of the Origin of the Narrative Account*, BZNW 81 (Berlin: Walter de Gruyter, 1997), 75–115.

"little faith" refers not to the absence of faith among non-believers but to the insufficient or anxious faith of those who have already accepted the call to serve.[20]

Along the same lines, it is worth pondering the various connections between our story in 8:18-27 and the mission discourse of chapter 10, where Jesus offers instructions for service directed specifically at the disciples (10:1). Having carried out a ministry of teaching (chapters 5–7) and healing (chapters 8–9) himself, Jesus now authorizes them to follow his example and do the same (10:1, 7-8). This is a way of life defined by itinerancy, hardship, and rejection (10:9-18; cf. 8:19-20). Indeed, because it is necessary to love Jesus more than one's father (10:37; cf. 8:21-22), such rejection is likely to come even from one's own family (10:21-22, 34-36). The disciples therefore must be fearless in carrying out their responsibilities (10:26-31; cf. 8:26). As followers of the Son of Man who has nowhere to lay his head (8:20), they await the Son of Man who will return in glory (10:23), confident that those who endure until the end will be "saved" (10:22; cf. 8:25).[21] Having received a call to ministry comparable to that of a prophet (8:21-22; cf. 1 Kgs. 19:20-21), each one of them goes forth as "a prophet in the name of a prophet" (10:41).[22] Read this way, it is possible to interpret 8:18-27 as both a narrative synopsis and rhetorical anticipation of chapter 10. In both passages, Jesus is seen interacting not with the crowds but with those called to share in his ministry, warning them of hardships but also assuring them of protection. In the midst of all these similarities, however, there is also an important difference: in 10:5-6 Jesus

---

20. Cf. Matt. 6:30; 16:8; Davies and Allison, *Saint Matthew*, 1:656; 2:69.

21. Note the use of the verb *apollumi* ("to perish, to lose") in 8:25 and 10:28, 39.

22. As we saw in Chapter Four, Matthew 8:21-22 is patterned after the story of Elijah's call of Elisha in 1 Kings 19:20-21. Also noteworthy are Jeremiah 16:1-9 and Ezekiel 24:15-24, where the prophets are directed to refrain from participating in mourning customs so as to focus on their particular calling (cf. Lev. 21:11; Num. 6:6).

instructs the disciples not to go "in the way of the Gentiles," while in 8:28 he leads them into Gentile territory. The disciples, then, will have some experience of ministry among the Gentiles, though, as we shall see, the meaning of this experience is far from clear.

Eschatology, Epiphany, and Discipleship

As this brief overview has suggested, in composing the mission discourse Matthew demonstrates a concern to situate the activities it prescribes for the disciples within a scenario of eschatological conflict (e.g., 10:22-23).[23] Indeed, it is only within the context of such a scenario that the full meaning of their ministry of teaching and healing can be properly understood. This is a scenario that applies to 8:18-27 as well, though in order to appreciate the implications of this fact it is necessary to engage in some comparative analysis.

Commentators have long noted similarities between the sea rescue narratives in the Gospels and the story of the prophet Jonah.[24] In the case of Matthew 8:23-27, the similarities extend even to the level of wording, as can be observed, for example, in the following texts:

(24) A windstorm arose on the sea, so great that the boat was being swamped by the waves; but he was asleep . . . (26) And he said to them, "Why are you afraid . . . ?" (Matt. 8:24, 26 NRSV)

(4) But the Lord hurled a great wind upon the sea, and such a mighty storm came upon the sea that the ship threatened to break up. (5)

---

23. On the eschatological character of Matthew 10, see Davies and Allison, *Saint Matthew*, 2:151, 158–59, 182, 186, 196–97, 202; R. T. France, *The Gospel of Matthew*, NICNT (Grand Rapids: Eerdmans, 2007), 389–90; Donald A. Hagner, *Matthew*, WBC 33 (Dallas: Word Books, 1993), 1:275–78; John K. Ridgway, *"Let Your Peace Come Upon It": Healing and Peace in Matthew 10:1-15*, Studies in Biblical Literature 2 (New York: Peter Lang, 1999), 265–68; Graham H. Twelftree, *In the Name of Jesus: Exorcism Among Early Christians* (Grand Rapids: Baker Academic, 2007), 164–68.

24. E.g., O. Lamar Cope, *Matthew, A Scribe Trained for the Kingdom of Heaven* (Washington, DC: Catholic Biblical Association, 1976), 96–98; John Nolland, *The Gospel of Matthew*, NIGTC (Grand Rapids: Eerdmans, 2005), 371.

> Then the mariners were afraid, and each cried to his god. . . . Jonah, meanwhile, had gone down into the hold of the ship and had lain down, and was fast asleep. (Jonah 1:4-5 NRSV)

Looking at both narratives in their entirety, we see that in each case the central figure is presented as someone through whom the power of the divine over the forces of nature is manifested. While Jonah is presented as the object of this power, however, Jesus is presented as its subject. Unlike the mariners in Jonah's story, Jesus does not "cry to his god" for help; rather he responds to the disciples' plea for help by stilling the tempest himself, acting just as God is sometimes commemorated as acting in the Psalms:

> You rule the raging of the sea; when its waves rise, you still them. (Ps. 89:9 NRSV)

> (5) You set the earth on its foundations, so that it shall never be shaken. (6) You cover it with the deep as with a garment; the waters stood above the mountains. (7) At your rebuke they flee; at the sound of your thunder they take to flight. (Ps. 104:5-7 NRSV)

> (28) Then they cried to the Lord in their trouble, and he brought them out from their distress; (29) he made the storm be still, and the waves of the sea were hushed. (Ps. 107:28-29 NRSV)

Here, as often in the Old Testament, the sea is imaged as a primordial force of chaos and destruction.[25] In keeping with this imagery, the sea is sometimes further personified (as in Ps. 104:7 above) as an adversary whom God "rebukes" with a mighty word.[26] Set within this sort of mythic framework, in terms of its *literary genre* the sea rescue story in 8:23-27 can be described as taking on the character of a divine

---

25. E.g., Job 9:8; 38:8-11; Pss. 33:7; 65:7; 74:13; 77:16; Prov. 8:27-29; Isa. 27:1; 51:10; Jer. 5:22; Hab. 3:15. In Matthew 7:25, 27, floods and winds symbolize eschatological trials.
26. E.g., Job 26:11-12; Ps. 106:9; Isa. 50:2; Nah. 1:4.

epiphany, while the story's protagonist can be described as taking on the character of an eschatological deliverer. The eschatological contours of the water imagery appear in even sharper relief when we recall the propensity among apocalypticists to use the sea storm as a symbol of eschatological tribulation.[27] Accordingly, they envisioned the renewed cosmos as incorporating not only the sea's defeat but also its complete annihilation: "Then I saw a new heaven and a new earth; for the first heaven and the first earth had passed away, and the sea was no more" (Rev. 21:1). The figure presented by our story appears to be the agent of just such a vision.

In keeping with its mythic background, there are a number of specific literary features at work in Matthew 8:23-27 that help to reinforce both the pericope's epiphanic significance and its eschatological character. Of these, there are four that warrant special attention.

The first feature concerns what is sometimes referred to as the motif of the sleeping deity.[28] In both Jonah 1:5 and Matthew 8:24, the central figure is presented as being asleep during the storm. While the former is best taken as a sign of human indifference, however, the latter is best taken as a sign of divine sovereignty, as consideration of the following passages suggests:

Wake up! Bestir yourself for my defense, for my cause, my God and my Lord! (Ps. 35:23 NRSV)

Rouse yourself! Why do you sleep, O Lord? Awake, do not cast us off forever! (Ps. 44:23 NRSV)

(9) Awake, awake, put on strength, O arm of the Lord!
Awake, as in days of old, the generations of long ago!
Was it not you who cut Rahab in pieces, who pierced the dragon?

27. E.g., Dan. 7:2-3; Rev. 13:1; 1QH 3:6, 12-18; 6:22-24; 7:4-5.
28. Bernard F. Batto, "The Sleeping God: An Ancient Near Eastern Motif of Divine Sovereignty," *Bib* 68 (1987): 153-77.

(10) Was it not you who dried up the sea, the waters of the great deep; who made the depths of the sea a way for the redeemed to cross over? (Isa. 51:9-10 NRSV)

Just as the disciples must rouse "Lord" Jesus from his slumber to rescue them from the storm, these poetic texts imagine a scenario in which the people must rouse the sleeping "Lord" to deliver them from danger. The last of these texts (Isa. 51:9-10) is of particular interest insofar as it includes a reminder about a sea rescue miracle of paradigmatic significance for salvation history, the parting of the Red Sea (Exod. 14:21-31). Interpreters going as far back as Eusebius have noted parallels between that story and the story in Matthew 8:23-27: "Scripture says, 'Moses stretched forth his hand over the sea, and the Lord drove back the sea with a strong south wind' . . . In a like manner, only much more grandly, our Savior 'rebuked the winds and the sea, and there was great calm'" (*Demonstration of the Gospel* 3.2). The similarities become even more pronounced when comparison is made with the account in LXX Ps. 105:9-10 (=106:9-10), according to which God "rebuked" (*epetimēse*) the Red Sea and "saved" (*esōsen*) the Israelites from their foes, while according to Matthew 8:25-26 Jesus "rebuked" (*epetimēsen*) the sea in response to the disciples' plea that he "save" (*sōson*) them. As this comparison suggests, what Jesus accomplishes in our story is analogous not so much to what Moses had accomplished at the Red Sea but to what God had accomplished at the Red Sea. As Paul Achtemeier puts it, here "Jesus is doing what in the OT God alone can do, still chaotic waters."[29]

Second, as the passage just cited illustrates, Old Testament authors imagined various scenarios in which God "rebukes" his primal enemy, the sea. It is important to bear in mind, however, that the term employed in Matthew 8:26 for Jesus' rebuking the sea (*epitimaō*)

29. Paul J. Achtemeier, *Jesus and the Miracle Tradition* (Eugene, OR: Cascade Books, 2008), 8. Cf. Job 26:12; Isa. 51:10.

is found elsewhere not only in the Old Testament but also in the New Testament, specifically, in some of the exorcism stories (Matt. 17:18; Mark 1:25; 9:25; Luke 4:35, 41; 9:42).[30] This lexical feature helps to shape the adversarial dynamics of our story in a particular way. Jesus is presented as rebuking the sea much in the same way he rebukes a demon, a tactic that in his cultural context would have made sense, given the common belief that demonic forces ("the spirit of the wind," "the spirit of the sea," etc.) were responsible for inclement weather.[31] Jesus' confrontation with the wind and the sea in 8:23-27, then, anticipates his more explicit confrontation with malevolent forces in the episode that immediately follows: the story of the Gadarene demoniacs (8:28-34).

Third, in Jonah 1:6, the ship's captain wakes Jonah from his slumber and implores him to pray that "we do not perish" (*mē apolōmetha*). In Matthew 8:25, the disciples use the same verb when they tell Jesus that "we are perishing" (*apollumetha*), though behind the exclamation in its Matthean context it is possible to discern a reference to the "perishing" or destruction (*apōleia*) associated with the eschatological judgment.[32] In the same vein, the plea to "save" in Matthew 8:25 can be interpreted as a metaphor for deliverance from such judgment.[33]

Finally, Matthew makes a noteworthy substitution in the term used to describe the tempest swamping the disciples' boat. While Mark describes the event as a "windstorm" (*lailaps*), Matthew chooses instead to describe it as an "earthquake" (*seismos*).[34] Earthquakes, of

---

30. John P. Meier, *A Marginal Jew: Rethinking the Historical Jesus* (New York: Doubleday, 1994), 2:926–27, cf. 2:589; Gordon J. Hamilton, "A New Hebrew-Aramaic Incantation Text from Galilee: Rebuking the Sea," *JSS* 41 (1996): 230.

31. E.g., *Jub.* 2:2; *1 En.* 60:11-25; 69:22; *2 En.* 19:4; *3 En.* 14:4; *T. Sol.* 16:1-5; *PGM* XXXVI.256-64.

32. Cf. Matt. 5:29-30; 7:13; 10:28, 39; 16:25; 21:41; 22:7; 2 Pet. 3:7; Rev. 17:8, 11.

33. Cf. Matt. 10:22; 16:25; 24:13, 22; Rom. 5:9; 1 Cor. 3:15; 5:5.

course, are often included among the various catastrophes or "signs" of the apocalypse, a feature that contributes to the depiction of the storm here as an eschatological symbol of death and destruction.[35] Moreover, in a pair of remarks unique to the First Gospel, Matthew also includes earthquakes among the events attending Jesus' death (27:54) and resurrection (28:2). In the same vein, if we recall that sleeping and rising sometimes function as metaphors for death and resurrection (e.g., Matt. 9:24-25) and that for Matthew "the sign of the prophet Jonah" points specifically to Jesus' being raised "after three days" (12:39-40; cf. 16:4; 27:63), then there is sufficient evidence to suggest that the events of our pericope represent what one commentator has referred to as "a preview of the risen Jesus' authority."[36]

Even though it lacks an account of healing, then, within the context of Matthew 8–9 the material in 8:18-27 contributes something vital to the overall portrait of Jesus and his healing ministry. The protagonist of the First Gospel is not just some charismatic healer, the evangelist is showing us, but a divine warrior and agent of eschatological deliverance, with his power extending not just over disease and disability but even over creation itself. Accordingly, every act of Jesus needs to be interpreted within a mythic framework, every healing representing a moment in a cosmic drama of conflict and transformation. There is indeed "something greater than Jonah" at work here (Matt. 12:41).

---

34. Cf. Ps. 46:1-2: "God is our refuge and strength, a very present help in trouble. Therefore we will not fear, though the earth should change, though the mountains shake in the heart of the sea" (NRSV).

35. Hag. 2:6; Matt. 24:7; Rev. 6:12; 8:5; 11:13, 19; 16:18. Cf. Petri Luomanen, *Entering the Kingdom of Heaven: A Study on the Structure of Matthew's View of Salvation*, WUNT 2.101 (Tübingen: Mohr Siebeck, 1998), 108.

36. Robert H. Gundry, *Matthew: A Commentary on His Literary and Theological Art* (Grand Rapids: Eerdmans, 1982), 155.

As we have seen, Matthew 8:18–27 is also very much about discipleship, and the observations made above have implications for how one approaches this theme as well. Specifically, in this unit Matthew clarifies what it means to follow Jesus by clarifying whom it is that the disciples must follow. Accordingly, both their experiences of tribulation and their acts of ministry need to be interpreted within the same mythic framework just described; every healing they carry out represents a moment in the same cosmic drama. In order to appreciate the nexus between Christology and discipleship in our passage, however, we need to engage in yet more comparative analysis.

As commentators often point out, the stilling of the storm episode can be compared with various tales from Greco-Roman literature where a god or hero demonstrates the ability to control the wind and sea. In fact, Wendy Cotter has catalogued over a dozen such tales, the following text being representative:[37]

> O universal light for all mankind, you who were recently manifested to us when, at the time that the vast sea rose from all sides and rushed upon us and nothing was visible except the destruction which was approaching and had well-nigh arrived, you stretched out your hand, revealed the hidden heavens, and granted us to behold the earth and to make port.

These lines are addressed to Serapis, a deity from Hellenized Egypt associated with the cult of Isis.[38] The language ("light . . . manifested . . . revealed") suggests that what the account describes is best understood as a divine epiphany. As noted earlier, the same characterization applies to Matthew 8:23-27 as well: Jesus' actions in calming the storm manifest divine power, thereby revealing

---

37. Aelius Aristides, *Orations* 45.33 (quoted from Wendy Cotter, *Miracles in Greco-Roman Antiquity* [London: Routledge, 1999], 137. For additional examples, see pp. 131–48; also Gerd Theissen, *The Miracle Stories of the Early Christian Tradition* [Philadelphia: Fortress Press, 1983], 99–103).
38. For the cult of Isis, see Chapter One.

something essential about his own person and ministry. It is no wonder, then, that the disciples respond with amazement, asking, "What sort of man is this?" Matthew's readers, of course, already know the answer, being familiar with the gospel message. Within the context of the narrative, however, an answer is not given until the disciples actually reach "the other side," where representatives of the same demonic forces that Jesus has just subdued refer to him as "Son of God," indeed, as the Son of God who comes as an agent of eschatological judgment (see 8:29 and the discussion in Chapter Seven). The disciples themselves will not provide an answer until the parallel storm-stilling episode in Matthew 14:22-33, which concludes with the twelve worshipping Jesus as the one who is "certainly God's Son" (14:33).[39]

In his role as God's Son, that is, as the one who acts with God's authority and manifests God's glory, Jesus is comparable to the sorts of Greco-Roman deities and heroes featured in the tales compiled by Cotter, mighty figures who wield divine power to protect and save their devotees from danger. While such comparative categories are applicable to understanding the nature of Jesus' actions in this story, however, they do not tell the whole story of Jesus' identity. In order to give an adequate response to the question of 8:27, we must read the storm-stilling episode in 8:23-27 in the manner that Matthew intended. That is, we must read the story together with the material on discipleship in 8:18-22. Viewed from this perspective, it is evident that the "sort of man" whom "even the winds and the sea obey" (8:27) is none other than "the Son of Man" who "has nowhere to lay his head" (8:20).[40] The implications of this observation for the Christology of our pericope are twofold. On one hand, the full

---

39. See also Matt. 3:17; 4:3, 6; 11:27; 16:16; 17:5; 26:63; 27:40, 43, 54; 28:19.
40. The cryptic title "Son of Man" would have recalled in the first instance the eschatological figure depicted in Daniel 7:13-14 (cf. *1 En.* 48:1-10; 62:1-16). It is probably significant that the first use of this title in the Gospel (i.e., Matt. 8:20; cf. 9:6) occurs in the context of an epiphany story

meaning of Jesus' identity as the Son of Man becomes apparent only in light of what is revealed about him in the sea rescue story: the Son of Man is not only the humble figure the disciples see before them (8:20) but also the agent of eschatological power whom they will see "coming on the clouds of heaven with power and great glory" (24:30). On the other hand, the full meaning of what is revealed about Jesus in the sea rescue story becomes apparent only in the light of his identity as the Son of Man, a man who knows what it is like to be separated from home and family, a man who knows what it means to give one's life over to serve others (20:26-28). Put differently, Jesus' conflict with the forces of death as Son of God and his conflict with the dominant social order as Son of Man are not for Matthew separate categories. Rather, they are aspects of Jesus' mission that mutually inform and support one another, reflecting a vital continuity in "the deep opposition that exists between the kingdom of God . . . and the world" described above.[41] As those summoned to follow him into the storm, this opposition is to be embodied in the ministry of the disciples as well, including their ministry of healing.

Another difference between Matthew 8:18-27 and the tales compiled by Cotter has to do with the matter of destination. In Greco-Roman tales, including the one cited above, the deity or hero ensures that the imperiled mariners reach their intended destination. In our story, by contrast, Jesus takes the disciples not to *their* destination but to *his* destination, the destination that he has determined for them, a region of the Gentiles. Here further comparison can be made with Jonah, who was summoned by God to be a prophet to the Gentiles. While Jonah sees traveling to the Gentiles as something to be resisted, however, Jesus sees it as an

---

that (as we have seen) displays various eschatological features. See further Douglas R. A. Hare, *The Son of Man Tradition* (Minneapolis: Fortress Press, 1990), 113–82.

41. See n. 15 above.

urgent priority. Accordingly, the sea storms in the two narratives take on different roles. In Jonah 1:1-16 the storm represents the means by which Jonah is set on his course to the Gentiles, while in Matthew 8:18-27 the storm represents an obstacle that Jesus must overcome in order to reach the Gentiles, suggesting yet another way in which the storm functions symbolically in our story. That a "mission" to the Gentiles would experience significant difficulty should not occasion surprise, especially when the events of 8:18-34 are examined within the broader context of the Gospel. The ambiguity surrounding Jesus' journey to a Gentile land reflects a narrative tension for the Gospel as a whole, a topic to which we will return in the next chapter.

7

On the Way, Before the Time: Matthew 8:28-34

As we learned in Chapter One, from a structural standpoint the pericope in Matthew 8:28-34 is of central importance for our study, representing as it does the middle story in the middle triad of miracle stories in chapters 8–9. With this episode, then, we reach the compositional heart of the evangelist's miracle discourse, an appropriate position given that what it reveals is nothing less than the underlying conflict informing Jesus' mission of healing. As we shall see, what is revealed about this conflict includes both the nature of the opposition that Jesus faces as healer and the nature of the power that he wields against it. In accord with this, the story also has a message for those called upon to participate in Jesus' ministry, that is, for those who would follow Jesus "wherever" he goes (8:19), revealing what is ultimately at stake for such followers in the starkest of terms.

The pericope opens in 8:28 with the report that Jesus' plan to visit "the other side"—a plan first announced in 8:18—has finally been fulfilled. The narrative tension created by 8:18 has yet to be fully resolved, however, because the reader has yet to learn the ultimate destination and true purpose of this rather peculiar journey. Abandoning his home and the security it represents (8:19-22), Jesus has traversed a symbolic and dangerous "nowhere" (8:23-27) in order to reach another kind of "place." Ironically, this is where Jesus will finally be acknowledged for who he truly is (8:29), though this acknowledgment will come not from those who have witnessed his mighty deeds, who seem uncertain about his identity (8:27), but from those who oppose him. Indeed, as we shall see, this is a place defined by opposition to Jesus and what he represents. It is only at this point within the broader narrative, then, that the reader starts to grasp the true nature of the destination to which Jesus has been leading his followers: "the other side" is not a symbolic place of acceptance but a symbolic place of judgment.

It is also only at this point in the narrative that the reader learns that "the other side" is in fact the land of the Gadarenes (8:28) in the Decapolis, a region populated largely by non-Jews and distinguished by its Hellenistic culture.[1] Having healed a Gentile's servant (8:5-13), Jesus now ventures into Gentile territory, doing so for the first time in his public ministry (cf. 2:13-15). Contributing to the otherness of the scene is the impurity that can be inferred regarding several of its major components, including references to what (from a Jewish perspective) were generally seen as unclean places (tombs), unclean people (Gentiles), and unclean animals (swine).[2] Implicit impurity applies to the narrative's most prominent accouterment as well, the

---

1. Jean-Paul Rey-Coquais, "Decapolis," *ABD* 2 (1992): 116–21.
2. Cf. Christine E. Hayes, *Gentile Impurities and Jewish Identities: Intermarriage and Conversion from the Bible to the Talmud* (Oxford: Oxford University Press, 2002), 45–67, 107–44. The presence of the swine underscores the fact that this is Gentile territory (cf. Lev. 11:7; Deut. 14:8; *m. B. Qam.* 7:7). Note that the swine are feeding "at a distance" (Matt. 8:30; cf. Mark 5:6): Matthew does not want to suggest that Jesus even approaches such animals!

two demoniacs, character types associated elsewhere in the Gospel with unclean spirits (Matt. 10:1; 12:43; cf. Mark 5:2, 8, 13). What the episode signifies, then, is an initial foray not only into the realm of the Gentiles but also into the realm of the demonic. The story in 8:28-34 is the first of Matthew's Gospel in another sense, that is, the first story that narrates Jesus performing an exorcism.[3]

In coming to terms with the significance of this exorcistic excursion for the Matthean depiction of healing, it is important to note that within any given society assumptions regarding the demonic do not represent isolated phenomena but contribute to an array of complex processes according to which cultural norms, boundaries, and limits are negotiated and enforced.[4] This fact has particular implications for explicating the potential function that demon-possessed individuals can have in the construction of symbolic narratives within a society, a point made by Amanda Witmer in her study of exorcism in the Gospel traditions:[5]

> Cross-cultural anthropological studies have demonstrated that the possessed person or spirit is . . . often associated with what is marginal or "other," either geographically, ethnically or religiously.

Insofar as all three of the analytical categories identified by Witmer apply to the encounter depicted in Matthew 8:28-34, what the demoniacs constitute for Jesus and his Jewish compatriots within the narrative world of the Gospel can be accurately described as wholly "other," that is, as constituting the "other" in all three senses of the term: geographical-political (Gadara, Decapolis), ethnic-cultural

---

3. The summary statements in Matthew 4:24 and 8:16 include demoniacs among those healed by Jesus. Note that Jesus' only other visit to Gentile territory (Matt. 15:21-28) also involves an exorcism.

4. Graham H. Twelftree, *In the Name of Jesus: Exorcism Among Early Christians* (Grand Rapids: Baker Academic, 2007), 25–33.

5. Amanda Witmer, *Jesus, the Galilean Exorcist: His Exorcisms in Social and Political Context*, Library of Historical Jesus Studies 10 (London: T&T Clark, 2012), 27.

(Gentile, Hellenistic), and religious-spiritual (non-Jewish, demonic). What we see unfolding with this journey, then, is not simply an incursion into a strange place but an epic confrontation between opposed realities. Delineating the nature of this confrontation as accurately as possible therefore constitutes a major priority for the interpreter.

As the narrative unfolds, however, it becomes apparent that Matthew is not always as clear as we might like about what it is that opposes Jesus, why it does so, and what consequences follow from this opposition. One thing that *is* clear about the confrontation in 8:28-34 is the evangelist's intent to dramatize its "biblical" proportions. As noted earlier, the immediately preceding episode of Jesus' stilling of the storm is conveyed in such a way as to recall Moses' parting of the Red Sea. The allusion to that biblical incident is strengthened here, especially through recourse to the motif of water.[6] Specifically, in both Exodus 14:26-31 and Matthew 8:28-34, the drowning of a multitude in the sea serves as a paradigmatic epiphany of God's power as well as a paradigmatic means by which God's people are saved from death. While the Exodus account culminates in the drowning of a multitude of Gentile soldiers, the Matthean account culminates in the drowning of a multitude of Gentiles' pigs. In keeping with the biblical worldview, the sea in Matthew 8:23-27 and 8:28-34 can be further conceptualized as a symbol both of primordial chaos and of eschatological tribulation.[7] Accordingly, as the protagonist in these stories, Jesus occupies the roles of divine warrior and eschatological deliverer, his actions constituting moments in a mythic, cosmic drama.

---

6. Eric Eve, *The Healer from Nazareth: Jesus' Miracles in Historical Context* (London: SPCK, 2009), 150.
7. See Chapter Six.

At this juncture, mention can be made of a prayer for protection against unclean spirits written in Greek and dated to the end of the first or the beginning of the second century CE.[8] In the text of the prayer, which appears to have functioned as a kind of amulet, the same power by which God liberated the Israelites from bondage in Egypt is invoked to liberate the petitioner from the grip of unclean spirits. Specifically, the angel of God who drowned Pharaoh's army in the Red Sea (Exod. 14:19) is summoned to cast the unclean spirits into the abyss (cf. *PGM* IV.3053-55). As Origen would later explain, the formula "the God who drowned the king of Egypt and the Egyptians in the Red Sea" was often used in exorcisms "to overpower demons and other evil powers" (*Against Celsus* 4.34).

Exorcistic connotations are evident at this point in the First Gospel as well. As noted earlier, when Jesus "rebukes" the winds and the sea in 8:26 he uses a verb (*epitimaō*) employed elsewhere in accounts of exorcisms.[9] In this respect, the story of the sea rescue anticipates the story of the Gadarene demoniacs, which is itself an exorcism story. Looking at Matthew 8:23-27 + 8:28-34 from the perspective of *form criticism*, then, it appears that a "nature" (or "sea") miracle with exorcistic features segues into an exorcism story with a feature borrowed from "nature" (i.e., the sea), the implication being that the same godlike power that informed Jesus' quelling of the demonic sea is now manifested in his subjugation of demonic men. Accordingly, an important item linking the two stories structurally is their shared adversarial dynamic. In both narratives, Jesus overcomes active demonic opposition, opposition that (as such) is associated with the power of death, symbolized in the former by an adversary that

---

8. On Papyrus Fouad 203, see Pieter W. van der Horst and Judith H. Newman, *Early Jewish Prayers in Greek*, Commentaries on Early Jewish Literature (Berlin: Walter de Gruyter, 2008), 125-33.

9. Matt. 17:18; Mark 1:25; 9:25; Luke 4:35, 41; 9:42. Cf. Twelftree, *In the Name of Jesus*, 116.

emerges from the sea and in the latter by adversaries who emerge from tombs only to be destroyed in the sea. Such symbolism further contributes to the episode's mythic, eschatological character.[10]

Read as a narrative pair, then, these two stories provide an important "biblical" lesson regarding the nature of evil. Having overcome demonic forces at work in the sea, Jesus arrives in Gadara only to be confronted by demonic forces at work on the land. Insofar as the combination of "land and sea" can be understood to signify the broadest possible scope of human activity (cf. Matt. 23:15), the progression of the narrative gives the impression that evil is indeed lurking everywhere, relentlessly seeking out opportunities to impede Jesus and corrupt human lives. By the same token, this narrative pair also provides an important lesson regarding the nature of the one who opposes evil. Evil may be restless and pervasive, but wherever it is to be found Jesus will be there as well, rooting it out. The mission of the healer who follows in his footsteps would seem to require the same sort of commitment.

(1) They came to the other side of the sea, to the country of the Gerasenes. (2) And when he got out of the boat, immediately a man from the tombs with an unclean spirit met him,	(28) When he came to the other side, to the country of the Gadarenes, two demoniacs met him coming out of the tombs. They were so violent that no one was able to pass by that way.
(3) a man who dwelt among the tombs; and no one was able to restrain him anymore, even with a chain; (4) for he had often been restrained with shackles and chains, but the chains he wrenched apart and the shackles broke in pieces; and no one was able to subdue him. (5) Night and day among the tombs and on the mountains he was crying out and cutting himself with stones. (6) Seeing Jesus from a distance, he ran up and bowed before him;	

10. For exorcism as a distinguishing characteristic of Jesus' ministry, see Joel Marcus, *Mark*, AB 27 (New Haven, CT: Yale University Press, 2000), 1:186–95; John P. Meier, *A Marginal Jew: Rethinking the Historical Jesus* (New York: Doubleday, 1994), 2:404–22, 646–77.

(7) and crying out with a loud voice, he said, "What do you have to do with me, Jesus, Son of the Most High God? I adjure you by God, do not torment me!"

(29) At once they cried out, saying, "What do you have to do with us, Son of God? Did you come here to torment us before the time?"

(8) For he was saying to him, "Come out of the man, you unclean spirit!" (9) And he was asking him, "What is your name?" And he said to him, "My name is legion, for we are many." (10) He implored him repeatedly not to send them out of the country.

(11) Now there on the hillside there was a large herd of swine feeding;

(30) Now there was a herd of many swine feeding at a distance from them.

(12) And they implored him, saying, "Send us into the swine, that we may enter into them."

(31) And the demons implored him, saying, "If you cast us out, send us into the herd of swine."

(13) And he gave them permission. And coming out the unclean spirits entered into the swine; and the herd rushed down the steep bank into the sea, about two thousand of them; and they were drowned in the sea.

(32) And he said to them, "Go!" And they came out and went into the swine, and at once the whole herd rushed down the steep bank into the sea and died in the waters.

(33) The swineherds fled, and went into the city and reported everything, including what had happened to the demoniacs.

(14) And the swineherds fled and reported it to the city and in the country; and they came to see what had happened.

(15) And they came to Jesus and saw the demoniac sitting, clothed and in his right mind, the same one who had had the legion, and they were afraid.

(34) At once the whole city came out to meet Jesus;

(16) And those who had seen it described how it had happened to the demoniac and about the swine.

(17) And they began to implore him to leave their borders.

and when they saw him they implored him to leave their borders. (Matt. 8:28-34)

(18) And as he was getting into the boat, the one who had been a demoniac implored him that he might go with him. (19) He did not allow him, but said to him, "Go to your home, to your own people, and report to them how much the Lord has done for you and how much mercy he showed you." (20) And he went away and began to proclaim in the Decapolis how much Jesus had done for him; and everyone was amazed. (Mark 5:1-20)

Immediately obvious is the fact that Matthew's account of the incident has two demoniacs in lieu of Mark's one, a "doubling" effect that we will encounter again in Matthew 9:27-31.[11] Also obvious is that even as he increases the number of demoniacs in the story Matthew decreases the story's length, reducing Mark's twenty verses to just seven. The resulting structure is therefore simpler and more direct. The focus is not on the men who are cured but on the man who cures them. Specifically, in his redaction Matthew demonstrates less interest than does Mark in (1) the techniques and (2) the results of the exorcism, and more interest in what the exorcism reveals about Jesus' messianic identity and mission.[12]

With regard to the *techniques* of the exorcism, it is noteworthy that Matthew omits the material in Mark 5:8-10. Presumably, he does so in order to avoid the impression that Jesus' initial command (Mark 5:8) was ineffective or that he could expel the demons only after learning their name (Mark 5:9). In lieu of a protracted exchange, Matthew reduces Jesus' dialogue to a single, imperious word, "Go!" (*hypagete*), the same command that he had used to repel Satan while being tempted in the wilderness (Matt. 4:10).[13] As with that incident,

---

11. For a discussion of Matthean doubling, see W. D. Davies and Dale C. Allison, *The Gospel According to Saint Matthew*, ICC (London: T&T Clark, 1988, 1991), 1:87; 2:80; Gerd Theissen, *The Miracle Stories of the Early Christian Tradition* (Philadelphia: Fortress Press, 1983), 54. Jewish tradition stressed the importance of having more than one witness; see Matthew 18:16 (quoting Deut. 19:15) and 26:60.

12. For Matthew's efforts to disassociate Jesus from exorcistic activities, see Chapter Thirteen.

what is highlighted here is the decisive and sovereign nature of the power Jesus employs against his opponents (cf. 8:9, 16). The parallelism of the one-word commands in 4:10 and 8:32 is also suggestive of the manner in which this opposition is conceptualized. Throughout the First Gospel, the corruption of human beings (13:19; 16:23) and the human world (4:8-9; 13:25, 38-39) by Satan is taken for granted.[14] One of the principal means by which this corruption occurs is through the activity of demons, entities over whom Satan is understood to have control (12:24; 25:41). Confronting demoniacs, then, brings the exorcist into conflict with the power of Satan, while each exorcism represents an assault on the kingdom of Satan carried out on behalf of the kingdom of God (12:25-29). In this regard, the activity of 8:28-34 can be contrasted with the non-eschatological exorcisms attributed to Apollonius of Tyana or the purveyors of the Greek Magical Papyri.[15] The protagonist of Matthew's Gospel is not some ordinary exorcist who has acquired the techniques necessary for "binding" individual demons (e.g., *PGM* IV.1245-48) but a cosmic warrior whose exorcising ministry portends the eschatological "binding" of Satan himself (Matt. 12:29; cf. Rev. 20:2).[16]

With regard to the *results* of the exorcism, it is noteworthy that Matthew omits the material in Mark 5:3-5, which describes the

---

13. This would seem to be a variation of the dismissal theme, for which cf. Matthew 8:4, 13; 9:6; Theissen, *Miracle Stories*, 67–68.
14. Robert Charles Branden, *Satanic Conflict and the Plot of Matthew* (New York: Peter Lang, 2006), 43–83.
15. For examples of narrated exorcisms, see Josephus, *Antiquities* 8.46-48; Philostratus, *Life of Apollonius* 4.20.1-3; Lucian, *The Lover of Lies* 16.
16. For the binding of Satan and his demons, see Tob. 8:3; *1 En.* 10:4, 11-12; 13:1-2; 14:5; 18:16; 21:3-6; 54:3-5; 69:28; 90:23; *2 Bar.* 56:13; *T. Levi* 18:12; *T. Sol.* 15:7; *Jub.* 5:6-10; 10:7-14; 48:15-19. Cf. Isa. 24:21-22; 2 Pet. 2:4; Jude 6; Christopher A. Faraone, "The Agonistic Context of Early Greek Binding Spells," in *Magika Hiera: Ancient Greek Magic and Religion*, eds. Christopher A. Faraone and Dirk Obbink (New York: Oxford University Press, 1991), 3–32; Richard H. Hiers, "'Binding' and 'Loosing': The Matthean Authorizations," *JBL* 104 (1985): 235–39; Eric Sorensen, *Possession and Exorcism in the New Testament and Early Christianity*, WUNT 2.157 (Tübingen: Mohr Siebeck, 2002), 140–42.

demoniac's state before the exorcism, and Mark 5:15, which describes his state after the exorcism.[17] Indeed, the Matthean narrative lacks any explicit indication as to what effect the exorcism has on the demoniacs. By contrast, what the Matthean narrative does *not* lack is an explicit indication from the demoniacs as to the identity of the one performing the exorcism.

> "What do you have to do with us, Jesus of Nazareth? Did you come to destroy us? I know who you are, the Holy One of God." (Mark 1:24)

> "What do you have to do with me, Jesus, Son of the Most High God? I adjure you by God, do not torment me!" (Mark 5:7)

> "What do you have to do with us, Son of God? Did you come here to torment us before the time?" (Matt. 8:29)

By omitting the material in Mark 5:3-5, Matthew's redaction has the effect of foregrounding the demoniacs' initial response to Jesus.[18] As the quotations above indicate, for its content this response appears to draw on elements not only of Mark 5:7 but also of Mark 1:24, which belongs to an exorcism story (Mark 1:21-28) that Matthew omits from his Gospel.[19] Being possessed by supernatural beings, the demoniacs articulate a supernatural perspective on the one who confronts them, the same perspective articulated by Satan while tempting Jesus in the wilderness (Matt. 4:3, 6; cf. 2:15; 3:17). Like Satan, the demoniacs seem to understand from the moment they see Jesus who he is and the threat he poses to their realm. Recognizing the conjunction of Matthew 8:28-34 with Matthew 8:23-27 (as noted above) is relevant for understanding how the narrative develops in

---

17. Note that Matthew also drops the reference to "he . . . bowed down before him" in Mark 5:6. In the First Gospel the demoniacs approach Jesus not as supplicants (cf. Matt. 8:2; 9:18) but as adversaries.

18. For the formula in 8:29 ("What do you have to do with us?") see Marcus, *Mark*, 1:187.

19. See Burton H. Throckmorton, *Gospel Parallels: A Comparison of the Synoptic Gospels*, 5th ed. (Nashville: Thomas Nelson, 1992), 20–21.

this regard: representatives of the same demonic forces that Jesus has just subdued using godlike power are now presented as explicitly acknowledging his authority as God's Son. In this they are very much unlike human characters in the Gospel, who have yet to perceive Jesus' true identity, a point underscored by the query just posed by the disciples in 8:27: "What sort of man is this, that even the winds and the sea obey him?" While the demoniacs are capable of answering this question immediately, the disciples will not be able to do so until later in the narrative, that is, until they witness a second miracle at sea (14:33; cf. 16:16; 17:5; 27:54).[20]

The questions in 8:27 and 8:29, then, can be seen as parallel responses to the epiphany of Jesus. While the former reveals uncertainty regarding Jesus' identity, however, the latter reveals uncertainty regarding Jesus' intent, a point underscored by the question that immediately follows, one whose phrasing is pregnant with eschatological meaning: "Have you come here to torment us before the time?" The word here for "torment" (*basanizō*) is appropriate to the context insofar as demons were sometimes thought to experience pain and anguish when being exorcised.[21] What makes Matthew's usage distinctive (cf. Mark 5:7) is that the verb is linked with the concept of the "time" (*kairos*), a term used elsewhere in the Gospel in reference to the eschatological age (13:30; 16:3; 21:34, 41; 24:45). In this case, comparison can be made with the sort of apocalyptic scenario envisioned by Revelation 20:10, according to which the devil, the beast, and the false prophet are cast into a lake of fire, where they "will be tormented (*basanisthēsontai*) day and night" for eternity.[22] A similar expectation is at work in the judgment scene

---

20. Cf. David B. Howell, *Matthew's Inclusive Story: A Study in the Narrative Rhetoric of the First Gospel*, JSNTSup 42 (Sheffield: JSOT, 1990), 221.
21. In Philostratus, *Life of Apollonius* 4.25, a demon begs an exorcist not to torment (*basanizein*) it.
22. Cf. Rev. 19:20; *1 En.* 10:13; 16:1; 55:3; 67:13.

of Matthew 25:41, with its reference to "the eternal fire which is prepared for the devil and his angels." It therefore appears that a term derived from exorcistic practice has been invested with eschatological meaning, much in the same way that Matthew has done with the language of "binding" in 12:29.

In calling Jesus the Son of God, then, and referring to his "tormenting" them before "the time," what the demoniacs are acknowledging is not simply his power as an exorcist but his authority as agent of eschatological judgment, an image consistent with depictions of Jesus elsewhere in the Gospel (e.g., 3:12; 19:28; 25:31-33).[23] As Jesus himself will put it: "If I by the Spirit of God cast out demons, then the kingdom of God has come upon you" (12:28). Insofar as the same forces that will usher in God's eschatological rule are already at work in the person of Jesus, his healing ministry can be interpreted as an advent of the kingdom. In this capacity, the healing event reveals not only the kingdom's power but also the kingdom's essence, the latter being conveyed symbolically in our pericope especially by the narrative action of 8:32:

> And they came out and went into the swine, and at once the whole herd rushed down the steep bank into the sea and died in the waters.

In keeping with ancient sensibilities, the demons are understood as both requiring a living host of some kind and possessing the ability to move from one host to another (cf. Matt. 12:43-45).[24] The type of animal into which the demons migrate illustrates their unclean nature, while the fate of the animals illustrates their deadliness.[25] The

---

23. Donald A. Hagner, *Matthew*, WBC 33 (Dallas: Word Books, 1993), 1:227: "the demons recognize that at the eschatological judgment they will experience God's judgment and the end of their power. The kingdom has come but in advance of its fullest and final coming."

24. For examples, see Witmer, *Jesus, The Galilean Exorcist*, 169. For more on Matthew's demonology, see Chapter Five, n. 1.

25. Rudolf Pesch, ("The Markan Version of the Healing of the Gerasene Demoniac," *Ecumenical Review* 23 [1971], 366–67) cites a Babylonian incantation that offers the unclean spirits a pig as

fact that the herd meets its demise in the sea is also significant insofar as certain apocalyptic texts envision demonic beings as emerging from the sea, the implication being that the sea represents their place of origin.[26] Given the parallels with Exodus 14:26-31 identified above, comparison can also be made with a report in the *Testament of Solomon*, according to which a demon named Abezethibou had been engulfed in the Red Sea when the water covered over Pharaoh's armies (25:7; cf. 25:1-6).

By sending the demons (back) into the sea, then, Jesus functions as the divine agent through whom demonic evil is thwarted and cosmic order restored.[27] The act of restoring order represents yet another way in which the story of the sea rescue and the story of the demoniacs have been integrated with one another. While in 8:23-27 the sea served as a symbol of chaos (i.e., as something to be controlled), however, here it functions as an instrument of destruction (i.e., as a means of judgment). Specifically, this act of healing prefigures the eschatological judgment, affording the reader a glimpse into the *kairos* of salvation history and the order it represents.

Of course in order to restore this order certain obstacles must be overcome, and in this respect the First Gospel presents us with yet more distinctive imagery. Among the Synoptics, Matthew is alone in stating that the demoniacs "were so fierce that no one could pass that way (*hodos*)" (8:28; cf. Mark 5:2; Luke 8:27). According to the Talmud, in a passage that explains how pairs of different kinds can

a substitute in place of the possessed man: "Give the pig in his stead, And give the flesh as his flesh, The blood as his blood, And let him take it! The heart . . . give as his heart and let him take it!"

26. E.g., Dan. 7:3; Matt. 17:15; Rev. 13:1; *1 En.* 60:7; *2 Bar.* 29:4; Tertullian, *On Baptism* 5 ("unclean spirits brood on waters"). Water was sometimes used in the performance of exorcisms, such as in *Numbers Rabbah* 19.8; *Testimony of Truth* 70.9-19; cf. Josephus, *Antiquities* 8.48. For the possibility that ancient incantation bowls (used to ward off or trap evil spirits) could be filled with water, see Witmer, *Jesus, the Galilean Exorcist*, 170.

27. Davies and Allison, *Saint Matthew*, 2:84.

be associated with demonic activity (*b. Pesah.* 109b-12a), the need for wariness in dealing with such pairs is said to arise "especially when one is setting out on the road" (*b. Pesah.* 110a).[28] This concern, in turn, reflects the notion, common in Jewish folklore, that demons can often be found lying in wait to ambush travelers,[29] a belief that may be applicable to the scenario depicted in Matthew 8:28, where Jesus encounters a pair of demoniacs while abroad in a strange land. Perhaps more relevant, especially given the allusions to Exodus 14 identified above, is Exodus 13:18:

> And God led the people round by the way (*hodon*) into the wilderness, to the Red Sea.

In their journey to and through the sea and what it represents (cf. Matt. 8:23-27), the people of God are led by God on the "way" to salvation (cf. Exod. 13:21). Similarly, as their messianic Lord, Jesus leads his followers on the "way" promised by the Old Testament prophets (Matt. 3:3; 11:10), that is, on the way from oppression and suffering to salvation through a revelation of divine power (cf. Isa. 40:3-5; Mal. 3:1). Accordingly, Jesus is the one who both teaches and embodies the "way" of God in truth (Matt. 22:16), the way that leads to life (Matt. 7:14).[30] Viewed from this perspective, the healings and exorcisms performed by Jesus can be understood figuratively as acts that remove even the most fearsome obstacles blocking the "way" of the Lord, opening it up for others to follow. Or perhaps it might be more correct to say that Jesus' ministry of healing *is* the way, that is,

---

28. Also from *b. Pesah.* 110a: "Ashmedai, king of the demons, is appointed over all pairs." Cf. Yaakov Elman, "The World of the 'Sabboraim': Cultural Aspects of Post-Redactional Additions to the Bavli," in *Creation and Composition: The Contribution of the Bavli Redactors (Stammaim) to the Aggada*, TSAJ 114, ed. Jeffrey L. Rubenstein (Tübingen: Mohr Siebeck, 2005), 398–405.

29. Eli Yassif, *The Hebrew Folktale: History, Genre, Meaning* (Bloomington: Indiana University Press, 1999), 147–48.

30. Cf. Gen. 18:19; Ps. 25:9; Acts 18:25-26.

the way by which suffering is alleviated and the power of evil is thrust back into the abyss.

An Enigmatic Mission

The story does not end there, however, but proceeds with a second scene, one that describes the response of the local population to Jesus' victory. Attention to the particular wording used in composing the two scenes is important:

> ... two demoniacs met (*hypēntēsan*) him, coming out (*exerchomenoi*) of the tombs. ... (31) And the demons implored (*parekaloun*) him ... (32) And they came out and went into (*apēlthon eis*) the swine ... (Matt. 8:28, 31, 32)

> (33) The swineherds ... went into (*apēlthon eis*) the city ... (34) At once the whole city came out (*exēlthen*) to meet (*hypantēsin*) Jesus; and ... they implored (*parekalesan*) him ... (Matt. 8:33, 34)

Matthew's version of this episode differs from those preserved by Mark and Luke in that it is structured using four pairs of similar verbs.[31] Furthermore, these pairs are used to structure the narrative in such a way that the actions of people in the story are made to mirror the actions of the demons. As we have seen, the response of the demons to Jesus is thoroughly negative: they confront Jesus only to be defeated by him. The response of the people is also negative, a point that becomes clearer when we compare Matthew 8:34 with 2 Samuel 19:16-18, where the people of Judah "come down" in order to "meet" the victorious King David and accompany him to the holy city.[32] Similarly, the report in Matthew 8:34 that the "whole" city came out to meet Jesus after his victory over the demons lends a

---

31. Note that *exerchomenoi* and *exēlthen* are based on the same verbal root.
32. Josephus sketches an analogous scene in *Antiquities* 11.327 where the people of Jerusalem go out to meet Alexander the Great (cf. *War* 7.100-101).

sense of drama and anticipation to the narrative. The reader might be forgiven for thinking at this point that the townspeople intend to greet him as a hero or benefactor, leading him into their city with honor, much as the Judeans had done for King David. But in contrast to other stories in the Gospel, where people respond to Jesus' miracles with awe and acclamation (e.g., Matt. 9:8), here the response is one of repudiation. While the demons had implored Jesus so that *they* might leave, the townspeople implore Jesus so that *he* might leave. What the story's parallel structure suggests, then, is that the response to the healer can take on different though parallel forms: the response may be human or it may be supra–human, but in either case it is one of resistance to the eschatological *kairos* that the healer represents.[33] According to Mark 5:15, the human response to Jesus is motivated by fear, presumably fear of the incredible power he has just unleashed on the demons.[34] For his part, Matthew leaves the people's motivation unclear.[35] As one commentator puts it, "[t]he only thing that is clear is that Jesus leaves no trace among the Gentile Gadarenes."[36] Jesus may possess the power to overcome those forces, even demonic forces, that block people from following the "way" of the Lord; but he does not compel people to follow that way.

The totality of the Gadarenes' rejection is heightened by Matthew's decision to delete the exchange narrated in Mark 5:18-20, in which the cured demoniac implores (*parekalei*) Jesus for permission to follow him, and Jesus responds by instructing him instead to proclaim throughout the Decapolis what "the Lord" has done for him.[37] The Markan conclusion to the story, then, is mixed, even

---

33. The phrase "came out to meet" (Matt. 8:34) is also found in Matthew 25:1 in the context of a parable about being prepared for the arrival of the eschatological bridegroom.

34. Perhaps like the Pharisees of Matthew 12:24 (cf. Mark 3:22) they suspect that his power is actually satanic in nature. Cf. Matt. 10:25.

35. If the response of the people in 8:34 was in fact one of fear, it would mirror that of the disciples in 8:26.

36. Ulrich Luz, *Matthew: A Commentary*, Hermeneia (Minneapolis: Fortress Press, 2005), 2:25.

hopeful: Jesus' rejection by the townspeople does not prevent the good news from spreading into non-Jewish territory. The Matthean conclusion, by contrast, is as enigmatic as it is anticlimactic. Ironically, the townspeople are able to accomplish what the demons could not: they prevent Jesus from proceeding on his "way" as a healer. Instead, Jesus rather unceremoniously turns around and goes back to his own city (9:1), leaving the reader wondering why he went to the trouble of such a perilous journey in the first place.

In order to address this question, it is helpful to consider what meaning this narrative may have had for Matthew and his community in the area of mission. However else one might evaluate Jesus' accomplishments in Matthew 8:28-34, from the perspective of evangelism his initial foray into Gentile lands can only be described as a failure, and the only conclusion we as readers can draw from the way the story ends is that "the time for the proclamation to the Gentiles has not yet come."[38] In this regard, the rejection that Jesus experiences in 8:28-34 as a missionary-healer can be interpreted as anticipating the instruction about missionary-healers in chapter 10. There Jesus authorizes the disciples to go out and, in effect, follow the example he has been providing them. Like Jesus, they are to proclaim the word, heal the sick, and cast out demons (10:1, 7-8).[39] Also like Jesus, they are to expect a fair amount of rejection, though the manner in which they are instructed to *respond* to such rejection shows a clear contrast with our pericope:

---

37. So while the Markan version draws attention to the *difference* between what the townspeople implore Jesus to do and what the *man* implores him to do, the Matthean version draws attention to the *similarity* between what the townspeople implore Jesus to do and what the *demons* implore him to do.

38. Luz, *Matthew*, 2:24.

39. In Matthew 17:14-21, it is assumed that Jesus' disciples perform exorcisms; cf. 7:22. Matthean redaction in 10:1 and 8 reinforces the parallels between Jesus' healing ministry and that of the disciples (cf. Mark 6:7, 13; Luke 9:1-2; 10:9). Note also the correlation of Matthew 10:1 with Matthew 9:35.

(14) Whoever does not receive you or hear your words, as you go out of that house or city, shake the dust off your feet. (15) Truly I say to you, it will be more tolerable for the land of Sodom and Gomorrah on the day of judgment than for that city. (Matt. 10:14-15)

In response to those who reject them, the disciples are instructed to enact a symbolic ritual of repudiation, prefiguring the judgment that awaits such people at the Parousia.[40] The story in 8:28-34, by contrast, contains no such ritual. When Jesus grants the plea of the demons to "leave" (8:31-32), the meaning of his action is clear: it ensures their fate and prefigures their eschatological destruction. When he grants the plea of the townspeople to "leave" (8:34—9:1), however, the meaning of his action is far from clear: the judgment that awaits them is left unspoken. In the light of 10:14-15, the reader might be tempted to conclude that the people of the Decapolis are being written off in favor of those who reside in Jesus' "own" city (9:1). It will not be long, however, before Jesus utters the following indictment:

(23) And you, Capernaum, will you be exalted to heaven? No, you will be brought down to Hades. For if the deeds of power occurred in Sodom that occurred in you, it would have remained until this day. (24) But I tell you that it will be more tolerable for the land of Sodom on the day of judgment than for you. (Matt. 11:23-24)

In the Gospel of Matthew, it is not the people of Gadara upon whom Jesus pronounces judgment but the people of Capernaum, the people with whom he lived (4:13) and for whom he performed many healings (8:16). The warning that Jesus delivers in chapter 11 is similar to one he had delivered earlier in the narrative, where he had prophesied that "the sons of the kingdom will be cast out" (8:12).[41]

---

40. Cf. Neh. 5:13; Acts 13:51; 18:6; Adela Yarbro Collins, *Mark*, Hermeneia (Minneapolis: Fortress Press, 2007), 300–302; John K. Ridgway, *"Let Your Peace Come Upon It": Healing and Peace in Matthew 10:1-15*, Studies in Biblical Literature 2 (New York: Peter Lang, 1999), 260–65.

In the same vein, it is important to note that in chapter 10, the people who reject the missionary-healers (and upon whom they are supposed to express judgment) are not Gentiles but fellow Israelites. Indeed, Jesus explicitly instructs the disciples not to go in the "way" (*hodos*) of the Gentiles (10:5). In this regard, the missionary-healers' experience of rejection mirrors the experience of Jesus himself, who, as we shall soon see, is rejected not only by the people of Gadara but by people in Capernaum as well (9:3, 24, 34).

Taken as a whole, these texts exhibit a noteworthy trend: the evangelist is more inclined to direct warnings of judgment to those who are inside the family of faith than to those who are outside it, an important message for the members of Matthew's own faith community, people who saw themselves as "sons of the kingdom" (13:38). Conversely, Matthew's message regarding Gentile outsiders is distinctively (one might even say notoriously) ambivalent. On one hand, there are instances where he casts Gentiles and what the Gentile world represents in a negative light (e.g., 5:47; 6:7-8, 31-32; 18:17; 20:25). In the same vein, and in contrast to Mark 5:19-20 (where the cured demoniac becomes a kind of proto-missionary), in the First Gospel there is no mention of a mission to the Gentiles led by Gentile believers.[42] On the other hand, there are also occasions where it is implied that, through Christ, the Gentiles will have a place in salvation history (e.g., 1:3, 5-6; 2:1-12; 4:15; 10:18; 12:38-42; 21:43; 24:14; 27:54). It is, accordingly, in Christ's name that they have "hope" (12:18-21).[43] The evangelist's ambivalence toward the Gentile world is expressed perhaps most pointedly in the story of the Canaanite woman (15:21-28).[44] Jesus is initially reluctant even to speak with the woman, insisting on his exclusive mission to Israel.

41. See the discussion in Chapter Three.
42. Anthony J. Saldarini, *Matthew's Christian-Jewish Community* (Chicago: University of Chicago Press, 1994), 75.
43. Note that this passage is attached to a summary account of Jesus' healing activity (12:15-16).

Nevertheless, her demonstration of "great faith," specifically, her faith in Jesus' ability to heal, overcomes his unwillingness to help her. As Donald Senior has suggested, the hesitation ascribed to Jesus in this narrative may reflect the hesitation about a Gentile mission harbored by members of Matthew's own community. In this case, the story has an important pastoral purpose: Jesus the healer models such hesitation *as well as* a willingness to accept faith wherever he finds it.[45]

As we have seen, this is not the only healing story in the Gospel involving an interaction between Jesus and Gentiles. Besides 8:5-13, the attentive reader will also recall the following:

> (24) The report about him spread to all Syria; and they brought to him all who were sick, those afflicted with various diseases and pains, demoniacs, epileptics, and paralytics, and he healed them. (25) And many crowds followed him from Galilee and the Decapolis and Jerusalem and Judea and from beyond the Jordan. (Matt. 4:24-25)

This report indicates that from the very beginning of his public ministry "crowds" of people from the Decapolis have been following Jesus.[46] Moreover, like the centurion in 8:5-13 and the Canaanite woman in 15:21-28, these Gentiles have come to Jesus specifically for healing: their belief in his ability to heal is how their faith is manifested, and it is through healing that Jesus responds to their faith. Consideration for this report raises the possibility that throughout the Gospel Matthew envisions the "crowds" as in fact being a mixed group of Jews and Gentiles, and that it is from this group that Jesus attracts followers.[47] However we interpret the evidence, it is apparent

44. Elaine M. Wainwright, *Towards A Feminist Critical Reading of the Gospel According to Matthew*, BZNW 60 (Berlin: Walter de Gruyter, 1991), 217–52.
45. Donald Senior, "Between Two Worlds: Gentiles and Jewish Christians in Matthew's Gospel," *CBQ* 61 (1999): 1–23.
46. Cf. Theissen, *Miracle Stories*, 205–206.
47. J. R. C. Cousland, *The Crowds in the Gospel of Matthew*, NovTSup 102 (Leiden: Brill, 2002), 53–73, esp. 58–61.

that Jesus' ministry of healing brings him into contact with people from the "other" side, that is, people from the margins of society, people like lepers, women, tax collectors, and, of course, what from Jesus' cultural location would have been the ultimate "other," the Gadarene demoniacs. What ultimately matters about these people from Matthew's perspective is not their social status or ethnicity but their response to Jesus. In texts like 4:24-25, this response is expressed as faith in Jesus' ability to heal; elsewhere it is expressed in doing the will of God his Father and bearing fruit worthy of God's kingdom (e.g., 12:46-50; 21:43).[48]

In coming to terms with the implications of all this for the missionary-healer, it is possible to interpret the example that Jesus has set for the disciples in Gadara as an anticipation not only of the commission that he will give them in chapter 10 but also of the final commission that he will give them in chapter 28:

> To me has been given all authority in heaven and on earth. (19) Go therefore and make disciples of all the nations . . . (Matt. 28:18-19).

Through his resurrection Jesus has become Lord of creation, while those who follow Jesus have entered into a new, eschatological age. The scope of the church's mission must "therefore" (28:19) reflect this new reality, expanding its ministry beyond previous understandings of insiders versus outsiders (cf. 24:14). The story of the Gadarene demoniacs functions particularly well in foreshadowing this "great" commission insofar as it illustrates the lengths to which Jesus himself was willing to go to heal those on the "other" side and combat the forces of evil, even if it meant being rejected by the very people who benefited the most from his actions. This story also foreshadows the

48. Cf. Saldarini, *Matthew's Christian-Jewish Community*, 68–83; Anders Runesson, "Judging Gentiles in the Gospel of Matthew: Between 'Othering' and Inclusion," in *Jesus, Matthew's Gospel and Early Christianity: Studies in Memory of Graham N. Stanton*, eds. Daniel M. Gurtner, Joel Willitts, and Richard A. Burridge (Edinburgh: T&T Clark, 2011), 133–51.

final commission insofar as it (like the sea rescue story to which it is attached) provided the disciples with a glimpse of Jesus' authority as cosmic Lord, as divine warrior and eschatological judge, as the one who brings new life from "the tombs" (8:28; cf. 27:52-53; 28:8-9). This is the Jesus who is always "with" the missionary-healers of Matthew's community as they endeavor to follow his example and heal those on the "other" side, even until the end of the age (28:20).

8

Practicing Healing in Community:
Matthew 9:1-8

In this passage, an important theme for the theology of the First Gospel makes its first appearance in the narrative of chapters 8–9: the theme of sin.[1] While Matthew 9:1-8 may introduce a new theme, however, it does not introduce a new section. Rather, it constitutes the third miracle story in the second triad of miracle stories within our unit. The context provided by 8:18-34, then, is of critical importance for understanding the particular perspective on sin, forgiveness, and healing that the evangelist wants to cultivate for his readers, a perspective that has at its center the identification of Jesus as the Son of Man (8:20; 9:6).

In the Second Gospel, the story of the Gerasene demoniac (Mark 5:1-20) is immediately followed by the story of Jairus's daughter and the woman with a flow of blood (Mark 5:21-43; cf. Matt. 9:18-26). In the First Gospel, the story of the Gadarene demoniacs (8:28-34)

1. Cf. Matt. 1:21; 3:6; 9:10-13; 11:19; 12:31; 18:15, 21; 26:45; 27:4; 26:28.

is immediately followed by a story about Jesus' encounter with a paralytic. A version of this story is also preserved by Mark, though it occurs at an earlier point in his narrative, namely, Mark 2:1-12 (cf. Luke 5:17-26).

(1) When he went back to Capernaum after some days, it was heard that he was at home.	(1) Getting into a boat, he crossed over and came to his own city.
(2) And many gathered together, so that there was no longer room, even at the door; and he was speaking the word to them.	
(3) And they came, bringing to him a paralytic, carried by four of them.	(2) And just then they brought to him a paralytic lying on a bed.
(4) And, not being able to get to him on account of the crowd, they removed the roof above where he was, and having dug an opening, they let down the pallet on which the paralytic was lying.	
(5) And seeing their faith, Jesus said to the paralytic, "Son, your sins are forgiven."	And seeing their faith, Jesus said to the paralytic, "Take courage, son; your sins are forgiven."
(6) Now some of the scribes were sitting there and reasoning in their hearts, (7) "Why does this man speak that way? He is blaspheming. Who can forgive sins but God alone?"	(3) And some of the scribes said to themselves, "This man blasphemes."
(8) Immediately Jesus, perceiving in his spirit that they were reasoning that way among themselves, said to them, "Why do you reason these things in your hearts?	(4) And seeing their thoughts, Jesus said to them, "Why do you think evil in your hearts?

(9) Which is easier, to say to the paralytic, 'Your sins are forgiven,' or to say, 'Rise up and take your pallet and walk'?	(5) For which is easier, to say, 'Your sins are forgiven,' or to say, 'Rise up and walk'?
(10) But so that you may know that the Son of Man has authority on earth to forgive sins"–he said to the paralytic– (11) "I say to you, rise up, take your pallet and go to your home."	(6) But so that you may know that the Son of Man has authority on earth to forgive sins" – he then said to the paralytic – "Rise up, take your bed and go to your home."
(12) And he rose up and immediately taking the pallet he went out before all of them, so that they were all amazed and glorified God, saying, "We have never seen anything like this!" (Mark 2:1-12)	(7) And he rose up and went to his home. (8) When the crowds saw this, they were afraid and glorified God, who had given such authority to the people. (Matt. 9:1-8)

As with other healing stories, Matthew both abbreviates the Markan account and does so in such a way as to make the element of dialogue more prominent. Specifically, he omits the report that Jesus was "at home" teaching to large crowds (Mark 2:1-2) as well as the description of the paralytic being let down through the house's roof on account of those crowds (Mark 2:4).[2] Among other things, this redaction lends a more concentric structure to the First Gospel's version of the story. At the literary and thematic center of the pericope we find Jesus' exchange with the scribes (9:3-6a), which is bracketed by his interactions with the paralytic (9:2-3, 6b-7), which in turn are bracketed by the story's introduction (9:1) and conclusion (9:8). By drawing attention to the exchange of 9:3-6a in this manner, the story's hybrid literary form is brought into relief. Specifically, Matthew 9:1-8 represents a healing story blended with elements of a controversy story, controversy representing an element that will also be of some importance to the two stories that immediately follow, 9:9-13 and 9:14-17.[3]

---

2. Matthew omits the indoor setting also in 12:22 (cf. Mark 3:19); 15:15 (cf. Mark 7:17), 21 (cf. Mark 7:24); 17:19 (cf. Mark 9:28); 19:7 (cf. Mark 10:10).

After being rebuffed in Gadara, Jesus returns by boat to Capernaum in order to resume the ministry of healing narrated in 8:5-17. Given the success of that ministry, as well as the fact that this was his "own" city (9:1; cf. 4:13), it would be natural for the reader to expect that Jesus will receive a warm welcome. Almost immediately, however, he finds himself embroiled in yet another confrontation.

The healing story as such begins in Matthew 9:2 with the report that a paralytic was "brought to" (*prosepheron*) Jesus by some people (their number and gender are left unspecified) and that Jesus "saw" their faith. Despite its compressed form, within this statement it is possible to discern several important lessons about the nature of faith, three of which can be mentioned here.

First, the verb *prospherō* recalls various statements in the Gospel in which we are told that the sick and suffering were "brought to" Jesus for healing (4:24; 8:16; 9:32; 12:22; 14:35; 17:16).[4] Like those individuals, the paralytic appears in our story as a rather passive figure, neither speaking nor initiating any action. Nevertheless, we can safely assume that his faith is included in what Jesus can "see" in 9:2 (cf. 9:22).[5] This suggests that faith in Jesus can be expressed in different ways, either by words and actions (e.g., 8:2) or by actions alone (cf. 9:20). Either form is legitimate as a sign of faith, it would seem, so long as it entails actually seeking out Jesus for help and not simply trusting in his ability to provide such help.[6]

---

3. The hybrid of healing (or exorcism) story and controversy story is a form that Matthew will employ elsewhere (i.e., 12:9-14, 22-37; and 21:14-17). See Boris Repschinski, *The Controversy Stories in the Gospel of Matthew*, FRLANT 189 (Göttingen: Vandenhoeck & Ruprecht, 2000), 65–75, 107–33, 187–93.

4. For a similar story involving someone being brought to Asclepius for healing, see Lynn R. LiDonnici, *The Epidaurian Miracle Inscriptions: Text, Translation and Commentary*, SBLTT 36 (Atlanta: Scholars, 1995), 105. Matthew 4:24 includes paralytics among those Jesus heals (cf. 8:6).

5. Donald A. Hagner, *Matthew*, WBC 33 (Dallas: Word Books, 1993), 1:232.

6. Heinz Joachim Held, "Matthew as Interpreter of the Miracle Stories," in *Tradition and Interpretation in Matthew*, eds. Günther Bornkamm, Gerhard Barth, and Heinz Joachim Held (Philadelphia: Westminster, 1963), 280–81.

Second, Jesus sees "their" faith, that is, what Jesus sees includes the faith of the paralytic's companions as well. This suggests that faith in Jesus can be expressed in different ways, not only by those who need healing themselves but also by those who help others in their moment of need, and that such faith matters to the one who heals. In this case, comparison can be made with the faith of the centurion, who advocates for healing on behalf of his servant (8:5-13), and the faith of the Canaanite woman, who advocates for healing on behalf of her child (15:21-28). While in those cases faith took the form of both words and actions, here it takes the form of actions alone.

Third, the fact that their faith is something that Jesus can "see" also offers food for thought, though here we encounter something of a puzzle, since in Matthew's version of the story what the paralytic and his companions offer Jesus in this regard seems rather minimal, especially in comparison with the heroic efforts narrated in Mark 2:4.[7] In addressing this issue, it is helpful to compare Matthew 9:2 with Matthew 9:4:

And Jesus, seeing (*idōn*) their faith, said . . .

And Jesus, seeing (*idōn*) their thoughts, said . . .

The parallelism of the two statements, a feature found only in Matthew's version of the episode, suggests that just as Jesus is able to see into the hearts of the scribes, he is able to see into the hearts of the paralytic and his companions.[8] This parallelism, together with the omission of the material in Mark 2:4, further suggests that in retelling

---

7. "Matthew reports nothing which can be seen as indicating their faith to Jesus" (John Nolland, *The Gospel of Matthew*, NIGTC [Grand Rapids: Eerdmans, 2005], 380). Elsewhere in the First Gospel faith is demonstrated through persistence in overcoming an obstacle of some kind (e.g., 8:10; 9:22, 29; 15:28).

8. Note that "seeing" in 9:4 is unique to Matthew's version of the story, though some ancient manuscripts have instead "knowing" (see W. D. Davies and Dale C. Allison, *The Gospel According to Saint Matthew*, ICC [London: T&T Clark, 1991], 2:91).

this story Matthew wanted to focus not on actions that demonstrate faith (though these are included) but on the inner conviction that informs such actions, an emphasis for the First Gospel generally.[9] As Jesus explains in 12:34-35, it is from the heart—that is, from the inner "treasure" of the human self—that each person brings forth either good things or evil things.

This emphasis on the "integrated" nature of faith (i.e., faith that integrates internal disposition with external action) also draws attention to the nature of Jesus' ability to "see" such faith. Elsewhere in the Gospel, Jesus exhibits this sort of supernatural acuity again in 12:25 ("Knowing their thoughts," etc.), an event that occurs in the context of another healing story (12:22-24; cf. 21:2-3). Passages like 9:2 and 12:25, in turn, are reminiscent of various Old Testament texts that assert the ability of God and God alone to see into human hearts, an ability that is often associated with God's role as judge.[10] The statement about sight in Matthew 9:2, then, is suggesting something not only about the nature of faith but also something about the God-like authority of the one who acknowledges faith, a matter of relevance for the ensuing controversy.

Still more teaching about faith is conveyed by Jesus' first words to the man: "Take courage, my son, your sins are forgiven" (9:2). In response to the expression of faith comes an expression of assurance and acceptance, one that presumably inspires deeper faith (cf. 9:22). The plea, "take courage" (*tharsei*), which is unique to Matthew's version of the story, has parallels outside of Scripture, for example, Tobit 5:10: "Take courage; the time is near for God to heal you."[11] As

---

9. E.g., Matt. 5:27-28; 6:3-4; 7:16-18. For Jesus' question in 9:4 ("Why do you think evil in your hearts?"), see especially 15:19 ("For out of the heart come evil thoughts," etc.).
10. E.g., 1 Sam. 16:7; 1 Kgs. 8:39; Ps. 139:1-2, 23; Prov. 24:12; Jer. 11:20; 17:9-10; cf. Matt. 6:6.
11. Cf. Tob. 11:11; Philostratus, *Life of Apollonius* 4.10.1; Lucian, *Lover of Lies* 11. There is also a narrative recorded in a third century BCE inscription (Emma J. Edelstein and Ludwig Edelstein, *Asclepius: Collection and Interpretation of the Testimonies* [Baltimore: Johns Hopkins University

in other extracanonical examples, here the word of encouragement relates specifically to the requested cure. In Matthew 9:2, by contrast, the word of encouragement introduces an unexpected topic, one whose meaning will dominate the rest of the pericope.

Also unexpected is the group of scribes that now appears on the scene.[12] In Matthew 8:19, one of the scribes had been mentioned as a potential follower. In Matthew 9:3, for the first time in the Gospel, the scribes appear as critics.[13] Specifically, they accuse Jesus of blasphemy, that is, of usurping the prerogative both of God, the only one who can forgive sins (e.g., Exod. 34:6-7; Ps. 86:5; Isa. 43:25), and of God's priests, the only ones authorized to enact such forgiveness (e.g., Lev. 4:20; 19:22; Num. 15:25). However, as Matthew 9:4 reveals, it is not Jesus who has spoken evil but the scribes. The first of Jesus' two rhetorical questions ("Why do you think evil in your hearts?") is reminiscent of prophetic texts like Jeremiah 4:14, 16:12, and Zechariah 8:17, reinforcing the image of Jesus as the agent of divine judgment.

With the second of Jesus' rhetorical questions ("Which is easier to say, 'Your sins are forgiven,' or to say, 'Get up and walk'?") we encounter yet another interpretive puzzle. This is because the appropriate answer to the question varies depending on the perspective from which one evaluates it. From the perspective of *external proof*, it is easier to declare that a person's sins have been forgiven than to declare that a person's illness has been cured because the latter is subject to observable verification in a way the former is not. In this case, Jesus is making an argument from the greater to

Press, 1945], 1:144), according to which the healing god Asclepius tells a supplicant, "Take courage (*tharsei*); at the right time I will return."

12. The presence of the scribes may be one reason why Matthew situates the action of the pericope not "at home" (as in Mark 2:1) but, apparently, in a public place.

13. The scribes appear frequently as Jesus' opponents (12:38; 15:1; 16:21; 20:18; 21:15; 23:13-15, 23, 25, 27, 29, 34; 26:57; 27:41). Cf. John P. Meier, *A Marginal Jew: Rethinking the Historical Jesus* (New York: Doubleday, 2001), 3:549–60.

the lesser: if he can accomplish something that is demonstrably more difficult (healing the paralytic) then logically he can accomplish the "easier" task as well (forgiving his sins).[14] The ensuing healing, then, serves as visible proof and public validation of the claim that Jesus makes in 9:2.

However, as we have just seen, in retelling the events of 9:2, Matthew's tendency is to focus not on external demonstrations of spiritual realities but on the spiritual realities themselves. If this priority applies to the rest of the episode as well, it has implications for how we evaluate the point behind Jesus' second rhetorical question. From the perspective of *internal actuality*, it is easier to cure someone's illness than to forgive someone's sins, since the former conceivably falls within the scope of human ability (Jesus, after all, was not the only charismatic healer), while the ability to absolve individuals of their guilt belongs to God alone.[15] Thus the act of forgiving the paralytic represents the more difficult and momentous accomplishment, since it is something that could be accomplished only if God's very self was acting in Jesus.

To claim even this much, however, understates the magnitude of what transpires in Matthew 9:1-8. In order to appreciate this fact, however, it is necessary to take a step back from the story itself and reconsider the distinctive context in which the evangelist has situated it.

As is his habit, in 9:1-8, Matthew not only rewrites the story he has received from the tradition, but also relocates it:

---

14. Jesus makes a similar kind of argument in 12:11-12, in the healing of the man with a withered hand, a story that resembles 9:1-8 formally.
15. In Lucian, *Lover of Lies* 11, a charismatic healer cures a snake-bitten man, who afterwards picks up the stretcher upon which he had been carried and walks off.

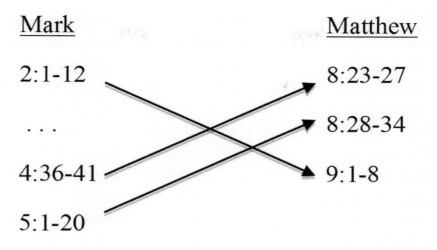

Mark	Matthew
2:1-12	8:23-27
. . .	8:28-34
4:36-41	9:1-8
5:1-20	

In the Second Gospel, the healing of the paralytic (Mark 2:1-12) is immediately preceded by the healing of the leper (Mark 1:40-45; cf. Matt. 8:1-4). In the First Gospel, the healing of the paralytic is immediately preceded by the stilling of the storm (Matt. 8:23-27) and the story of the Gadarene demoniacs (Matt. 8:28-34), episodes that in Mark occur at a later point in the narrative (4:36—5:20). In addition, Matthew's way of structuring the material in chapters 8–9 indicates that these three miracle stories (8:23-27, 8:28-34, and 9:1-8) are meant to be read together, as a discrete sub-unit, much like the triads in 8:1-15 and 9:18-34 (see Chapter One). As one might expect, this re-contextualization of the paralytic's story, a feature found only in the First Gospel, has critical implications for interpretation. Specifically, when 9:1-8 is read in the aftermath of 8:23-34, it is possible to discern a meaningful progression in terms of the specific types of adversaries and obstacles against which Jesus must act.

As we saw earlier, in Matthew 8:23-27, Jesus' adversary was the sea, an image of primordial death and chaos, while in Matthew 8:28-34 his adversary was a pair of demoniacs, representatives of satanic defiance and corruption. In both episodes the exorcistic features of the narration were deployed in such a manner so as to illustrate not only the confrontational nature of Jesus' ministry but also the eschatological significance of that confrontation. Specifically, the mighty deeds of Jesus were seen to function as enacted symbols of God's impending kingdom, dramatizing how the power of God interrupts human lives and expels a rival power, claiming those lives as its own. Matthew's way of structuring the narrative suggests that he understands the mighty deeds of 9:1-8 in the same vein, that is, as an extension of both Jesus' eschatological struggle with Satan and his eschatological judgment of evil. While 8:28-34 had shown Jesus liberating people from the *presence* of evil, however, 9:1-8 shows him liberating people from the *effects* of evil, indeed, from the most insidious effect of evil, namely, sin.[16] What transpires in 9:1-8, then, is not simply the forgiveness of someone's sins but a symbolic act that advances the depiction of Jesus as eschatological warrior and judge, the one empowered by God to overcome everything that corrupts human existence and usher in a new era of human wholeness. The transposition of the paralytic's story from its original Markan setting to its new Matthean setting contributes to this depiction in a vital way: the eschatological warrior's victory over the forces that corrupt human life is incomplete until it attends to the problem of sin.

This fact is signaled in the story itself by the specific wording employed by Jesus in 9:6: "But so that you may know that the Son of Man has authority on earth to forgive sins." To begin with, the introductory formula ("so that you may know") recalls Old Testament texts in which God's sovereignty over the earth is asserted (Exod. 8:22; 9:14), thereby contributing to the general solemnity of the scene. The impressiveness of Jesus' declaration is amplified further

16. For the connection of exorcism (8:32), forgiveness (9:2), and healing (9:6-7) in Matthew we have a parallel in 4QPrNab, a fragmentary text from Qumran describing how King Nabonidus of Babylon was forgiven his sins and cured of a disease by a Jewish exorcist. For a translation, see Florentino García Martínez, *The Dead Sea Scrolls Translated: The Qumran Texts in English*, 2nd ed. (Leiden: Brill, 1996), 289.

by his use of the title "the Son of Man" (*ho huios tou anthrōpou*).[17] Elsewhere in the Gospel when Jesus speaks of himself this way he is usually speaking of his role as eschatological judge (e.g., 10:23; 13:41; 16:27-28; 19:28; 24:30; 25:31; 26:64). In forgiving the paralytic, then, Jesus is not acting on his own initiative but by virtue of the authority, or *exousia*, that has been invested in him as the Son of Man (9:6), a figure familiar especially from Daniel 7:13-14:

> (13) I saw in the night visions, and, behold, there came with the clouds of heaven one like a son of man (*huios anthrōpou*), and he came even to the ancient of days, and was brought before him. (14) And there was given to him dominion and honor and a kingdom, so that all the peoples, nations, and languages should serve him: his authority (*exousia*) is an everlasting authority, which shall not pass away, and his kingdom shall not be destroyed.

Like the Danielic Son of Man, Jesus is an eschatological figure granted authority to carry out God's will on earth (cf. Matt. 28:18). Unlike the Danielic Son of Man, for Jesus this authority entails not only defeating evil but also forgiving sins.[18] With regard to the latter, it is important to remember that the forgiveness of sins is a regular element in the eschatological scenarios envisioned by both biblical and extrabiblical authors.[19] According to *Pesiqta Rabbati* 37.2, for example, "the utterance of the Messiah's tongue is pardon and forgiveness for Israel." Within the context of ancient Judaism, then, the claim that Jesus makes in Matthew 9:6 would not represent an entirely unexpected expansion of the Son of Man's role. What *would*

---

17. Douglas R. A. Hare, *The Son of Man Tradition* (Minneapolis: Fortress Press, 1990), 113–82.

18. Cf. Chrys C. Caragounis, *The Son of Man: Vision and Interpretation*, WUNT 38 (Tübingen: Mohr Siebeck, 1986), 187–90.

19. E.g., Isa. 44:21-23; Jer. 31:34; Ezek. 16:62-63; *T. Levi* 18:9; CD 14:19; 11QMelch 4-9. Cf. Joseph M. Baumgarten, "Messianic Forgiveness of Sin in CD 14:19," in *Provo International Conference on the Dead Sea Scrolls: Technological Innovations, New Texts, and Reformulated Issues*, STDJ 30, eds. Donald W. Parry and Eugene Charles Ulrich (Leiden: Brill, 1999), 537–44.

have been unexpected against such a background is the declaration that Jesus makes about himself in Matthew 20:28:

> The Son of Man came not to be served but to serve, and to give his life as a ransom for many.

Unlike the Danielic Son of Man, the Matthean Son of Man is a servant who suffers on behalf of others (cf. Isa. 53:4-5, 10-12, and note the quotation of Isa. 53:4 in Matt. 8:17).[20] The event to which Matthew 20:28 refers, of course, is the crucifixion, an event given a sacrificial interpretation by Jesus himself during the Last Supper:

> This is my blood of the covenant, which is poured out for many for the forgiveness of sins. (Matt. 26:28)

The expression, "for the forgiveness of sins"—an expression that Matthew has added to his source material (cf. Mark 14:24)—clarifies the meaning of Jesus' death both as an offering for sin (cf. Isa. 53:12) and as the basis of a covenant (cf. Exod. 24:8). This emphasis on forgiveness is in keeping with both the theological and the social priorities of the First Gospel as a whole.[21] Specifically, for Matthew the covenant through which Jesus' followers are bound to him and to one other has forgiveness as both its basis (in his death) and its expression (in their lives). Jesus' entire ministry can be summed up as saving people from their sins (1:21). Accordingly, the dynamic of sin and forgiveness informs a whole range of practices through which people participate in covenantal solidarity, including, besides the Eucharist (26:26-29), baptism (3:1-17), prayer (6:12, 14-15), fasting (6:16-18), and fraternal correction (18:15-22). Forgiveness, then, is

---

20. This is consistent with passages in the First Gospel where Jesus speaks of the Son of Man as one who is betrayed and condemned to death (e.g., 17:22; 20:18; 26:2, 24, 45). See further the discussion of Matthew 8:20 in Chapter Six.

21. Thomas W. Buckley, *Seventy Times Seven: Sin, Judgment, and Forgiveness in Matthew* (Collegeville, MN: Liturgical, 1991), 9–29, 73–87.

not only something that is bestowed once and for all; it is also something that it lived out on a daily basis. The fact that the forgiveness Jesus represents is conferred in the context of a healing story brings its "incarnational" nature into relief: the forgiveness that the paralytic bears on his healed body is bestowed by one whose own body will be broken and blood shed for the forgiveness of sins.

The relevance of these observations for Matthew 9:1-8 is borne out by two of the story's specific literary features, the first of which has a parallel in chapter 18:

> ... the Son of Man has authority on earth (*epi tēs gēs*) to forgive sins ... (Matt. 9:6)

> Truly I tell you, whatever you bind on earth (*epi tēs gēs*) will be bound in heaven, and whatever you release on earth will be released in heaven. (Matt. 18:18)

The Son of Man's authority to forgive is something that he exercises "on (the) earth" (*epi tēs gēs*), that is, something that he exercises in the realm of human affairs in advance of the Parousia, when the heavenly kingdom will appear to transform that realm.[22] As Matthew 18:18 (cf. 16:19) indicates, however, this authority is not something that he exercises alone: just as authority has been bestowed on Jesus, he bestows authority on others.[23] The immediate literary context of the statement in 18:18 (cf. 18:15-22) makes it clear that the language of "binding" and "releasing" refers to the authority to forgive or not forgive sins (cf. 1 Kgs. 8:31-34).[24] Any decision in this regard must involve the participation of at least two or three believers, since

---

22. Hagner, *Matthew*, 1:233–34.
23. The bestowal of authority (*exousia*) also figures in Matthew 10:1; cf. 28:18.
24. For Matthew 18:15-22, see Petri Luomanen, *Entering the Kingdom of Heaven: A Study on the Structure of Matthew's View of Salvation*, WUNT 2.101 (Tübingen: Mohr Siebeck, 1998), 248–52; Stephenson H. Brooks, *Matthew's Community: The Evidence of His Special Sayings Material*, JSNTSup 16 (Sheffield: JSOT, 1987), 99–107.

"where two or three have gathered together in my name, I am there in their midst" (18:20). The Son of Man's authority to forgive is valid wherever he is, and he is "with" his followers when they gather in his name (cf. 1:23; 28:20). They can forgive sins, then, because he is with them and they can forgive sins only when he is with them. The practice of forgiveness, then, is one of the ways in which believers experience his presence as a community as well as one of the ways in which the community becomes a living expression of that presence.[25]

The second specific literary feature can be found in the distinctive conclusion that Matthew has provided for the story:[26]

> They were all amazed and glorified God, saying, "We never saw anything like this!" (Mark 2:12)

> And the crowds, seeing this, were afraid and glorified God, who had given such authority to the people. (Matt. 9:8)

While Mark's ending draws attention to the miracle, Matthew's ending draws attention to the church.[27] The authority given by God to "the people" is the authority of the Son of Man, a point that comes across more clearly in a literal translation of Matthew 9:6 and 8:

> . . . the son of the person (*tou anthrōpou*) has authority (*exousian*) . . .

> . . . had given such authority (*exousian*) to the persons (*tois anthrōpois*).

---

25. Cf. Richard B. Hays, *The Moral Vision of the New Testament: Community, Cross, New Creation* (San Francisco: HarperSanFrancisco, 1996), 101–104.

26. Evidently, Matthew has transposed the declaration in Mark 2:12 from the story of the paralytic to the story of the mute demoniac (Matt. 9:33). In lieu of "were afraid" in Matthew 9:8 (cf. Luke 5:26), some manuscripts have "were amazed" (for which see 8:27 and 9:33). On fear as a response, see Gerd Theissen, *The Miracle Stories of the Early Christian Tradition* (Philadelphia: Fortress Press, 1983), 69–71.

27. "Matt 9:8 steers the admiration of the onlookers into the direction of forgiveness of sins and away from the miracle" (Repschinski, *Controversy Stories*, 71). On the same page, Repschinski also notes how Matthew changes Mark's "all" to "the crowds," thus avoiding the implication that the scribes joined the rest in glorifying God.

As we saw above, the Matthean Son of Man differs from the Danielic Son of Man in that only the former is invested with the authority to forgive sins. As noteworthy as this may be, the statement in Matthew 9:8 reveals an even more profound difference: it is only through the former that humanity can participate in this authority as well, a reality confirmed by Jesus' directives to his followers in 18:15-22. The element of participation is subtly reinforced by yet another item unique to Matthew's version of the story, the reference to what the bystanders "saw" when Jesus healed the paralytic. Note the following parallels:

And Jesus, seeing (*idōn*) their faith . . . (9:2)

And Jesus, seeing (*idōn*) their thoughts . . . (9:4)

And the crowds, seeing (*idontes*) this . . . (9:8)

Like Jesus himself, the people are presented as being able to "see" beyond the externals, that is, they are able not only to observe the visible demonstration of healing (9:7) but also to perceive the spiritual reality that the healing demonstrates (9:8). Significantly, what the bystanders are reported as perceiving is not the individualist aspect of this reality (i.e., that the paralytic had been forgiven) but the implications this reality has for "the people." Presumably, it is just this sort of communal insight into the nature of forgiveness that Matthew hopes to cultivate among his readers.

Collective Faith, Eschatological Healing

At this point, however, it might seem that with all this talk of forgiveness we have strayed rather far from the topic of healing. In defense of the discussion above, it can be pointed out that the paralytic and his companions probably had the same kind of response.

After all, we have to assume that they, like so many others in the Gospel, came to Jesus for healing (cf. 8:16). The pronouncement recorded in 9:2, then, would have seemed to them incongruous with the demands of the situation, and we as interpreters are left wondering why so much of a healing narrative (and this healing narrative in particular) is devoted to the theme of forgiveness.

Of course, Jesus' pronouncement only *seems* unexpected until we remember that various biblical traditions posited a causal connection between sin and illness (e.g., Lev. 26:14-16; Deut. 28:15, 22, 27-28; Ps. 38:3; John 5:14) as well as a corresponding connection between forgiveness and healing (e.g., Ps. 103:3; Isa. 33:24; James 5:14-15).[28] While acknowledging the pertinence of these traditions for explicating the logic of our passage, however, we should also remember that Scripture as a whole does not provide us with a unified perspective on the theme. Alongside the texts just mentioned are images of righteous people suffering (e.g., Job 9:15-18) and of unrighteous people thriving (e.g., Ps. 73:3-5).[29] As Frederick Gaiser observes, "the Old Testament never claims that all illness is the result of breaking the divine law, or that righteousness according to the law always results in full health."[30] It would thus be incorrect to

---

28. The persistence of these views is evidenced by *b. Ned.* 41a, which offers a striking parallel to our text: "a sick person does not arise from his illness until all his sins are forgiven him." For the connection between sin and illness in the Greco-Roman world, see Angelos Chaniotis, "Illness and Cures in the Greek Propitiatory Inscriptions and Dedications of Lydia and Phrygia," in *Ancient Medicine in its Socio-Cultural Context*, eds. Ph. J. van der Eijk et al. (Amsterdam: Rodopi, 1995), 2:323–43; Angelos Chaniotis, "Ritual Performances of Divine Justice: The Epigraphy of Confession, Atonement and Exaltation in Roman Asia Minor," in *From Hellenism to Islam: Cultural and Linguistic Change in the Roman Near East*, eds. Hannah M. Cotton et al. (Cambridge: Cambridge University Press, 2009), 115–53.

29. Cf. Kathy Black, *A Healing Homiletic: Preaching and Disability* (Nashville: Abingdon, 1996), 19–42, 104–23; Colleen C. Grant, "Reinterpreting the Healing Narratives," in *Human Disability and the Service of God: Reassessing Religious Practice*, eds. Nancy L. Eiesland and Don E. Saliers (Nashville: Abingdon, 1998), 72–87; Amos Yong, *The Bible, Disability, and the Church: A New Vision of the People of God* (Grand Rapids: Eerdmans, 2011), 57–63.

30. Frederick J. Gaiser, *Healing in the Bible: Theological Insight for Christian Ministry* (Grand Rapids: Baker Academic, 2010), 24.

assume that in a biblical worldview sickness and disability necessarily function as signs of divine condemnation. As scholars in the field of disability studies point out, there are in fact a number of biblical texts in which disability is associated not with divine displeasure but with divine acceptance: on the Day of the Lord people with disabilities are shown being accepted just as they are (Isa. 33:17-24; Jer. 31:7-9; Mic. 4:6-8; Zeph. 3:19-20), a view with which our author appears to agree (Matt. 5:29-30; 18:8-9; cf. Luke 14:16-24).[31]

Along the same line, it is important to note that in the First Gospel, 9:1-8 is the only text on healing that implies some sort of link between sin and illness: elsewhere people are cured without reference to their personal guilt.[32] Conversely, in the First Gospel, 9:1-8 is the only text on forgiveness that mentions healing; elsewhere, people are forgiven without reference to their bodily ailments.[33] Moreover, even within the story itself there is no indication that the paralytic is in particular need of forgiveness, just as there is no indication that the "tax collectors and sinners" with whom Jesus dines in the passage that immediately follows are in particular need of healing (9:9-13). Their sins have indeed made them "sick" (9:12) but it is clear that this does not refer to sickness in the physical sense. Thus while Matthew is aware of the link between sin and illness, he seems uninterested in making that link explicit or in applying it to individual cases. In the end, perhaps the best commentary on Matthew 9:1-8 is a passage derived not from the First Gospel but the Fourth. To those who would fixate on identifying the cause of a particular person's disability, Jesus responds, "Neither this man nor his parents sinned; he

31. E.g., Saul M. Olyan, *Disability in the Hebrew Bible: Interpreting Mental and Physical Differences* (Cambridge: Cambridge University Press, 2008), 81–85. Cf. Thomas E. Reynolds, *Vulnerable Communion: A Theology of Disability and Hospitality* (Grand Rapids: Brazos, 2008), 225–28.
32. Birger Gerhardsson, *The Mighty Acts of Jesus According to Matthew* (Lund: CWK Gleerup, 1979), 80.
33. Matt. 6:12, 14-15; 12:31-32; 18:15-35.

was born blind so that God's works might be revealed in him" (John 9:3).[34]

The theme of divine revelation is applicable to Matthew 9:1-8 as well, though in addressing this theme we would do well to resist the sorts of individualistic approaches that sometimes accompany its interpretation.[35] After all, what precipitates the forgiveness of the paralytic's sins (i.e., what Jesus "sees" in 9:2) is not his faith alone but his faith together with that of his companions. In contemplating this fact, I find it to be highly significant that the only story in the First Gospel that suggests a connection between healing and forgiveness is also a story that shows the healed person being—both literally and figuratively—supported by others. Insofar as the paralytic receives forgiveness within the context of a *collective* expression of faith, this episode is especially wellisuited to its Matthean setting, where (as we have seen) there is an emphasis on forgiveness as an experience and practice that is lived out in community (9:8; cf. 18:15-22), a point that will be applicable to the interpretation of 9:9-13 as well.

Complementing and clarifying the social dimension of healing in our story is an eschatological dimension, and it is in this respect that the theme of divine revelation becomes most apparent. After all, the one who forgives the paralytic's sins is not simply a man but the Son of Man, and it is in accord with the Son of Man's authority and presence that forgiveness is experienced within the community (9:8; cf. 18:15-22). The community's practice of forgiveness, then, can be properly understood as an eschatological practice insofar as the Son of Man himself is an eschatological figure. Moreover, as we have seen, the identification of Jesus as an eschatological figure in the story of the paralytic is not anomalous but actually extends the

---

34. Joel Marcus, *Mark*, AB 27 (New Haven, CT: Yale University Press, 2000), 1:221. Cf. Gaiser, *Healing in the Bible*, 151–64.
35. E.g., Michael L. Brown, *Israel's Divine Healer* (Grand Rapids: Zondervan, 1995), 230.

narrative arc of the two stories that immediately precede it, where Jesus is depicted overpowering primordial forces of chaos (8:23-27) and passing judgment on satanic agents of corruption (8:28-34). Accordingly, the narrative element of confrontation helps to unite the three stories structurally and thematically. Thus both the need for forgiveness and the announcement of forgiveness are properly understood with the context of an unfolding eschatological drama, one in which all humanity is implicated. Within this drama, sin and sickness are connected not because one leads to the other but because both are products of the human condition and manifestations of human fallenness. Conversely, forgiveness and healing are related not as cause and effect but as mutually informing manifestations of the impending kingdom and its power to transform this condition.[36]

In assessing the implications of this narrative development, it behooves us to recall the very active role assigned to Satan in our author's worldview.[37] In the First Gospel, Satan is presented as a corruptor of both human morals (e.g., 5:37) and human society (e.g., 4:8-9). It is no wonder that the community is instructed to pray for deliverance from "the evil one" (6:13), the implication being that God alone can provide such salvation. Perhaps the most disturbing reminder of Satan's power in the world of human affairs comes from the parable of the Tares (13:24-30) and the explanation that Jesus provides for the parable in 13:36-43:

> The one who sows the good seed is the Son of Man, (38) and the field is the world, and the good seed are the children of the kingdom; and the tares are the children of the evil one, (39) and the enemy who sowed them is the devil . . . (41) The Son of Man will send his angels, and they will gather out of his kingdom all the stumbling blocks and those who

---

36. Black, *A Healing Homiletic*, 113; Reynolds, *Vulnerable Communion*, 227.
37. Robert Charles Branden, *Satanic Conflict and the Plot of Matthew* (New York: Peter Lang, 2006), 43–83.

commit lawlessness (42) and throw them into the furnace of fire. (Matt. 13:37-39, 41-42)

Here sinners are referred to both as "those who commit lawlessness" (drawing attention to individual human responsibility) and as "children of the evil one" who have been "sowed" by the devil (drawing attention to the causal influence of forces that transcend individual human responsibility). The Matthean understanding of sin, then, is complex. On one hand, there is no question that the First Gospel establishes for each of its readers high standards of moral accountability (e.g., 5:48). Indeed, their righteousness is expected to surpass even that of the scribes and the Pharisees (5:17-20). By the same token, the problem of sin for Matthew is more than a matter of personal decision-making. As 13:36-43 suggests, it is also part of a cosmic struggle between the Son of Man and Satan for human souls, one that will be resolved only in the final judgment.[38]

Consideration for this cosmic dimension has implications for the interpretation of 9:1-8. The authority that Jesus claims here as Son of Man is not simply the authority to forgive the sins of individuals. It is the authority of the one empowered by God to defeat everything that corrupts human existence and usher in a new era of human wholeness. What transpires in 9:1-8, then, is not simply the forgiveness of someone's sins but a symbolic act that advances the depiction of Jesus in 8:23-34 as eschatological warrior and judge. Insofar as the church participates in the Son of Man's authority to forgive (chapter 18), it becomes an agent and symbol of his eschatological work.

It is from this perspective that we can affirm that for Matthew the paralytic functions not as an *individual* believer but as a *typical* believer

---

38. For the dualistic, deterministic explanation of evil advanced here, see John K. Riches, *Conflicting Mythologies: Identity Formation in the Gospels of Mark and Matthew*, Studies of the New Testament and Its World (Edinburgh: T&T Clark, 2000), 199–200, 240–43.

and as a lesson in the dynamics of healing. The paralytic is well-suited to this representative role insofar as the nature of his condition dramatizes the debilitating effects of sin, his physical incapacitation bringing to mind biblical images of sin as binding, enslaving, or disabling people.[39] Indeed, the man's situation is so helpless that he cannot even approach Jesus on his own, but must rely on the faith of others to bring him to his liberator. The paralytic is also well-suited to this representative role insofar as he illustrates the importance of being responsive to the surprising nature of grace.[40] The man does not come to Jesus for forgiveness yet forgiveness is what the healer has discerned he needs. Moreover, the man receives forgiveness without really having to "do" anything: it is simply a matter of faith reaching out for help.

In all this, Matthew is teaching his readers something about the nature of forgiveness. Being in need of forgiveness themselves (6:12), they can identify with the paralytic's situation and see themselves in him. Together with the companion stories in 8:23-34, this story serves as a reminder that all people are susceptible to forces beyond their control or comprehension. Such forces are so insidious and incapacitating that individuals cannot free themselves but must rely for liberation on the cosmic power of the Son of Man and the supporting faith of the community he authorizes. This means that the announcement of forgiveness is not the end of the story but the beginning. Having been transformed into both recipients and agents of the Son of Man's authority, the forgiven are now drawn into a social and eschatological drama, and it is only from this perspective that one can understand the full meaning of healing.

39. E.g., Pss. 31:10; 38:4; 40:12; Prov. 29:6; Isa. 50:1; Lam. 1:14; Hos. 10:10; John 8:34; Acts 8:23; Rom. 6:6, 17; Heb. 12:1.
40. Cf. Molly C. Haslam, *A Constructive Theology of Intellectual Disability: Human Being as Mutuality and Response* (New York: Fordham University Press, 2012), 104–106.

9

Unexpected Guests: Matthew 9:9-13

As we have just learned, those who would "follow" Jesus (8:19, 22) and the example that he sets in Matthew 8:18–9:8 are encouraged to see themselves as participants in an unfolding eschatological drama. Accordingly, they approach the dynamics of sin and forgiveness not as matters of individual concern but as fundamentally social realities, that is, as realities in which all humanity is implicated. One of the consequences of this commitment is that those who would follow Jesus' example as *healers* implicate themselves in communal practices of forgiveness (e.g., 6:12-18; 18:15-22; 26:26-29). After all, before beginning his ministry of healing even Jesus submitted to a baptism for the repentance of sins (3:11, 14-15). The sort of wholeness that these healers mediate, then, is a product of the grace that they experience in community, an experience that is instrumental in shaping their self-understanding and agency as healers. Keeping these considerations in mind is essential when pondering the contribution of our next pericope, Matthew 9:9-13, to this eschatological drama, a pericope that illustrates yet another practice expressive of forgiveness, namely, hospitality.

In terms of literary genre, the material in 9:9-13 presents us with something distinctive, consisting as it does of a call story (9:9) joined to a controversy story (9:10-13).[1] As we have seen, Matthew 8–9 is comprised largely of healing stories, and so the inclusion of such formally disparate material would seem to require some explanation. The reference to Jesus as a physician to the sick in 9:12, even if it is metaphorical, represents an obvious fit from a thematic perspective, though it is important to note that these verses contribute to the development of the narrative in other ways as well.

(13) He went out again beside the sea; and the whole crowd came to him and he was teaching them. (14) Going on he saw Levi son of Alphaeus sitting at the tax booth; and he said to him, "Follow me." And he got up and followed him.

(9) Going on from there, Jesus saw a man called Matthew sitting at the tax booth; and he said to him, "Follow me." And he got up and followed him.

(15) And he was reclining in his house, and many tax collectors and sinners were reclining with Jesus and his disciples; for there were many of them, and they were following him.

(10) And while he was reclining in the house, many tax collectors and sinners came and were reclining with Jesus and his disciples.

(16) When the scribes of the Pharisees saw that he was eating with sinners and tax collectors, they said to his disciples, "Why is he eating with tax collectors and sinners?"

(11) When the Pharisees saw this, they said to his disciples, "Why is your teacher eating with tax collectors and sinners?"

---

1. P.Oxy. 1224 (translation in Burton H. Throckmorton, *Gospel Parallels: A Comparison of the Synoptic Gospels*, 5th ed. [Nashville: Thomas Nelson, 1992], 44) provides evidence that in the pre-synoptic tradition the story of Jesus reclining with sinners was not originally attached to the call of Levi.

(17) When he heard this, Jesus said to them, "It is not those who are healthy who have need of a physician but those who are sick.	(12) When he heard this, he said, "It is not those who are healthy who have need of a physician but those who are sick.
I came to call not the righteous but sinners." (Mark 2:13-17)	(13) Go and learn what this means, 'I desire mercy and not sacrifice.' For I came to call not the righteous but sinners." (Matt. 9:9-13)

To begin with, it is important to note that Matthew 9:10-13 is not the only controversy story in chapter 9.[2] The same designation applies to the pericope that immediately follows it (9:14-17), which may explain why the two stories are coupled in the tradition (cf. Mark 2:13-22).[3] The object of the controversy in 9:14-17 (i.e., fasting) is a practice often associated with repentance, a theme that is relevant to the subject matter of 9:10-13 as well.

Matthew 9:9-13 is also linked to the pericope that immediately precedes it (9:2-9), specifically, by the theme of sin (9:2, 5-6, 10-11, 13). The continuity between the two episodes is enhanced by Matthew's omission of the transitional material in Mark 2:13.[4] The basic point behind this imbrication is clear enough: Jesus' ministry to sinners reveals something about the nature of his ministry to the sick, while his ministry to the sick can be properly understood only in light of his ministry to sinners. In the case of the paralytic, sin is associated with the man's physical condition. In the case of the tax collector, sin

2. A controversy story is a brief narrative in which Jesus responds to an opponent's objection. In his redaction Matthew structures the elements of such stories more concisely than his sources and makes the transitions between elements more distinct, thereby drawing attention to the form's dialogical nature. See Boris Repschinski, *The Controversy Stories in the Gospel of Matthew*, FRLANT 189 (Göttingen: Vandenhoeck & Ruprecht, 2000), 264–73.

3. Cf. Joanna Dewey, *Markan Public Debate: Literary Technique, Concentric Structure, and Theology in Mark 2:1—3:6*, SBLDS 48 (Chico, CA: Scholars, 1980), 79–94.

4. By ignoring Mark 2:13, Matthew also passes over its scenario of Jesus *teaching* by the lakeside, thereby reinforcing the distinction between the ministry of word (chapters 5–7) and the ministry of deed (chapters 8–9).

is associated with the man's chosen profession (see below). In both cases the men are in need of the sort of forgiveness that Jesus alone can provide. After all, Jesus was sent to "save his people from their sins" (1:21) and preach a message of eschatological repentance (4:17; cf. 3:1-2).[5] In the case of the paralytic, this forgiveness is signaled by an act of healing. In the case of the tax collector, this forgiveness is signaled by an act of hospitality. In both cases the forgiveness that the men receive is presented as a matter not so much of anything that they themselves do or say but rather of what Jesus "sees" in them (9:2, 9). In other words, forgiveness is presented as a matter of both Jesus' initiative and the sovereign grace that this initiative enacts. This is particularly true in the case of the latter, who does not even approach Jesus for help but is found simply "sitting in the tax collector's booth" (9:9). Accordingly, in relating these stories the evangelist seems more interested in what the men do *after* their encounter with Jesus than what they do before it. Specifically, in both cases the men are presented as responding positively to Jesus, the parallelism between the two extending to the specific language used:

> And he got up and went home. (9:7)
> And he got up and followed him. (9:9)

Unlike the would-be disciple of Matthew 8:21-22, the tax collector makes no special requests before following Jesus. He simply hears and obeys.

This last point suggests yet another way in which Matthew 9:9-13 relates to its literary context. Form critics agree that Matthew 9:9 belongs to the category of "call" story and as such exhibits a structure comparable to that of the discipleship stories in Matthew 4:18-22.[6]

---

5. For the problem of sin, see also Matthew 3:6; 11:19; 12:31; 18:15, 21; 26:28. And for repentance, cf. Matt. 3:8, 11; 11:20-21; 12:41. Cf. Petri Luomanen, *Entering the Kingdom of Heaven: A Study on the Structure of Matthew's View of Salvation*, WUNT 2.101 (Tübingen: Mohr Siebeck, 1998), 220–28.

While the pair of pronouncement stories preserved in 8:18-22 are not call stories in the strict sense, they also deal with the theme of discipleship and in this respect correspond with the stories in 9:9-13, thus creating a formal and thematic frame around the triad of miracle stories in 8:23—9:8. This correspondence is reinforced by the repetition of several key terms, including "disciples" (8:21; 9:10-11), "teacher" (8:19; 9:11), and "follow me" (8:22; 9:9).[7] In the midst of these similarities, however, there is also an important difference. While in 8:18-22 it is the would-be disciples who initiate the action, in 9:9 it is Jesus who does so, with attention again being drawn to his sovereign (and intrusive) authority.

Another difference can be discerned in terms of *who* Jesus calls, though here the difference is not between Matthew 8:18-22 and Matthew 9:9 but between the First Gospel and the Second. In the former, the name of the tax collector has been changed from "Levi, son of Alphaeus" (Mark 2:14) to "Matthew" (Matt. 9:9), a redaction that corresponds with a change made in chapter 10, where the unadorned reference to "Matthew" (Mark 3:18) in a roster of the twelve disciples has been expanded to "Matthew the tax collector" (Matt. 10:3). Commentators have long puzzled over the reasons for these changes, and it is unlikely that we will ever arrive at a definitive explanation for them.[8] Evidently, it was important for the evangelist to show that the individuals specially "called" by Jesus to "follow" him were among the circle of the twelve, that is, that they were among those specially chosen by him to symbolize the eschatological re-gathering of the twelve tribes (19:28) and, as such, to carry out his

---

6. E.g., R. T. France, *The Gospel of Matthew*, NICNT (Grand Rapids: Eerdmans, 2007), 350; John Nolland, *The Gospel of Matthew*, NIGTC (Grand Rapids: Eerdmans, 2005), 385. Cf. A. J. Droge, "Call Stories," *ABD* 1 (1992): 821–23.

7. Note that the references to "teacher" in both 8:19 and 9:11 are redactional.

8. W. D. Davies and Dale C. Allison, *The Gospel According to Saint Matthew*, ICC (London: T&T Clark, 1991), 2:98–99.

mission to "the lost sheep of the house of Israel" (10:6).⁹ Insofar as these twelve are explicitly identified as disciples (10:1), the change to "Matthew" in Matthew 9:9 supplements the reference to disciples in 9:10-11 and reinforces the correspondence between Matthew 9:9-13 and Matthew 8:18-22, which, as we have just seen, also refers to disciples (8:21).¹⁰

The change of name in 9:9 may also suggest something more specifically regarding Matthew's understanding of healing and healers. In his version of the tax collector's story, acceptance is extended not simply to one of Jesus' followers (as in Mark) but to one of the twelve, that is, to one of those specially chosen by Jesus to carry out his ministry of healing (Matt. 10:1, 8). In other words, among those commissioned by Jesus to heal others is an individual who himself was once "sick" and in need of a "physician" (9:12). This Matthean healer, then, knows what it means to be healed, a fact that would have given Jesus' words in 10:8 special meaning: "Freely you received, freely give" (cf. 2 Kgs. 5:15-16).¹¹ Jesus not only forgives sinners (9:2-8); he calls them (9:9-13). He not only cures the "sick" (9:9-13); he calls on them to cure the sick themselves (10:1-8).

Like other disciples in the Gospel, when Matthew is called in 9:9, he gets up and "follows" Jesus. Exactly to *where* he follows Jesus, though, is unclear. At this point comparison with the parallel accounts in both Mark and Luke is in order:

> And while he was reclining in the house, many tax collectors and sinners came and were reclining with Jesus and his disciples. (Matt. 9:10)

9. Cf. John P. Meier, *A Marginal Jew: Rethinking the Historical Jesus* (New York: Doubleday, 2001), 3:148–63.
10. Insofar as "Matthew" (*Matthaios*) resembles "disciple" (*mathētēs*), "through assonance the name helps stress the theme of discipleship" (Davies and Allison, *Saint Matthew*, 2:98).
11. Note that these words are found only in Matthew's Gospel (cf. Mark 3:15; 6:13; Luke 10:9).

And he was reclining in his house, and many tax collectors and sinners were reclining with Jesus and his disciples; for there were many of them, and they were following him. (Mark 2:15)

And Levi gave a great banquet for him in his house; and there was a large crowd of tax collectors and others who were reclining with them. (Luke 5:29)

Luke states plainly that the meal was held in the house of Levi, while Mark speaks ambiguously of "his" house, which logically could refer either to Levi's house or to Jesus' house (cf. Matt. 4:13; 9:1). Matthew, meanwhile, speaks of "the" house, presumably alluding to the last reference in the narrative to a house, that is, the reference to Peter's house in Matthew 8:14. The likelihood that Matthew has in mind Peter's (or perhaps Jesus') house is reinforced by the fact that in 9:9 it is the tax collector who follows Jesus and not vice versa.[12] The fact that 9:10 reports how the tax collectors and sinners "came" and reclined "with Jesus" (and not Jesus who came to recline "with" them) further suggests that it is Jesus and not Matthew who is acting as host.[13] Finally, it is important to note that the verb "to call" (*kalesai*) in 9:13 is operating on two levels of meaning. In Greek the same word that Jesus uses to "call" tax collectors and sinners to discipleship could also be used to "call" (i.e., invite) someone to a meal.[14] This usage underscores the symbolic meaning of what transpires in 9:10. The gathering to which Jesus calls tax collectors and sinners is no ordinary meal but rather a foretaste of the messianic banquet, an eschatological event that in Matthew's mind can be hosted by none other than the Messiah himself (cf. 9:15).[15]

---

12. In Matthew 9:28, two men in need of healing follow Jesus into "the" house, which again is most likely a reference to either Peter's or Jesus' house. Given what they say in 9:11, it is also difficult to imagine Pharisees loitering in the house of a tax collector.
13. Repschinski, *Controversy Stories*, 76.
14. E.g., Matt. 22:3, 9; Luke 14:7-14; John 2:2; 1 Cor. 10:27; Rev. 19:9. Cf. Dennis E. Smith, *From Symposium to Eucharist: The Banquet in the Early Christian World* (Minneapolis: Fortress Press, 2003), 22-23, 229.

That meal imagery was of significance to the evangelist's presentation of Jesus can be discerned from a variety of texts.[16] In the parable of the Wedding Banquet, for example, the king's servants "call" (*kalesai*) the expected guests to attend a grand banquet that he is throwing for his son, the bridegroom (22:3-4). When they ignore the invitation and mistreat the servants, the king destroys "their city" (22:7) and instructs the servants to "call" anyone they can find, both good and bad, to attend the feast (22:9-10). This is reminiscent of a text discussed in Chapter Three, where Jesus announces that "many will come from east and west" to dine with the patriarchs in the heavenly banquet, while "the sons of the kingdom will be cast out" (8:11-12).

Another relevant "meal" text can be found in Matthew 26:20-30. Like Mark, Matthew presents the Last Supper as an anticipation of a meal to be celebrated in the eschatological kingdom (26:29; cf. Mark 14:25). Unlike Mark, however, Matthew explicitly associates this meal with the forgiveness of sins (26:28; cf. Mark 14:24), a feature that resonates with the meal in 9:10, where Jesus dines with sinners, that is, with those in greatest need of forgiveness. Attention to the language employed by the evangelist to introduce the two scenes is also instructive:

And as he was reclining (*katakeisthai*) in his house . . . (Mark 2:15)

And as he was reclining (*anakeimenou*) in the house . . . (Matt. 9:10)

When it was evening, he reclined (*anekeito*) with the twelve. (Matt. 26:20)

15. For the imagery of the messianic banquet, see Isa. 25:6-8; 55:1-2; 65:13-14; Zeph. 1:7; Luke 14:15; 22:28-30; Rev. 19:9 . See further Chapter Three, n. 23.
16. James P. Grimshaw, *The Matthean Community and the World: An Analysis of Matthew's Food Exchange*, Studies in Biblical Literature 111 (New York: Peter Lang, 2008), 187–90; Peter-Ben Smit, *Fellowship and Food in the Kingdom: Eschatological Meals and Scenes of Utopian Abundance in the New Testament*, WUNT 2.234 (Tübingen: Mohr Siebeck, 2008), 201–58.

A subtle change in the wording of Matthew's version of the story in 9:10-13 reinforces its similarity with the Last Supper: the covenant for the forgiveness of sins that Jesus announces at a meal there is prefigured by the solidarity with sinners that he expresses at a meal here. Insofar as "reclining was usually reserved for feasts,"[17] the wording of 9:10 underscores the special, celebratory nature of the occasion, which would help to explain why it attracts the attention of onlookers in 9:11.

However we construe the exact relationship between the meal texts in Matthew 8:11-12, 9:10-13, 22:1-14, and 26:20-30, behind them all it is possible to discern a basic point: the kingdom of God is like a great banquet that will be attended by unexpected guests. Jesus anticipates and enacts this reality through his dining practices, not only forgiving sinners (cf. 9:2) but also welcoming them to his table (9:9-13). There can be little doubt that Jesus intended this act of acceptance to be interpreted as a prophetic act, one meant to challenge prevailing norms and attitudes. His choice of the common *table* as a venue for issuing this challenge would have been culturally appropriate, given the scrutiny paid by ancient Mediterranean people generally to meals as occasions for displaying social solidarity and social status.[18] It is not just that "Jesus' choice of companions offers him no social advantage," however.[19] Rather, his particular choice of companions brings him into conflict with the arbitrators of such advantage, represented in 9:11 by the Pharisees.[20]

---

17. Davies and Allison, *Saint Matthew*, 2:99.
18. See Smith, *From Symposium to Eucharist*, 42–46 and s.v. "social status." Ancient dining practices "reflected and reinforced hierarchical order, social relations, and status through invitations, different qualities and quantities of food, types of tableware and eating utensils, and seating order (Pliny, *Letters* 2.6)" (Warren Carter, *Matthew and the Margins: A Socio-Political and Religious Reading* [Sheffield: Sheffield Academic, 2000], 219).
19. Nolland, *The Gospel of Matthew*, 386.
20. Note that "the scribes of the Pharisees" in Mark 2:16 has become simply "the Pharisees" in Matthew 9:11. Evidently, Matthew wanted to differentiate the group with which Jesus interacts

In order to appreciate the nature of this conflict, it is helpful to know something about the status of tax collectors in ancient Israelite society.[21] A tax collector (*telōnēs*) like Matthew would have been a minor functionary in the employ of Herod Antipas, his tax booth (*telōnion*) serving as a place for collecting tolls on transported goods. Members of this profession were generally castigated as dishonest, greedy, and traitorous, and so would have been routinely categorized with other unseemly groups, including Gentiles (18:17) and prostitutes (21:31-32).[22] Two judgments about tax collectors rendered in rabbinic sources are especially relevant for understanding the socio-religious dynamics of our text. First, the entry of a tax collector into a house was thought to render the domicile ritually unclean (*m. Tehar.* 7:6). Second (and no doubt in part because of this), it was thought difficult for a tax collector to make repentance (*t. B. Mes.* 8.26).

Opinions like these help to create a backdrop for the Pharisees' question in Matthew 9:11, though there were priorities specific to their movement that are worth bearing in mind as well. Note that the Pharisees do not ask why Jesus is seen associating with tax collectors and sinners or talking with them, but why he is seen *eating* with them. Various sources (e.g., Matt. 15:2) suggest that the purity concerns of the Pharisees often focused on matters of food and table.[23]

---

in 9:1-9 from the one with which he interacts in 9:9-13. For comparable editorial alterations, see Matthew 12:24 (cf. Mark 3:22); 22:34 (cf. Mark 12:28), 41 (cf. Mark 12:35).

21. Adela Yarbro Collins, *Mark*, Hermeneia (Minneapolis: Fortress Press, 2007), 194: "The tax collectors of Galilee in the time of Jesus were employees of Herod Antipas, not of Rome." See further, Richard A. Horsley, *Jesus and the Spiral of Violence: Popular Jewish Resistance in Roman Palestine* (San Francisco: Harper & Row, 1987), 212–23; John R. Donahue, "Tax Collector," *ABD* 6 (1992): 337–38; Donahue, "Tax Collectors and Sinners," *CBQ* 33 (1971): 39–61; Craig S. Keener, *A Commentary on the Gospel of Matthew* (Grand Rapids: Eerdmans, 1999), 292–93.

22. Collins, *Mark*, 193: they engage in activities "regarded as base and unseemly by humanity," and in this regard are similar to brothel keepers (Dio Chrysostom, *Orations* 14.14).

23. J. Patrick Mullen, *Dining with Pharisees* (Collegeville, MN: Liturgical, 2004), 39–77; Anthony J. Saldarini, *Pharisees, Scribes and Sadducees in Palestinian Society: A Sociological Approach* (Grand Rapids: Eerdmans, 2001), 199–237. Cf. Mark 7:3-4; John 2:6; Roger P. Booth, *Jesus and the*

In fact, such concerns were so pronounced (and so fundamental to their identity as a group) that the Pharisees formed voluntary eating fellowships in order to protect themselves from impure people and impure food (i.e., non-kosher or non-tithed food).[24] Referring to the work of Jacob Neusner, John Meier summarizes the agenda informing these practices as follows: "the Pharisees sought by strict observance of purity rules to extend the holiness of the temple into the sphere of everyday Jewish living and eating."[25] By contrast, eating with tax collectors, whose very presence was a source of defilement, and sinners, who by definition were lax when it came to ritual matters, would have been seen as a threat to such holiness.[26] In a very important sense, then, the conflict between Jesus and the Pharisees in our story is a conflict about holiness, that is, about who is holy and what makes one holy.

The Pharisees' question in 9:11 does not go unanswered, of course, but (in keeping with the conventions of the controversy story genre) is followed immediately by Jesus' decisive response, which brings the episode to an end. In contrast to the response in Mark 2:17, which has two parts, the response in Matthew 9:12-13 has three parts, in keeping with the evangelist's predilection for triadic groupings. Below I analyze each of these three elements in turn.

As commentators frequently note, for the first element of his response (9:12) Jesus draws on a proverbial concept.[27] Typical in this

Laws of Purity: Tradition History and Legal History in Mark 7, JSNTSup 13 (Sheffield: JSOT, 1986), 151–54, 190–92; Eyal Regev, "Pure Individualism: The Idea of Non-Priestly Purity in Ancient Judaism," *JSJ* 31 (2000): 180–81, 186–89.

24. Smith, *From Symposium to Eucharist*, 150–52; Joel Marcus, *Mark*, AB 27 (New Haven, CT: Yale University Press, 2000), 1:519–24. As Jacob Neusner (*The Idea of Purity in Ancient Judaism*, SJLA 1 [Leiden: Brill, 1973], 65) puts it, they "held one must eat his secular food, that is, ordinary, everyday meals, in a state of purity *as if one were a Temple priest* . . . The table of every Jew in his home was seen to be like the table of the Lord in the Jerusalem Temple" (emphasis original).

25. Meier, *A Marginal Jew*, 3:312.

26. Marcus, *Mark*, 1:227.

27. E.g., Donald A. Hagner, *Matthew*, WBC 33 (Dallas: Word Books, 1993), 1:239.

regard is a popular saying preserved by the Greek author Plutarch: "Physicians are wont to spend their time, not among the healthy, but where the sick are."[28] What commentators note less frequently is that this concept was often used metaphorically by moral philosophers of the time to depict themselves as "physicians" of the soul and their teaching as a "therapy" for the "disease" of immorality.[29] According to one source, for example, the Cynic philosopher Demonax "was never known to make an uproar or excite himself or get angry, even if he had to rebuke someone; though he assailed sins, he forgave sinners, thinking that one should pattern after doctors, who heal sickness but feel no anger at the sick."[30] Like Demonax, the "patients" that Jesus seeks out are sinners whom he "heals" with forgiveness even as he calls on them to repent of their sins.

As apt (and plentiful) as such comparisons may be, they still do not capture the full meaning of the imagery at work in Matthew 9:12, especially in light of what Jesus says in the second and third elements of his response. Consider the following texts:

> The Lord will strike Egypt, striking and *healing*; they will return to the Lord, and he will listen to their supplications and *heal* them. (Isa. 19:22 NRSV)

> I have seen their ways, but I will *heal* them; I will lead them and repay them with comfort. (Isa. 57:18 NRSV)

> For I will restore *health* to you, and your wounds I will *heal*, says the Lord, because they have called you an outcast. (Jer. 30:17 NRSV)

> Come, let us return to the Lord; for it is he who has torn us, and he will *heal* us; he has struck down, and he will bind us up. (Hos. 6:1 NRSV)

---

28. Plutarch, *Moralia* 230F.
29. Martha C. Nussbaum, *The Therapy of Desire: Theory and Practice in Hellenistic Ethics* (Princeton, NJ: Princeton University Press, 1994), 13–47, 484–510.
30. Lucian, *Demonax* 7. Cf. Ps.-Diogenes, *Epistles* 38.4; Dio Chrysostom, *Orations* 8.5; 13.32; 17.1-6; 27.7-8; Diogenes Laertius, *Lives of the Philosophers* 2.70; 6.6.

In an essay on representations of disability in the latter prophets, Sarah Melcher observes that the metaphor of "God as healer" is often used in Scripture to characterize God's restorative work on behalf of the people.[31] That the evangelist found this metaphor applicable to the restorative work of Jesus is apparent from Matthew 13:15, where he quotes Isaiah 6:10:[32]

> For the heart of this people has grown hard,
> And with their ears they hear poorly,
> And they have shut their eyes,
> Lest they should see with their eyes
> And hear with their ears
> And understand with their heart,
> And they repent, and I heal them.

If the people repent, that is, if they accept Jesus and his proclamation of the kingdom, they will experience eschatological "healing" from the Lord.[33] From this perspective, healing can be said to sum up the whole purpose of Jesus' mission, with the sorts of physical healings performed in chapters 8–9 serving as visible signs of the divine healing promised by Isaiah and the other biblical prophets (cf. 8:17).[34]

As Melcher notes, in the Old Testament the depiction of God as healer often belongs to a "pattern of punishment then restoration for God's people, with 'healing' as a primary metaphor of restoration: Jer. 33:1-13; Hos. 6:4–7:10; 11:1–12:1; and so on."[35] The reference to Hosea 6:4–7:10 here (note also the quote of Hos. 6:1 above) is particularly interesting, given that the second element in Jesus'

---

31. Sarah Melcher, "With Whom Do the Disabled Associate? Metaphorical Interplay in the Latter Prophets," in *This Abled Body: Rethinking Disabilities in Biblical Studies*, eds. Hector Avalos, Sarah J. Melcher, and Jeremy Schipper (Atlanta: Society of Biblical Literature, 2007), 115–29. Other examples include Exod. 15:26; 2 Chron. 30:20; Ps. 147:2-3; Isa. 30:26; Jer. 3:22; 8:22; 17:14; Hos. 7:1; 14:4.
32. Translation from Hagner, *Matthew*, 1:370.
33. Cf. John 12:39-40; Acts 28:26-27.
34. France, *The Gospel of Matthew*, 380–81.
35. Melcher, "With Whom Do the Disabled Associate?" 119.

response to the Pharisees (Matt. 9:13a), an element found only in Matthew's version of the story, includes a quotation of Hosea 6:6:[36]

> But go and learn what this means: "I desire mercy (*eleos*) and not sacrifice" . . .

The introductory phrase ("go and learn") may be a rabbinic expression, and so would be appropriate to an exchange that Jesus is having with the Pharisees.[37] The Scripture quote itself is noteworthy for introducing the topic of mercy (*eleos*) into the presentation of Jesus' healing ministry in chapters 8–9.[38] Thematically, such a move is appropriate, seeing how the concept represents for Matthew a cardinal virtue (cf. 5:7; 12:7; 18:33; 23:23), especially in the context of healing stories, where supplicants are often depicted addressing Jesus with pleas for mercy (9:27; 15:22; 17:15; 20:30-31). As such stories suggest, mercy is among the preeminent qualities required of a healer. It is this, and not sacrifice, that God "desires" of those who minister to the sick.[39] Jesus both clarifies and dramatizes the meaning of this mercy through his ministry to society's outcasts, represented in 9:10-11 by the tax collectors and sinners.[40]

In evaluating the significance of Hosea 6:6 within its Matthean context, it should be noted that the Scripture verse not only grounds

---

36. Note that the quotation of Hosea 6:6 in Matthew 12:7 is also redactional and also occurs in the context of a controversy with the Pharisees.

37. Davies and Allison, *Saint Matthew*, 2:104; Nolland, *The Gospel of Matthew*, 387. Charles H. Talbert (*Matthew*, Paideia [Grand Rapids: Baker Academic, 2010], 119) also notes a parallel with *Avot of Rabbi Nathan* 4 (which also quotes Hos. 6:6): "This tradition seems to indicate that the Matthean Jesus was challenging the Pharisees on the basis of their own accepted values."

38. Cf. David Hill, "On the Use and Meaning of Hosea VI.6 in Matthew's Gospel," *NTS* 24 (1977): 107–19.

39. This should not be interpreted as a wholesale rejection of the cultic system. After all, in 8:4 Jesus instructed the cleansed leper to show himself to the priest and make the required offering. Cf. 5:18-19, 23-24; 23:23-28; Ulrich Luz, *Matthew: A Commentary*, Hermeneia (Minneapolis: Fortress Press, 2005), 2:33–34.

40. Heinz Joachim Held, "Matthew as Interpreter of the Miracle Stories," in *Tradition and Interpretation in Matthew*, eds. Günther Bornkamm, Gerhard Barth, and Heinz Joachim Held (Philadelphia: Westminster, 1963), 257–59.

the healing ministry of Jesus in biblical revelation (as in Matt. 8:17 or 13:15) but also associates this ministry with a specific image of God:

(2) You will return to the Lord your God and hearken to his voice . . .
(3) Then the Lord will heal your sins and have mercy (*eleēsei*) on you ... (Deut. 30:2-3)

Have mercy (*eleēson*) on me, Lord, for I am weak. Heal me, Lord, for my bones are dismayed. (Ps. 6:2)

Lord, have mercy (*eleēson*) on me! Heal me, for I have sinned against you. (Ps. 41:4)

Consideration for these verses underscores the importance of reading the first two elements of Jesus' response to the Pharisees in tandem with one another. In his role as "physician" to sinners, Jesus embodies the biblical image of God as healer of the penitent, the mercy he extends to outcasts serving as a reflection of the mercy that God extends to the people when healing (that is, forgiving) their sins.

The unity of Jesus' actions with God's will is further implied by the structural correspondence between the second and third elements of his response to the Pharisees in 9:13:

I desire mercy and not sacrifice.
I came to call not the righteous but sinners.

The parallelism of the two sentences is reinforced by their antithetical structure as well as by the repeated used of first-person singular verbs. The latter feature draws attention to the complex nature of the "self"-attestation that Jesus is offering at this point in the narrative: the reason why "I" came to call sinners, he says, is because "I" desire mercy. Jesus' actions accord with God's will because Jesus himself accords with God's will. He manifests God's will in what he does, what he says, and who he is.

It is from this perspective that we can perhaps best appreciate the literary form of the third element in Jesus' response to the Pharisees. In evaluating the significance of Matthew 9:13b, scholars often compare it with other "I came" (*elthon*) statements in the Gospel,[41] the first and most programmatic of which is Matthew 5:17:

> Do not think that I came (*elthon*) to abolish the law or the prophets; I came not to abolish but to fulfill.

It is possible to read the Scripture quote in 9:13a as a commentary on this statement: one of the ways in which Jesus "fulfills" the prophets is by manifesting the mercy of which Hosea spoke. The statement in 9:13b then extends the thought by specifying those to whom this mercy is directed, that is, to sinners (cf. Luke 19:10; 1 Tim. 1:15).

As helpful as such comparisons are, a more compelling line of inquiry is presented by a different saying in the Gospel, one that includes not only the same verb as the "I came" sayings but also a reference to tax collectors and sinners:

> (16) "To what shall I compare this generation? It is like children sitting in the marketplaces, who call to each other, (17) saying, 'We played the flute for you, and you did not dance; we sang a dirge, and you did not mourn.' (18) For John came neither eating nor drinking, and they say, 'He has a demon!' (19) The Son of Man came (*elthen*) eating and drinking, and they say, 'Look, a gluttonous man and a drunkard, a friend of tax collectors and sinners!' Yet wisdom is justified by her works." (20) Then he began to denounce the cities in which most of his deeds of power were done, because they did not repent. (Matt. 11:16-20)

The reference to Jesus as a friend (*philos*) of tax collectors and sinners is consistent with the presentation of his activities in 9:10-13 insofar

---

41. Cf. Matt. 10:34-35; 20:28; Luke 12:49, 51; John 5:43; 6:38, 42; 11:27; 12:27, 46-47; 18:37; Warren Carter, "Jesus' 'I Have Come' Statements in Matthew," *CBQ* 60 (1998): 44–62; Simon J. Gathercole, *The Pre-existent Son: Recovering the Christologies of Matthew, Mark, and Luke* (Grand Rapids: Eerdmans, 2006), 148–76.

as sharing a meal with someone could be understood as a gesture of friendship.[42] The statements in 11:18-19 indicate that this sort of "eating and drinking" was something for which Jesus was well-known as well as something that distinguished him from John the Baptist (see Chapter Ten). The reference to "works" (*erga*) in 11:19 most obviously recalls "the works of the Messiah" (*ta erga tou christou*) in 11:2, that is, Jesus' messianic "works" of preaching and healing as summarized in 11:5, which in turn looks back to his activities in chapters 5–9.[43]

What is most intriguing about 11:19, of course, is its reference to wisdom. In contrast to the version of this saying in Luke 7:35,[44] Jesus is presented here as acting not as an emissary of wisdom but as an incarnation of wisdom. In Matthew's opinion, divine *Sophia* herself is active in Jesus' works, including his works of healing—both physical healing and the sort of healing that occurs when he eats and drinks with outcasts.[45] As Celia Deutsch observes, texts like this (cf. Matt. 11:25-30; 12:38-42; 13:53-58; 23:34-39) issue an implicit invitation to reflect on the identity and significance of Jesus in terms of the prevailing "Wisdom myth," especially as it can be reconstructed from the books of Proverbs and Sirach.[46] Looking specifically at chapter

---

42. For friendship in meal ethics, see Smith, *From Symposium to Eucharist*, 55.

43. For more on Matthew 11:2-5, see Chapter Twelve.

44. "Yet wisdom is justified by all her children." Cf. Joel B. Green, *The Gospel of Luke*, NICNT (Grand Rapids: Eerdmans, 1997), 304–305.

45. For a more nuanced view, see Russell Pregeant, "The Wisdom Passages in Matthew's Story," in *Treasures New and Old: Recent Contributions to Matthean Studies*, eds. David R. Bauer and Mark Allen Powell (Atlanta: Scholars, 1996), 197–232, especially p. 201: "if we grant that for Matthew Jesus' deeds are in fact to be identified with those of Wisdom, this does not necessitate the view that Jesus *is* Wisdom." For sapiential themes in Matthew, see also Grant Macaskill, *Revealed Wisdom and Inaugurated Eschatology in Ancient Judaism and Early Christianity*, JSJSup 115 (Leiden: Brill, 2007), 115–95; M. Jack Suggs, *Wisdom, Christology, and Law in Matthew's Gospel* (Cambridge, MA: Harvard University Press, 1970), 99–127; Ben Witherington, *Jesus the Sage: The Pilgrimage of Wisdom* (Minneapolis: Fortress Press, 1994), 341–68.

46. Celia M. Deutsch, *Lady Wisdom, Jesus, and the Sages: Metaphor and Social Context in Matthew's Gospel* (Valley Forge, PA: Trinity Press International, 1996), 21, 42, 142–47.

11, she explains that the reason why Matthew presents Jesus as personified Wisdom is "because, for him, Jesus, like Wisdom, is prophet of repentance and sage. Like Wisdom he, too, is both accepted and rejected."[47]

As instructive as Deutsch's comments are, they fail to account adequately for the fact that Matthew 11:19b, the most explicit reference to Jesus as Wisdom in the Gospel, occurs in a context not only where he is depicted as a preacher of repentance (11:20) but also where he is identified as a friend of tax collectors and sinners (11:19a). If we include Matthew 9:9-13 in such reflections, a passage where such identification also figures prominently, it is possible to develop an even deeper appreciation for how the story of Wisdom informs the story of Jesus. Note in particular how the book of Proverbs depicts *Sophia* as reproving the wayward and "calling" them to repentance (Prov. 1:20-23; 8:1-5), summoning them to her "house" (Prov. 9:1; cf. Sir. 14:23-27), and inviting them to "eat and drink" from the banquet that she has prepared (Prov. 9:2-6; cf. Sir. 24:19-22). As we have seen, these elements are also present in Matthew 9:9-13: Jesus "calls" sinners (9:9, 13), reclines with them in "the house" (9:10), and shares a meal with them (9:10-11). The theme of Wisdom's rejection (e.g., Prov. 1:24-25) is hinted at as well (Matt. 9:11), a theme driven home by Matthew 11:20, where we learn that the people of Capernaum failed to repent despite the "mighty works" that they witnessed (i.e., the works narrated in chapters 8–9).

If elements of the Wisdom myth are indeed at work structuring the action of 9:9-13, such a depiction would be relevant to the evangelist's sectarian agenda as described in Chapter One. What the Pharisees (and their successors) see as offensive, Matthew and his readers see as an extension of salvation history.[48] Jesus is not just

47. Ibid., 53.

some "teacher" (9:11) but Wisdom incarnate; his works of healing are not violations of ritual purity but revelations of Wisdom's ongoing activity in the world, "a pure emanation of the glory of the Almighty" into which "nothing defiled gains entrance" (Wis. 7:25). Insofar as *Sophia* was also thought to be active in creation (e.g., Prov. 8:22-31; cf. Wis. 7:22; 9:9; Sir. 1:9-10) and the source of life (e.g., Prov. 3:13-22; cf. Sir. 1:20), in his role as personified Wisdom Jesus can be properly understood as the agent of new creation and the source of new life, manifested in the restored bodies and reformed lives of the people he heals.

48. Jewish sages were not supposed to associate with sinners (e.g., *m. Avot* 1:7), as noted by Eric Ottenheijm, "The Shared Meal—A Therapeutic Device: The Function and Meaning of Hos 6:6 in Matt 9:10-13," *NovT* 53 (2011): 1, 9.

10

Things Old and New: Matthew 9:14-17

In chapter 9, Jesus engages in debates with the scribes (9:1-8), with the Pharisees (9:9-13), and, now, with the disciples of John (9:14-17). Structurally, this triad of consecutive controversy-laden stories helps to connect the triad of miracle stories in 8:23—9:8 with the triad of miracle stories in 9:18-34. Thematically, the stories in 9:1-17 have a notable cumulative effect: the rift between Jesus and the "old" order (9:16-17) is substantive, wide-ranging, and expanding. The healing ministry of Jesus generates debate and, ultimately, rejection (9:34).

Matthew 9:14-17 continues from 9:10-13 with no indication of a transition in time or place. Evidently, Jesus and the disciples are still in "the house" dining with tax collectors and sinners. Having responded to a question about his eating practices from the Pharisees, he responds now to a question about his eating practices from another group, the disciples of John the Baptist. In both cases the interlocutors appear rather abruptly, and in both cases it is clear that their questions are meant as objections. Thus the two stories in 9:10-17 exhibit continuity in setting, form, and theme.

In evaluating the social and religious significance of the question in Matthew 9:14, it is important to remember that Jesus was not the only prophetic figure of the time who successfully called tax collectors to repentance.[1] According to Matthew 21:32, John did so as well. As we have just seen (in Chapter Nine), however, Matthew 11:18-19 indicates a fundamental contrast between Jesus and John in terms of the form of their respective ministries, which would presumably correspond to a fundamental contrast in the way of life embraced by their followers. For his part, John "came neither eating nor drinking" (11:18), a hyperbolic statement implying that he and his disciples took the practice of ritual fasting (and perhaps other ascetical practices) to extreme lengths (cf. 3:4).[2] Jesus, meanwhile, is castigated as "a gluttonous man and a drunkard, a friend of tax collectors and sinners" (11:19), no doubt a reference to the sort of incident narrated in 9:10-13. From this perspective John and Jesus can be seen as competitors, reaching out to the same audience (tax collectors and sinners) but doing so with markedly different approaches (asceticism versus celebration).

(18) John's disciples and the Pharisees were fasting. And they came and said to him, "Why do John's disciples and the disciples of the Pharisees fast, but your disciples do not fast?"	(14) Then the disciples of John came to him, saying, "Why do we and the Pharisees fast, but your disciples do not fast?"
(19) And Jesus said to them, "The attendants of the bridegroom cannot fast while the bridegroom is with them, can they? As long as they have the bridegroom with them, they cannot fast. (20) But days will come when the bridegroom is taken from them, and then they will fast on that day.	(15) And Jesus said to them, "The attendants of the bridegroom cannot mourn as long as the bridegroom is with them, can they? But days will come when the bridegroom is taken from them, and then they will fast.

1. As this passage also reminds us, Jesus is not the only character in the narrative whose ministry attracts disciples. For John's disciples, see also Matthew 11:2; 14:12.
2. For more on John the Baptist, see John P. Meier, *A Marginal Jew: Rethinking the Historical Jesus* (New York: Doubleday, 1994), 2:19–233.

(21) No one sews a piece of unshrunk cloth on an old cloak; otherwise, the patch pulls away from it, the new from the old and a worse tear occurs.	(16) No one puts a piece of unshrunk cloth on an old cloak; for the patch pulls away from the cloak and a worse tear occurs.
(22) And no one puts new wine into old wineskins; otherwise, the wine will burst the skins and the wine is destroyed, and also the wineskins; rather new wine is put into fresh wineskins." (Mark 2:18-22)	(17) Neither do they put new wine into old wineskins; otherwise, the wineskins burst and the wine pours out and the wineskins are destroyed; but they put new wine into fresh wineskins, and both are preserved." (Matt. 9:14-17)

In addition to further connecting this pericope with the one that precedes it, the reference to the Pharisees in 9:14 serves as a reminder that ritual fasting was widely observed in Second Temple Judaism, a fact that makes the absence of fasting among Jesus' followers even more striking. We should not assume, however, that John necessarily agreed with the Pharisees regarding the exigencies of this practice (cf. 3:7). On the contrary, it is apparent that communal decisions about how, when, and why to fast functioned as conspicuous markers of both group identity and group differentiation at the time.[3]

Given this function, it is not surprising that both parties in the exchange narrated in Matthew 9:14-15 take it for granted that fasting bears not only social but also theological significance. The precise nature of this significance, however, is not made explicit in the text, and we should not assume that the practice had the same meaning at all times for all participants. In light of the prominence attached to the theme in his preaching (Matt. 3:2, 8, 11), it is likely that John understood fasting specifically as a sign or ritual of *repentance*, an interpretation that would have been grounded in various biblical

---

3. Matthew 6:16-18 provides further evidence that fasting was a contested practice, at least in terms of how and why it was observed. Cf. Matt. 4:2; 17:21; Mark 9:29; Luke 2:37; 5:33-35; 18:12; Acts 10:30; 13:2-3; 14:23; 27:9; 1 Cor. 7:5; 2 Cor. 6:5; 11:27; *Did.* 8.1; David A. Lambert, "Fast, Fasting," *New Interpreter's Dictionary of the Bible* (Nashville: Abingdon, 2007), 2:431–34.

traditions (e.g., 1 Sam. 7:6; 1 Kgs. 21:27-29; Joel 2:12-16; Jonah 3:5-9).[4] Such an interpretation would certainly have been germane to a conversation taking place in the presence of "many" sinners (Matt. 9:10). As the broader context of the Gospel makes clear, neither the practice of fasting (Matt. 4:2; 6:16-18) nor the need for repentance (Matt. 4:17; 11:20-21; 12:41) were matters about which Jesus was unconcerned. Yet it is also clear that he parted ways with the Baptist when it came to the meaning of such matters for those awaiting the advent of God's kingdom.[5] As Jesus' reply in Matthew 9:15 specifies, if he differs from John in the role that he assigns fasting in the lives of his disciples, it is because he differs from John in the role that he himself has been assigned in salvation history.

At first glance, Jesus' talk of a bridegroom and his attendants seems incongruous with the narrative situation. After all, up to this point there has been no mention of weddings or wedding plans. When we as readers recognize the metaphorical impact of his answer, however, we see that it is his interlocutors and not Jesus who are acting incongruously.

As we saw above in Chapter Three, the messianic age was sometimes likened to a great banquet.[6] In certain biblical traditions, this banquet is likened specifically to a wedding feast (e.g., Rev. 19:9), imagery that draws on the biblical metaphor of God being married to Israel (e.g., Hos. 2:19-20) or of God being Israel's bridegroom (e.g., Isa. 62:5).[7] The application of such imagery to Matthew's

---

4. Cf. Tob. 12:8-10; *Pss. Sol.* 3:8; *m. Ta'an.* 2:1; *Gos. Thom.* 104; E. P. Sanders, *Jesus and Judaism* (Philadelphia: Fortress Press, 1985), 206–207.

5. Tobias Hägerland, "Jesus and the Rites of Repentance," *NTS* 52 (2006): 166–87.

6. E.g., Isa. 25:6-8; Matt. 8:11-12; Luke 22:28-30; *4 Ezra* 6:52; *5 Ezra* 2:38; *1 En.* 62:14; *3 En.* 48A:10; *2 Bar.* 29:4-7; 1QSa 2:14-22. Cf. Peter-Ben Smit, *Fellowship and Food in the Kingdom: Eschatological Meals and Scenes of Utopian Abundance in the New Testament,* WUNT 2.234 (Tübingen: Mohr Siebeck, 2008), 201–58.

7. Marianne Blickenstaff, *While the Bridegroom is With Them: Marriage, Family, Gender and Violence in the Gospel of Matthew,* JSNTSup 292 (London: T&T Clark, 2005), 26–29.

presentation of Jesus is evident especially in Matthew 22:1-14, where we learn that "the kingdom of heaven may be compared to a king who gave a wedding feast for his son" (22:2), and 25:1-13, where we learn that "the kingdom of heaven may be compared to ten virgins, who took their lamps out to meet the bridegroom" (25:1).[8] The application of such imagery in 9:15 both clarifies the symbolic significance of the meal in 9:10-13 and introduces a thematic shift in the narrative. It is only at this point that the characters in the story learn that the one who has called (i.e., invited) sinners to the table is in fact the bridegroom and that the meal he shares with them is in fact a foretaste of the wedding feast.[9] Through Jesus they are in the very presence of God's healing mercy and eschatological blessing. The time of messianic fulfillment has come, and to respond with fasting would be to misunderstand the nature of that fulfillment.

This is not, however, the totality of Jesus' answer. In the second half of 9:15 he continues with a prediction that plays a critical role within the context of 9:14-17 insofar as it not only refines but also redirects the conversation. Jesus does not object to the practice of fasting as such; rather, its observance must suit the occasion. To clarify this he draws a distinction between two periods of time, one of celebration when the bridegroom is present and one of sorrow when the bridegroom will be absent. While this distinction is clear enough on the metaphorical level, commentators have long struggled to explain its meaning on a practical level. Some suspect that the latter refers to the time between the resurrection and the Parousia.[10]

---

8. Bridegroom imagery is applied to Jesus elsewhere in John 3:29; 2 Cor. 11:2; Eph. 5:22-27; Rev. 19:7; 21:2, 9. Cf. Blickenstaff, *While the Bridegroom is With Them*, 46–109; Smit, *Fellowship and Food*, 229–48.

9. Joel Marcus, *Mark*, AB 27 (New Haven, CT: Yale University Press, 2000), 1:233: "In Jewish law wedding guests were freed from certain religious obligations that were deemed to be incompatible with the joy of the occasion; e.g., *b. Sukk.* 25b."

10. E.g., W. D. Davies and Dale C. Allison, *The Gospel According to Saint Matthew*, ICC (London: T&T Clark, 1991), 2:111. Cf. Meier, *A Marginal Jew*, 2:439–50.

This interpretation would not be consistent, however, with texts like Matthew 18:20 and 28:20, which assert the ongoing presence of the risen Lord with his followers, and Matthew 24:42-44 and 25:13, which characterize the period of the post-resurrection church as a time of preparedness and vigilance, not mourning. Other commentators think that what is being referred to in 9:15b is not the period of the post-resurrection church at all but rather the period of the Passion.[11]

Even as the metaphorical language of 9:15 generates such questions, focusing too much on finding their answer may cause us to miss the more fundamental point being made. As is often the case, attention to changes that the evangelist has made in his source material helps to illuminate his priorities as a storyteller. An especially important clue in this regard occurs in 9:15a, where Matthew has substituted "mourn" for "fast" in Mark 2:19a:[12]

> The attendants of the bridegroom cannot *fast* while the bridegroom is with them, can they? . . . (20) But days will come when the bridegroom is taken from them, and then they will fast on that day. (Mark 2:19-20)

> The attendants of the bridegroom cannot *mourn* as long as the bridegroom is with them, can they? But days will come when the bridegroom is taken from them, and then they will fast. (Matt. 9:15)

As W. D. Davies and Dale Allison note, the redaction in 9:15a "strengthens the allusion to Jesus' death" in 9:15b, which ominously forecasts a time when the bridegroom will no longer be with his attendants.[13] As they also note, the expression "days will come" is used elsewhere in Scripture to preface eschatological predictions, and

---

11. E.g., John Nolland, *The Gospel of Matthew*, NIGTC (Grand Rapids: Eerdmans, 2005), 390–91. Note that Matthew drops the reference in Mark 2:20 to "on that day."
12. As is his custom, Matthew abbreviates, dropping Mark 2:19b.
13. Davies and Allison, *Saint Matthew*, 2:109. For the association of fasting with grief, see 2 Sam. 1:12; 12:22; Zech. 7:5; Bar. 1:5 (cf. Matt. 6:16-18). *4 Ezra* 10:1-4 relates a vision in which a woman mourns and fasts after the death of her son, the bridegroom.

so its use here encourages the audience to interpret this death as an eschatological event.[14] What is important to recognize, however, is that the order of Jesus' statements in 9:15a+b has the effect of turning conventional eschatological expectations on their head: the time of eschatological mourning was supposed to give way to the time of eschatological fulfillment, not vice versa.[15] The meaning of this reversal becomes clearer as we read further into the pericope. Logically, the declaration in 9:15a should have been sufficient as an answer to the query of 9:14. The continuation in 9:15b not only digresses from the topic but creates a jarring juxtaposition: how are the guests supposed to celebrate knowing that the bridegroom will be taken from them?

To the parabolic analogy that Jesus introduced in 9:15 he attaches two further analogies (9:16 and 17), creating a three-part answer corresponding to the three-part answer he had given earlier at the dinner (9:12-13). The three segments in 9:15-17 are connected logically insofar as all involve nonsensical combinations: mourning at a wedding feast, patching an old garment with unshrunk cloth, and putting new wine into old wineskins. At the same time, it is crucial to observe how these additional analogies do more than just further ground Jesus' argument in traditional imagery. They also extend his argument to its "logical" conclusion: such combinations are not only nonsensical but as such also lead to unwanted results.

By this point it is apparent that Jesus is no longer simply responding to the question posed in 9:14. He is also looking back at the events of 9:1-14 as a whole, asserting the incompatibility of

---

14. E.g., Isa. 39:6; Jer. 7:32; 23:5; 31:31; Amos 4:2; 9:13; Luke 17:22; 21:6.
15. Marcus, *Mark*, 1:237: "in a startling reversal of the usual Jewish eschatological pattern, the period of messianic redemption . . . is *followed* rather than preceded by the period of messianic woes" (emphasis original). The point of the passage, however, is not to reorient the eschatological timetable but to reorient one's understanding of the eschatological bridegroom. Cf. Boris Repschinski, *The Controversy Stories in the Gospel of Matthew*, FRLANT 189 (Göttingen: Vandenhoeck & Ruprecht, 2000), 85–87.

the "old" (represented by the scribes, the Pharisees, and John) with the "new" (represented by Jesus and his followers). The latter cannot be contained by the former: new wine requires new wineskins. In 9:15-17, then, Jesus transforms a question about a specific practice into a sweeping assertion about the nature of salvation history. The appearance of the bridegroom is not an isolated event but the sign of a new era that transforms the old. It is not therefore just fasting but all theological practices that must be reevaluated in the light of this reality.[16]

The logic informing this reality, however, entails more than the incompatibility of the old and the new. In this regard, we should bear in mind that the combinations presented in 9:16 and 17 lead to results that are not just unwanted but disastrous. In order to appreciate the full impact of the scenarios that Jesus depicts in his response to John's disciples, however, it is necessary to recognize the level of violence implicit in their symbolism. To begin with, the bridegroom of 9:15 is not simply absent. Rather, he is "taken away" (*aparthē ap'*) from his attendants, a possible allusion to Isaiah 53:8: "For his life is taken away (*airetai apo*) from the earth" (cf. Gen. 5:24; 2 Kgs. 2:10; Prov. 24:11; Jer. 11:19).[17] The use of a passive verb here brings to mind the passion predictions that speak of Jesus being "handed over" to the authorities (Matt. 17:22; 20:18) as well as passages in the passion narrative itself that speak of him being "seized" (Matt. 26:50) and "led away" to the authorities (Matt. 26:57; 27:2) and to his crucifixion (Matt. 27:31). A specific lexical connection between the statements in 9:15 and 9:16

16. An analogy can be drawn with 5:17-20 and the way this passage creates a conceptual framework for reevaluating the practices discussed in 5:21—6:18, including fasting (6:16-18).
17. Meier, *Marginal Jew*, 2:500. Cf. Donald Juel, *Messianic Exegesis: Christological Interpretation of the Old Testament in Early Christianity* (Philadelphia: Fortress Press, 1987), 119–33; Adrian M. Leske, "The Influence of Isaiah 40–66 on Christology in Matthew and Luke: A Comparison," *SBLSP* 33 (1994): 897–916. Note that Matt. 8:17 cites Isa. 53:4, Matt. 27:12 alludes to Isa. 53:7, Matt. 27:57 alludes to Isa. 53:9, Matt. 20:28 alludes to Isa. 53:10-12, and Matt. 12:29, 26:27-28, and 27:38 allude to Isa. 53:12.

provides some additional insight as to how the evangelist may have understood the meaning of Jesus' death:

> . . . the bridegroom is taken away (*aparthē ap'*) from them . . .

> . . . for the patch pulls away (*airei . . . apo*) from the garment . . .

The former utilizes a verbal construction (*apairō apo*) similar to that found in the latter (*airō apo*), suggesting a correlation between the events they describe. The old order will "take away" Jesus because what he represents "takes away" from its very fabric (cf. Matt. 21:43), the eschatological power he embodies in essence tearing the world apart. As Joel Marcus observes, the word used in 9:16 for "tear" (*schisma*) is used elsewhere in the New Testament of "schisms" between different social groups.[18] Given the allusion in 9:15 to Jesus' death, however, a more compelling analogy comes from an event with which his death coincides:

> And Jesus cried out again with a loud voice, and yielded up his spirit. (51) And at once the veil of the temple was torn (*eschisthē*) in two from top to bottom . . . (Matt. 27:50-51)

The tearing of the old garment in 9:16 foreshadows the tearing of the temple's veil in 27:51, the implicit violence in both cases being linked to the violent end of Jesus himself.[19] Viewed from this perspective, the veil can be seen as another symbol of the "old" order that opposes Jesus, while the veil's rending serves as a portent of its destruction (cf. 24:2; 27:40).[20]

---

18. Marcus, *Mark*, 1:234. See John 7:43; 9:16; 10:19; 1 Cor. 1:10; 11:18; 12:25; cf. Acts 14:4; 23:7.

19. Cf. Daniel M. Gurtner, *The Torn Veil: Matthew's Exposition of the Death of Jesus*, SNTSMS 139 (Cambridge: Cambridge University Press, 2007), 170. Note that Matthew 9:16 is the only place in the Gospel where *schisma* is used, and that Matthew 27:51 is the only place in the Gospel where *schizō* is used.

The symbolism of violence extends into 9:17, the final verse of the pericope. The reference to wine in the context of a meal scene would have been natural enough, especially insofar as it was traditionally included among the items served at the messianic banquet.[21] In 9:17b, however, the reference to wine is employed to depict not a scene of fulfillment but a scene of destruction:[22]

> . . . the wine will burst the skins and the wine is destroyed, and also the wineskins. (Mark 2:22)

> . . . the wineskins burst, and the wine pours out (*ekcheitai*) and the wineskins are destroyed. (Matt. 9:17)

Note how Matthew has expanded the imagery of his source by adding a reference to how the wine "pours out" of the wineskins (cf. Luke 5:37). This redaction has the effect of creating a metaphorical link with another passage in the First Gospel, one in which Jesus is shown using the occasion of a meal to interpret the eschatological significance of his death:[23]

> . . . this is my blood of the covenant, which is poured out (*ekchunnomenon*) for many for forgiveness of sins. (26:28)

Within the symbolic world of the Gospel, the imagery of wine being poured out signifies the blood that will be poured out of Jesus' body at his death, the blood of a sacrifice that inaugurates a new covenant, one defined by the forgiveness of sins.[24] The relevance of

---

20. See Davies and Allison, *Saint Matthew*, 3:630–31, including especially the quotation of *Lives of the Prophets* 12:12. They also note patristic sources that liken the rending of the veil to the tearing of a garment (in mourning), e.g., Origen, *Commentary on Matthew: Fragments* 560.

21. Isa. 25:6; *2 Bar.* 29:5; 1QSa 2:17-20. Cf. John 2:1-11.

22. For the imagery of bursting wineskins, see Josh. 9:13; Job 32:19.

23. The verb *ekcheō* is often used with reference to sacrifice (e.g., Exod. 29:12; Lev. 4:7, 18, 25, 30, 34; Sir. 50:15) or violent death (e.g., Gen. 9:6; Num. 35:33; Deut. 19:10; Jer. 7:6; Joel 4:19). For the association of wine with blood, see Gen. 49:11; Deut. 32:14; Isa. 49:26; Sir. 39:26; 50:15.

24. Note that the reference to forgiveness of sins in Matthew 26:28 is redactional (cf. Mark 14:24).

this signification for the interpretation of 9:17 is increased by the fact that Jesus has just alluded to his death (9:15b) and employed imagery suggesting the violence attending that death (9:16). Bear in mind, too, that Jesus utters these words in the presence of "many" sinners (9:10). The imagery of 9:15b-17, then, serves as a reminder that the grace and redemption conveyed by Jesus' act of dining with such people will be fully realized "for many" (26:28) only through his death.

This death, of course, will not be a natural one:

> (34) Therefore I am sending to you prophets and sages and scribes, some of whom you will kill and crucify, and some of whom you will scourge in your synagogues and pursue from city to city, (35) so that upon you may come all the righteous blood poured out (*ekchunnomenon*) on the earth … (Matt. 23:34-35)

If 26:28 explicates the meaning of Christ's death, 23:34-35 explicates its nature. It is, like the deaths of all those who represent the new order, the result of violent conflict with the old order. This disturbing reality is underscored in our pericope by one last image. When new wine is put into old wineskins, the wine not only pours out of the wineskins; the wineskins themselves are "destroyed" (9:17). The verb employed here (*apollumi*) is found scattered throughout the Gospel to describe both the efforts of the old order to kill Jesus (2:13; 12:14; 27:20) as well as the divine judgment awaiting those who murder the righteous (21:41; 22:7). The relation between the old and the new is, in essence, defined by destruction:

> Do not think that I came to bring peace on the earth; I came to bring not peace but a sword. (Matt. 10:34)

The struggles to which this statement alludes (cf. 11:12) foreshadow the time of the apocalyptic tribulation, a time of war, death, deceit, and lawlessness (24:4-28). Indeed, as 9:15-17 implies, with the advent of the bridegroom the eschatological conflict has already been joined, a conflict into which the bridegroom's attendants are necessarily caught up. As Jesus will soon warn them (10:5-42), in carrying out their mission of preaching and healing (10:1, 7-8) the disciples will be scourged, betrayed, hated, persecuted, and maligned—experiences that confirm the eschatological nature of that mission.[25]

The sort of conflictual scenario projected by these texts has profound implications for understanding the presentation of healing in the First Gospel. In a sense, the analogies that Jesus draws in 9:15-17 look back not only to the controversies of 9:1-14 but also to all of the miracles that he has performed up to this point in the narrative. These mighty deeds must now be reevaluated not only in the shadow of the cross (see on 8:17) but also in terms of the power of the cross to overturn the world. Jesus and those who follow him are acting as agents of eschatological transformation through whom the power of the new order "bursts" through the old, with each healing serving as a sign and enactment of a broader confrontation with everything that opposes the impending kingdom.

Is there hope beyond the conflict? In a statement unique to Matthew's version of the story, Jesus concludes his response to John's disciples with the promise that when new wine is put into fresh (*kanous*) wineskins both are "preserved" (9:17). In light of the discussion above, this can be read as an anticipation of Jesus' promise to the disciples at the Last Supper that he will drink the fruit of the vine "afresh" (*kainon*) with them in his Father's kingdom (26:29), another reference to the messianic banquet. While it is apparent that the statement about "preserving" applies grammatically to the new

---

25. Davies and Allison, *Saint Matthew*, 2:180–97; Donald A. Hagner, *Matthew*, WBC 33 (Dallas: Word Books, 1993), 1:274–80; Douglas R. A. Hare, *The Theme of Jewish Persecution of Christians in the Gospel According to Saint Matthew*, SNTSMS 6 (Cambridge: Cambridge University Press, 1967), 96–114; Stephen C. Barton, *Discipleship and Family Ties in Mark and Matthew*, SNTSMS 80 (Cambridge: Cambridge University Press, 1994), 155–78.

wine and the new wineskins (i.e., the immediate subject of the verb), it is possible that the statement applies logically to the old (*palaious*) wineskins in some manner as well.[26] After all, even if the scribes as a group are representative of the old order, Jesus can still proclaim that, "every scribe who has been made a disciple for the kingdom of heaven is like a man who is a householder, who brings out of his treasure new (*kaina*) and old (*palaia*) things" (Matt. 13:52).[27] This suggests that the relationship between the old and the new is not defined entirely by conflict, a point consistent with the person and mission of Jesus himself, who came not to abolish the law and the prophets but to fulfill them (5:17).

26. Davies and Allison, *Saint Matthew*, 2:115.
27. Cf. Matt. 23:34; Celia M. Deutsch, *Lady Wisdom, Jesus, and the Sages: Metaphor and Social Context in Matthew's Gospel* (Valley Forge, PA: Trinity Press International, 1996), 111–41; David E. Orton, *The Understanding Scribe: Matthew and the Apocalyptic Ideal*, JSNTSup 25 (Sheffield: Sheffield Academic Press, 1989), 137–76.

11

Daughters in the Borderland:
Matthew 9:18-26

A triad of stories defined by controversy (9:1-8, 9-13, 14-17) gives way to a triad of stories defined by the miraculous: the story of the official's daughter and the woman with a flow of blood (9:18-26), the story of the two blind men (9:27-31), and the story of the mute demoniac (9:32-34). While in each of the previous triads of miracle stories (8:1-15; 8:23—9:8) Jesus cured a total of three individuals, in this triad, the total increases to five. In addition, one of these episodes (9:18-19, 23-26) involves a revivification, arguably the most impressive of his miracles. Jesus will refer to this and related wonders later in the narrative:

> . . . the blind receive sight and the lame walk, the lepers are cleansed and the deaf hear, the dead are raised up . . . (Matt. 11:5)

Here Jesus recapitulates "the works of the Messiah" (11:2), deeds that, as such, accord with biblical prophecy.[1] Note that three of the five events enumerated in 11:5 are narrated in 9:18-34 (for the other two see 8:1-4 and 9:1-8), suggesting that this final triad of miracle stories plays a more substantive role in anticipating 11:2-5, with the latter being a passage of programmatic significance within the Gospel for articulating Jesus' christological status.[2] In concert with this, in the final triad we also see the matter of *publicity* emerging more overtly as both a narrative and theological concern, each of the three stories being punctuated with a report about Jesus' expanding reputation (9:26, 31, 33).[3] Despite his efforts to maintain secrecy (9:25, 30), word of Jesus' fame as a healer is getting out, culminating in the contrasting responses of 9:33 and 9:34, responses that appear to look back not only to the miracle in 9:32 but also to the whole set of miracles in chapters 8–9. The evangelist's point in structuring the narrative this way seems clear enough: Jesus' ministry of healing has the effect of creating a division between the people and their religious leaders, a theme upon which subsequent passages in the Gospel will elaborate (e.g., 12:1-45).

For his account of the official's daughter and the woman with a flow of blood (9:18-26), it is apparent that Matthew relies on Mark 5:21-43. It is also apparent, however, that Matthew has altered the story's context. In the Second Gospel, the story is preceded by the story of the Gerasene demoniac (Mark 5:1-20). In the First Gospel, it is preceded by a story in which Jesus dines with sinners (9:10-13) and answers a question about fasting (9:14-17), events that Mark places at an earlier point in the narrative (Mark 2:15-22).

1. See the discussion of this passage in Chapter Twelve.
2. On Matthew 11:5 and its bearing on Matthew's presentation of the Davidic Messiah, see Lidija Novakovic, *Messiah, the Healer of the Sick: A Study of Jesus as the Son of David in the Gospel of Matthew*, WUNT 2.170 (Tübingen: Mohr Siebeck, 2003), 152–84.
3. As John Nolland (*The Gospel of Matthew*, NIGTC [Grand Rapids: Eerdmans, 2005], 398) observes, in designing chapters 8–9 the evangelist has postponed references in his source material to the spread of Jesus' reputation until the end of the unit; for example, Matt. 9:26 is based on Mark 1:28, Matt. 9:31 is based on Mark 1:45, and Matt. 9:33 is based on Mark 2:12.

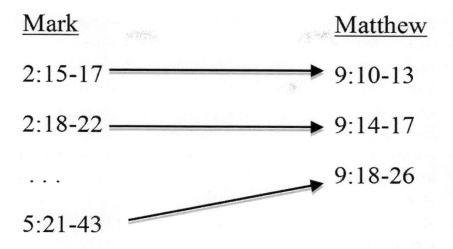

Mark	Matthew
2:15-17 ⟶	9:10-13
2:18-22 ⟶	9:14-17
. . .	9:18-26
5:21-43 ⟶	

In addition to changing the story's context, Matthew also changes its introduction:

> (21) When Jesus had crossed again in the boat to the other side, a large crowd gathered around him; and he was by the sea. (22) Then one of the synagogue officials named Jairus came up . . . (Mark 5:21-22)

> While he was saying these things to them, suddenly a certain official came in . . . (Matt. 9:18)

In the Second Gospel, the scene opens with Jesus disembarking from a boat in a public place. In the First Gospel, the scene opens with Jesus still reclining at table in "the house" (Matt. 9:10), talking "to them," that is, to the disciples of John (Matt. 9:14).[4] It is likely that Matthew's inspiration for this transition comes from Mark:

> While he was still speaking . . . (Mark 5:35)

> While he was speaking these things . . . (Matt. 9:18)

---

4. Boris Repschinski, *The Controversy Stories in the Gospel of Matthew*, FRLANT 189 (Göttingen: Vandenhoeck & Ruprecht, 2000), 83: "The reader can imagine Jesus in the house of the meal until he gets up in 9:19."

Despite the similarities in form, however, the two phrases serve different functions. Mark's version of the phrase creates a narrative overlap between the story of the daughter and the story of the woman, highlighting the dramatic link between the two figures: the former dies "while" Jesus is detained interacting with the latter. Matthew's version of the phrase, by contrast, creates a narrative overlap between the story of the official and the story involving John's disciples: the former approaches Jesus "while" Jesus addresses the latter.

Through his manner of both rearranging and rewriting his source material, then, the evangelist appears to be inviting his readers to ponder how Matthew 9:10-17 and Matthew 9:18-26 might relate to one another. Unfortunately, commentators have had little to say about the possible significance of this relationship. An exception in this regard is John Nolland, who suggests that what Matthew presents in 9:18-26 serves as "a further instance of what Jesus has just been speaking of" in 9:14-17, namely, the "rubric" identified by Jesus in 9:17: "new wine into fresh wineskins."[5] Accordingly, the wondrous deeds that follow in 9:18-34 attest to "the newness of what God is now doing" in Jesus, such events being "unmatched in the history of Israel" (cf. 9:33b).[6] While Nolland focuses on the miracles themselves, Elaine Wainwright understands 9:18-26 to be connected to 9:10-17 by the theme of social inclusion. In 9:18-26, "Jesus confronts powerful taboos relating to women and uncleanness." This narrative is then "placed alongside the parables of the new and old. Just as Jesus called a tax collector and ate with sinners, thus breaking down the categories for inclusion or exclusion set up by religious leaders (9:9-13), so too he breaks down the

---

5. Nolland, *The Gospel of Matthew*, 394.
6. Ibid., 399.

boundaries which exclude women and girls" from participating in salvation.[7]

Yet another option is to sidestep the question altogether and posit a structural break between the two pericopes. W. D. Davies and Dale C. Allison, for example, divide the contents of chapters 8–9 into three units (8:1-22, 8:23—9:17, and 9:18-38), with each unit consisting of three miracle stories followed by "teaching material."[8] When analyzing the third unit, though, they wrestle with the question of why Matthew places the story of the official's daughter before rather than after the pair of redactional healing stories in 9:27-34. As they observe, its account of raising the dead (insofar as it constitutes the most impressive of Jesus' miracles) would have made more sense as the climax of both the triad of miracle stories in 9:18-34 and the cycle of miracle stories assembled in chapters 8–9. Such an arrangement also would have aligned more precisely with the catalog of miracles in 11:5, where raising the dead is mentioned last (cf. Isa. 35:5-6). Their opinion is that the evangelist concludes with the story of the mute demoniac (9:32-34) rather than with the story of the official's daughter because "he needed an exorcism in order to conclude with the Pharisees' charge about Beelzebul, for this charge is part of the introduction to chapter 10."[9] While this may explain why Matthew places the story of the mute demoniac last in the triad of miracles in 9:18-34, it fails to explain why he places the story of the daughter and the woman first.

My own opinion is that Matthew placed this story first in the triad because he wanted to connect its imagery with that of 9:10-17,

---

7. Elaine M. Wainwright, *Towards A Feminist Critical Reading of the Gospel According to Matthew*, BZNW 60 (Berlin: Walter de Gruyter, 1991), 213. As Clinton Wahlen (*Jesus and the Impurity of Spirits in the Synoptic Gospels*, WUNT 2.185 [Tübingen: Mohr Siebeck, 2004], 116) points out, in both 9:9-17 and 9:18-26, "Jesus is depicted as unhindered by ritual concerns."

8. W.D. Davies and Dale C. Allison, *The Gospel According to Saint Matthew*, ICC (London: T&T Clark, 1988, 1991), 1:67; cf. 1:69, 102; 2:1–5.

9. Ibid., 2:125.

especially that of 9:15-17. In contrast to Davies and Allison, then, I am accepting the evangelist's invitation to interpret the story of the daughter and the woman in the light of the material that precedes it. In contrast to Nolland and Wainwright, on the other hand, my orientation in developing this interpretation derives from neither the newness of Jesus' miracles nor the newness of his social agenda, but rather from the newness of what the evangelist believes has been wrought through Jesus' death. In explicating this point, special attention will be paid to how the meaning of Jesus' death is signified through the narrative's symbolic discourse.

(21) When Jesus crossed over again in the boat to the other side, a large crowd gathered around him; and he was by the sea.

(22) And one of the synagogue officials, named Jairus, approached, and seeing him fell at his feet

(18) While he was saying these things to them, suddenly a certain official came and bowed before him,

(23) and implored him repeatedly, saying, "My daughter is at the point of death; come and lay your hands on her so that she may be made well and live.

saying, "My daughter has just died; but come and lay your hand on her, and she will live."

(24) And he went with him. And a large crowd followed him and was pressing in on him.

(19) And rising up Jesus followed him, with his disciples.

(25) Now there was a woman who had had a hemorrhage of blood for twelve years,

(20) Then suddenly a woman who had been hemorrhaging blood for twelve years came up from behind and touched the fringe of his cloak;

(26) and had endured much under many physicians and spent all that she had and was not helped at all, but rather grew worse-(27) when she heard about Jesus, she came up from behind in the crowd and touched his cloak;

(28) for she was saying, "If I just touch his clothes, I will be made well."

(29) And immediately the flow of her blood dried up and she knew in her body that she was healed of her affliction. (30) Immediately, Jesus, perceiving in himself that power had gone forth from him, turned around in the crowd and said, "Who touched my clothes?" (31) And his disciples said to him, "You see the crowd pressing in on you, and you say, 'Who touched me?'" (32) And he looked around to see who had done this. (33) But the woman, with fear and trembling, knowing what had happened to her, came and fell down before him and told him the whole truth.

(34) And he said to her, "Daughter, your faith has made you well; go in peace and be healed of your affliction."

(35) While he was still speaking, some people from the synagogue official's house came, saying, "Your daughter has died; why trouble the teacher anymore?" (36) But overhearing what they were saying, Jesus said to the synagogue official, "Do not fear; only believe." (37) And he allowed no one to follow with him, except for Peter and James and John, the brother of James.

(38) They went to the house of the synagogue official, and he saw a commotion and much weeping and wailing.

(39) When he entered, he said to them, "Why do you make a commotion and weep? The child did not die but is sleeping.

(40) And they laughed at him. But putting them all out, he took the child's father and mother and those with him and went in where the child was.

(21) for she was saying to herself, "If only I touch his cloak, I will be made well."

(22) Jesus turned, and seeing her he said, "Take courage, daughter; your faith has made you well." And from that hour the woman was made well.

(23) When Jesus came to the official's house and saw the flute players and the crowd in turmoil,

(24) he said, "Go away! For the girl did not die but is sleeping." And they laughed at him.

(41) And taking the child by the hand, he said to her, "Talitha coum," which means, "Little girl, rise!"	(25) But when the crowd had been put out, he went in and took her by the hand, and the girl rose up.
(42) Immediately the girl got up and walked around (for she was twelve years old). And they were utterly amazed.	
(43) And he strictly ordered them that no one should know this, and told them to give her something to eat. (Mark 5:21-43)	(26) And the report of this spread throughout all that land. (Matt. 9:18-26)

As we have seen, Matthean redaction not only brings the story of the daughter and the woman into contact with the question about fasting but also incorporates the story into a whole suite of formally similar accounts of healing in chapters 8–9. Comparison with such accounts is a good place to begin in explicating both what is "old" and what is "new" about 9:18-26.

To begin with, the official of 9:18-19 recalls the centurion of 8:5-13. Both men are supplicants pleading on behalf of subordinates within their respective households. Both are also men in positions of authority who, unlike the religious leaders of the people, show respect for Jesus, the former by his words (8:8-9), the latter by his actions (9:18). The official's act of bowing, in turn, brings to mind the actions of the leper in 8:2, who bows before Jesus while making a request for healing. Jesus responds by stretching out his hand and touching the leper (8:3), gestures that figure in the story of the official's daughter as well (9:18).[10] When Jesus arrives at the official's house, he goes alone into the room where the girl is lying, takes her by the hand, and makes her "rise up" (9:25), much as he had done earlier for Peter's mother-in-law (8:14-15).[11] The story of the

10. Note that in 9:18 Matthew speaks of Jesus' "hand" (not "hands," as in Mark 5:23), probably alluding to "the hand of God" in passages like Deut. 3:24; 5:15; 7:19; 9:26; 32:39; 1 Sam. 6:3; Ps. 10:12; Isa. 11:11; 41:10. Cf. Matt. 8:3; 12:49; 14:31.

centurion anticipates 9:18-26 in another way, insofar as the man's "great faith" (8:10, 13) can be compared with the "saving faith" of the woman with a flow of blood (9:22; cf. 9:28-29).[12] As in the story of the paralytic, when Jesus "sees" faith in a suppliant he responds by telling the person to "take courage" (9:2, 22). The story of the leper, meanwhile, anticipates 9:18-26 insofar as the impurity of the man's condition can be compared with the impurity attaching to both the woman and the daughter. Indeed, as Numbers 5:2 indicates, it would not have been unusual to group the conditions represented by these sorts of character types together:

> Command the Israelites to put out of the camp everyone who is leprous, or has a discharge, and everyone who is unclean through contact with a corpse. (Num. 5:2 NRSV)

In each case Jesus overcomes both ritual impurity and the social stigma associated with it through a manifestation of sacred power, and in each case this occurs through some manner of touch (8:3; 9:20, 25).[13]

Taking all these variables into consideration, it is tempting to characterize 9:18-26 simply as a recapitulation of what has transpired so far in chapters 8–9. It certainly is the case that by the time the reader reaches this point in the narrative a sense of familiarity has developed in terms of how the story unfolds. By the same token, it is also the case that the material in 9:18-26 evidences a number of distinctive features, and it is through attention to such features that

---

11. Matthew drops the second half of Mark 5:41 because he "wants to dissociate Jesus from magical activity" (Davies and Allison, *Saint Matthew*, 2:133; cf. Ulrich Luz, *Matthew: A Commentary*, Hermeneia [Minneapolis: Fortress Press, 2005], 2:42).

12. Note also the use of the phrase "in/from that hour" in 8:13 (*en tē hōra ekeinē*) and 9:22 (*apo tēs hōras ekeinēs*).

13. Cf. Louise J. Lawrence, *Sense and Stigma in the Gospels: Depictions of Sensory-Disabled Characters* (Oxford: Oxford University Press, 2013), 76–97.

we can recognize the special contribution that the story makes to the Gospel.

First, in 9:18-19 + 23-26 we have the Gospel's only account of a revivification.[14] Regardless of Jesus' assertion that the girl is only "asleep" (9:24), there is little question that she is in fact dead, as the official states in 9:18. This diagnosis is confirmed through comparison with 10:8 and 11:5, both of which look back to this incident. While tales about individuals being brought back from the dead were not unheard of in the ancient Mediterranean world,[15] the most relevant precedents for Jesus' miracle come from the exploits of two other biblical figures, namely, the prophets Elijah (1 Kgs. 17:17-24) and Elisha (2 Kgs. 4:18-37). In fact, at several points Matthean redaction has the effect of highlighting parallels with the latter.

Note, for example, that in contrast to the Second Gospel, in the First Gospel the girl is dead from the beginning of the story (Matt. 9:18; cf. Mark 5:23), just as the story of the Shunammite woman's son begins with an account of his death (2 Kgs. 4:18-20). This change in the girl's initial status both strengthens the connection between the two stories and dramatizes the depth of the official's "resurrection faith." Like the Shunammite woman, he believes that the healer has power not only over illness but even over death itself.[16] Also significant is the healer's response:

---

14. The episode in Matthew 27:52-53 is not a revivification but an anticipation of the eschatological resurrection of the dead. Cf. Ezek. 37:12-13.

15. Concerning Asclepius, Diodorus Siculus writes, "it was believed that he had brought back to life many who had died" (*Library of History* 4.71.1). For further examples, see Nolland, *The Gospel of Matthew*, 394; Wendy Cotter, *Miracles in Greco-Roman Antiquity* (London: Routledge, 1999), 13–15, 24–30, 33–34, 45–47. See also Apuleius, *Metamorphoses* 2.28-29, where an Egyptian necromancer dressed like a priest of Isis raises someone from the dead.

16. John P. Meier, *A Marginal Jew: Rethinking the Historical Jesus* (New York: Doubleday, 1994), 2:781. The ruler evidently assumes Jesus' authority over death, despite the fact that there is "no basis in the narrative so far for such an assumption" (R. T. France, *The Gospel of Matthew*, NICNT [Grand Rapids: Eerdmans, 2007], 362). Cf. Gerd Theissen, *The Miracle Stories of the Early Christian Tradition* (Philadelphia: Fortress Press, 1983), 178.

And he went with him. And a large crowd followed him . . . (Mark 5:24; cf. 5:37)

And rising up Jesus followed him . . . (Matt. 9:19)

And Elisha arose and went after her. (2 Kgs. 4:30)

It is worth noting how uncharacteristic it is for Jesus to be seen following someone, rather than the other way around.[17] The most likely reason for Matthew's creation of this peculiar scenario is to strengthen the connection with the actions of Elisha, who follows the mother of the dead child to the house where his body has been laid.[18] A final observation in this regard can be made regarding the setting of the revivification itself. While Mark has Jesus enter the house accompanied by the child's parents and some of the disciples (5:40), Matthew has him enter alone (Matt. 9:25), a detail that recalls 2 Kings 4:33, where Elisha enters the dead youth's room alone (cf. 1 Kgs. 17:19).[19] Jesus' act of raising someone from the dead, then, is not simply an impressive accomplishment but an event in salvation history. It is, in other words, an event that both fulfills biblical prophecy (cf. Matt. 8:17; 11:5) and accords with precedents set by biblical prophets. At the same time, even as Matthew 9:18-26 resembles 2 Kings 4:18-37 with respect to specific details, it also contains a major compositional feature that 2 Kings 4:18-37 does not, a point that leads to our next observation.

A second distinctive feature of Matthew 9:18-26 concerns the text's literary structure. Here we have the Gospel's only example of intertwined healing stories. In this respect, the evangelist follows his source material, though the manner in which he does so reveals

---

17. Cf. Matt. 4:20, 22, 25; 8:1, 10, 19, 22, 23; 9:9, 27; 10:38; 12:15; 14:13; 16:24; 19:2, 21, 27, 28; 20:29, 34; 21:9; 26:58; 27:55.
18. Nolland, *The Gospel of Matthew*, 395.
19. France, *The Gospel of Matthew*, 365; Meier, *Marginal Jew*, 2:779.

important differences. In Mark, the connection between the two stories relies in no small part on the narrative suspense generated by the inserted story: the child dies while Jesus is unexpectedly detained interacting with the woman, thus necessitating a more dramatic test of the father's faith (Mark 5:36).[20] In Matthew, as we have seen, the child is dead from the beginning, leaving the narrative function of the woman's story *as an inserted story* less apparent. As Davies and Allison observe, the "interpolation of the healing of the woman with a hemorrhage makes sense only in Mark," since it is only in Mark's account that the daughter dies while this healing is taking place.[21]

At this point it is helpful to examine another place in the Gospel where Matthew encounters a Markan "sandwich," namely, the cleansing of the temple and the cursing of the fig tree:[22]

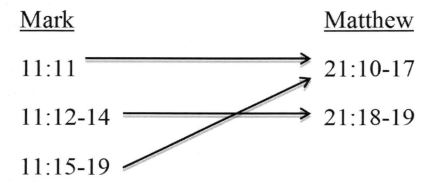

As a comparison of the two passages attests, the author of the First Gospel had no compunction about converting a set of intertwined stories in his source material into a set of parallel stories. Given the availability of this redactional option, it seems fair to inquire after

20. Mark constructs a clearer parallel on the narrative level between the faith of the woman and the faith of the official: having witnessed the former's demonstration of faith (5:33-34), the latter is called upon to demonstrate faith himself (5:36).

21. Davies and Allison, *Saint Matthew*, 2:122.

22. Cf. William R. Telford, *The Barren Temple and the Withered Tree*, JSNTSup 1 (Sheffield: JSOT, 1980), 69–94.

what reasons Matthew may have had for *not* undoing the Markan intercalation he encountered in the story of the daughter and the woman. Such a question seems especially relevant given the change that Matthew *does* make regarding the daughter's initial condition.

Perhaps the best way to address this question is by actually reading 9:18-26 as a set of intertwined narratives, that is, by reading the stories of the daughter and the woman in light of one another. Once again, however, differences between the two Gospels can be discerned. In keeping with his editorial proclivities, Matthew's is the more economical rendition.[23] Note in particular how references to the disciples in Mark 5:31, 37, 40, 42, to the crowd in Mark 5:24, 27, 30-31, to the physicians in Mark 5:26, to the messengers in Mark 5:35, and to the girl's family in Mark 5:40, 42 have been dropped.[24] By reducing the profile of the story's secondary characters, Matthew not only offers a shorter account but also brings the roles played by the story's primary characters into sharper relief. This latter change, in turn, has implications for the way that we read the two stories in light of one another. In what follows, I compare and contrast these primary roles as a way of illuminating the text's narrative logic.

The Official and the Woman

We begin with the official and the woman with the flow of blood. Both individuals approach Jesus for help: the former on behalf of a member of his household, the latter on behalf of herself. Both approach him with a stooping gesture: the former by bowing down before Jesus while making his request, the latter by bowing down

---

23. Heinz Joachim Held, "Matthew as Interpreter of the Miracle Stories," in *Tradition and Interpretation in Matthew*, eds. Günther Bornkamm, Gerhard Barth, and Heinz Joachim Held (Philadelphia: Westminster, 1963), 166–67, 179–80, 233; Theissen, *Miracle Stories*, 175–78.

24. J. R. C. Cousland (*The Crowds in the Gospel of Matthew*, NovTSup 102 [Leiden: Brill, 2002], 41) notes how Matthew's compression of Markan miracle stories sometimes involves eliminating references to the crowds. Cf. Matt. 9:27//Mark 10:46.

in order to touch the fringe of his cloak.[25] Both also have their expectations met on a rather specific linguistic level: note the repetition of "hand" in 9:18, 25 and of "made well" in 9:21-22. Finally, and in contrast to the Second Gospel, both are also anonymous, a feature that broadens their potential representative function for Matthew's readers (cf. Mark 5:22).[26]

In the midst of these similarities one finds significant differences as well. Whatever its precise connotation, the title "official" (*archōn*) suggests for the man a position of power, and the opening of the narrative suggests that he is not reluctant to use this power.[27] Despite the deferential gesture, he is shown acting rather boldly, entering the house (apparently) uninvited, interrupting Jesus' dinner, asking him to leave the meal in order to perform a service for him in his own house and (as if that were not enough) to incur ritual contamination in the course of doing so. Such seeming temerity can be interpreted as a reflection of the man's social status. As the male head of a household, a person of authority, and someone who is ritually clean, he can enter the house where the banquet is being held and approach Jesus directly. All this contrasts with the socially restricted movements of the woman, who remains outside the house and approaches Jesus furtively.[28] Like the official, her actions can be interpreted as a reflection of her social status. Unlike the official's

25. Referring to 1 Samuel 15:27 and Zechariah 8:23, Luz (*Matthew*, 2:42) suggests that her manner of touching Jesus' garment should be interpreted as "a petitionary gesture" (see also *b. Taʾan.* 23b). Matthew 9:20 and Luke 8:44 agree against Mark 5:27 in adding "the fringe," for which see Mark 6:56; Matt. 14:36; 23:5; and cf. Num. 15:38-40; Deut. 22:12.
26. Note that in Matthew 20:30 the name of Bartimaeus will be dropped (cf. Mark 10:46).
27. Matthew changes "synagogue official" (Mark 5:22, 35-36, 38) to simply "official" (9:18, 23), perhaps so as to disassociate the man from what for Matthew's readers would have been a problematic institution (see Chapter One).
28. In contrast to the official, she hopes to obtain healing from Jesus without his permission or even his awareness. A contrast can also be made with Matthew 14:36 (cf. Mark 6:56), where those in need of healing *ask* Jesus to touch the fringe of his cloak.

daughter or the centurion's servant, she has no one to supplicate on her behalf.

In her analysis of the healing stories in chapters 8–9, Wainwright has suggested that by this point in the narrative "the space of the house is emerging symbolically as a borderland space."[29] When it comes to this particular story, however, it might be more correct to state that it is the space *between* houses that functions as a borderland, that is, as the venue in which Jesus encounters those who stand outside the symbolic space of the male household and its attendant systems of power and purity. The fact that the woman is healed outside of a domestic setting reinforces her lack of both a family network and access to patriarchal resources.[30] The woman's diminished status relative to the man is further intimated by their respective speaking roles. For his part, the man speaks directly to Jesus (9:18). The woman, by contrast, speaks only to herself (9:21), the Markan report that she told Jesus "the whole truth" (5:33) having been expunged.[31] This redactional detail has the effect of both underscoring the woman's isolation and highlighting Jesus' perspicacity. Like his Father in heaven, Jesus knows what she needs without her having to ask (cf. 6:8). Accordingly, what he "sees" (cf. 6:6) is not simply the woman herself but also the woman's faith, to which he responds with a word of encouragement (9:22; cf. 9:2). The lesson to be drawn from this seems clear enough: Jesus answers the plea for help whether it is spoken aloud (as in 9:18) or not (as in 9:21).[32]

---

29. Elaine M. Wainwright, *Women Healing/Healing Women: The Genderization of Healing in Early Christianity* (London: Equinox, 2006), 147.

30. Note that Matthew drops Mark 5:26. The indication that (at some point, at least) the woman had access to professional help and the means to pay for such help has been deleted.

31. Nolland, *The Gospel of Matthew*, 396: "the woman's condition remains a private matter between her and Jesus."

32. In this regard, the official can be compared with the centurion, the woman with the paralytic. Cf. Held, "Matthew as Interpreter," 178–80.

The content of Jesus' encouraging word in 9:22 indicates yet another way in which the woman differs from the man. While what the latter does in 9:18 could certainly be interpreted as a demonstration of faith, Jesus does not verbally acknowledge it as such (cf. 8:10, 13).[33] In fact, he does not speak to the man at all (cf. Mark 5:36).[34] He does, however, speak to the woman: "Take courage, daughter, your faith has made you well/saved you" (9:22). Matthew's reformulation of the narrative draws attention not only to the power of Jesus' perception but also to the power of Jesus' word (cf. 8:8, 16). In contrast to Mark, in Matthew the woman is healed after Jesus speaks, not before (cf. Mark 5:29). Like Mark, Matthew has Jesus both attribute to the woman saving faith and address her as "daughter" (cf. Mark 5:34). As Wainwright observes, this form of address would have been especially significant to the woman given her social station.[35] With this title she is now not only relieved of her physical malady but also included in a new set of meaningful social relations, relations defined not by the patriarchal household but by the divine kingdom: in the language of medical anthropology, she has been both "cured" and "healed." The act of inclusion that accompanies the story's first miracle contrasts with the act of exclusion that accompanies its second. While the woman had to wait outside the house to approach Jesus, the man has to wait outside the house while Jesus heals a member of his household (9:25). The daughter's healing may occur inside a house but it occurs without the presence of the house's master.

---

33. France, *The Gospel of Matthew*, 362.

34. As Theissen (*Miracle Stories*, 137) notes, this is not the only time that Matthew removes the concept of *pistis* ("faith") from a Markan miracle story.

35. Wainwright, *Feminist Critical Reading*, 203. Cf. Matt. 12:49-50.

The Woman and the Daughter

This leads to the next line of comparison, which is between the woman and the daughter. We begin with differences between the two, some of which have already been noted. For her part, the daughter is presented primarily in terms of her relationship to the (patriarchal) head of the household, who serves as her petitioner. As if to solidify this role, her body is placed physically within the private, "domestic" space of the father's house. The girl's dependency, domestication, and docility contrast with the initiative attributed to the woman, an unattached female operating on her own behalf in the public, "borderland" space between households.

In the midst of these differences, the two figures exhibit also a significant number of similarities. Both are females in need of Jesus' help. Both are referred to as "daughter" (9:18, 22). In both cases touch is involved.[36] In both cases Matthean redaction emphasizes the personal nature of their encounters with Jesus: in 9:20-22 the disciples and the crowd are written out of the story (cf. Mark 5:27-31), while in 9:25 everyone except the healer is put out of the house (cf. Mark 5:40).[37] Both are also associated with ritual impurity. The girl's body, of course, is a source of pollution by virtue of being deceased.[38] In the case of the woman, it is likely that her bleeding is uterine and, as such, a source of pollution as well. The term that Matthew uses in 9:20 to describe her condition (*haimorroeō*) is found elsewhere in

36. Wainwright (*Women Healing*, 150) suggests that by initiating the touch the woman takes on the role of healer, though this observation seems to apply more to Mark's version of the story than to Matthew's. For the idea that healing is communicable through an individual's personal effects, see 2 Kings 13:20-21; Matthew 14:36; Mark 6:56; Acts 19:12; Plutarch, *Sulla* 35.3-5; Lucian, *The Lover of Lies* 18-21; Emma J. Edelstein and Ludwig Edelstein, *Asclepius: Collection and Interpretation of the Testimonies* (Baltimore: Johns Hopkins University Press, 1945), 1:231.

37. Matthew's more "private" version of the story accordingly drops the report of the witnesses' response (Mark 5:42b), Jesus' subsequent instructions to them (Mark 5:43a), and the demonstration of the miracle's effectiveness (Mark 5:43b). Cf. Theissen, *Miracle Stories*, 61.

38. Num. 19:11-22; cf. Lev. 21:1-4, 11; *m. Ohal.* 1:1-4.

biblical literature only in Leviticus 15:33, which accompanies statutes set down regarding the ritual uncleanness incurred by a woman who "has a discharge of blood for many days" beyond her period (Lev. 15:25-32).[39] The fact that menstrual impurity can be transmitted through touch (Lev. 15:19-24; cf. *m. Zabim* 5:1, 6)[40] would help to explain why the woman approaches Jesus surreptitiously: "she believes that to be healed she must physically touch Jesus or at least his clothing; yet to do so would constitute a brazen act of a ritually unclean woman communicating her uncleanness to a holy man whom she otherwise does not know."[41] It would also help to explain why she touches his cloak and not his person: "impurity contracted through contact with clothes is less serious than impurity contracted through contact with flesh."[42] As in the case of the daughter, the power of Jesus to overcome a physical disorder includes the power to overcome a cultural taboo.

The similarity between the woman and the girl is not restricted to matters of ritual impurity, however. As David Tabb Stewart explains, in the ancient world a chronic menstrual condition would have "disabled" a woman not only ritually but also socially. This was especially true insofar as such a condition would have been perceived as a threat to fertility and thus "a symbol of death."[43] Among some authors, contact with menstrual fluid or with a menstruating woman was thought to cause death or infertility in certain plants and animals.

39. Mark 5:25 has a different formulation, for which cf. Lev. 15:19, 25; 20:18.
40. For a nuanced discussion, see Charlotte Fonrobert, "The Woman with a Blood-Flow (Mark 5.24-34) Revisited: Menstrual Laws and Jewish Culture in Christian Feminist Hermeneutics," in *Early Christian Interpretation of the Scriptures of Israel*, eds. Craig A. Evans and James A. Sanders (Sheffield: Sheffield Academic Press, 1997), 121–40.
41. Meier, *Marginal Jew*, 2:709.
42. Joel Marcus, *Mark*, AB 27 (New Haven, CT: Yale University Press, 2000), 1:359 (referring to Lev. 15:7). Cf. *m. Ohal.* 1:5; Jacob Milgrom, *Leviticus*, AB 3 (New York: Doubleday, 1991), 1:914.
43. David Tabb Stewart, "Sexual Disabilities in the Hebrew Bible," in *Disability Studies and Biblical Literature*, eds. Candida R. Moss and Jeremy Schipper (New York: Palgrave Macmillan, 2011), 71–78.

According to Pliny, for instance, "crops touched by it [i.e., menstrual fluid] become barren, grafts die, seeds in gardens are dried up, the fruit of trees falls off."[44] According to the Talmud, meanwhile, if a menstruating woman passes between two men "she kills one of them."[45] Wainwright suggests that the linkage with death may be grounded in the biblical text itself, insofar as the instructions regarding the woman with an irregular discharge conclude with a warning to keep the people separated from impurity, "so that they will not die in their uncleanness by their defiling my tabernacle" (Lev. 15:31 NASB).[46] As Jacob Milgrom writes in his commentary on Leviticus 15, "[v]aginal blood and semen represent the forces of life; their loss – death."[47] All this points to another similarity between the two females in our story: both are somehow "dead," one physically, the other symbolically.[48] Given that when it comes to women, "the patriarchal world values their breeding bodies more than anything else," the fact that the latter cannot participate in "the self-validating act of procreation" further underscores her marginalization vis-à-vis patriarchal structures and agendas.[49]

The Woman, the Daughter, and Jesus

Yet another similarity between the two females in our story concerns their relationship with the story's protagonist: the two can be compared not only with one another but also with Jesus. In

---

44. Pliny, *Natural History* 7.64; cf. 17.266-67; 28.77-81; Aelian, *Nature of Animals* 6.36; Columella, *On Agriculture* 10.359-66; 11.3.38. See further Jean-Jacques Aubert, "Threatened Wombs: Aspects of Ancient Uterine Magic," *GRBS* 30 (1990): 421–49.

45. *b. Pesah.* 111a. This happens if it is the beginning of her menstrual period. If it is the end of her period, she causes a quarrel between them. Cf. *Hekhalot Rabbati* 18.226.

46. Wainwright, *Feminist Critical Reading*, 199.

47. Milgrom, *Leviticus*, 1:1002. For the "abhorrence of the menstruant" in antiquity, see 1:948–53.

48. Wainwright, *Feminist Critical Reading*, 199.

49. Carole R. Fontaine, "Disabilities and Illness in the Bible: A Feminist Perspective," in *A Feminist Companion to the Hebrew Bible in the New Testament*, ed. Athalya Brenner (Sheffield: Sheffield Academic Press, 1996), 291.

developing this point, Wainwright's work on the healing narratives becomes especially important. As she explains, in the Gospel of Matthew, healed women "carry in their restored bodies the signification of those aspects of transformation that Jesus himself represents and enacts."[50] In the case of 9:18-26, each woman signifies a particular aspect of transformation, and in each instance this aspect is conveyed through a particular verb: the daughter is "raised" (*egeirō*) while the woman is "saved" (*sōzō*).

Taking the daughter first: the same term used to describe her act of "rising" in 9:25 will be used later in the Gospel with reference to Jesus' resurrection (16:21; 17:9, 23; 20:19; 26:32; 27:63; 28:6-7). For the evangelist, "it would have seemed appropriate that the one raised from the dead should have the power to conquer death in others, and stories of raising people from the dead would serve to symbolize the eschatological salvation Jesus was believed to bring."[51] As if to underscore the point, Matthew modifies Mark's account of Jesus' response to the official:

And he went with him. (Mark 5:24)

And rising up (*egertheis*) Jesus followed him . . . (Matt. 9:19)

Jesus responds to the father's plea for a miracle by symbolically "rising" from his place at the table. Of course, whereas the "rising" of the daughter involves the revivification of someone who will die again, Matthew's readers know that the "rising" of Jesus constitutes nothing less than the transcendence of death itself, his resurrection inaugurating a new era in salvation history.[52] In the light of this

---

50. Wainwright, *Women Healing*, 152. As we saw in Chapter Four, this signification applies to the case of Peter's mother-in-law (Matt. 8:14-15), especially the actions associated with her healing: "rising" and "serving."

51. Eric Eve, *The Healer from Nazareth: Jesus' Miracles in Historical Context* (London: SPCK, 2009), 157. As we shall see, however, applying the language of "salvation" to the daughter in Matthew's version of the story presents certain problems.

reality, death is properly understood as "sleep" (9:24), that is, as an interim state that ultimately gives way to new life.[53] The girl, then, can be said to signify certain aspects of transformation associated with Jesus insofar as the same eschatological power by which God will raise him from the dead is manifested in her restored body.[54]

The restored body of the woman can also be understood to signify certain aspects of transformation associated with Jesus, though her body is not "raised"—it is "saved." In fact, in Matthew's version of the story, hers is the *only* body that is said to be saved:

> Come and lay your hands on her, so that she may be made well/saved (*sōthē*) and live. (Mark 5:23)

> But come and lay your hand on her, and she will live. (Matt. 9:18)

Matthew seems intent on particularizing the ways in which the two females signify different aspects of transformation associated with Jesus. In contrast to the Second Gospel, which speaks of both the woman and the daughter being "saved," in the First Gospel it is the woman alone. Moreover, the act of "saving" functions as a leitmotif for her story:

> (28) For she said, "If I but touch his clothes, I will be made well/saved (*sōthēsomai*)." . . . (34) He said to her, "Daughter, your faith has made you well/saved you (*sesōken*)." (Mark 5:28, 34)

---

52. France, *The Gospel of Matthew*, 364.

53. Cf. Marcus, *Mark*, 1:371. For sleep as a euphemism for death, cf. Matt. 27:52; John 11:11-14; 1 Cor. 15:6; Eph. 5:14; 2 Pet. 3:4.

54. The crowds who laugh at Jesus in 9:24, meanwhile, can be understood to represent those who view the possibility of life after death with skepticism (cf. Matt. 22:23). Amy-Jill Levine ("Discharging Responsibility: Matthean Jesus, Biblical Law, and Hemorrhaging Woman," in *A Feminist Companion to Matthew*, ed. Amy-Jill Levine [Cleveland, OH: Pilgrim, 2001], 87), on the other hand, thinks that they represent the people who mock Jesus during his execution. For the theme of unreceptiveness, see Birger Gerhardsson, *The Mighty Acts of Jesus According to Matthew* (Lund: CWK Gleerup, 1979), 68.

(21) For she said to herself, "If I only touch his cloak, I will be made well/saved (*sōthēsomai*)." (22) Jesus turned, and seeing her he said, "Take courage, daughter; your faith has made you well/saved you (*sesōken*)." And from that hour the woman was made well/saved (*esōthē*). (Matt. 9:21-22)

In keeping with his redactional proclivities, Matthew increases the number of references to *sōzō* in the woman's story from two to three.[55] Moreover, the term's rapid repetition supports a rather remarkable progression of occurrences: the substance of the woman's unspoken wish (9:21) is promptly articulated as Jesus' spoken word (9:22a), which (being Jesus' word) is immediately translated into action (9:22b).[56] In reshaping this narrative, then, Matthew disassociates the daughter's story from "salvation" even as he emphasizes its structural role in the story of the woman. The woman wants to be saved, Jesus says she has been saved, and then she *is* saved.

As we seek out an explanation for this change, there is a temptation to seize upon some of the characterological distinctions identified above: the individual who is said to be "saved" in the story is the one who exhibits the active, not passive role. Matthew, then, is teaching his readers that salvation is more than the restoration of physical existence but is predicated upon the sort of courageous faith that brings one into an intimate, familial relationship with Jesus. While this explanation has its merits, it fails to account for another important fact: this is the only place in the Gospel where the verb *sōzō* is applied to an individual healed by Jesus.[57] Even in other stories

---

55. For Matthew's love of triads, see Davies and Allison, *Saint Matthew*, 1:62–72, 86–87.
56. In Mark, Jesus' word to her functions as the confirmation of a healing that has already taken place (5:29), while in Matthew it is what enacts the healing (as in 8:13). Cf. Vernon K. Robbins, "The Woman Who Touched Jesus' Garment: Socio-Rhetorical Analysis of the Synoptic Account," *NTS* 33 (1987): 505–506.
57. France, *The Gospel of Matthew*, 358–61. Of particular interest is Matthew 20:34, where the evangelist similarly deletes the reference to being "saved/made well" from a healing story (cf. Mark 10:52). While 9:20-22 is the only Matthean healing story in which *sōzō* is used, the

where the petitioner's faith is explicitly acknowledged, this language is absent (8:10; 9:2, 29; 15:28). Evidently, then, there was something about this woman for Matthew that made her singularly suitable as a representative of what it means to be "saved" by Jesus. If it was not a matter of her faith (or only a matter of her faith), then other possibilities need to be considered.

In pursuing this line of inquiry, it is important to remember that within the Gospel *sōzō*, like *egeirō*, evokes a double horizon of meaning. Indeed, as Wainwright has argued, the only way to grasp the significance of the term for our story is in terms of "the fullness of what that word entails within the symbolic universe of the Matthean narrative" as a whole.[58] Viewed from this perspective, it is evident that the application of "saving" language to the woman not only denotes her physical healing (her being "made well") but also signifies her participation in the saving work of Jesus more broadly. Specifically, Wainwright says, the application of saving language situates the woman's experience paradigmatically within an eschatological framework, one that "carries with it connotations of . . . preservation from eternal death."[59] This much is apparent from the way that the term is employed elsewhere in the Gospel, in passages like 8:25, 14:30, 16:25, and 19:25. Viewed from this perspective, the woman is seen to be "saved" not only from her affliction but symbolically from the realm of the dead as well.

While other interpreters have made similar observations,[60] what makes the approach embraced by Wainwright instructive for our purposes is the attention it draws to the narrative's somatic dynamics:

---

summary statement in 14:36 (which also speaks of people touching the fringe of Jesus' garment) has the related verb *diasōzō*.

58. Wainwright, *Women Healing*, 152.

59. Ibid., 151.

60. Luz, *Matthew*, 2:42–43; France, *The Gospel of Matthew*, 361, 363; Donald A. Hagner, *Matthew*, WBC 33 (Dallas: Word Books, 1993), 1:249. Cf. Marcus, *Mark*, 1:365–66.

in 9:22 "the healed body of a woman is written with language associated with Jesus . . . Transformation results in her carrying on her healed body the mark of Jesus."[61] Unfortunately, Wainwright expounds on neither what this "mark" of transformation might be nor why it is the woman—and *not* the daughter—who "carries" this mark on her body. After all, it is the daughter (by virtue of being physically raised from the dead) who would seem to be the more likely candidate for signifying salvation, that is, for signifying "preservation from eternal death." Yet, as we have seen, Matthean redaction actually discourages the reader from making such an identification.

In spite of these unanswered questions, let me suggest that we follow Wainwright's lead and investigate the story of the daughter and the woman with special attention to how its language functions within the symbolic matrix of the Gospel as a whole. In particular, the attention she draws to the language of "marked" bodies can be of value in addressing the relation of 9:18-26 to 9:14-17, a matter to which we now turn.

Poured Out for Many

As we have seen, 9:18a represents a redactional transition that links the story of the daughter and the woman with the scene that immediately precedes it. Jesus is still at the table, holding a conversation, appropriately enough, about eating practices. The evangelist's efforts to integrate 9:14-17 with 9:18-26 are further evidenced by a change he makes in Jesus' response to the question with which the former begins:

> The attendants of the bridegroom cannot *fast* while the bridegroom is with them, can they? (Mark 2:19)

61. Wainwright, *Women Healing*, 151.

> The attendants of the bridegroom cannot *mourn* as long as the bridegroom is with them, can they? (Matt. 9:15)

Jesus' dinner with tax collectors and sinners (9:10–13), we now learn, is no ordinary meal. Rather, as we saw above, Jesus here likens himself to the eschatological bridegroom and his followers to the bridegroom's attendants. The meal they share together is, by implication, a foretaste of the messianic banquet. As Gerd Theissen has suggested, in 9:15a Matthew replaces "fast" (in Mark 2:19) with "mourn" in anticipation of 9:23, reinforcing the narrative link between what transpires in the house of 9:10-19 and what transpires in the house of 9:23-25.[62] In each case, the presence of Jesus makes mourning practices inappropriate: just as there is no need for fasting in the former there is no need for flute players in the latter.[63] Moreover, what transpires in the latter will validate what is asserted in the former: mourning is not appropriate in the presence of Jesus because what he represents is no less than life from death.

As Davies and Allison have suggested, the change from "fast" to "mourn" also reinforces the link between 9:15a and 9:15b:[64]

> But days will come when the bridegroom is taken away from them, and then they will fast.

As commentators agree, Jesus here alludes to his death. What had started out as a justification for the current practice of not fasting now suddenly veers into an ominous revelation about future events, one

---

62. Theissen, *Miracle Stories*, 210. Insofar as its action both begins (9:18) and ends (9:25) in a house, Matthew's version of the daughter's story evidences a spatial unity that Mark's version does not. In both cases, Jesus' presence and activity transform the domestic space, which here can be understood as representing the "old" or patriarchal order.

63. Flute players are associated with mourning in Jeremiah 48:36; Josephus, *War* 3.437; *m. Sabb.* 23:4; *m. Ketub.* 4:4; *m. B. Mes.* 6:1.

64. Davies and Allison, *Saint Matthew*, 2:109–10. They also note (2:111) that the phrase "days will come" in 9:15 encourages the reader to interpret Jesus' death as an eschatological event (cf. Isa. 39:6; Jer. 7:32; 23:5; 31:31; Amos 4:2; 9:13; Luke 17:22; 21:6).

that creates a disconcerting juxtaposition of images: the bridegroom of joy will become the bridegroom of woe.

As we learned in Chapter Ten, the imagery of 9:16-17 expands on this theme. Just as the old cloak "tears" in 9:16, the temple veil will tear at the moment of Jesus' death (27:50-51). Just as the old wineskins are "destroyed" in 9:17a, the authorities will seek to destroy Jesus (27:20). Just as the new wine is "poured out" in 9:17a, ceremonial wine will be poured out at the Last Supper:

> . . . the wine will burst the skins and the wine is destroyed, and also the wineskins. (Mark 2:22)

> . . . the wineskins burst, and the wine *pours out* and the wineskins are destroyed. (Matt. 9:17)

> . . . this is my blood of the covenant, which is *poured out* for many for forgiveness of sins. (Matt. 26:28)

Within the symbolic world of the Gospel, the imagery of wine being poured out signifies the blood that will be poured out of Jesus' body at his death, the blood of a sacrifice that inaugurates a new covenant, one defined by the forgiveness of sins.[65] The relevance of this signification for the interpretation of 9:17 is increased by the fact that Jesus has just alluded to his death (9:15b) and employed imagery suggesting the violence attending that death (9:16). Bear in mind, too, that Jesus utters these words in the presence of "many" sinners (9:10). The imagery of 9:15b-17 serves as a reminder that the grace and redemption conveyed by Jesus' act of dining with such people will be fully realized "for many" (26:28) only through his death.

That such redemption is to be construed specifically as an event of *salvation* is indicated at various points in the Gospel. There are, to

---

65. The verb *ekcheō* is often used with reference to sacrifice (e.g., Exod. 29:12; Lev. 4:7, 18, 25, 30, 34; Sir. 50:15) or violent death (e.g., Gen. 9:6; Num. 35:33; Deut. 19:10; Jer. 7:6; Joel 4:19).

begin with, the three uses of *sōzō* in the passion narrative, where the language of saving is put into the mouths of those mocking Jesus on the cross, for example, in 27:42: "He saved others; himself he cannot save" (cf. 27:40, 49).[66] The evangelist's readers, of course, recognizing the irony of the situation, understand that it is precisely by not saving himself from death on the cross that he saves others (cf. 16:25). They also understand that saving others constitutes the purpose of Jesus' life and mission:

> You shall call his name Jesus, for he will save (*sōsei*) his people from their sins. (1:21)

What Jesus ultimately "saves" people from is sin, and the way he does this is by pouring out his blood on the cross "for the forgiveness of sins" (26:28).[67] It is only through the pouring out of his blood, then, that people can properly be understood to be "saved." As Davies and Allison observe, 1:21 not only points forward to the cross but also provides an orientation for everything that follows in the narrative: "The passion already comes into the picture, for it is at the crucifixion that Jesus pours out his lifeblood *eis aphesin hamartiōn* ["for the forgiveness of sins"] (26:28). Thus the entire Gospel is to be read in the light of its end."[68] For Matthew, the shedding of Jesus' blood on the cross is the definitive event in salvation history. As such, it represents a uniquely generative image within his symbolic world.

Images of fulfillment and celebration (9:15a), then, are interrupted by images of death and destruction (9:15b–17b). In this much Matthew follows Mark. Matthew departs from Mark, however, in

---

66. Note that the reference to saving in Matthew 27:49 (cf. Mark 15:36) is redactional. Cf. Raymond E. Brown, *The Death of the Messiah: From Gethsemane to the Grave* (New York: Doubleday, 1994), 2:994–96, 1063.

67. Cf. Boris Repschinski, "'For He Will Save His People from Their Sins' (Matthew 1:21): A Christology for Christian Jews," *CBQ* 68 (2006): 248–67.

68. Davies and Allison, *Saint Matthew*, 1:210.

continuing the narrative not with a story about Sabbath observance (Mark 2:23-28) but with a story about resurrection. Having just announced his own death, Jesus learns of a death that has just occurred. But the official does not simply issue a report: he asks Jesus for life from death. By asking for the impossible, it seems as though he grasps the significance of what Jesus has just said about putting "new wine into fresh wineskins" (9:17c). Jesus' response, of course, is to "rise up" (9:19), in anticipation of the "rising up" of the official's daughter (9:25), which in turn anticipates Jesus' own rising (28:6-7). So images of death and destruction do not have the last word but give way to new life.

The way that leads to life, however, is not easy (cf. 7:14). In order to reach the official's house Jesus must traverse a liminal "borderland" space, a venue in which he transcends the "old" systems of power and purity and encounters a bleeding woman, one whose ailment signifies death and whose faith prompts a miraculous recovery. The story about resurrection, then, is interrupted by a story about being "saved."

The Mark of Jesus

In a recent article, Candida Moss has examined Mark's account of the woman with a flow of blood from the perspective of disability studies. As she notes, "the specifically gynecological nature of her medical condition and the contrast with Jairus's daughter have led scholars to focus on her identity as a woman to the neglect of her disability."[69] One of the repercussions of this negligence is that:

[w]hile many scholars have concentrated on the parallels between the woman with the flow of blood and Jairus's daughter, they have neglected the obvious comparison between Jesus and the woman. In the

---

69. Candida R. Moss, "The Man with the Flow of Power: Porous Bodies in Mark 5:25-34," *JBL* 129 (2010): 509.

narrative, the flow of power from Jesus mirrors the flow of blood from the woman . . . Both the diseased woman with the flow of blood and the divine protagonist of Mark are porous, leaky creatures.[70]

Accordingly, "the Markan Jesus appears weak and sickly . . . his physiological makeup resembles that of the sick and diseased."[71]

For his part, Matthew demonstrates little interest in a "sickly" Jesus. Nevertheless, in the First Gospel there is still an important sense in which the woman's flow of blood "mirrors" what happens to Jesus, though what it mirrors is different. The reference in Mark 5:30 to power pouring out of Jesus' body has been dropped and instead we have a reference to wine pouring out of a ruptured wineskin, an allusion to the blood that pours out of Jesus' body on the cross. So while in Mark the blood pouring out of the woman's body mirrors the power pouring out of Jesus' body when she is healed, in Matthew the blood pouring out of the woman's body mirrors the blood pouring out of Jesus' body on the cross. It is in this latter sense, I would suggest, that the woman carries "the mark of Jesus" on her body (cf. Gal. 6:17). Just as the daughter's body signifies Jesus' resurrected body, the woman's body signifies Jesus' crucified body.[72]

This interpretation offers answers to several of the questions that have been posed over the course of the discussion above. First, it provides a new perspective from which to consider the relationship between 9:14-17 and 9:18-26. The presentation of the latter as a continuation of the former encourages the reader to construe the elements of the two pericopes as participating in a cohesive symbolic matrix. Most prominent in this regard is the imagery of wine/blood

---

70. Ibid., 516.

71. Ibid.

72. Wainwright (*Women Healing*, 151) thinks of the woman as "marked" only with reference to her healed body. But it seems that this designation can be applied to both aspects of her experience: her bleeding body signifies Jesus' death while her healed body signifies salvation through his death. Cf. Levine, "Discharging Responsibility," 87.

flowing from a ruptured vessel/person. Matthean redaction clarifies both how the signifiers supporting this imagery inform one another and how they function within the narrative world projected by the Gospel as a whole (cf. 23:35; 26:28).

Second, it offers an explanation as to why the evangelist has left the intercalation of 9:18-26 intact. Just as images of fulfillment (9:15a) are interrupted by images of death (9:15b-17b), only to give way to images of restoration (9:17c) and a story signifying resurrection (9:18-19), the story signifying resurrection (9:18-19, 23-26) is itself interrupted by a story that signifies the cross (9:20-22). The logic informing Matthew's narrative theology dictates that the two kinds of imagery must be held together, indeed, intertwined: new life is only possible through death. This represents one of the ways in which the evangelist communicates both the central and the intrusive nature of the cross within his symbolic universe.

Third, this interpretation explains why for Matthew it is the woman alone who is said to participate in salvation. While the initial conditions of both females in our story can be understood as signifying death, the fact that the woman's body is hemorrhaging blood makes her uniquely suitable to signify what it means to be "saved" by Jesus, inasmuch as it is only through his blood shed on the cross that he saves people from their sins (1:21; 26:28).[73] The fact that the woman had been suffering from a hemorrhage "for twelve years" may have reinforced her representational quality in this regard, inasmuch as it is understood to be "his" people, that is, the people of Israel, whom Jesus saves from their sins (1:21; cf. 10:5-6; 19:28).[74]

---

73. Wainwright's approach (*Women Healing*, 146–53) tends to depict the two females as parallel rather than distinct representations: the daughter's experience signifies being raised from death; the woman's experience signifies being saved from death.

74. Matthew 1:21 may allude to Psalm 130:8, which mentions Israel by name. In the Gospel, *laos* usually refers to the people of Israel (e.g., 2:4, 6; 13:15; 15:8; 21:23; 26:3, 47; 27:1). Cf. Stuart L. Love, "Jesus Heals the Hemorrhaging Woman," in *The Social Setting of Jesus and the Gospels*, eds. Wolfgang Stegemann, Bruce J. Malina, and Gerd Theissen (Minneapolis: Fortress Press,

Finally, the fact that the individual hemorrhaging blood is female may also be relevant for understanding her representational quality. As Ulrich Luz has noted, in the Gospel of Matthew, women "stand by Jesus precisely in his suffering."[75] While Luz applies this observation to the women of the passion story (26:6-13; 27:55-56; 28:1-10), it seems to apply to Jesus' "daughter" as well.

2002), 97. Note that Matthew 9:20 is the only place in the Gospel where the duration of a person's condition is indicated; cf. Mark 9:21; Luke 13:11; John 5:5; 9:1; Acts 3:2; 4:22; 9:33; 14:8.

75. Luz, *Matthew*, 3:337.

12

Sensing the Son of David: Matthew 9:27-31

In the ancient Mediterranean world, eye ailments were treated by a range of healthcare systems.[1] The goddess Isis, for example, was thought to aid her devotees through nocturnal visions:

> For standing above the sick in their sleep she gives them aid for their diseases and works remarkable cures upon such as submit themselves to her; and many who have despaired of their physicians because of the difficulty of their malady are restored to health by her, while those who have altogether lost the use of their eyes or some other part of their body, whenever they turn to this goddess, are restored to their previous condition.[2]

That the cure of blindness is mentioned specifically in this otherwise generic description stands to reason insofar as Isis was sometimes associated with the "solar eye," that is, with the power of celestial

---

1. For other healings of blindness, see Wendy Cotter, *Miracles in Greco-Roman Antiquity* (London: Routledge, 1999), 17–18, 40–41, 43, 193, 214–16.
2. Diodorus Siculus, *Library of History* 1.25.5. Cf. Pausanias, *Description of Greece* 7.5.7–8; 10.38.13; Ovid, *Letters from the Black Sea* 1.1.51–58; Jane Draycott, *Approaches to Healing in Roman Egypt*, BAR International Series 2416 (Oxford: Archaeopress, 2012), 34.

light.[3] According to Pliny, on the other hand, diseases of the eye are relieved not by appealing to some deity but by the application of beef suet boiled with oil,[4] while in the book of Tobit the protagonist's blindness is healed when (at the direction of the angel Raphael) his eyes are smeared with the gall of a fish.[5] Different again is the *Testament of Solomon*, where we learn that the king (occasionally referred to as the "Son of David") has been granted authority over thirty-six demons responsible for various human ailments, including the demon responsible for causing "damage to the eyes" (18:7).[6]

The last of these examples may provide a relevant background for interpreting Matthew 12:22-24, a story in which a blind and mute man is described as "demon-possessed" (Matt. 12:22) and onlookers respond to his healing by wondering if his healer might be the "Son of David" (Matt. 12:23). By the same token, what makes this and other healings of blindness recorded in the First Gospel (Matt. 9:27-31; 11:5; 15:30-31; 20:29-34; 21:14) distinctive is their *eschatological* bearing, a point made perhaps most clearly in Matthew 11:2-5 (cf. Luke 7:18-23), a text that functions as a recapitulation of Jesus' public ministry up to this point in the narrative, especially as recounted in chapters 5–9:

> (2) When John heard in prison about the deeds of the Messiah (*ta erga tou christou*), he sent word through his disciples (3) and asked him, "Are you the Coming One (*ho erchomenos*), or are we to wait for another?" (4) Jesus answered them, "Go and tell John what you hear and see: (5) the blind receive their sight, the lame walk, lepers are cleansed, the deaf

---

3. J. Assmann, "Isis," in *Dictionary of Deities and Demons in the Bible*, eds. Karel van der Toorn et al. (Leiden: Brill, 1999), 456–58.

4. *Natural History* 28.167.

5. Tob. 11:7-15; cf. Pliny, *Natural History* 32.24; Larry P. Hogan, *Healing in the Second Temple Period*, NTOA 21 (Göttingen: Vandenhoeck & Ruprecht, 1992), 27–37.

6. Cf. *T. Sol.* 12:2; 13:4. The *Testament* refers to Solomon as "Son of David" in its prologue as well as in 1:7 and 20:1. Cf. Peter Busch, "Solomon as a True Exorcist: The Testament of Solomon in Its Cultural Setting," in *The Figure of Solomon in Jewish, Christian and Islamic Tradition: King, Sage and Architect*, ed. Joseph Verheyden (Leiden: Brill, 2013), 183–95.

hear, the dead are raised, and the poor have good news proclaimed to them."

The final verse of this passage (Matt. 11:5) is a conflation of allusions to several Isaianic oracles, including Isaiah 29:18, 35:5, 42:7 and 18 (all of which refer to the blind receiving sight) as well as Isaiah 26:19, 35:6, and 61:1.[7] The miraculous events listed in this verse (the blind receiving sight, the lame walking, lepers being cleansed, the deaf hearing, the dead being raised) all refer back to the series of miracle stories in chapters 8–9, in which instances of just such events had been related (see especially Matt. 8:1-4; 9:1-8, 18-34). What Matthew is doing in 11:2-5, then, is reminding his readers that these events are to be understood not simply as wondrous deeds but as the fulfillment of biblical prophecies of eschatological deliverance.[8] The application of the phrase *ta erga tou christou* in Matthew 11:2 (absent from the parallel passage in Luke 7:18) further indicates that these events are to be interpreted messianically: they are not just signs generally associated with the messianic era but "works" performed by the Messiah himself.[9] The same messianic intent can be inferred from the application of the phrase *ho erchomenos* in Matthew 11:3, especially when comparison is made with Matthew 21:9:

Hosanna to the Son of David: Blessed is the one who comes (*ho erchomenos*) in the name of the Lord. (cf. Ps. 118:26)

7. According to a fragmentary poetic text found at Qumran, the Messiah will "heal the sick, raise the dead, and preach good news to the poor" (4Q521 frag 2 II.12-13). For discussion, see John J. Collins, *The Scepter and the Star: The Messiahs of the Dead Sea Scrolls and Other Ancient Literature* (New York: Doubleday, 1995), 117–22.

8. Note also the quotation of Isaiah 53:4 in Matthew 8:17 and of Hosea 6:6 in Matthew 9:13.

9. While the messianic era was understood in contemporaneous Judaism to be a time of healing generally (e.g., *1 En.* 96:3; *2 Bar.* 73:1-3; *4 Ezra* 7:121-26; *Jub.* 23:26-30), the Messiah himself was not expected to be a healer and/or exorcist. See Hans Kvalbein, "The Wonders of the End-Time: Metaphoric Language in 4Q521 and the Interpretation of Matthew 11.5 par.," *JSP* 18 (1998): 87–110.

Jesus is the Coming One, that is, he is the royal Messiah of the Davidic line, the promised ruler of the nation of Israel, and, as Matthew 11:2-5 asserts, proof of this is to be found in his healings.[10] References elsewhere in the Gospel to Bethlehem, to sheep and shepherds, and to being anointed with the Spirit of God help to reinforce Jesus' identification as the Son of David, a designation used by Matthew more often than by any other New Testament author.[11]

That so many of the Isaianic prophecies alluded to in Matthew 11:5 specifically mention the healing of *the blind* is noteworthy, especially given the passage's messianic overtones. This is because the era of eschatological restoration was sometimes depicted symbolically as a time when the reign of "darkness" over human existence would give way to a realm of "light" (e.g., Isa. 58:8, 10; 60:1-3; Mal. 4:2; Rev. 22:5; 1QM 1:8). That the author of the First Gospel was familiar with such depictions is evident especially from Matthew 4:16:

> The people who were sitting in darkness saw a great light, and upon those sitting in the region and shadow of death light has dawned.

This quotation is a modified version of Isaiah 9:2, which in turn belongs to a prophetic oracle (Isa. 9:1-7) that promises Israel a deliverer, specifically, a son from the house of David (Isa. 9:6-7). The Davidic Messiah, then, brings to his people not only healing but also the light and life of a new era in salvation history.[12]

---

10. Note that the reference to the Son of David in Matthew 21:9 is redactional (cf. Mark 11:9-10). On Matthew 11:5 and its bearing on Matthew's presentation of the Davidic Messiah, see Lidija Novakovic, *Messiah, the Healer of the Sick: A Study of Jesus as the Son of David in the Gospel of Matthew*, WUNT 2.170 (Tübingen: Mohr Siebeck, 2003), 152–84.

11. Cf. Matt. 1:1, 6, 17, 20; 21:15; 22:42. For Bethlehem, see Matt. 2:1, 6 (cf. 1 Sam. 17:12; Mic. 5:2). Sheep and shepherds: Matt. 2:6; 9:36; 10:6; 15:24; 18:12; 25:32; 26:31 (cf. 1 Sam. 16:19; 2 Sam. 5:2; Ezek. 37:24). Being anointed with the Spirit: Matt. 3:16; 12:18, 28 (cf. 1 Sam. 16:13; Isa. 11:1-2). See further Young S. Chae, *Jesus as the Eschatological Shepherd: Studies in the Old Testament, Second Temple Judaism, and in the Gospel of Matthew*, WUNT 2.216 (Tübingen: Mohr Siebeck, 2006), 247–326.

When all of these priorities are taken into consideration, it is not surprising that within the First Gospel we find the designation "Son of David" being applied to Jesus in the context of healing stories, and especially in the context of stories that involve Jesus healing the blind (Matt. 9:27; 12:23; 20:30-31; 21:14-15; cf. 15:22). From the evangelist's perspective, the application of such a "nationalistic" title in these stories stands to reason, since for him the nation as a whole is not only living in darkness (Matt. 4:16; 13:13-15) but also being led by "blind guides" (Matt. 15:14; 23:16-26). The ability of blind people in these stories to recognize their Messiah (not to mention his ability to *heal* their blindness) contrasts ironically with the response accorded him by Israel's religious leaders (e.g., Matt. 9:34; 12:24), who are unable to heal their own "blindness," much less the blindness of those they lead. When blind people in these stories entreat Jesus as "Son of David" for healing, then, they sound like subjects petitioning their king for a boon (cf. 2 Sam. 14:4).[13]

In coming to terms with the different levels of meaning that Matthew attaches to the concept of blindness, it is important to bear in mind that the imagery of light and darkness occurs fairly often in the First Gospel (e.g., 6:22-23; 10:27; 17:2; 24:29; 27:45), constituting a basic polarity within the symbolic world it projects.[14] Examined in terms of their contribution to this world, stories about the healing of blindness can be understood to function as eschatological parables, that is, as narrated metaphors in which the experience of the blind

---

12. The connection created between 4:16 and 4:23 by the repetition of references to the "people" (*laos*) suggests that the "light" would include healing. Cf. J. R. C. Cousland, *The Crowds in the Gospel of Matthew*, NovTSup 102 (Leiden: Brill, 2002), 81.

13. In this regard, comparison can be made with a story preserved by Suetonius (*Vespasian* 7.2-3), according to which Vespasian miraculously healed a blind man who appealed for help to the emperor while he was holding court. Cf. Tacitus, *History* 4.81; Dio Cassius, *History* 65.8.1.

14. This is a common feature in ancient religious literature generally; see Menelaos Christopoulos, Efimia Karakantza, and Olga Levaniou, eds., *Light and Darkness in Ancient Greek Myth and Religion* (Lanham, MD: Lexington, 2010).

symbolizes the experience of humanity living "in the land and shadow of death," waiting for the dawn of a new age. The "great light" that appears in their midst is, of course, Jesus himself (Matt. 4:16), while Jesus' followers can be similarly described as a "light" to the world around them (Matt. 5:14-16; cf. Rom. 2:17-20). The imagery of "outer darkness," on the other hand, is used to represent the condition of those who stand under divine judgment (Matt. 8:12; 22:13; 25:30).[15]

To be sure, such symbolic valences are as powerful as they are pervasive. They can also become problematic, however, especially when consideration is given to how they shape the reader's attitude toward blind persons themselves. As Kathy Black observes, the words "blind" and "blindness" are among the most common terms in our religious vocabulary. Yet such terms

> are always used in a negative connotation; usually in reference to our refusal to obey or pay attention to what God wills for our lives. The presence of persons who are blind in our congregations and communities seems to go unnoticed as pastors consistently use "blind" and "blindness" as metaphors for living in some state of sin. These terms are also used to denote a "pre-Christian" state – a time before coming to know Jesus. This is made clear in the popular hymn "Amazing Grace": "I once was lost, but now am found; was blind, but now I see."[16]

Such negative connotations, of course, are grounded in the text of Scripture itself, where the blind are often depicted as bearers of divine judgment and blindness often serves as a symbol for weakness, ignorance, and death.[17] In the words of one commentator, "to be blind means to lack understanding or to live in the darkness of

---

15. Similar imagery can be found in contemporaneous Judaism. The Essenes, for example, described members prior to joining the eschatological sect as "like blind persons and like those who grope for the path," while current members are "children of light" guided by "the Prince of light." See John K. Riches, *Conflicting Mythologies: Identity Formation in the Gospels of Mark and Matthew*, Studies of the New Testament and Its World (Edinburgh: T&T Clark, 2000), 78–85.

16. Kathy Black, *A Healing Homiletic: Preaching and Disability* (Nashville: Abingdon, 1996), 58.

the old eon."[18] As disability scholars frequently point out, uncritical appropriations of such symbolism have profound implications for the social existence of blind people in our communities, who must bear the burden of serving as living reminders of humanity's need for "light" and life.

These sorts of concerns extend to the depiction of other disabilities as well. Generally speaking, in the Gospels, Jesus is not presented as accommodating people with disabilities or honoring the somatic difference they represent. Instead, in the healing stories such individuals serve as objects of Jesus' transformative power and (as we have seen) instruments through which his messianic status is demonstrated. Meanwhile, for their part, people with disabilities are presented not as agitating for their inclusion in the people of God *as* people with disabilities but as pleading with Jesus to make their disabilities go away.[19] Such depictions reinforce the notion that "God is glorified not in disability but only in its overcoming," and that in order to become a disciple or even to model certain aspects of discipleship one must conform to a particular somatic norm.[20]

17. For example: Gen. 19:11; Exod. 4:11; Lev. 21:18; Deut. 28:8-9; 2 Kgs. 6:18; Lam. 4:14; Isa. 6:9-10; 42:18; 43:8; 56:10; 59:9-10; Zeph. 1:17; John 9:2; Acts 13:11; 2 Pet. 1:9; 1 John 2:11; Rev. 3:17. See further Saul M. Olyan, *Disability in the Hebrew Bible: Interpreting Mental and Physical Differences* (Cambridge: Cambridge University Press, 2008), s.v. "blindness and the blind." As Yael Avrahami (*The Senses of Scripture: Sensory Perception in the Hebrew Bible* [New York: T&T Clark, 2012], 212) puts it, in the Bible generally, "[s]ight symbolizes knowledge and thought. Symbolically, someone who cannot see, cannot know."

18. Ulrich Luz, *Matthew: A Commentary*, Hermeneia (Minneapolis: Fortress Press, 2005), 2:47.

19. David Mitchell and Sharon Snyder, "'Jesus Thrown Everything Off Balance': Disability and Redemption in Biblical Literature," in *This Abled Body: Rethinking Disabilities in Biblical Studies*, eds. Hector Avalos, Sarah J. Melcher, and Jeremy Schipper (Atlanta: Society of Biblical Literature, 2007), 178–80; James A. Metzger and James P. Grimshaw, "Reading Matthew's Healing Narratives from the Perspectives of the Caregiver and the Disabled," in *Matthew*, Texts @ Contexts, eds. Nicole Wilkinson Duran and James P. Grimshaw (Minneapolis: Fortress Press, 2013), 137–38.

20. Amos Yong, *The Bible, Disability, and the Church: A New Vision of the People of God* (Grand Rapids: Eerdmans, 2011), 53.

The perspective articulated by Black and other disability scholars is one that needs to be taken seriously in any general assessment of the ways in which people with disabilities are depicted in the Gospel of Matthew. Let me suggest, however, that this prevailing representation of disability in the Gospel is disrupted, at least momentarily, by the particular manner in which the evangelist has formulated the healing story in Matthew 9:27-31, a story about how two blind men receive their sight from a man they call "Son of David."

Following, Secrecy, and Disobedience

We begin our analysis of Matthew 9:27-31 with how the story ends:

> But they went out and spread the news (*diephēmisan*) about him in all that land (*en holē tē gē ekeinē*). (Matt. 9:31)

This verse corresponds with the conclusion of the passage that immediately precedes, namely, the story of the official's daughter and the woman with a flow of blood (Matt. 9:18-26):[21]

> The news (*phēmē*) of this went out to all that land (*eis holēn tēn gēn ekeinēn*). (Matt. 9:26)

The pair of observations in 9:26 and 9:31, in turn, anticipates both the declaration of the crowds in 9:33, according to which Jesus' healings are unprecedented "in Israel," as well as the summary statement in 9:35, according to which Jesus traveled through "all the cities and villages" teaching and healing (cf. 4:23-25). The sequence of verses 26 + 31 + 33 + 35, taken as a whole, creates an insistent narrative trajectory for the second half of chapter 9: the scope of both Jesus' activity and Jesus' reputation is expanding throughout the nation of

---

21. Matthew 9:26 (like Matt. 4:24) appears to be based on Mark 1:28: "And the report about him went out immediately everywhere to all the surrounding district of Galilee." Cf. Mark 1:45.

Israel, a fact that would not have been lost on the nation's leaders (9:34).

The similarities between Matthew 9:18-26 and 9:27-31 extend to other narrative features as well. In both stories, a pair of individuals is healed, two women in the former, two men in the latter. In both stories, people approach Jesus for healing (9:20, 28).[22] Both stories involve touch (9:25, 29), and in both stories Jesus says something about faith (9:22, 29). The most intriguing similarity, however, has to do with the role of "the house" as a venue for healing. In 9:25, Jesus dismisses the crowd from the official's residence, entering the house alone to resuscitate his daughter. In 9:28, Jesus enters "the house," apparently alone, followed by the two men. Which house the evangelist has in mind here is difficult to say, since references have been made previously to what appear to be different houses in 8:14, 9:10, and 9:23.[23] Perhaps for our author the question of which house Jesus enters in 9:28 is less important than what the house represents, namely, a secluded place in which the performance of the miracle can be shielded from the gaze of third-party witnesses. The theme of secrecy becomes explicit in 9:30, where Jesus commands the men to tell no one about what he has done for them.[24] Together, then, the stories in 9:18-26 and 9:27-31 present the reader with an unsettling incongruity: the scope of Jesus' reputation is expanding, but this is happening despite his efforts to the contrary.[25] In presenting this

---

22. Forms of the same verb are used in the Greek, namely, *proselthousa* in 9:20 and *proselthon* in 9:28.

23. See also the discussion in Chapter Nine.

24. For a discussion of the secrecy motif in ancient healing stories, see Gerd Theissen (*The Miracle Stories of the Early Christian Tradition* [Philadelphia: Fortress Press, 1983], 61, 64–65, 68–69, 78, 140–52, 156, 187–88), who gives examples from other religious traditions, especially the Greek Magical Papyri, where the exclusion of the public from the revelation of the sacred safeguards divine secrets and lends an aura of mystery to the proceedings.

25. The rationale for Jesus' command in 9:30 is unspecified, though see 12:15-21 (and the discussion in Chapters Five and Thirteen). R. T. France (*The Gospel of Matthew*, NICNT [Grand Rapids: Eerdmans, 2007], 368) suggests that the need for secrecy is prompted specifically by the fact that the blind men refer to Jesus as Son of David, a politically sensitive

incongruity, it appears that the evangelist wants to impress upon his readers something about the nature of the Messiah's deeds: they are so exceptional in nature that knowledge of them cannot be suppressed, even by Jesus himself.[26]

In order to achieve a better understanding of the interplay between public and private in the unfolding of the narrative, it is necessary to take a closer look at Matthew's source material for his story of the two blind men. In so doing, however, we face an unusually complex literary situation. Experts agree that Matthew 9:27-31 is based at least partly on the story of Bartimaeus in Mark 10:46-52 (cf. Luke 18:35-43). They also agree, however, that Matthew draws on the Bartimaeus story two times, once in Matthew 9:27-31 and then again in Matthew 20:29-34. In terms of both its internal composition and its location within the narrative as a whole, the version of the story offered in 20:29-34 coheres more closely with the Markan prototype.[27] The "doublet" in 9:27-31, by contrast, looks more like Matthew's own composition, created in anticipation of the summarizing statement in Matthew 11:5, which, as we have seen, refers specifically to the blind receiving sight.

Other concerns become apparent when we compare Matthew 9:27-31 directly with Mark 10:46-52:

---

title. Cf. Graham N. Stanton, *A Gospel for a New People: Studies in Matthew* (Edinburgh: T&T Clark, 1992), 183.

26. Adela Yarbro Collins, *Mark*, Hermeneia (Minneapolis: Fortress Press, 2007), 180, 374; Heikki Räisänen, *The 'Messianic Secret' in Mark* (Edinburgh: T&T Clark, 1990), 60–62, 144–49.

27. I will return to this topic later in the chapter.

(46) And as he was setting out from Jericho with his disciples and a large crowd, the son of Timaeus, Bartimaeus, a blind beggar, was sitting by the road.

(27) As Jesus went on from there, two blind men followed him,

(47) And when he heard that it was Jesus the Nazarene, he began to cry out and say, "Jesus, Son of David, have mercy on me!"

(48) Many were rebuking him to be quiet, but he cried out all the more, "Son of David, have mercy on me!"

crying out and saying, "Have mercy on us, Son of David!"

(49) Stopping, Jesus said, "Call him." And they called the blind man, saying to him, "Take courage, get up! He is calling for you."

(50) Throwing aside his cloak, he jumped up and went to Jesus. (51) And answering him Jesus said, "What do you want me to do for you?" And the blind man said to him, "My teacher, that I might regain my sight!"

(28) When he entered the house, the blind men came up to him, and Jesus said to them, "Do you believe that I can do this?" They said to him, "Yes, Lord."

(52) And Jesus said to him, "Go! Your faith has made you well."

(29) Then he touched their eyes, saying, "According to your faith let it be done to you."

And at once he regained his sight and followed him on the road. (Mark 10:46-52)

(30) And their eyes were opened. And Jesus strictly charged them, saying, "See that no one knows about this!"

(31) But they went out and spread the news about him in all that land. (Matt. 9:27-31)

In keeping with his redactional proclivities, Matthew offers a more condensed version of the narrative. Also typical is Matthew's penchant for more "biblical" language, evidenced here especially by the expression chosen to depict the healing itself: according to Mark 10:52 the man "regained his sight," while Matthew 9:30 reports that "their eyes were opened," the latter echoing the same Isaianic texts alluded to in Matthew 11:5.[28] In addition, note that Matthew has two blind men in lieu of Mark's one, a feature that recalls the dual demoniacs of Matthew 8:28-34 (cf. Mark 5:1-20) and anticipates the two blind men of Matthew 20:29-34.[29] Note further that Matthew drops Mark's references to Bartimaeus and his father, lending his version of the tale a more representational quality.[30] It is also significant that both the crowds and the disciples have been written out of the story. Like other episodes in chapters 8–9, Matthew's focus is on the encounter between Jesus and the person(s) being healed.[31] Following Mark 10:47-48, Matthew has the two men plead with Jesus to "have mercy" on them (Matt. 9:27; cf. 15:22; 17:15; 20:30-31), a request reminiscent especially of appeals found in the Psalms:

> Have mercy on me, O Lord, for I languish; heal me, O Lord, for my bones shake with terror. (Ps. 6:2 JPS; cf. Pss. 27:7; 41:4)

As in Mark, the healing in Matthew does not occur at once: after making their initial appeal (Matt. 9:27; cf. Mark 10:47-48), the blind men must approach Jesus for further interaction (Matt. 9:28; cf. Mark 10:50-51), an exchange rendered more personal by Matthew's having Jesus actually touch the men's eyes (Matt. 9:29).[32] As in Mark, this

28. Isa. 35:5; 42:7. For the use of the phrase elsewhere in the Old Testament, see Avrahami, *The Senses of Scripture*, 71–72.
29. For a survey of some of the possible reasons for Matthew's doubling the number of persons healed in these stories, see W. D. Davies and Dale C. Allison, *The Gospel According to Saint Matthew*, ICC (London: T&T Clark, 1988, 1991), 1:87; 2:80. Jewish tradition stressed the importance of having more than one witness; see Matthew 18:16 (quoting Deut. 19:15); 26:60.
30. Similarly, in Matthew 9:18 the evangelist drops the name of Jairus (cf. Mark 5:22).
31. Heinz Joachim Held, "Matthew as Interpreter of the Miracle Stories," in *Tradition and Interpretation in Matthew*, eds. Günther Bornkamm, Gerhard Barth, and Heinz Joachim Held (Philadelphia: Westminster, 1963), 233–37. Also see above on 8:14-15 (Chapter Four) and 9:23-25 (Chapter Eleven).
32. Cf. Mark 10:52; Matt. 20:34. For the act of touching in other healing stories, see especially Mark 1:41//Matt. 8:3 and Mark 8:22-23. For an example from the cult of Asclepius, see Lynn R. LiDonnici, *The Epidaurian Miracle Inscriptions: Text, Translation and Commentary*, SBLTT 36 (Atlanta: Scholars, 1995), 99.

interaction also involves dialogue, though a shift occurs in the topic of conversation. The question in Mark 10:51 about the petitioner's wish ("What do you *want* me to do for you?") becomes in Matthew 9:28 a question about the petitioners' faith ("Do you *believe* that I can do this?"), a feature that figures in other healing stories.[33] The change in topic is accompanied by a change in address: in the response to his query, Jesus is referred to not simply as "teacher" (Mark 10:51) but with the more elevated title "Lord" (Matt. 9:28), the latter being a feature that figures in other healing stories as well (and again cf. Ps. 6:2).[34] The use of the formula "to believe that" (*pisteuō hoti*), which is found only here in the First Gospel, together with the acknowledgement of Jesus as Lord, transforms the exchange in Matthew 9:28 into something that sounds like a confessional statement, in which case comparison can be made with the following:[35]

Yes, Lord. I have come to believe that you are the Christ . . . (John 11:27)

If you will confess with your mouth the Lord Jesus and believe in your heart that God raised him from the dead . . . (Rom. 10:9)

In this regard, it is significant that Matthew departs from Mark by having the exchange take place in the private space of "the house" (Matt. 9:28; cf. Mark 10:46), a reference that for his readers would have brought to mind the experience of gathering in the house-*church*, that is, in the place of Christian worship.[36] As Heinz Joachim Held points out, this shift in the nature of the exchange

---

33. Matt. 8:10, 13; 9:22; 15:28; cf. 17:20; Held, "Matthew as Interpreter," 239–41; Theissen, *Miracle Stories*, 137.

34. Matt. 8:2, 6, 8; 15:22, 25, 27; 17:15; 20:30, 31, 33. For the use of the title, "teacher," see above on 8:19 (Chapter Six) and 9:11 (Chapter Nine).

35. Cf. also John 20:31; 1 Thess. 4:14; James 2:19.

36. For the social and symbolic significance of "the house" in Matthew, see Michael H. Crosby, *House of Disciples: Church, Economics, and Justice in Matthew* (Maryknoll, NY: Orbis Books, 1988), 49–75, 99–125. For houses as centers of healing, see the discussion in Chapter Five.

between Jesus and the petitioner(s) entails a shift also in Jesus' word of healing:

> Your faith has saved you. (Mark 10:52)

> According to your faith let it be done to you. (Matt. 9:29)

As Held puts it, Mark's pronouncement about "saving faith" has been replaced by Matthew with a pronouncement about "praying faith," the latter corresponding more plainly with what can be pieced together regarding the cultic practices of the Matthean community (cf. Matt. 6:10).[37] The account in Matthew 20:29-34, meanwhile, contains no such pronouncement, thus lacking any reference to the blind men's faith.

Another significant difference between Mark 10:46-52 and Matthew 9:27-31 concerns how the two stories end. The former ends with Bartimaeus following Jesus on the road. The latter ends with Jesus enjoining the men to secrecy and with both of them immediately ignoring his command.[38] Put differently, a command for silence attributed to the crowds (Mark 10:48) is changed into a command for secrecy attributed to Jesus and shifted to the end of the pericope (Matt. 9:30). Mark's blind man disobeys the crowds; Matthew's blind men disobey Jesus.[39]

For the basis of this alternative conclusion we must again turn to Mark. Not to the conclusion of his story about Bartimaeus, however, but to a healing story that occurs earlier in the Second Gospel:

---

37. Held, "Matthew as Interpreter," 287–88. Cf. the discussion of Matt. 9:18//Mark 5:23 in Chapter Eleven.

38. No rationale is provided for the men's disobedience. Evert-Jan Vledder (*Conflict in the Miracle Stories: A Socio-Exegetical Study of Matthew 8 and 9*, JSNTSup 152 [Sheffield: Sheffield Academic Press, 1997], 220–21) conjectures that it represents a failure on their part to recognize the full extent to which Jesus embodies divine mercy.

39. Theissen, *Miracle Stories*, 187–88.

(40) And a man with a scale-disease came up to him pleading with him, and kneeling he said to him, "If you are willing, you can (*dunasai*) cleanse me." (41) And moved with compassion, he stretched out his hand and touched (*hēpsato*) him and said to him, "I am willing; be cleansed!" (42) And at once the scale-disease left him and he was cleansed. (43) And strictly charging him (*embrimēsamenos*), he at once cast him out, (44) and he said to him, "See that (*hora*) you tell no one (*mēdeni*) anything; but go show yourself to the priest and offer for your cleansing what Moses commanded, as a testimony to them." (45) But he went out (*exelthōn*) and began to proclaim it freely and to spread (*diaphēmizein*) the word, so that he was no longer able to enter a city openly, but stayed out in deserted places; and they were coming to him from everywhere. (Mark 1:40-45)

(2) And coming up to him, a man with a scale-disease bowed down before him, saying, "Lord, if you are willing, you can (*dunasai*) cleanse me." (3) And stretching out his hand he touched (*hēpsato*) him, saying, "I am willing; be cleansed!" And at once his scale-disease was cleansed. (4) And Jesus said to him, "See that (*hora*) you tell no one (*mēdeni*); but go show yourself to the priest and offer the gift that Moses commanded, as a testimony to them." (Matt. 8:2-4)

(27) As Jesus went on from there, two blind men followed him, crying out and saying, "Have mercy on us, Son of David!" (28) When he entered the house, the blind men came up to him, and Jesus said to them, "Do you believe that I can (*dunamai*) do this?" They said to him, "Yes, Lord." (29) Then he touched (*hēpsato*) their eyes, saying, "According to your faith let it be done to you." (30) And their eyes were opened. And Jesus strictly charged (*enebrimēthē*) them, saying, "See that no one (*horate mēdeis*) knows about this!" (31) But they went out (*exelthontes*) and spread the news (*diephēmisan*) about him in all that land. (Matt. 9:27-31)

It appears that Matthew has shifted certain elements from Mark's version of the healing of the "leper" to the story of the two blind men in Matthew 9:27-31, elements that are *not* to be found in the story of Bartimaeus.[40] Note that some of these elements occur in Matthew's version of the leper's story (Matt. 8:2-4) while others do not.[41] Among the latter, most significant is the report that despite being "strictly charged" by Jesus, the healed man disobeyed Jesus' command to tell "no one" but instead "went out" and "spread" the word about his healer (Mark 1:44-45; cf. Matt. 9:30-31). It appears that Matthew was intent on preserving the major features of Mark 1:40-45, but that he did so by distributing those features across two stories, Matthew 8:2-4 and Matthew 9:27-31. Why the evangelist would utilize some of the elements of Mark 1:40-45 in Matthew 8:2-4 seems obvious enough, since both stories concern the cleansing of a man with a scale-disease. But why he would shift some of these elements, especially the motif of disobedience, to Matthew 9:27-31, a story about two blind men, remains something of a puzzle.[42]

Similar comments can be made regarding the command to secrecy. Consider, for example, the way in which Mark and Matthew conclude the story of the official's daughter:

And he strictly ordered them that no one should know about this. (Mark 5:43)

The news of this went out to all that land. (Matt. 9:26)

Matthew has dropped the Markan command to secrecy in 5:43 or, put differently, he has *shifted* the command from the story of the official's daughter (Matt. 9:18-19 + 23-26) to the story that immediately follows it, the story of the two blind men (Matt.

---

40. Note also that the phrase, "moved with compassion," has been shifted from Mark 1:41 to Matthew 20:24. Cf. John Nolland, *The Gospel of Matthew*, NIGTC (Grand Rapids: Eerdmans, 2005), 829.
41. E.g., both Matthew 8:2 and 9:28 (cf. Mark 1:40) have the verb *dunamai* (= "can" in the translation), though the focus in the former is on Jesus' *willingness* to heal while in the latter it is on his *ability* to heal. For the act of touching (*hēpsato*) in Matthew 8:3 and 9:29, see n. 32 above.
42. Presumably, he deletes the motif from 8:1-4 in part so as to avoid the scenario of Jesus' instruction regarding the law being disobeyed by someone who has just called him "Lord" (see 5:17-20 as well as the discussion in Chapter Two). This does not explain, however, why he transfers the motif to 9:27-31.

9:27-31). Again, the rationale for this redaction is not immediately apparent. Mention should also be made of the story of Jesus and a deaf man (*kōphon*) in Mark 7:32-37, in which the healing takes place "in private" (Mark 7:33; cf. Matt. 9:28) and which concludes with Jesus ordering those who brought the man to tell no one, and with them disobeying his order.[43] Matthew drops the story in Mark 7:32-37 (see Matt. 15:30-31) but includes the secrecy + disobedience sequence elsewhere, namely, in Matthew 9:30-31. Not coincidentally (it would seem), the story of the two blind men is immediately followed by a story (9:32-34) in which Jesus heals a man who is mute (*kōphon*).

Seclusion and secrecy motifs are also evident in another Markan healing story that Matthew does not retell, namely, Mark 8:22-26:

> (22) And they came to Bethsaida. And they brought to him a blind man and implored him to touch him. (23) And taking the blind man by the hand he led him out of the village; and after spitting on his eyes and laying his hands on him, he asked him, "Do you see anything?" (24) And looking up, he said, "I see people, because I see them like trees, walking around." (25) Then again he laid his hands on his eyes, and his sight broke through and he was restored and saw everything clearly. (26) And he sent him to his home, saying, "Do not even enter the village."

Functionally, Jesus' act of leading the blind man out of the village in Mark 8:23 (cf. Mark 7:33) corresponds with his leading the two men into the house in Matthew 9:28, while his command for the man not to enter the village in Mark 8:26 corresponds with his command for the two men to tell no one in Matthew 9:30b, even as Mark 8:26 notably *lacks* the disobedience motif of Matthew 9:31.[44] The references to saliva and healing by degrees in Mark 8:23-25 may explain why Matthew omits this story, though in a way the account

---

43. Mark 7:36: "And he ordered them to tell no one; but the more he ordered them, the more widely they proclaimed it."
44. The manuscript tradition for Mark 8:26 adds a command for secrecy; see Collins, *Mark*, 389–90.

in Matthew 9:27-31 (with its "extra" blind man) compensates for the omission.[45]

As commentators often note, the stories about blind men in 8:22-26 and 10:46-52 have deep symbolic value for Mark, with the ability of these men to see their surroundings signifying the ability of the disciples to discern who Jesus truly is (cf. Mark 8:17-18, 27-30).[46] In this regard, it is significant that Mark 10:46-52 concludes with Bartimaeus "following" Jesus (10:52), an obvious metaphor for discipleship (Mark 8:34; 10:28; etc.). Some scholars have even gone so far as to categorize the Bartimaeus episode formally as a "call" story, analogous to episodes elsewhere in the Gospel where Jesus calls individuals to be his disciples.[47] For his part, Matthew frequently understands "following" Jesus as a metaphor for discipleship as well (Matt. 4:20, 22; 8:19, 22-23; 9:9; 10:38; 16:24; 19:21, 27-28; 27:55) and similarly concludes the story in Matthew 20:29-34 with the two men following Jesus (20:34).[48]

The two men in Matthew 9:27-31 follow Jesus, too, though the symbolic value of their action is less apparent. In order to recognize some of the possibilities in this regard, it is helpful to submit for comparison not another healing story but the story of the "call" of Matthew the tax collector (Matt. 9:9-13).[49] Note in particular the nearly identical openings to the two stories:[50]

> And going on from there Jesus . . . (*kai paragōn ho Iēsous ekeithen . . .*) (Matt. 9:9)

---

45. Note also the theme of touching in Mark 8:22 and Matthew 9:29.

46. E.g., Joel Marcus, *Mark*, AB 27 (New Haven, CT: Yale University Press, 2009), 2:592–602, 757–66.

47. Paul J. Achtemeier, "'And He Followed Him': Miracles and Discipleship in Mark 10:46-52," *Semeia* 11 (1978): 115–45; cf. Riches, *Conflicting Mythologies*, 69–113.

48. Cf. Jack D. Kingsbury, "The Verb *akolouthein* ("To Follow") as an Index of Matthew's View of His Community," *JBL* 97 (1978): 56–73.

49. Luz, *Matthew*, 2:46–47.

50. Note that 9:9 and 9:27 are the only two places in the Gospel where Matthew uses the *paragō* + *ekeithen* construction.

And going on from there Jesus . . . (*kai paragonti ekeithen tō Iēsou* . . .) (Matt. 9:27)

In 9:9-10, the tax collector "follows" (*ēkolouthēsen*) Jesus and then interacts with him in "the house" (*hē oikia*), actions that parallel those of the blind men in 9:27-28, who "follow" Jesus (*ēkolouthēsan*) and then interact with him in "the house" (*hē oikia*). The actions of Jesus in 9:9-13, meanwhile, are identified as an expression of mercy, or *eleos* (9:13), a concept that figures prominently in the healing story as well, where the two men plead with Jesus to "have mercy" (*eleēson*) on them (9:27).[51] Looking at this set of parallels as a whole (and taking into consideration the proximity of the two episodes), it looks as though the evangelist is encouraging the reader to see how the experience of the men healed by Jesus in 9:27-31 resembles the experience of the man called by Jesus to be one of his disciples in 9:9-13 (cf. 10:3).

In the First Gospel, then, there are two stories about Jesus healing two blind men, and in both stories the men are represented as "following" Jesus, a likely metaphor for discipleship.[52] Despite these basic similarities, however, a crucial difference can be discerned: while the two men in Matthew 20:29-34 follow Jesus *after* they are healed, the two men in Matthew 9:27-31 follow Jesus *before* they are healed. In addition, the confession + pronouncement of faith in Matthew 9:28-29 is lacking in Matthew 20:29-34. Another feature lacking in Matthew 20:29-34 is found in Matthew 9:30-31,

51. Warren Carter (*Matthew and the Margins: A Socio-Political and Religious Reading* [Sheffield: Sheffield Academic Press, 2000], 227) characterizes their request for mercy as a "trait of discipleship." For the theme of mercy, see also Matt. 5:7; 9:13; 12:7; 15:22; 17:15; 18:33; 20:30-31; 23:23. Chae (*Jesus as the Eschatological Davidic Shepherd*, 255) discusses how the theme of mercy connects 9:13 with 9:27.

52. In some of the summary statements (Matt. 4:24-25; 12:15; 14:13-14; 19:2), depictions of the crowds as "following" Jesus are accompanied by accounts of healing (cf. Cousland, *The Crowds in the Gospel of Matthew*, 163–68). The two blind men are differentiated from such crowds by their interactions with Jesus in the house, including their confessional statement.

where the healed men are enjoined by Jesus to secrecy and then promptly disobey his command.[53] In what follows, I want to explore what implications this difference in Matthew's utilization of both the following motif and the secrecy/disobedience motif might have for the representation of disability in his Gospel.

Senses of Scripture

The differences between Matthew 9:27-31 and Matthew 20:29-34 outlined above can be attributed in part to differences in how the stories function within their respective narrative contexts.[54] On one hand, like the Markan text upon which it is based (Mark 10:46—11:10), the story in Matthew 20:29-34 is closely linked with the story that immediately follows, the account of the triumphal entry (Matt. 21:1-10): the healing of two men who call Jesus "Son of David" in the former (20:30-31) provides added legitimation for the public acclamation of Jesus as "Son of David" in the latter (21:9; cf. 21:15).[55] Accordingly, the men are healed not in the private space of "the house" but in the public space of the road, while after their healing the men are not enjoined to secrecy but rather join the crowd following Jesus and making this acclamation (20:29, 34; 21:9).[56] The story in Matthew 9:27-31, on the other hand, belongs to a series of miracle stories that reveal both different aspects of Jesus'

53. Note that Matthew 20:34 drops Jesus' command for the healed man to "Go!" in Mark 10:52, eliminating even the hint of disobedience. Cf. Marcus, *Mark*, 2:761, 764–65.
54. Cf. W. R. G. Loader, "Son of David, Blindness, Possession, and Duality in Matthew," *CBQ* 44 (1982): 572–80. Janice Capel Anderson ("Double and Triple Stories, the Implied Reader, and Redundancy in Matthew," *Semeia* 31 [1985]: 77–78) contends that the pair of blind men in 20:29-34 is presented more favorably than the pair in 9:27-31 but, as we shall see, this is a matter of perspective.
55. Note that the reference to Son of David in Matthew 21:9 is redactional (cf. Mark 11:9-10). The reference to Son of David in Matthew 21:15 (cf. Mark 11:18) is also redactional.
56. This accounts for another difference between 9:27-31 and 20:29-34. The former opens with the blind men following Jesus while the latter opens with the crowd following Jesus (20:29) and the two blind men sitting by the road (20:30). Cf. Mark 10:46.

healing ministry and different ways in which people respond to that ministry (chapters 8–9).[57] Matters relating to publicity are at work in this narrative context as well, though the manner in which these matters unfold is complicated. As we have seen, the story of the two blind men in 9:27-31 is connected structurally to the pericope that immediately precedes it, the story of the official's daughter (9:18-26).

It is also important to note how the two stories are connected logically. The same verb used to describe the daughter's "rising up" in Matthew 9:25 will be used later in the Gospel with reference to Jesus' resurrection (Matt. 16:21; 17:9, 23; 20:19; 26:32; 27:63; 28:6-7), the implication being that the same eschatological power by which God will raise him from the dead is manifested in her restored body.[58] Moreover, in a statement that Matthew adds to his source material, we learn that "the news" about Jesus being the agent of such power "went out to all that land" (Matt. 9:26; cf. Mark 5:43). Assuming that the two men mentioned in the verse that immediately follows (Matt. 9:27) are inhabitants of that land—indeed, that they are representative of those "sitting in the land and shadow of death" (Matt. 4:16)—then we can also assume that they are among those who have heard the good news. From this perspective, 9:26 and 9:27 can be seen as complementing one another: the former indicates what is being *spoken* about Jesus while the latter introduces characters into the story who must rely entirely on what they *hear* about Jesus.

An important conclusion follows from all this: the first characters in the narrative to know and follow Jesus as the Son of David do

---

57. Cf. David B. Howell, *Matthew's Inclusive Story: A Study in the Narrative Rhetoric of the First Gospel*, JSNTSup 42 (Sheffield: JSOT, 1990), 133–35; and the discussion of reader-response criticism in Chapter One.

58. As Eric Eve (*The Healer from Nazareth: Jesus' Miracles in Historical Context* [London: SPCK, 2009], 157) puts it, for the evangelist, "it would have seemed appropriate that the one raised from the dead should have the power to conquer death in others, and stories of raising people from the dead would serve to symbolize the eschatological salvation Jesus was believed to bring."

so on the basis of non-visual modes of sense perception. Specifically, any understanding the men have come to have of Jesus depends on the power of hearing, not on the power of sight. Indeed, within the context of the story itself the acquisition of sight provides no apparent advantage in their ability to perceive Jesus' identity or respond appropriately to his demands. In fact, it may be interpreted as representing a liability, inasmuch as it is only *after* receiving their sight that the men disobey Jesus and the *only* agency attributed to the men after receiving their sight entails an act of disobedience. Being blind, the men are unable to see Jesus or the effects of his messianic deeds. It is apparent from the narrative, however, that they *are* able to hear him, a fact that has implications for understanding their representative function for the reader.

For such a compressed narrative, it is striking how much agency is assigned to these two men. In this regard, a clear contrast can be made between Matthew 9:27-31, which concerns individuals who are unable to *see*, and the story that immediately follows, Matthew 9:32-34, which concerns an individual who is unable to *hear*: the latter does not follow Jesus (or manifest any attribute of discipleship) but must be "brought to him" by others (9:32).[59] In the Matthean scheme of sensory impairment, deafness appears to carry greater consequences for agency than blindness, probably because the deaf are unable to hear either Jesus' words (9:28) or the reports that are being disseminated about him (9:26). The parallelism of 9:26 and 9:31 highlights another dimension of the blind men's agency, namely, that after their healing they become agents in disseminating the same good news of which they were the apparent beneficiaries though, as we have seen, a certain ambiguity attaches to this agency insofar as they carry it out in contradiction to Jesus' own orders. In this

59. Cf. Matt. 4:24; 8:16; 9:2; 12:22; 14:35.

regard a distinction can be made between the two blind men, whose proclamation of "the news" in 9:31 is prohibited by Jesus, and the disciples, whose proclamation of the kingdom is authorized by Jesus (10:7, 19-20, 27).[60]

Consideration of such facts raises questions regarding the role of both sensory experiences and sensory metaphors in the depiction of discipleship in the First Gospel. In coming to terms with the various dimensions of this role, it is important to bear in mind that Matthew actually has a fair amount to say about both seeing and hearing. Given what was discussed above regarding the significance of light imagery in the First Gospel, it is not surprising that in contemporary scholarship the evangelist's understanding of vision has been studied rather extensively.[61] His understanding of audition, on the other hand, has received comparatively little attention.[62] What follows represents an effort to remedy this imbalance.

One place where the evangelist mentions both seeing and hearing has already been mentioned, namely, the "deeds of the Messiah" passage in Matthew 11:2-5. John the Baptist has been in prison since the beginning of Jesus' public ministry (Matt. 4:12) and so can be taken as representative of those who have not witnessed those deeds with their own eyes but rely on what they have "heard" (Matt. 11:2) from others about them. Jesus begins his response to John's query with a statement that has a parallel in the Gospel of Luke:

---

60. This distinction can be set within the larger context of speech ethics in the Gospel, where a contrast is made between prohibited speech acts (e.g., 5:22, 34-36; 6:7; 7:4) and authorized speech acts (e.g., 5:37, 44; 6:9-13). The speech of the blind men belongs to the former.

61. E.g., Candida R. Moss, "Blurred Vision and Ethical Confusion: The Rhetorical Function of Matthew 6:22-23," *CBQ* 73 (2011): 757-76.

62. E.g., Jeannine K. Brown, "The Rhetoric of Hearing: The Use of the Isaianic Hearing Motif in Matthew 11:2–16:20," in *Built Upon The Rock: Studies in the Gospel of Matthew*, eds. Daniel M. Gurtner and John Nolland (Grand Rapids: Eerdmans, 2008), 248–69; Louise J. Lawrence, "Reading Matthew's Gospel with Deaf Culture," in *Matthew*, Texts @ Contexts, eds. Nicole Wilkinson Duran and James P. Grimshaw (Minneapolis: Fortress Press, 2013), 158–62.

Go and tell John what you hear and see. (Matt. 11:4)

Go and tell John what you have seen and heard. (Luke 7:22)

In both passages, it is implied that the two modes of perception (seeing and hearing) serve to complement one another, though there is a difference in the order of presentation.[63] In the Third Gospel, seeing precedes hearing. In the First Gospel, it is the other way around. The reason for the difference has to do with the function of Matthew 11:2-5 as a recapitulation of chapters 5–9, a unit in which the presentation of "the Messiah of the Word" (referring to the Sermon on the Mount in chapters 5–7) precedes the presentation of "the Messiah of Deed" (referring to the suite of miracle stories in chapters 8–9).[64] The point seems to be that it is possible to discern the full meaning of the miracles that one sees Jesus perform only after one hears Jesus proclaim the gospel.[65] Moreover, the Isaianic allusions of the verse that follows (Matt. 11:5) play an important hermeneutical role in relation to the contents of chapters 8–9. What the evangelist is teaching his readers in 11:5 is that the miracles recounted in those chapters are not self-interpreting, that is, the miracles are not in and of themselves proof of Jesus' messianic status.[66] Rather, the christological meaning of the miracles that the characters in the story have witnessed in chapters 8–9 must be clarified through

---

63. For the correlation between seeing and hearing in the Old Testament, see Avrahami, *The Senses of Scripture*, 69–74.

64. Held, "Matthew as Interpreter," 246. Similarly, the summary statements in Matthew 4:23 and 9:35 (which together create a narrative frame around chapters 5–9) mention teaching and proclaiming before healing. Cf. Matt. 13:14, and note also the summary statement in Matt. 11:1 (cf. Mark 1:39; 6:6).

65. Craig Koester ("Hearing, Seeing, and Believing in the Gospel of John," *Bib* 70 [1989]: 327–48) makes similar observations about the Fourth Gospel. Regarding John 1:35–2:25, for example, he writes, "The sign they (i.e., the disciples) saw at Cana did not evoke an initial faith. Rather, the sign confirmed and was perceived by a faith that had been engendered through hearing. In contrast, the people who came to Jesus because of what they saw him do were later confounded by what they heard him say" (pp. 332–33).

66. Held, "Matthew as Interpreter," 255.

the application of certain Isaianic prophecies, prophecies that Jesus speaks and that characters in the story hear. As Matthew 11:20-24 will go on to explain, witnessing miracles, even many miracles, does not necessarily generate the right kind of response to the gospel.[67] What is essential, then, for John (and, presumably, for anyone in John's position) is not seeing Jesus' miracles but hearing Jesus' explanation of their messianic significance.[68]

The need for verbal interpretation informs the narration of other revelatory events in the Gospel as well, even events in which the visual experience is nothing less than theophanic. In the transfiguration story, for example, the meaning of the visual elements in Matthew 17:2-5a (the change in Jesus' appearance, the appearance of Moses, Elijah, and the "bright cloud") remains indeterminate until we reach the decisive explication of the event in Matthew 17:5b.[69] What is noteworthy about this explication is that it has not only a verbal *form* ("A voice out of the cloud said . . . ") but also a verbal *reference*:

This is my beloved Son, with whom I am well pleased: listen to him!

The divine command for the disciples to "listen" to what Jesus says entails a likely allusion to the book of Deuteronomy:

---

67. In this passage, Jesus denounces the cities (including Capernaum, the setting for Matt. 9:27-31) in which he had performed most of his healings because they failed to repent; that is, they failed to recognize that the deeds of the Messiah make a claim on those who experience them.

68. Cf. Luz, *Matthew*, 2:134: "Unlike Luke 7:21, Matthew does not find it necessary to have John's disciples immediately experience Jesus' miracles; the reports of chaps. 8–9 that are here summarized (i.e., in Matt 11:4-5) are sufficient."

69. Cf. Matt. 4:16-17. Speaking of biblical theophanies generally, George Savran ("Seeing is Believing: On the Relative Priority of Visual and Verbal Perception of the Divine," *BibInt* 17 [2009]: 325) states, "In order to take in the significance of the object which has been glimpsed there often must be clarification, and this is best accomplished through words. The meaning of an initial vision is often not self-evident, and the details of the message necessitate verbal clarification in order to convey the central import of the theophany."

(15) The Lord your God will raise up for you a prophet like me from among you . . . you shall listen to him . . . (18) I will put my words in his mouth, and he shall speak to them all that I command him. (Deut. 18:15, 18 NASB)

This allusion, in turn, not only further intimates the verbal character of Jesus' identity but also provides a background for understanding what is asserted later in the narrative regarding the eternal (i.e., divine) authority of Jesus' verbal ministry: "Heaven and earth will pass away, but my words will not pass away" (Matt. 24:35).[70]

If the oral-aural medium applies to the manner in which Jesus communicates the gospel, it applies as well to the manner in which people in the narrative receive it, a point evidenced perhaps most vividly by what one scholar has labeled the "parables of hearing" in Matthew 13:3-23.[71] Here humanity is grouped into different types of hearers, distinguished specifically by the different ways in which they respond to "the word of the kingdom" (13:19). Within this schema, the evangelist's anthropological ideal is realized by the person who not only hears but also understands the word. This is because, as the quotation of Isaiah 6:9-10 in Matthew 13:14-15 makes plain,[72] "hearing" is a matter not of the ears but of the heart, or *kardia*, a common metaphor in the Gospel for the seat of human understanding, volition, and emotion.[73] As Matthew 13:19 indicates,

---

70. Note how the verbal clarification continues in Matthew 17:9-13. Similar is the resurrection account: the meaning of the visual elements (Matt. 28:1-4) for the participants is elucidated by subsequent verbal instructions (Matt. 28:5-10). The magi, meanwhile, are led to their intended destination not by what they see (2:2, 10) but by a combination of what they see and what they hear (2:9). Cf. Jack D. Kingsbury, "The Rhetoric of Comprehension in the Gospel of Matthew," *NTS* 41 (1995): 358–77.

71. Gerhard Kittel, "*akouō*," *TDNT* 1 (1964): 219. Note especially 13:9: "He who has ears, let him hear."

72. Significantly, even though the quotation of Isaiah 6:9-10 in Matthew 13:14-15 also makes reference to "seeing" (which, again, is mentioned after "hearing"), this mode of sense perception is *not* applied to the interpretation of the parable in Matthew 13:18-23. Cf. Deut. 29:4; Jer. 5:21-23; Ezek. 12:2.

73. Cf. Matt. 5:8, 28; 6:21; 9:4; 11:29; 12:34; 15:8, 18-19; 18:35; 22:37; Avrahami, *The Senses of Scripture*, 158.

what is "sown" in the heart is not something that one sees but something that one hears (cf. 12:34; 15:8, 18). Because the commitment of the heart is determinative for human comportment (Matt. 6:21; 12:34; 15:19), the one who hears and understands the word will also bear "fruit" (i.e., actions) worthy of the word, as the conclusion to the pericope (Matt. 13:23) stipulates.[74] Put differently, the only proof of true understanding—that is, of true "hearing"—is to be found in actions informed by that understanding (cf. 7:16-20; 12:33-37). Similarly, in Matthew 7:24, Jesus identifies the "wise" person (that is, the person with understanding) as the one "who hears these words of mine and acts on them," a likely allusion to Deuteronomy 28:15 ("But it shall come about, if you do not hear the Lord your God and act to do all his commandments," etc.).[75]

That our survey of Matthean texts has encountered yet another allusion to a passage from Deuteronomy should not go unnoticed, especially in light of what disability scholars have characterized as the latter's "audiocentricity," a term that refers to the book's propensity to portray hearing as the most reliable mode for apprehending divine revelation, while casting aspersions on other senses (especially sight) as potentially deceptive.[76] A fundamental contrast is made in this regard between idols, which can be seen but not heard (Deut. 4:28; etc.), and the Sinai theophany, which is recast as a predominantly auditory experience: "You heard the sound of words but you saw no form—only a voice" (Deut. 4:12). As Stephen Geller has argued,

---

74. "And the one sown on the good soil, this is the one who hears the word and understands it; who indeed bears fruit and brings forth, some a hundredfold, some sixty, and some thirty."
75. Davies and Allison, *Saint Matthew*, 1:719.
76. The text "depicts hearing as the religiously decisive sense, the one on which contact with God depends" (Rebecca Raphael, "Whoring after Cripples: On the Intersection of Gender and Disability Imagery in Jeremiah," in *Disability Studies and Biblical Literature*, eds. Candida R. Moss and Jeremy Schipper [New York: Palgrave Macmillan, 2011], 109). Cf. Hector Avalos, "Introducing Sensory Criticism in Biblical Studies: Audiocentricity and Visiocentricity," in *This Abled Body: Rethinking Disabilities in Biblical Studies*, 50–55; Rebecca Raphael, *Biblical Corpora: Representations of Disability in Hebrew Biblical Literature* (New York: T&T Clark, 2008), 40–44.

one way in which Deuteronomy's articulation of such perceptual priorities can be assessed is in terms of its contribution to the development of biblical *wisdom* traditions. Indeed, in asserting this particular hierarchy of sensory modes, Deuteronomy appears to be reconceptualizing the basis of wisdom itself. Whereas with what Geller calls the "Old Wisdom" (that is, the conception of wisdom received by Deuteronomy) it is the case that "ultimate authority continually rests on the visual," with the "New Wisdom" (that is, the conception of wisdom advanced by Deuteronomy itself) it is the case that "seeing validates the initial, constitutive event, but thenceforth all authority rests on hearing, on teaching the young."[77] While Old Wisdom involves observing nature, New Wisdom involves learning a tradition, one that within the narrative world of the text is communicated by words that Moses speaks and that the Israelites hear.

That an argument about the senses can be construed as an argument about wisdom is relevant to the interpretation of the First Gospel as well, insofar as Matthew's proclivity for sapiential themes and forms has long been acknowledged by biblical scholarship.[78] In keeping with this proclivity, particular emphasis is placed in the Gospel both on presenting Jesus as a teacher (e.g., Matt. 7:28-29; 11:29; 23:8; 26:18) and on showing that the disciples understand what Jesus teaches them (e.g., Matt. 13:23, 51-52; 23:34). The latter is critical because for Matthew being a disciple means becoming not only a learner but also a teacher oneself. Indeed, the Gospel culminates with Jesus commissioning the disciples to "teach them (i.e., all the nations) to observe all that I commanded you" (Matt.

---

77. Stephen A. Geller, *Sacred Enigmas: Literary Religion in the Hebrew Bible* (New York: Routledge, 1996), 50.

78. E.g., Celia M. Deutsch, *Lady Wisdom, Jesus, and the Sages: Metaphor and Social Context in Matthew's Gospel* (Valley Forge, PA: Trinity Press International, 1996), 142–47. See further Chapter Nine.

28:20; cf. 5:19; 10:24-25). What Jesus has "commanded" the disciples refers in the first place to the five major discourses of the Gospel (chapters 5–7, 10, 13, 18, 23–25), discourses that in the narrative world of the text Jesus speaks and the disciples hear.[79] Thus, as Ulrich Luz puts it, in Matthew "the disciples are basically designated as *hearers* of Jesus' message," since "discipleship is always related to the teaching of the earthly Jesus."[80] It is from this perspective that we can best appreciate the appeal in Matthew 15:10 for characters in the story (and, by implication, individuals in Matthew's audience) to "hear and understand," an appeal that, not surprisingly, has analogues in the book of Deuteronomy (Deut. 5:1; 6:3-4; 12:28; etc.).

Commenting on the situation more generally, disabilities scholar Yael Avrahami has remarked on the need for biblical researchers "to liberate themselves . . . from the Western bias that prioritizes the sense of sight."[81] The analysis above has shown how Matthew 9:27-31 not only dramatizes the role of hearing within the narrative world of the text but does so in a manner consistent with priorities expressed elsewhere in the Gospel. In this way it serves as a partial corrective to the emphasis placed in the scholarly literature on Matthew's semantics of vision and light. To be sure, the First Gospel does not privilege hearing to the same degree or with the same intent that Deuteronomy does. After all, as we have seen, passages like Matthew 4:16, 5:14-16, and 6:22-23, with their imagery of light and vision, figure prominently in structuring the author's symbolic world, while passages like Matthew 11:4 and 13:14-15 present hearing and seeing as complementary modes of sense perception. Rather than indicating

---

79. Note Matthew's consistency in indicating that the disciples are actually present to hear each discourse (Matt. 5:1; 10:1; 13:36; 18:1; 23:1). In some cases the discourses are even formulated in such a way as to underscore their oral-aural nature. For example, in the antitheses (Matt. 6:21-48), the content is presented as something that the disciples have heard ("You have heard . . .") and about which Jesus will speak ("But I say to you . . .").

80. Ulrich Luz, *Studies in Matthew* (Grand Rapids: Eerdmans, 2005), 124–25 (my emphasis).

81. Avrahami, *The Senses of Scripture*, 26.

a consistent hierarchy, it is probably better to interpret the sorts of auditory concerns identified above within the broader web of a complex sensory dynamic, one that incorporates and communicates various perspectives on how human beings make "sense" of their experiences, including their experience of the gospel/Gospel itself.[82] Given the generally low rates of literacy in antiquity, we can assume that the majority of Matthew's "readers" interacted with the content of his Gospel not visually, by looking at a written text, but aurally, by hearing the recitation of an "oral-performative tradition."[83] In this case, the auditory priorities projected by the Gospel's narrative world would accord with the oral-aural medium through which the Gospel itself was being transmitted.

Signs of (Un)receptiveness

Commentators sometimes struggle trying to project a realistic scenario for the action attributed to the two blind men in Matthew 9:27. John Nolland, for instance, speculates that the men were able to follow Jesus by listening to the noise created by his entourage.[84] As we have seen, however, in Matthew 9:27-31 all references to third-party characters have been dropped: for Matthew everything revolves around the men's personal interaction with Jesus. The evangelist,

---

82. A deeper appreciation for such dynamics would need to take into account the various ways in which the different modes of perception complement one another, e.g., just as true "hearing" is presented as a matter not of the ears but of the heart (13:14-15), true "sight" penetrates beyond what is observable to the eyes. Besides Matthew 4:18, 21; 9:2, 9, see Walter T. Wilson, "Seen in Secret: Inconspicuous Piety and Alternative Subjectivity in Matthew 6:1-6, 16-18," *CBQ* 72 (2010): 475–97.

83. For an overview of matters attending the study of this tradition, see Richard A. Horsley, "Oral Communication, Oral Performance, and New Testament Interpretation," in *Method and Meaning: Essays on New Testament Interpretation in Honor of Harold W. Attridge*, eds. Andrew B. McGowan and Kent Harold Richards (Atlanta: Society of Biblical Literature, 2011), 125–55. For an analysis of the synoptic healing stories "as products of the oral medium and of oral mentality," see Werner H. Kelber, *The Oral and the Written Gospel: The Hermeneutics of Speaking and Writing in the Synoptic Tradition, Mark, Paul, and Q* (Philadelphia: Fortress Press, 1983), 45–52.

84. Nolland, *The Gospel of Matthew*, 400.

it seems, is more concerned with *that* these blind men follow Jesus than with *how* they follow Jesus, indicating that this act of following conveys a symbolic meaning. This meaning is consistent with the depiction of such acts elsewhere in the Gospel, for example, in Matthew 9:9-13, where a man called by Jesus to be a disciple similarly "follows" him into "the house" and experiences his "mercy" there. The symbolic meaning conveyed by the men's action is further clarified when our pericope is compared with similar healing stories. In Matthew 9:27-31, the evangelist departs from both Mark 10:46-52 and Matthew 20:29-34 by stating that the blind men followed Jesus before and not after they were healed. In addition, their action is accompanied by several other marks of discipleship, all of which are assigned to the men before their eyes are opened: they follow Jesus into "the house," they acknowledge him as "Lord," and they confess their belief in his ability to heal them (9:28).[85]

Especially striking, of course, is the form of address that the blind men use for Jesus in Matthew 9:27 (cf. 20:30-31). Here, for the first time in the narrative, someone is depicted as referring to Jesus as "Son of David." Evidently, these blind men are able to "see" something about Jesus that sighted people cannot, namely, that Jesus is the Messiah of Israel, the one sent by God to bring eschatological "light" to his people. If the imagery of blindness in the Gospels usually denotes "a time before coming to know Jesus,"[86] then here we have a story in which the blind are represented as "coming to know Jesus" before their sight is restored, exercising a kind of prophetic insight comparable to that of blind seers like Eli (1 Sam. 3) or Ahijah (1 Kgs. 14).[87] Moreover, in contrast to Mark 10:46-52

---

85. As noted above, the account in 20:29-34 lacks any reference to the men's faith.
86. Black, *A Healing Homiletic*, 58.
87. Cf. Mary Ann Beavis, "From the Margin to the Way: A Feminist Reading of the Story of Bartimaeus," *JFSR* 14 (1998): 37; Olyan, *Disability in the Hebrew Bible*, 9. For the motif of the blind seer in Greco-Roman literature, see Beavis, "From the Margin to the Way," 26–27.

and Matthew 20:29-34, the two men in Matthew 9:27-31 are able both to perceive who Jesus is *and* to act on this perception (i.e., by "following" Jesus) without the benefit of physical sight. In so doing, their experience draws attention to the power of hearing in the formation of disciples, which in turn draws attention to the power of what is heard, power that is nothing less than eschatological in its implications (9:25-26). The example that the two men set for the readers, then, is in keeping with texts like Matthew 7:24 and 13:3-23, texts in which the substance of the Gospel is presented as something to be received by way of hearing, with hearing, understanding, and doing being presented as integrated activities that together constitute the appropriate response to Jesus. What is important to note is that this integrative perspective on discipleship is applied to the blind men of Matthew 9:27-31 *as blind men*, insofar as they hear what Jesus says, understand who he is, and act in ways that express their faith in him, all without benefit of sight. Thinking again of the story as a kind of parable, the two men can be understood to signify those who follow and confess and believe and "see" the truth about Jesus without having visual evidence of Jesus' miracles to guide them through the eschatological "darkness." In keeping with this, it is probably significant that, because it occurs in the private space of "the house" (9:28), the blind men's miracle is an event about which other characters in narrative hear (9:31) but which they do not see.

That the two men are paradigmatic of something *after* their healing is evident as well, though in this instance what they provide us with is not an inspiring example but a cautionary tale. In Matthew 9:27-31, the evangelist departs from both Mark 10:46-52 and Matthew 20:29-34 not only in the manner in which the story begins but also in the manner in which the story ends, namely, with Jesus enjoining the healed men to secrecy and with the men disobeying Jesus' command (cf. Mark 1:44-45; 5:43; 7:36; 8:26), the latter constituting the only act assigned to the men after their healing. Moreover, this is the only story in the Gospel in which a command from Jesus for secrecy is said to be disobeyed (cf. Matt. 8:4; 12:16; 16:20; 17:9). Evidently, there was something from the evangelist's perspective that made these two men uniquely suitable as participants in such a scenario. His point seems to be that one may be able to *perceive* the truth before being made whole but being made whole is itself no guarantee that one will always *obey* the truth. If the men's blindness is a symbol of receptiveness to revelation, then their sightedness is a symbol of unreceptiveness to what has been revealed, specifically, unreceptiveness to the demand that revelation makes on its recipients (cf. 11:20-24).[88] As we know from Matthew 7:21-23, entering the kingdom of God is more than a matter of calling Jesus "Lord": it also entails obedience to God's will.

A certain irony presents itself, then, insofar as the two men can be understood to signify discipleship more effectively before they are healed than after they are healed. As noted above, the acquisition of sight provides the men with no apparent advantage in their ability to discern Jesus' identity or respond appropriately to his demands, and may in fact represent something of a liability in this regard. From this vantage point, the example they set disrupts the prevailing biblical notion (observed above) that "God is glorified not in disability but only in its overcoming."[89] Put differently, being "healed" (i.e., miraculously acquiring bodies that better conform to the somatic norm) does not turn the men into better disciples; for Matthew, physical healing is not necessarily accompanied by spiritual illumination, even in a story that involves the healing of blindness. To

---

88. Cf. Colleen C. Grant, "Reinterpreting the Healing Narratives," in *Human Disability and the Service of God: Reassessing Religious Practice*, eds. Nancy L. Eiesland and Don E. Saliers (Nashville: Abingdon, 1998), 72–87.

89. Yong, *The Bible, Disability, and the Church*, 53.

be sure, in their failure the two men are no worse than other followers of Jesus (cf. 8:25-26; 14:29-31; 16:7-11, 22-23; 17:19-20; etc.) and, as we have seen, the unwanted publicity that the men provide for Jesus helps to advance the plot (cf. 9:26, 33-34). Nevertheless, it is apparent that the actions of the healed men do not illustrate an appropriate response to Jesus, a point that generates an important observation for thinking about the representation of disability in the Gospel as a whole: the signification that Matthew assigns to people with disabilities is not fixed, but can vary from story to story. In some cases their healing attracts positive associations (e.g., 20:29-34), while in other cases the meaning is more ambiguous (9:27-31).[90] In terms of their representative function, then, such individuals amount to more than "flat" or one-dimensional characters; rather they manifest certain nuances and variations with respect to their agency. Accordingly, even as the two stories about blind men in the First Gospel resemble each other formally, what we as readers are supposed to learn from these stories differs.

Such difference extends to the representation of human bodies as well. Insofar as they exemplify positive responses to Jesus before being healed, the two blind men illustrate somatic differentiation in terms of how different aspects of discipleship are being modeled for the readers within the overall narrative. That the evangelist's eschatological horizon embraced such dissimilarity is suggested by a statement that Jesus makes in one of his major discourses:

> If your eye causes you to sin, tear it out and throw it away; it is better for you to enter life with one eye than to have two eyes and to be thrown into the hell of fire. (Matt. 18:9; cf. 5:29)

---

90. In this regard, perhaps comparison can be made with the lame man of John 5:1-18, for which see Andrew T. Lincoln, *The Gospel According to Saint John*, BNTC 4 (London: Continuum, 2005), 190–200.

Significantly, Matthew identifies the eye (and not the ear!) as the sensory organ that can lead one into sin, suggesting that vision is being problematized morally in a way that hearing is not.[91] Moreover, the symbolic language that Matthew employs in 18:8-9 makes room for people with disabilities (including specifically people with visual impairments) in the economy of salvation. Just as human beings do not need to be healed (that is, "normalized") in order to "see" and "follow" Jesus, they do not need to conform to a particular somatic norm in order to become participants in the kingdom.[92]

91. See 5:28, and cf. Plutarch, *Moralia* 681A: "A person both experiences and produces many effects through the eyes; he is possessed and governed by either pleasure or displeasure exactly in proportion to what he sees." Contributing to this characterization are passages like 6:23 and 20:15, which suggest that Matthew was also familiar with the notion of the evil eye, a widespread belief that certain individuals can inflict harm on others through a malignant gaze (John H. Elliott, "The Evil Eye and the Sermon on the Mount," *BibInt* 2 [1994]: 51–84).

92. Cf. Olyan, *Disability in the Hebrew Bible*, 81–85.

13

Healing Every Disease: Matthew 9:32-38

In this chapter we examine two units, an account of an exorcism
(9:32-34) followed by a transitional paragraph (9:35-38). With the
former, we reach the third miracle story in the third triad of miracle
stories preserved in Matthew 8–9. If the previous episode drew
attention to the power of hearing, this episode draws attention to the
power of speech. It is noteworthy, then, that in contrast to the first
two stories of the third triad (9:18-26 and 9:27-31), in 9:32-34 Jesus
is not represented as saying anything (cf. 8:14-15). Instead, attention
shifts to the speech of other characters, especially that of third-party
witnesses.

In ancient Greek, the term *kōphos* could refer to the inability to
speak ("mute"), to the inability to hear ("deaf"), or to both.[1] Since
Matthew 9:33 presents the remedy to this condition as the ability to
speak, the first of these options is probably in view here, which is the

---

1. Adela Yarbro Collins, *Mark*, Hermeneia (Minneapolis: Fortress Press, 2007), 370; W. D. Davies
and Dale C. Allison, *The Gospel According to Saint Matthew*, ICC (London: T&T Clark, 1991),
2:139.

case in Matthew 15:31 as well.[2] By contrast, in Matthew 11:5 (which, as we have seen, refers back to 9:18-34), those with this condition are reported as obtaining the ability to hear, which most likely entails an allusion to Isaiah 35:5:

> Then the eyes of the blind will be opened, and the ears of the deaf (*kōphōn*) will hear.

Here, as often in the biblical tradition (Exod. 4:11; Lev. 19:14; Isa. 29:18; 42:18-19; 43:8), *kōphos* appears together with *tuphlos* ("blind"), which helps to explain the contiguity of Matthew 9:27-31 (a story about two blind men) and 9:32-34.[3] As with 9:27-31, the event recorded in 9:32-34 is meant to convey eschatological significance. If the messianic era is a time when those living in darkness will see the light (Matt. 4:16), it is also a time when those with no voice will be empowered to speak out. The *War Scroll*, for example, envisions God's final deliverance of Israel as including the following:

> In judgment he has lifted up the melting heart; he has opened the mouth of the mute to sing God's marvels. (1QM 14:5-6)

In this scenario, the mute are associated with those who have a "melting heart," that is, those dispirited by fear or grief (cf. Ps. 22:14; Isa. 13:7; Ezek. 21:7). In the eyes of the Scroll's author(s), the participation of such individuals in praising God is to be interpreted as a sign of divine mercy and redemption (1QM 14:4-5).

---

2. The Greek *Life of Aesop*, an anonymous biography from the first century CE, begins by describing how the protagonist was mute and unable to speak until Isis and the Muses healed him (ch. 1–8). See Pavlos Avlamis, "Isis and the People in the *Life of Aesop*," in *Revelation, Literature, and Community in Late Antiquity*, TSAJ 146, eds. Philippa Townsend and Moulie Vidas (Tübingen: Mohr Siebeck, 2011), 65–67. Cf. Christian Laes, "Silent History? Speech Impairment in Roman Antiquity," in *Disabilities in Roman Antiquity: Disparate Bodies A Capite ad Calcem*, eds. Christian Laes, C. F. Goodey, and M. Lynn Rose (Leiden: Brill, 2013), 145–80.
3. References to the blind and the deaf/mute are also found together in Matthew 11:5; 12:22; 15:30-31.

Our story has another, less obvious point of comparison with the one that precedes it: like Matthew 9:27-31, Matthew 9:32-34 is an example of a redactional "doublet." The source of this doublet, however, is not a passage from Mark but a passage from the Q source:[4]

> (32) As they were going out, they brought to him a mute, demon-possessed man. (33) And when the demon was cast out, the mute man spoke. And the crowds were amazed, saying, "Nothing like this has ever been seen in Israel!" (34) But the Pharisees were saying, "He casts out the demons by the ruler of the demons." (Matt. 9:32-34)

> (22) Then they brought to him one who was demon-possessed, blind and mute, and he healed him, so that the mute man was able to speak and see. (23) And all the crowds were astonished and were saying, "Can this be the Son of David?" (24) But when the Pharisees heard this, they said, "This man casts out the demons only by Beelzebul, ruler of the demons." (Matt. 12:22-24)

> (14) And he was casting out a demon, and it was mute. When the demon had gone out, the mute man spoke and the crowds were amazed. (15) But some of them said, "He casts out the demons by Beelzebul, the ruler of the demons." (Luke 11:14-15)

Each story recounts an exorcism that elicits a divided response from onlookers. As with the story of the two blind men (9:27-31), it appears that Matthew has created the doublet in 9:32-34 in order to round out the suite of miracle stories in chapters 8–9 and create a basis for Jesus' summation in 11:4-6.[5] In terms of its placement within the broader narrative, the version of the story in Matthew 12:22-24 accords better with Luke 11:14-15 than does the version in Matthew 9:32-34.[6] Matthew 12:22-24 also accords better with

---

4. Note that apparently this is the only narration of an exorcism in the Q source. Cf. John S. Kloppenborg, Q, The Earliest Gospel: An Introduction to the Original Stories and Sayings of Jesus (Louisville: Westminster John Knox, 2008), 69–72.
5. See Chapter Twelve.

Luke 11:14-15 in mentioning the ruler of the demons, Beelzebul, by name. At the same time, the two Matthean accounts agree with one another against Luke 11:14-15 in certain respects, most notably in attributing the pericope's concluding accusation to the Pharisees, in keeping with Matthew's proclivity to cast that group as Jesus' principal opponents (in Mark 3:22 a similar accusation is attributed to the scribes).[7] The two Matthean accounts also *disagree* with one another in certain respects, most notably in the latter's referring to the man as being both mute and blind (12:22) and to the crowds' speculation about Jesus being the Son of David (12:23).[8] Matthew 12:22-24 thus appears to be a composite story, combining features familiar from both 9:27-31 (where two blind men call Jesus "Son of David") and 9:32-34.[9]

If we were to look for a parallel to Matthew 9:32-34 in the Second Gospel, the closest analogy would be Mark 7:32-37:

> (32) And they brought to him a deaf man (*kōphon*) who had a speech impediment and they implored him to lay his hand on him. (33) Taking him aside from the crowd, in private, he put his fingers into his ears, and after spitting he touched his tongue; (34) and looking up to heaven he sighed and said to him, "Ephphatha," that is, "Be opened!" (35) And his ears were opened and the impediment of his tongue was released and he spoke plainly. (36) And he ordered them to tell no one; but the more he

6. Burton H. Throckmorton, *Gospel Parallels: A Comparison of the Synoptic Gospels*, 5th ed. (Nashville: Thomas Nelson, 1992), 46, 70.

7. See the discussion of Matthew 9:11 (in Chapter Nine) and 9:14 (in Chapter Ten). Also Anthony J. Saldarini, *Matthew's Christian-Jewish Community* (Chicago: University of Chicago Press, 1994), 44–67; Margaret Davies, "Stereotyping the Other: The 'Pharisees' in the Gospel According to Matthew," in *Biblical Studies/Cultural Studies: The Third Sheffield Colloquium*, JSOTSup 266, eds. Cheryl J. Exum and Stephen D. Moore (Sheffield: Sheffield Academic Press, 1998), 415–32.

8. The two Matthean accounts also disagree with one another with regard to the verb used to describe the crowds' reaction, with Matthew 9:32 (like Luke 11:14) using "amazed" (*thaumazō*), while Matthew 12:23 has "astonished" (*existēmi*). The former is also found in Matthew 8:27 and in some of the ancient manuscripts for Matthew 9:8. The latter occurs nowhere else in the First Gospel, though cf. Mark 2:12; 3:21; 5:42; 6:51.

9. W. R. G. Loader, "Son of David, Blindness, Possession, and Duality in Matthew," *CBQ* 44 (1982): 576–78.

ordered them, the more widely they proclaimed it. (37) And they were utterly astounded, saying, "He does all things well; he even makes the deaf to hear and the speechless to speak."

The use of techniques associated with magic in 7:33-34 is probably the reason why Matthew (like Luke) omits this story from his narrative.[10] Nevertheless, the pericope contains a number of specific features that we find elsewhere in the First Gospel. For example, in Mark 7:32, as in Matthew 9:32 and 12:22 (but not Luke 11:14), the person in need of healing is "brought" to Jesus (cf. Matthew 8:16; 9:2). As we have seen, however, the most intriguing parallels that Mark 7:32-37 exhibits with the First Gospel are to be found not in Matthew 9:32-34 or 12:22-24 but in Matthew 9:27-31, the story of the two blind men.[11] Indeed, even though both stories concern a *kōphon*, Mark 7:32-37 and Matthew 9:32-34 exhibit more differences than similarities. For example, while the healing in Mark 7:33 takes place "in private" (cf. Matt. 9:28), the healing in Matthew 9:32 occurs as "they" (i.e., Jesus and the two men from 9:27-31) are leaving the house, presumably in view of the crowds. In keeping with the public setting, the story in 9:32-34 does not include a command to silence (as in Mark 7:36 and Matt. 9:30) but proceeds directly to a pair of responses to the healing, only the first of which has an analogue in Mark 7:37. Finally, while *kōphon* in Mark 7:32-37 refers to the inability to hear, in Matthew 9:32-34 (as we have seen) it refers to the inability to speak.

It is with these observations in mind that we turn to the matter of the story's *literary form*. To begin with, it is obvious that 9:32-34 is an exorcism story: the man is described as "demon-possessed" (cf.

---

10. No mention is made of demonic possession, though as Joel Marcus (*Mark*, AB 27 [New Haven, CT: Yale University Press, 2000], 1:478) notes, the methods employed by Jesus here would be open to exorcistic interpretation. See further Louise J. Lawrence, *Sense and Stigma in the Gospels: Depictions of Sensory-Disabled Characters* (Oxford: Oxford University Press, 2013), 57–75.

11. See Chapter Twelve.

Matt. 4:24; 8:16, 28, 33; 12:22; 15:22) and the demon is "cast out" of him (cf. Matt. 7:22; 8:16, 31; 10:1, 8; 12:24, 26-28; 17:19). As R. T. France observes, up to this point in the Gospel it has been implied that demonic possession constitutes a distinct category over against sickness and physical disability (e.g., 4:24; 8:16).[12] Here, by contrast, we learn that the former can cause the latter, in which case comparison can be made with a source like the *Testament of Solomon*, where muteness is attributed to a demon that looks like "a three-headed dragon with awful skin" (*T. Sol.* 12:2; cf. 18:9).[13] The same causal connection is made by the parallel story in Matthew 12:22-24, though note that there the verb "heal" (12:22) is used together with the verb "cast out" (12:24) to describe Jesus' activity, suggesting an imbrication in conceptualizing both the etiology of the disability and the means of its cure (cf. 17:14-21). In 15:30-31, by contrast, muteness and other disabilities are not explicitly attributed to demonic influence at all, in which case Jesus is said simply to "heal" people with these conditions, with no reference to "casting out" evil spirits.[14]

In conjunction with this, it is important to remember that in redacting his source material Matthew exhibits a tendency to curtail Jesus' profile as an exorcist, thereby distancing his healing activity as a whole from exorcistic associations.[15] For instance, as we saw

12. R. T. France, *The Gospel of Matthew*, NICNT (Grand Rapids: Eerdmans, 2007), 369.
13. The idea may be that the tongue of the mute person was "bound" by a demon (Adolf Deissmann, *Light from the Ancient East* [Grand Rapids: Baker, 1978], 304–307). In Mark 9:25 and Luke 11:14, by contrast, the demon responsible for muteness is itself mute. As Graham H. Twelftree (*In the Name of Jesus: Exorcism Among Early Christians* [Grand Rapids: Baker Academic, 2007], 124) explains, mute spirits were considered particularly difficult to exorcise because they cannot hear the incantations or provide information about themselves.
14. Gerd Theissen, *The Miracle Stories of the Early Christian Tradition* (Philadelphia: Fortress Press, 1983), 85–91. For *therapeuō* used in the context of an exorcism, see also 4:24; 17:18. In Matthew 8:16; 10:1, 8, there seems to be a distinction between healing an illness and casting out a demon.
15. John M. Hull, *Hellenistic Magic and the Synoptic Tradition* (Naperville, IL: Allenson, 1974), 128–41.

earlier (Chapter Seven), in 8:28-34 the evangelist offers a substantially abridged version of the exorcism recounted in Mark 5:1-20. Elsewhere, he omits references to exorcisms (Matt. 4:23; cf. Mark 1:39), an account of an exorcism (Mark 1:23-28), and distinctive elements of exorcism stories, especially in Matthew 8:16 (cf. Mark 1:34), 12:15-16 (cf. Mark 3:11), 15:28 (cf. Mark 7:29-30), and 17:17-18 (cf. Mark 9:20, 25-26).[16] This redactional activity makes the duplication of the exorcism story in the case we are now considering all the more noteworthy.

In addition to classifying the pericope as an exorcism story, W. D. Davies and Dale Allison have suggested that it is also possible to think of 9:32-34 as a pronouncement story, in which case comparison can be made with the story of the centurion (8:5-13), which, as argued above, represents a hybrid of healing story and pronouncement story.[17] Matthew 9:32-34 is a rather odd pronouncement story, however, in that the story's protagonist does no pronouncing. In fact, no speech is attributed to Jesus at all. Moreover, the story concludes with not one but two pronouncements, the first attributed to the crowds, the second to Jesus' opponents.

These formal features should be borne in mind as we evaluate the rhetorical function of Matthew 9:32-34 both as a self-contained unit and as the concluding miracle story of 8:1—9:34. The pericope is unusual in lacking the same dyadic focus that we have encountered so frequently in the preceding healing accounts. No mention is made of dialogue or interaction between Jesus and the person being healed (a clear contrast with the story in Mark 7:32-37). Unlike the woman with the flow of blood or the two blind men, the mute man communicates no expression of faith in Jesus, either implicitly

16. Loader, "Son of David," 580; Lidija Novakovic, *Messiah, the Healer of the Sick: A Study of Jesus as the Son of David in the Gospel of Matthew,* WUNT 2.170 (Tübingen: Mohr Siebeck, 2003), 104–105. See also the comments on Matthew 8:2-3 (cf. Mark 1:41-43) in Chapter Two.

17. Davies and Allison, *Saint Matthew,* 2:138.

or explicitly. It is not even made plain that Jesus is the one who effects the man's cure ("And when the demon was cast out," etc.). Afterwards, we are told that the man "spoke" (9:33), but we are not told what he had to say. From a narrative perspective, it appears that the primary function of his speech is to serve as a prompt for the speech of others.

In presenting the latter (i.e., the speech of these "others"), a noteworthy difference can be discerned between Matthew and Luke:

> And when the demon was cast out the mute man spoke. And the crowds were amazed, saying, "Nothing like this has ever been seen in Israel!" (Matt. 9:33)

> When the demon had gone out, the mute man spoke and the crowds were amazed. (Luke 11:14)

The Third Gospel reports the people's reaction but not their words. The First Gospel, on the other hand, reports both, drawing attention to the role of speech in the account and highlighting the contribution that the crowds make to the development of the plot (cf. 9:8). In keeping with this, the declaration in 9:33 offers the reader a vital perspective on what is happening in the narrative, a perspective that can be analyzed according to both its *temporal* and its *spatial* dimensions.

As for the temporal dimension, the word "ever" in 9:33 should not be taken lightly. The crowd recognizes that what they are witnessing occupies a unique place in salvation history, reinforcing the idea that in its original context an event like this would have carried eschatological significance (cf. Judg. 19:30). Within the context of the story itself, the crowds' declaration (like that of the Pharisees in 9:34) refers to the exorcism that Jesus has just performed. At the same time, the story's position within the narrative also invites the reader to interpret the declaration as a commentary on everything that has transpired in chapters 8–9.[18] In this case, what is unprecedented about Jesus' accomplishments is not the exorcism per se (after all, exorcists were not that uncommon; see 7:22; 12:27) but the range and scale of Jesus' miracles in their entirety.

As for the spatial dimension, it is helpful to compare Matthew 9:33 with the texts that Mark and Matthew use to conclude the story of the paralytic:

> And he rose up and immediately taking the pallet he went out before all of them, so that they were all amazed and glorified God, saying, "We have never seen anything like this!" (Mark 2:12)

> When the crowds saw this, they were afraid and glorified God, who had given such authority to the people. (Matt. 9:8)

It appears that Matthew has transposed the declaration in Mark 2:12 from the story of the paralytic to the story of the mute demoniac.[19] Moreover, in the course of doing so he has modified the scope of the statement so as to encompass the entire history of "Israel," that is, the entire experience of God's people.[20] Within the context of Matthew 9:33, this redaction creates specific associations, recalling as it does the identification of Jesus in the preceding story as the Son of David (9:27), that is, the Messiah of Israel. The reference also lends some specificity to the reports in 9:26 and 31 that the news of Jesus' miracles was spreading "throughout all that land." The crowds' declaration reminds the reader that these events are occurring not just

---

18. Heinz Joachim Held, "Matthew as Interpreter of the Miracle Stories," in *Tradition and Interpretation in Matthew*, eds. Günther Bornkamm, Gerhard Barth, and Heinz Joachim Held (Philadelphia: Westminster, 1963), 247. The correspondence of Matthew 9:33 with Matthew 7:28 also gives the former something of a structural role: the units in both chapters 5–7 and chapters 8–9 end with reports about the crowds' response to Jesus.

19. Cf. J. R. C. Cousland, *The Crowds in the Gospel of Matthew*, NovTSup 102 (Leiden: Brill, 2002), 136–40.

20. John Nolland, *The Gospel of Matthew*, NIGTC (Grand Rapids: Eerdmans, 2005), 403. References to "Israel" are made elsewhere in Matthew 2:6, 20, 21; 8:10; 10:6, 23; 15:24, 31; 19:28; 27:9, 42.

in any "land," but in the land of Israel, and that the one ultimately responsible for these events is not just any god but "the God of Israel," who should be praised accordingly (as in 15:31). The reference to Israel in 9:33 also points forward in the narrative, especially to the mission discourse, where Jesus instructs the apostles to "go to the lost sheep of the house of Israel" (10:6; cf. 10:23), the reference to sheep (cf. 9:36; 10:16) reinforcing the identification of Jesus as the Son of David in 9:27 (cf. 1 Sam. 16:19; 2 Sam. 5:2; Ezek. 37:24).

The declaration of the crowds in Matthew 9:33, then, conveys a vital perspective on the scope and nature of Jesus' ministry. By the same token, it is apparent that there is nothing particularly christological about this perspective. The crowds are not shown drawing any conclusions about the source of the healer's power, the implications of what they have witnessed, or the identity of the healer himself. In this regard, their words contrast not only with those of the two blind men, who acknowledge Jesus as "Son of David" (9:27), but even with those of the crowds in 12:23, who, upon seeing Jesus heal the blind and mute demoniac ask themselves, "Can this be the Son of David?" (cf. 21:9). As Ulrich Luz observes, the reaction reported in 9:33 exposes the limitations of those who attempt to understand Jesus' miracles "from the outside," that is, from outside the circle of faith.[21] To the extent that the observation in 9:33 can be interpreted positively, the crowds should be understood as representing potential followers of Jesus but no more than that. This is because they have yet to comprehend who Jesus is or to respond accordingly (cf. 11:20-24).[22]

The crowds' response is not the final word, however, but (together with the exorcism itself) provides the basis for a second response:

21. Ulrich Luz, *Matthew: A Commentary*, Hermeneia (Minneapolis: Fortress Press, 2005), 2:50.
22. Cousland, *The Crowds in the Gospel of Matthew*, 138.

> But the Pharisees were saying, "He casts out the demons by the ruler of the demons." (Matt. 9:34)

> But when the Pharisees heard this, they said, "This man casts out the demons only by Beelzebul, ruler of the demons." (Matt. 12:24)

> But some of them said, "He casts out the demons by Beelzebul, the ruler of the demons." (Luke 11:15)

> The scribes who came down from Jerusalem were saying, "He has Beelzebul," and, "He casts out the demons by the ruler of the demons." (Mark 3:22)

Like its counterpart in Matthew 9:33, the statement in Matthew 9:34 looks both (1) back and (2) forward in the narrative.

(1) Beginning with the former, we should recall that this is not the first time in the cycle of miracle stories that Jesus' work has generated a mixed response. As discussed above, in the story of the paralytic, the crowds react to what Jesus says and does by glorifying God (9:8), while the scribes accuse him of blasphemy (9:3). Jesus meets with a less than favorable reception also in 8:34, where the Gadarenes ask him to leave their land, and in 9:24, where the crowds laugh at his assessment of the dead girl's condition. Building on these references, the statement in 9:34 (coming as it does at the end of the cycle of miracle stories in chapters 8–9) drives home an important point: Jesus' messianic ministry of healing not only meets resistance; it also produces adversaries.

Specifically, as in Matthew 12:24 (but not Mark 3:22 or Luke 11:15), the negative evaluation of Jesus' exorcistic activity is attributed to the group that will emerge as Jesus' chief adversaries in the Gospel, namely, the Pharisees. As in Matthew 9:11 (their first appearance in the cycle of miracle stories), no explanation is given either for the Pharisees' presence or their motivation.[23] While the question they had posed earlier (as to why Jesus ate with tax collectors and sinners) was obviously critical in nature, it is only at this point in the narrative that their condemnation of Jesus becomes overt. By alleging demonic collusion, the Pharisees are in essence accusing Jesus of being a sorcerer and false prophet: according to Leviticus 20:27, such individuals should be put to death.[24] In this regard, it is important to remember that the practice of distinguishing "true" from "false" types of charismatic activity constituted a basic form of self-definition and social control for many groups in antiquity, including Matthew's own (cf. 7:15-23; 24:24).[25] Note that the Pharisees do not deny the fact that Jesus has performed a miracle. What remains a matter of dispute is the *meaning* of the miracle, suggesting that what the Pharisees are responding to in 9:34 is not just the exorcism itself but also the crowds' reaction to the exorcism. The healing ministry of Jesus is having the effect of separating the people from their religious leaders. Consequently, a struggle is now under way for the hearts and minds of the people (the people of "Israel"), a struggle that will generate dramatic tension for the remainder of the narrative. The response of the Pharisees in 9:34 contrasts not only with that of the crowds in 9:33 but also with that of the two blind men in 9:27: the failure of Israel's religious leaders to recognize Israel's Messiah precipitates a crisis with which the ministry of Jesus and his followers will have to contend.

(2) It is from this perspective that we can better appreciate the function of 9:32-34 as a hinge passage, one that links chapters 8–9

23. Perhaps their condemnation is fueled in part by Jesus' recent acclamation as Son of David (9:27). Cf. France, *The Gospel of Matthew*, 368; Novakovic, *Messiah, the Healer of the Sick*, 135.
24. Cf. Lev. 19:31; CD 12:2-3; *m. Sanh.* 7:7; Philo, *On the Special Laws* 4.50-52.
25. Susan R. Garrett, *The Demise of the Devil: Magic and the Demonic in Luke's Writings* (Minneapolis: Fortress Press, 1989), 11–36; Amanda Witmer, *Jesus, The Galilean Exorcist: His Exorcisms in Social and Political Context*, Library of Historical Jesus Studies 10 (London: T&T Clark, 2012), 109–32; Dwight D. Sheets, "Jesus as Demon-Possessed," in *Who Do My Opponents Say I Am? An Investigation of the Accusations Against Jesus*, eds. Scot McKnight and Joseph B. Modica (London: T&T Clark, 2008), 27–49.

with chapter 10 and the material beyond. If the crowds' response in 9:33 pointed forward to the mission discourse (as we saw above), the same can be said of the Pharisees' response in 9:34. In the face of mounting opposition, Jesus not only presses on with his own mission but now summons twelve (a symbolically significant number) apostles to assist him in bringing the Gospel to Israel (10:1-4; cf. 19:28). As interpreters often observe, in chapter 10 the theme of opposition is as ominous as it is pervasive.[26] The people may be like sheep without a shepherd (9:36; 10:6), but the apostles themselves are also like sheep, that is, sheep being sent out in the midst of wolves (10:16). Matthew 10:25 makes it painfully clear that the apostles will face the same sort of rejection Jesus himself has faced:

> If they have called the head of the house Beelzebul, how much more those of his household.

The events of Matthew 9:32-34, then, set an example for the apostles in at least two ways, modeling both the type of exorcism that Jesus charges them to perform (10:1, 8) and the type of response they are likely to experience as a result of performing such exorcisms.

The events of 9:32-34 also set an example for the apostles in another, more subtle and symbolic way. Jesus' words of warning in 10:25 continue with words of reassurance, reassuring in the sense that they situate both the apostles' experience and their obligation within an eschatological context:

> (26) Therefore do not fear them. For there is nothing concealed that will not be revealed or hidden that will not be made known. (27) What I say to you in the darkness, speak in the light; and what you hear in the ear, proclaim on the housetops. (Matt. 10:26-27)

---

26. France, *The Gospel of Matthew*, 389–90; Donald A. Hagner, *Matthew*, WBC 33 (Dallas: Word Books, 1993), 1:275; Craig S. Keener, *A Commentary on the Gospel of Matthew* (Grand Rapids: Eerdmans, 1999), 321–25.

As with the two blind men (9:27-31), the darkness that the apostles experience will ultimately give way to light.[27] And as with the mute demoniac (9:32-34), the apostles will be enabled to "speak" in the light, that is, to speak out publically ("upon the housetops"), a point elaborated earlier in the chapter:

> (19) But when they hand you over, do not be anxious about how or what you will speak; for it will be given you in that hour what you will speak. (20) For it is not you who is speaking but the Spirit of your Father who is speaking in you. (Matt. 10:19-20)

The entity that inspires the apostles is not (as their adversaries allege) Beelzebul but rather the Spirit of God, the same divine Spirit bestowed on Jesus at his baptism (3:16; cf. 12:18). [28] As 12:28 explains, this is also the same Spirit by which Jesus casts out demons, which would presumably include the demon he casts out in 9:33. Put differently, the same Spirit by which Jesus gives the mute demoniac voice gives the apostles voice when they proclaim the Gospel, participation in the Spirit representing yet another way in which their ministry of word and deed is modeled after that of Jesus himself.[29] The ministry of Jesus, in turn, reflects the activity of God in salvation history, as comparison with Exodus 4:11-12 suggests:

> (11) Who gives speech to mortals? And who makes them deaf and mute (kōphon), seeing and blind? Is it not I, God? (12) And now go, and I will open your mouth and I will teach you what you are to say.

---

27. Cf. Mark 4:22; Luke 8:17; 12:2-3; *Gos. Thom.* 5–6, 33; *2 Bar.* 83:3-4.

28. This outpouring of the Spirit would have been perceived as an eschatological event, as noted by Davies and Allison, *Saint Matthew*, 2:186; Marcus, *Mark*, 2.883.

29. Cf. Blaine Charette, *Restoring Presence: The Spirit in Matthew's Gospel* (Sheffield: Sheffield Academic Press, 2000), 65–67, 133–34. Note that up to this point in the narrative the disciples have not had much to say (8:21, 25, 27).

As Warren Carter puts it, "Jesus does God's work in giving speech."[30] In other words, what God's Spirit is doing through Jesus and his followers can be seen as an extension of what God had done through Moses, the God who bestows on humankind both the capacity to speak and words with which to speak (cf. Ps. 119:41-46; Jer. 1:6-10).

The Warrior Servant

Like its counterpart in Matthew 9:33, then, the statement in Matthew 9:34 points forward to material in chapter 10. As we have seen, the incident in 9:32-34 also helps to create a foundation for the material in chapter 11, especially the summation of Jesus' messianic activity in 11:4-6. As we have also seen, 9:32-34 has a close parallel in 12:22-24, raising the question of how the former relates to the latter within the overall narrative. In order to address this question, we need to look at both incidents within their broader literary contexts.

As Boris Repschinski has observed, the context of the latter (i.e., 12:22-24) is dominated by four controversy stories (12:1-8, 9-14, 22-37, 38-45), each of which involves a dispute between Jesus and the Pharisees (12:2, 14, 24, 38).[31] A dispute about Sabbath observance (12:1-8) concludes with Jesus citing Hosea 6:6, the same text he had cited to the Pharisees in Matthew 9:13. Controversy over the Sabbath carries over into the ensuing healing story (12:9-14), a story whose conclusion dramatically heightens the acrimony between Jesus and the Pharisees: the latter are no longer simply implying that he is worthy of death (9:34) but actively conspiring to destroy him

---

30. Warren Carter, *Matthew and the Margins: A Socio-Political and Religious Reading* (Sheffield: Sheffield Academic Press, 2000), 229.

31. Boris Repschinski, *The Controversy Stories in the Gospel of Matthew*, FRLANT 189 (Göttingen: Vandenhoeck & Ruprecht, 2000), 92–144.

(12:14).[32] Once again the ministry of healing meets resistance and produces adversaries.

In response to this, Jesus withdraws, healing those who "followed" him (12:15; cf. 9:27) and ordering those healed not to make him known (12:16; cf. 9:30). Unlike the earlier directive to the two blind men, here the command to silence comes with a rationale (12:17-21). Citing a modified version of Isaiah 42:1-4, 9, the evangelist explains to the reader that the secrecy motif is in keeping with Jesus' identity as the Servant prophesied by Isaiah.[33] Among the various elements of the fulfillment quotation, the following are of particular interest for our study:

> (18) I will put my Spirit upon him . . . (19) He will not quarrel, nor cry out; neither will anyone hear his voice in the streets. (12:18-19)

The narrative proceeds without interruption to the next episode, where we learn that among those being healed by Jesus is a blind and mute demoniac (12:22-24),[34] and that it is by the Spirit that Jesus is able to accomplish such healings (12:28). A certain irony presents itself, then: having just been identified as the Spirit-endowed one whose "voice" is not heard publically (i.e., "in the streets"), Jesus is empowered by the Spirit to give voice to another person through the public performance of an exorcism. This, too, would seem to be in keeping with Jesus' identity as Isaiah's Servant, who is "mute" in the face of oppression and affliction (Isa. 53:7; cf. 42:19) even as he bears the infirmities of others (Matt. 8:17; cf. Isa. 53:4).[35]

---

32. This is the story of the man with the withered hand, for which see Repschinski, *Controversy Stories*, 107–16; John P. Meier, *A Marginal Jew: Rethinking the Historical Jesus* (New York: Doubleday, 1994), 2:681–84; Yong-Eui Yang, *Jesus and the Sabbath in Matthew's Gospel*, JSNTSup 139 (Sheffield: Sheffield Academic Press, 1997), 195–214.
33. For analysis of 12:15-21, see Novakovic, *Messiah, the Healer of the Sick*, 133–51; Richard Beaton, *Isaiah's Christ in Matthew's Gospel*, SNTSMS 123 (Cambridge: Cambridge University Press, 2002), 122–73; Yang, *Jesus and the Sabbath*, 214–21.
34. Like the demoniac of 9:32, he is "brought" to Jesus (12:22).

As with the healing of the mute demoniac, the healing of the blind and mute demoniac provokes responses both from the crowds (12:23; cf. 9:33) and from the Pharisees, who, upon hearing the crowds' response, again accuse Jesus of collusion with Satan (12:24; cf. 9:34). While the parallel account in 12:22-24 may seem repetitious, especially coming only a few chapters after the episode in 9:32-34, it nevertheless contributes to the development of the plot in several ways.[36] To begin with, the second healing, involving a man who is both blind and mute, is more impressive than the first, which would help to explain why the crowd is not only amazed but also wonders if Jesus might be the Son of David (12:23; cf. 9:33), an identification that corresponds with the report of Jesus being endowed with the Spirit in 12:18 and 28 (cf. 1 Sam. 16:13; Isa. 11:1-2). In addition, the narrative repetition makes the Pharisees look persistent in their opposition to Jesus.[37] While the accusation that the Pharisees make against Jesus in 12:24 resembles the earlier one in 9:34, it takes on greater weight in light of the fact that they are now actually plotting to kill Jesus (12:14). This heightened seriousness, in turn, helps to justify Jesus' response: rather than moving on with his mission (as he had in 9:35), he now stops to repudiate the Pharisees' allegation. Indeed, in contrast to 9:32-34, the debate about the meaning of Jesus' actions in 12:22-24 precipitates a protracted defense from Jesus regarding his exorcistic ministry (12:25-37).

The defense that Jesus offers is rhetorically complex, encompassing numerous interrelated elements, only a few of which can be

---

35. Cf. Simon Horne, "Those Who are Blind See: Some New Testament Uses of Impairment, Inability, and Paradox," in *Human Disability and the Service of God: Reassessing Religious Practice*, eds. Nancy L. Eiesland and Don E. Saliers (Nashville: Abingdon, 1998), 94.

36. Janice Capel Anderson, "Double and Triple Stories, the Implied Reader, and Redundancy in Matthew," *Semeia* 31 (1985): 71–89, esp. 74–75. See also David B. Howell, *Matthew's Inclusive Story: A Study in the Narrative Rhetoric of the First Gospel*, JSNTSup 42 (Sheffield: JSOT, 1990), 139–40.

37. Note how in Matthew 12:24 they reappear on the scene even though Jesus has withdrawn from them in Matthew 12:15.

mentioned here.[38] To begin with, note how Jesus asserts that he casts out demons not "by Beelzebul" (12:24) but rather "by the Spirit of God" (12:28; cf. 12:18). His exorcistic ministry, then, is nothing less than a manifestation of God's dominion breaking into the world, that is, breaking the power of Satan's control over humanity (12:25-26, 28-29). As the agent of this transformation, Jesus is properly understood not simply as someone who has acquired the techniques necessary for "binding" individual demons (12:27) but as the divine warrior incarnate, the one whose ministry portends the eschatological "binding" of Satan himself (12:29; cf. Rev. 20:2).[39] Through the exorcisms that he and his disciples perform, the people of Israel are experiencing the power of this eschatological reality in their own lives. The struggle between the Son of David and the Pharisees on the human level, then, is properly understood against the background of a cosmic conflict between the kingdom of God and the kingdom of Satan.[40]

These observations, taken as a whole, shed light on a critical narrative trajectory for Matthew's Gospel. The theme and practice of healing are seen not only uniting the contents of chapters 8–9 but also integrating these chapters with the ensuing narrative. Specifically: (1) acts of healing help to establish Jesus' messianic identity, (2) the ministry of healing is shown to be essential to the vocation and mission of his disciples, and (3) claims about the theological significance of healing serve as the basis of debate between the Jesus movement and its detractors. Subsequent chapters build on these narrative loci even as they offer clarification as to their basic character. For example, as we have seen, it is a priority for

---

38. On this passage see Meier, *A Marginal Jew*, 2:407–23; Repschinski, *Controversy Stories*, 116–33.
39. For the binding of Satan and his demons, see Tob. 8:3; *1 En.* 10:4, 11-12; 13:1-2; 14:5; 18:16; 21:3-6; 54:3-5; 69:28; 90:23; *2 Bar.* 56:13; *T. Levi* 18:12; *Jub.* 5:6-10; 10:7-14; 48:15-19. See further in Chapter Seven, n. 16.
40. Beaton, *Isaiah's Christ in Matthew's Gospel*, 182.

Matthew to indicate how the healings performed by Jesus manifest the eschatological work of God's Spirit, an assertion that has implications for understanding the themes of Christology (e.g., 12:18), discipleship (e.g., 10:20), and polemic (e.g., 12:28) within the Gospel. The nexus of healing, identity, and opposition achieves a certain rhetorical focus in 9:32-34, a story in which the characters must make a decision regarding their assessment of Jesus. The open-ended nature of the conclusion to the cycle of miracle stories in chapters 8–9 not only creates narrative suspense but also, by implication, confronts the readers with a similar decision: which side are they on?[41]

The Eschatological Shepherd

Having finished recounting the series of nine miracle stories, Matthew transitions to the next major unit of his Gospel, the mission discourse of chapter 10. It is at this point that the reader begins to recognize the alternating pattern of action (chapters 1–4, 8–9, etc.) and speech (chapters 5–7, 10, etc.) that structures the overall narrative. The transitional paragraph itself consists of three short segments: a formulaic summary of Jesus' ministry in chapters 5–9 (9:35), a report of Jesus' personal response to the people he encounters in this ministry and the reason for his response (9:36), and Jesus' statement to the disciples about the need for "workers" to extend this ministry (9:37-38).

As noted in Chapter One, 9:35 recalls 4:23, matching the language of the earlier verse with only minor variations:[42]

---

41. Cf. Howell, *Matthew's Inclusive Story*, 134–35.
42. Matthew 4:23 is based on Mark 1:39, while the reference to teaching in the villages in Matthew 9:35 derives from Mark 6:6 (cf. Luke 8:1).

> He went about in all Galilee teaching in their synagogues and proclaiming the good news of the kingdom and healing every disease and every sickness among the people. (Matt. 4:23)

> Jesus went about all the cities and the villages teaching in their synagogues and proclaiming the good news of the kingdom and healing every disease and every sickness. (Matt. 9:35)

Note in particular how a triad of activities (teaching, proclaiming, and healing) structures each verse.[43] Together, the pair of statements create a frame around the material in chapters 5–9, summarizing Jesus' ministry up to this point in the narrative and inviting the readers to see his ministry of word (chapters 5–7) and his ministry of deed (chapters 8–9) as an integrated whole.[44] By the time they reach 9:35 the readers will be in a better position (having read the contents of chapters 8–9) to appreciate the fact that Jesus is capable of healing "every" disease and "every" sickness among the people.[45] By the time they reach 9:35 the readers will also be in a better position to appreciate the distancing involved when Matthew refers to the places where Jesus teaches as "their" synagogues, passages like 9:3, 11, and 34 having dramatized the less than hospitable reception he receives from the people's religious leaders (cf. 6:2, 5; 12:9; 13:54). It is probably safe to assume that both the kind of ministry Jesus carried out in Capernaum and the kind of response that ministry received in Capernaum were replicated in the other locales he visited (cf. 11:20-24). Note finally that while 4:23 has Jesus traveling throughout "all Galilee," 9:35 has him traveling throughout "all the cities and

---

43. The connection between Matthew 4:23 and 9:35 is reinforced by the parallelism between Matthew 5:1 and 9:36, which have the same opening: "And seeing the crowds" (*idōn de tous ochlous*), etc.

44. As with other summary statements in the Gospel (4:23-25; 8:16; 12:15-16; 14:13-14, 35-36; 15:29-31; 19:1-2), attention is drawn to the scope of Jesus' healing ministry. Cf. Cousland, *The Crowds in the Gospel of Matthew*, 108–17; Birger Gerhardsson, *The Mighty Acts of Jesus According to Matthew* (Lund: CWK Gleerup, 1979), 20–37.

45. For the comprehensiveness of Jesus' healing ministry, cf. Chapter Five, n. 2.

the villages," subtly suggesting that the scope of his ministry has expanded (cf. 9:26, 31, 33).[46]

The integrated presentation of Jesus' ministry in chapters 5–9 is important in another way, in that it provides both a basis and a model for the ministry that Jesus will commission the disciples to carry out in chapter 10. As with Jesus himself, this will be a ministry of word and deed, the latter including healings and exorcisms (10:7-8).[47] As with Jesus himself, this ministry will be itinerant in nature: note in particular the correspondence of "cities and villages" in 9:35 with "city or village" in 10:11. As with Jesus himself (9:36), this ministry will focus on the lost "sheep" of the people (10:6). And as with Jesus himself, this ministry will meet with opposition from the leaders of "their" synagogues (10:17; cf. 23:34). Reinforcing this point is an additional framing device:

A. The Call of the First Disciples (4:18-22)
   B. Summary Statement (4:23)
      C. Ministry of Word (chapters 5–7)
      C'. Ministry of Deed (chapters 8–9)
   B'. Summary Statement (9:35)
A'. The Summoning of the Twelve Disciples (9:36–10:1)

Right before the first summary statement and right after the second summary statement Matthew has placed material in which Jesus appoints individuals to assist in his ministry, either to "fish" for people (4:19) or to bring in the Lord's "harvest" (9:37), thereby furnishing the intervening material with a missional outlook.[48] News about Jesus

---

46. Cousland, *The Crowds in the Gospel of Matthew*, 90.
47. Note the verbal correlation of 9:35 with 10:1, 7-8.
48. Nolland, *The Gospel of Matthew*, 406.

has spread throughout the land (9:26, 31); Jesus himself has traveled throughout the land (9:35); now his disciples must do likewise.[49]

The rationale for this ministry is further elaborated by the next verse in the transitional paragraph, Matthew 9:36:

> And when he got out (of the boat) he saw a large crowd and he had compassion for them, because they were like sheep without a shepherd, and he began to teach them many things. (Mark 6:34)

> Seeing the crowds, he had compassion for them, because they were harassed and downtrodden like sheep without a shepherd. (Matt. 9:36)

Matthew shifts a statement that had been associated with miraculous feeding (Mark 6:34; cf. Mark 6:30-44; Matt. 14:13-21) to a setting where it is associated with miraculous healing (Matt. 9:36; cf. Matt. 9:35). The crowds that Jesus encounters in his travels through the land are likened to "sheep without a shepherd," a reference that evokes several biblical texts (e.g., Num. 27:17; 1 Kgs. 22:17; Jer. 50:6), the most significant of which (especially given the new Matthean setting) is Ezekiel 34.[50] This chapter begins by condemning "the shepherds of Israel" for their failure to lead the people: "Those who are sickly you have not strengthened, the diseased you have not healed, the broken you have not bound up, the scattered you have not brought back, nor have you sought for the lost" (34:4). The people, therefore, "were scattered for lack of a shepherd" (34:5).[51] Judgment

---

49. As Dorothy Jean Weaver (*Matthew's Missionary Discourse: A Literary Critical Analysis*, JSNTSup 38 [Sheffield: JSOT, 1990], 72–73) notes, 9:35 is also correlated verbally with 11:1 (both verses referring to teaching, proclaiming, and cities), the bracketed text in 9:35—11:1 interlocking with the bracketed text in 4:23—9:35 and reinforcing the parallelism between Jesus and the disciples. This also means that 11:1 looks back to 4:23, forming a lengthier bracketed text (4:23—11:1), for which 9:35 functions as a hinge verse.

50. Wayne Baxter, "Healing and the Son of David: Matthew's Warrant," *NovT* 48 (2006): 36–50; Joel Willitts, *Matthew's Messianic Shepherd-King: In Search of 'The Lost Sheep of the House of Israel'*, BZNW 147 (Berlin: Walter de Gruyter, 2007), 117–34. The translations of Ezekiel 34 that follow are from the NASB.

51. Matthew's redactional reference to the crowds as "harassed and downtrodden" strengthens the allusion to Ezekiel 34:4-6. Cf. Jer. 23:1-2; Zech. 10:2-3; Young S. Chae, *Jesus as the*

does not have the final word, however. Rather God promises to rectify the situation: "I will seek the lost, bring back the scattered, bind up the broken and strengthen the sick . . . Then I will set over them one shepherd, my servant David" (34:16, 23).[52] The title of "shepherd" carries messianic connotations elsewhere (e.g., Jer. 3:15; *Pss. Sol.* 17:40), especially in Micah 5:4, which is cited (together with Mic. 5:2) in Matthew 2:6:

> And you Bethlehem, land of Judah,
> Are in no way least among the leaders of Judah,
> For out of you shall come forth a ruler,
> Who shall shepherd my people, Israel.

For Matthew, Jesus is the eschatological shepherd, the one promised by the prophets, and as comparison with Ezekiel 34 suggests, Jesus' nationwide ministry of healing represents an anticipated manifestation of this identity, one of the ways in which the shepherd will "seek the lost" (Ezek. 34:16; cf. Matt. 10:6; 15:24; 18:11).[53] Like other references in the Gospel to sheep and shepherds (10:6; 15:24; 18:12; 25:32; 26:31), the description in 9:36 reinforces the identification of Jesus as the messianic Son of David (cf. 1 Sam. 16:19; 2 Sam. 5:2; Ezek. 37:24), a designation that was applied to Jesus by the two blind men in 9:27. Thus, as Young Chae observes, the transitional paragraph in 9:35-38 "links the picture of the healing Son of David in chapters 8–9 with the mission of the disciples among

---

Eschatological Shepherd: Studies in the Old Testament, Second Temple Judaism, and in the Gospel of Matthew, WUNT 2.216 (Tübingen: Mohr Siebeck, 2006), 208–10; Charlene McAfee Moss, *The Zechariah Tradition and the Gospel of Matthew*, BZNW 156 (Berlin: Walter de Gruyter, 2008), 41–60.

52. Cf. Jer. 23:3-4; Ezek. 37:24; Zech. 11:16; *Apocr. Ezek.* frag. 5. For the connection between shepherding and healing, see also CD 13:7-9: "the Inspector of the camp . . . will heal all the strays like a shepherd his flock."

53. Reports of crowds *following* Jesus, and specifically following him for healing (4:24-25; 12:15; 14:13-14; 19:2), accord with his image as the people's shepherd. Cf. Cousland, *The Crowds in the Gospel of Matthew*, 86–94.

the lost sheep of the house of Israel (10:1-6)."[54] In the same vein, the description of 9:36 can also be interpreted as a commentary on the events of 9:32-34. The people are without shepherds because their religious leaders, the Pharisees, have rejected their Messiah, that is, they oppose Jesus *as* the Son of David on account of the claim to authority the title implies. Consequently, the Pharisees are being replaced by Jesus and his disciples as the leaders of the people. In this regard, it is significant that 10:1-5 is the first time in the Gospel that the evangelist mentions a group of *twelve* disciples. Like the twelve patriarchs, they represent the twelve tribes of Israel and thus the ingathering of God's people. As 10:1 explains, they share in Jesus' authority (cf. 19:28), embodying and extending the patterns of ministry laid out in chapters 5–9. This point is reinforced by Matthew's redaction of 10:1 (as well as 10:8), which has the effect of emphasizing both the healing ministry of the twelve (cf. Mark 6:7, 13; Luke 9:1-2; 10:9) and the verbal correlation of 10:1 with 9:35,[55] thereby strengthening the connection between chapter 10 and chapters 8–9.[56]

Matthew 9:36 identifies another fundamental rationale for the disciples' mission, namely, the "compassion" that Jesus feels when he witnesses the plight of the people, the same emotion he feels in 14:14 and 20:34 in response to the people's need for healing.[57] As in those passages (cf. 15:32), Jesus' response does not terminate with an expression of emotion but is promptly translated into action:[58]

---

54. Chae, *Jesus as the Eschatological Shepherd*, 255, cf. 205–12.
55. In Greek, the two verses end with the same seven words.
56. Cf. Cousland, *The Crowds in the Gospel of Matthew*, 112; John K. Ridgway, *"Let Your Peace Come Upon It": Healing and Peace in Matthew 10:1-15*, Studies in Biblical Literature 2 (New York: Peter Lang, 1999), 224–37.
57. Cf. Matt. 15:32; 18:27; also the discussion of Jesus' mercy (*eleos*) in 9:13 (Chapter Nine) and 9:27 (Chapter Twelve).
58. "In each case there is not only sympathy with a person's need, but also a practical response which meets that need" (France, *The Gospel of Matthew*, 373). While Mark has Jesus respond

(37) Then he said to his disciples, "The harvest is great, but the workers are few. (38) Therefore beg the Lord of the harvest to send out workers into his harvest." (Matt. 9:37-38)

And he said to them, "The harvest is great, but the workers are few. Therefore beg the Lord of the harvest to send out workers into his harvest." (Luke 10:2)

The imagery shifts from that of sheep in want of a shepherd (Matt. 9:36, drawing on Mark 6:34) to that of a harvest in want of laborers (Matt. 9:37-38, drawing on Q/Luke 10:2). In this instance the harvesting imagery appears to combine scenarios of eschatological ingathering (e.g., Isa. 27:12) with scenarios of eschatological judgment (e.g., Jer. 51:33).[59] Either way, the disciples' missionary work is made to take on eschatological dimensions (cf. Matt. 13:24-30, 36-43), an observation that applies to the contents of the mission discourse itself (e.g., Matt. 10:17-23; cf. Mark 13:9-13). As commentators often observe, from a narrative standpoint the mission discourse in the First Gospel is unusual, in that Jesus is not reported as actually sending the twelve on a mission (11:1; cf. Mark 6:7-13).[60] It appears that his instructions (including the instruction to heal the sick) are meant to apply principally to the work of missionaries beyond the time narrated by the Gospel, that is, in the time after Easter (cf. 28:18-20), which would presumably include the time of the evangelist himself.[61]

To sum up: The imagery of the transitional paragraph invites the reader to reconsider the events of chapters 8–9 as a dimension of Jesus' identity as the compassionate shepherd, seeking out the lost,

---

to the need by teaching (Mark 6:34), Matthew has him respond by summoning disciples (Matt. 9:37–10:1).

59. Cf. Matt. 3:12; 13:30, 39; John 4:35-38; Rev. 14:15-16.

60. Davies and Allison, *Saint Matthew*, 2:239; Luz, *Matthew*, 2:123; France, *The Gospel of Matthew*, 416–17; cf. Twelftree, *In the Name of Jesus*, 164–68.

61. Cf. the discussion of reader-response criticism in Chapter One.

providing needed leadership for the people, and inaugurating a time of national restoration. Put differently, the healing stories can now be understood as showing what the messianic Son of David is like, what his reign will mean for the people, and how those called by the Messiah will participate in this reign.[62]

---

62. "[T]he healings in Matthew appear to be linked to a broader concern for justice and the renewal/reconstitution of the people of God. Central to this theme is Jesus' role as ideal Davidic King" (Beaton, *Isaiah's Christ in Matthew's Gospel*, 185).

14

Conclusion

As we have just seen, the final miracle story in Matthew 8–9 recounts the exorcism of a mute demoniac (9:32-34). In terms of the physical ailment involved, comparison can be made with the following testimony from a fourth century BCE inscription found at Epidaurus cataloguing various cures attributed to the god Asclepius:[1]

> A voiceless boy. He came as a supplicant to the Temple for his voice. When he had performed the preliminary sacrifices and fulfilled the usual rites, thereupon the temple servant who brings in the fire for the god, looking at the boy's father, demanded he should promise to bring within a year the thank-offering for the cure if he obtained that for which he had come. But the boy suddenly said, "I promise." His father was startled at this and asked him to repeat it. The boy repeated the words and after that became well.

---

1. Translation from Emma J. Edelstein and Ludwig Edelstein, *Asclepius: Collection and Interpretation of the Testimonies* (Baltimore: Johns Hopkins University Press, 1945), 1:230–31. Cf. Lynn R. LiDonnici, *The Epidaurian Miracle Inscriptions: Text, Translation and Commentary*, SBLTT 36 (Atlanta: Scholars, 1995), 88–89 (with introductory comments on pp. 5–82).

Like the story of the man in Matthew 9:32-34, this account is immediately preceded by a story describing a miraculous healing of blindness, suggesting a traditional connection between the two kinds of disability.[2] For their part, the testimonies at Epidaurus were displayed prominently for visitors to read as they entered the sanctuary, bolstering the deity's reputation and fostering a general atmosphere of hope and anticipation. Like the contents of Matthew 8–9, the healings commemorated by the inscriptions pertain to a range of healthcare problems: paralysis, dropsy, headaches, consumption, and so on. By the same token, the testimonials themselves do not evidence nearly as much variation in their narrative form as what we find in the First Gospel. The "ritualized" character of the storytelling at Epidaurus no doubt reflects the institutional setting and priestly ethos informing the healing practices of the Asclepius cult, where the importance of performing the necessary rites is stressed as a matter of routine.[3] The stories in Matthew 8–9, by contrast, while similarly episodic in nature, demonstrate far more internal drama and unpredictability. On more than one occasion Jesus even faces entrenched opposition, a feature lacking from the Epidaurian inscriptions. To be sure, at the heart of both the Asclepian and Gospel accounts there is a manifestation of the sacred, that is, a tangible revelation of divine power that addresses people's urgent needs, eliminates suffering, and restores physical health. Nevertheless, there is also a crucial difference between the accounts in terms of social function. While the inscriptions are meant to inspire confidence and promote conformity, the stories in chapters 8–9 evidence an orientation that is distinctly

---

2. See the beginning of Chapter Thirteen.

3. As Elaine Wainwright (*Women Healing/Healing Women: The Genderization of Healing in Early Christianity* [London: Equinox, 2006], 86) notes, control of the narratives in their final compositional form probably belonged to the priests. See further the discussion of the Asclepius cult in Chapter One.

prophetic in character. Unlike the healings of Asclepius, the healings of Jesus are disruptive and controversial. Unlike the healings of Asclepius, the healings of Jesus demand a personal response, one that entails a decision not only about the source of healing power and the identity of the healer but also about the claim that the healer makes on the lives of those he encounters. Accordingly, Jesus' healings engender a movement that is itself prophetic in character, a movement defined by risk, controversy, and commitment.

Matthew 9:32-34 also differs from the Epidaurian testimonial cited above in that the afflicted man is identified as a demoniac and his cure entails the expulsion of a demon, concepts of this sort being foreign to the worldview endorsed by the Asclepius cult. For a somewhat closer parallel in this regard we can turn to the following tale from the Babylonian Talmud:

> One time Agrath encountered Hanina ben Dosa. She said to him, "Were it not that they proclaim in Heaven regarding you, 'Be cautious of Hanina ben Dosa and his Torah learning!' I would endanger you." He said to her, "If in fact I am highly regarded in Heaven, I decree upon you and all demons never to pass through populated areas." She said to him, "I beg of you, leave me a little leeway." He acquiesced and left her the eves of the Sabbaths and the eves of Wednesdays. (b. Pesah. 112b)

The principal figure here, Hanina ben Dosa, was a Palestinian Jew of the first century CE known for the exceptional power of his prayers, including his prayers for healing.[4] His confrontation with the demon Agrath here bears some resemblance to Jesus' confrontation with

---

4. For his healing prayers, see m. Ber. 5:5 and b. Ber. 34b. For the complexities that attend reconstructing the life of the "historical" Hanina ben Dosa, see John P. Meier, A Marginal Jew: Rethinking the Historical Jesus (New York: Doubleday, 1994), 2:581–88; Eric Eve, The Jewish Context of Jesus' Miracles, JSNTSup 231 (London: Sheffield, 2002), 279–95. As Joseph Blenkinsopp ("Miracles: Elisha and Hanina ben Dosa," in Miracles in Jewish and Christian Antiquity: Imagining Truth, ed. John C. Cavadini [Notre Dame, IN: University of Notre Dame Press, 1999], 57–81) points out, Hanina's miracles can be compared with those of Elisha, an observation that applies to the miracles of Jesus as well (see Chapters Two, Three, and Four).

the Gadarene demoniacs, who similarly acknowledge the holy man's authority and then secure a concession from him (8:29-32). While Hanina's authority derives from his knowledge of the law, however, Jesus' authority derives from his status as the Son of God (8:29), that is, as one who comes as an agent of eschatological judgment. Note, too, that Hanina is not presented as performing an exorcism: Agrath is not in possession of a human body but appears to Hanina in her own (presumably female) form.[5] Finally, for all the power that Hanina appears to possess over the realm of the demonic, his actions are not given an eschatological interpretation, while within the broader context of the Gospel those of Jesus are understood to represent a turning point in salvation history. As we have seen, the latter's binding of individual demons gives rise to messianic hopes of the binding of Satan himself (12:22-29), a scenario depicted in apocalyptic texts like Revelation 20:1-3.

For all their differences, however, these stories about Asclepius, Jesus, and Hanina ben Dosa do have at least one important feature in common: they all are communicated *as stories*, a point that reflects the fact that most of our information about healing in Mediterranean antiquity is preserved in narrative form. That this is a matter of not only historical but also methodological interest becomes apparent when one takes into account recent trends in the field of medical anthropology, especially trends that have drawn attention to the relationship between healing and storytelling. Studies such as those conducted by Cheryl Mattingly and Linda Garro, for instance, focus on the phenomenon of "illness narratives" and the different forms of "therapeutic emplotment" that sustain them.[6] As a basic medium of communication, they argue, narrative is particularly well-suited not

5. Comparison with *b. Qidd.* 81a suggests that this form would have been an alluring one, adding another dimension to the encounter in *b. Pesah.* 112b absent from Matthew 8:28-34 or 9:32-34.
6. Cheryl Mattingly, *Healing Dramas and Clinical Plots: The Narrative Structure of Experience* (Cambridge: Cambridge University Press, 1998), 1–24; Cheryl Mattingly and Linda C. Garro,

only for conveying but also for interpreting experiences of healing. This is on account of the capacity of stories to convey the *eventful* character of such experiences—"eventful" both in the sense that the stories effectively recount moments of singular, often life-altering significance and in the sense that the sequencing of events essential to any act of storytelling effectively captures the manner in which the experience of illness and healing is marked by changes that occur in time. These are stories that belong to a "literature of extreme situations," exposing both the forces that move someone's life beyond the mundane and the means by which one personally comes to term with such forces. Narrative accomplishes this by situating the disruption caused by an illness or disability (as well as the response to such disruption) within a coherent structure and context, thereby functioning as a strategy "for organizing personal experiences into culturally intelligible scripts."[7]

The criteria of singularity, temporality, and cultural intelligibility are all worth bearing mind as we turn our attention to the "illness narratives" of Matthew 8–9 and the manner of their "therapeutic emplotment." As we have seen, consideration for matters of narrative analysis represents a priority for the interpreter insofar as the evangelist has introduced wide-ranging changes into the traditional material upon which these chapters are based, reconfiguring both the content and the arrangement of these stories into a new and evocative whole. Such analysis can be carried out with respect to two different but mutually supportive structures. The first of these, which I refer to simply as the *narrative structure* of Matthew 8–9, attends to the manner in which these chapters recount a succession of events connected in time and place.

Narrative and the Cultural Construction of Illness and Healing (Berkeley: University of California Press, 2000), 1–49.
7. Mattingly, *Healing Dramas*, 13.

Triads and Interludes

The description of this structure properly begins not with 8:1 but with 4:23, a summary statement indicating that Jesus' activity comprises two kinds of ministry, namely, a ministry of teaching and a ministry of healing (cf. 4:24-25). What follows elaborates on the substance and character of this activity, chapters 5–7 on the ministry of teaching and chapters 8–9 on the ministry of healing. A summary statement in 9:35 recalls the statement in 4:23, enclosing the intervening material into a narrative whole: the Messiah of Word is also the Messiah of Deed. His ministry of teaching can only be fully understood in light of his ministry of healing and vice versa.

The dominant narrative feature of Matthew 8–9 itself is a series of miracle stories divided into three structurally parallel triads (8:1-17; 8:23—9:8; and 9:18-34), a feature that not only lends cohesiveness to the unit but also reinforces its juxtaposition with the Sermon on the Mount, which itself is divided into triads.[8] Like the contents of his teaching, then, the events of Jesus' ministry fall into meaningful patterns. The correspondence between the two units is further signaled by the first story in chapter 8, which demonstrates Jesus' positive relationship with the Mosaic law (8:1-4), a concern addressed in the first section of the body of the Sermon (5:17-48). Separating the three triads of miracle stories are two thematically and formally analogous units or "interludes" that do not recount miracles (8:18-22 and 9:9-17). Besides playing a structural role (making the division into triads more apparent), this alternation of miracle and non-miracle material reflects the balance in the two kinds of ministry presented in chapters 5–9 as a whole.

---

8. Walter T. Wilson, "A Third Form of Righteousness: The Theme and Contribution of Matthew 6.19–7.12 in the Sermon on the Mount," NTS 53 (2007): 303–24. Note also how chapters 5–7 and chapters 8–9 conclude similarly with a report that "the crowds were amazed" (7:28; 9:33).

The first triad of miracle stories (8:1-4, 5-13, 14-17) is distinguished from the other two in that it consists entirely of healing stories, specifically, healing stories that have been blended by Matthew with other literary forms: the first pericope is a healing story with elements of a commissioning story, the second is a healing story with elements of a pronouncement story, and the third is a healing story with elements of a call narrative, to which has been appended a summary statement and a fulfillment quotation. Such blending enhances the manner in which each episode points beyond itself, connecting with incidents and themes communicated elsewhere in the text. Thus the cleansed man is charged by Jesus to go ahead of him and give testimony in the temple, foreshadowing the "cleansing" of the temple itself (cf. 21:14). The inserted material in 8:11-12, meanwhile, announces that unexpected guests will be welcome at the messianic banquet, a theme that anticipates the action of 9:10-13. The domestic service of Peter's mother-in-law, lastly, prefigures the public service rendered to Jesus by both his male and female followers (cf. 27:55).[9]

This triad is further distinguished by its prophetic character, insofar as each of its stories alludes to a healing performed by the prophet Elisha, the first two stories recalling 2 Kings 5:1-14 and the third recalling 2 Kings 4:18-37. This narrative feature is extended and concretized by the quotation of Isaiah "the prophet" in 8:17: Jesus has come to fulfill not only the law, then, but also the prophets (5:17). The feature is further developed by the manner in which the story of Peter's mother-in-law alludes to 1 Kings 19:19-21, anticipating the pronouncement stories on discipleship that Matthew has inserted into the narrative at 8:19-22, which allude to the same Old Testament

---

9. As we saw in Chapter Four, complementary forms of narrative "contraction" in 8:1-15 draw attention both to the "privatized" nature of the woman's encounter with Jesus and to the domestic setting in which this encounter occurs.

text. From this perspective, 8:14-15 can be seen to function as a narrative hinge, serving both as the third of three stories (8:1-4, 5-13, 14-15) that evoke healings performed by Elisha (2 Kgs. 4:18-37; 5:1-14) and as the first of three stories (8:14-15, 19-20, 21-22) that evoke the prophet's call (1 Kgs. 19:19-21).

The second triad of miracle stories is from a literary perspective the most miscellaneous of the unit, consisting of a nature miracle (8:23-27), an exorcism (8:28-34), and a healing story with elements of a controversy story (9:1-8). This triad also contains the only miracle story in chapters 8–9 in which the disciples have a speaking role (8:23-27), building on the discipleship material of 8:18-22.[10]

In terms of basic narrative dynamics, elements of conflict and adversity figure more prominently in this triad than in the first, as Jesus is shown overcoming a series of related threats to human salvation. Thus the first story demonstrates his power to deliver people from the sea, a symbol of primeval chaos and eschatological tribulation. The second story demonstrates his power to liberate people from demons, that is, from supra-human forces of evil and corruption. The motif of water not only connects these two stories but also links them with the Red Sea incident (Exod. 14:21-31), a rescue miracle and epiphany of paradigmatic significance for salvation history.[11] The third story, finally, demonstrates Jesus' authority to save people from the most insidious effect of evil, namely, sin, an authority he possesses by virtue of his status as the Son of Man (cf. Dan. 7:13-14). All of this establishes Jesus as the divine warrior and judge, one who has entered into a cosmic struggle

---

10. The first triad of miracle stories does not refer to the disciples at all, while the third triad mentions them only in passing (9:19). It is only in chapter 10 that they are given a "voice" (e.g., 10:7, 20).

11. In both episodes, the exorcistic features are deployed in such a manner so as to illustrate not only the confrontational nature of Jesus' ministry but also the eschatological significance of that confrontation.

with the kingdom of Satan for human souls (cf. 12:25-29; 13:36-43), each story serving as an anticipation of the sorts of transformations associated with the eschatological *kairos* (8:29).

In keeping with the adversarial dynamic, another feature that distinguishes the second triad from the first is that its stories report different kinds of corporate reactions to Jesus, with the reports being sequenced in such a way as to suggest increasing narrative tension. Thus in the first story the amazed disciples wonder "what kind of man" Jesus might be (8:27) while in the second story the Gadarenes implore Jesus to leave their land (8:34). In the third story, finally, we hear of a split response, one that divides the people from their religious leaders: the awestruck crowds glorify God (9:7) while the scribes accuse Jesus of blasphemy (9:3). The dynamic of social conflict carries over into 9:9-13 and 9:14-17, controversy stories in which Jesus responds to objections posed, respectively, by the Pharisees and the disciples of John. From this perspective, 9:1-8 can be seen to function as a second narrative hinge, serving both as the third of three stories (8:23-27, 28-34, 9:1-8) in which Jesus confronts eschatological opposition and as the first of three stories (9:1-8, 9-13, 14-17) in which he confronts opposition from different religious groups.

The third triad of miracle stories presents a series of progressively shorter episodes, the first a healing story intercalated into a revivification story (9:18-26), the second a healing story (9:27-31), and the third an exorcism story with elements of a pronouncement story (9:32-34). With this final triad the matter of publicity emerges more plainly as a narrative and theological motif, each story being punctuated with a report about Jesus' expanding reputation (9:26, 31, 33). With this triad it also becomes apparent that the venue for both Jesus' ministry and the response to that ministry is "the land" (9:26, 31), that is, "Israel" (9:33), a disclosure that accords with the identification of Jesus as the Son of David (9:27), that is, the messianic agent of Israel's restoration (cf. 11:2-5).

Given the political or "nationalistic" character of such developments, it is not surprising that both oppositional and eschatological themes continue to be in evidence. Thus allusions to Jesus' violent death in 9:15-17 (cf. Isa. 53:8; Matt. 26:28; 27:51) give way to interwoven stories about life from death (9:18-26), the body of the hemorrhaging woman signifying Jesus' crucified body, the body of the raised daughter signifying Jesus' resurrected body. The experience of the two blind men (9:27-31), meanwhile, symbolizes the light of the messianic age breaking through the darkness currently enveloping the land (cf. 4:15-16). Like the final story of the second triad (9:1-8), the final story of the third triad (9:32-34) shows Israel's Messiah eliciting a mixed response from Israel's people, one that separates the crowds, who respond with amazement, from their religious leaders, who accuse Jesus of collusion with Satan. The contrasting reactions, which appear to look back at the contents of chapters 8–9 in their entirely, also set the stage for what follows: the Pharisees' rejection of the Son of David explains why the people are like sheep without a shepherd (9:36; cf. Ezek. 34:5, 23) and thus why Jesus must summon workers to help him bring in the eschatological harvest (9:37-38). This sets the stage in turn for chapter 10, in which Jesus instructs the twelve regarding their mission "to the lost sheep of the house of Israel" (10:6). From this perspective, 9:32-34 can be seen to function (much like 8:14-15 and 9:1-8) as a narrative hinge, serving both as the third of three miracle stories (9:18-26, 27-31, 32-34) dramatizing the incompatibility of the new with the old (9:16-17) and as a segue to chapter 10 and a foreshadowing of Jesus' struggle with the Pharisees for the hearts and minds of God's people (12:1-45, etc.).

As indicated above, the triads in 8:1-17, 8:23—9:8, and 9:18-34 are separated by two segments or "interludes" (8:18-22 and 9:9-17) distinguished from their surroundings in that they do not recount miracles. These segments resemble one another formally in that each includes two parallel stories with the same narrative setting. Thus the first segment contains two pronouncement stories on discipleship (8:19-20, 21-22) prompted by Jesus' command to leave Capernaum (8:18), while the second contains two controversy stories (9:10-13, 14-17) that take place while Jesus is reclining with sinners in "the house" (9:10).

The two segments are connected topically as well, a point illustrated most clearly by their common vocabulary, especially the terms "teacher" (8:19; 9:11), "disciple" (8:21, 23; 9:10, 11, 14), and "follow" (8:19, 22, 23; 9:9). Together these words signal the particular contribution made by the interludes within the overall narrative. As we have seen, the triads of miracle stories convey both the impressive power of Jesus to transform people's lives and an impressive array of christological indicators (Lord, Son of God, Son of Man, Son of David). Within this context, the interludes drive home the point that Jesus is not a solitary (albeit messianic) figure but is properly understood as the leader and teacher of a community of disciples who follow him by sharing in his ministry. The focus of 8:18-22 and 9:9-17, then, is on the call to discipleship and what it means to accept this call.

The surrounding miracle stories relate to the development of this theme in at least three important ways. First, by making the one who issues the call more impressive, they make the call itself more compelling and authoritative. Second, the miracles show what the call entails, setting an example for the disciples to "follow," a point that becomes explicit in the mission discourse, especially 10:1 and 8, where they are authorized to engage in the same healing ministry as

Jesus himself. Third, the miracles reveal the disruptive nature of this ministry, dramatizing the manner in which it generates both change and opposition. The interludes dilate on this point by identifying the disciples as those who have chosen "the other side" (8:18), separating themselves from the established social and religious order, represented in 8:18-22 by the household and in 9:9-17 by the Pharisees and the disciples of John. In all this, of course, Jesus' disciples follow their teacher's example as well (see 10:16-25). As attendants of the eschatological bridegroom, they serve as representatives and agents of the "new" order that is "pulling away" from and "bursting" through the old (9:15-17).

Insofar as the transitional segment in 9:35-38 also mentions the ministry to which Jesus summons the disciples, it can be understood as having a connection with the two interludes as well. Its imagery certainly contributes to the separation motif, differentiating the workers from the people, who are likened to sheep without a shepherd and a harvest to be brought in. The alternating pattern established in 8:1—9:34 between triads of miracle stories and material on discipleship, then, appears to carry over into 9:35-38, albeit in a weakened fashion, since 9:35-38 lacks the sorts of formal and topical parallels between 8:18-22 and 9:9-17 identified above.

Finally, superimposed on this overarching structure are two further triads that help both to link the triads of miracle stories with one another and to integrate the triads of miracle stories with the intervening non-miracle material. The first of these is the sea journey narrative (cf. 14:22-36) demarcated by 8:18, where Jesus announces the journey, and 9:1, where he returns from the journey. Enclosed within these framing verses are three narrative elements: conversations about who will accompany Jesus on the journey (8:18-22), the journey itself (8:23-27), and Jesus' exploits upon reaching the journey's destination (8:28-34). Each element identifies a different kind of obstacle and form of adversity that Jesus' followers must face, signified respectively by the household, the stormy sea, and the demon-possessed men. The triad also contributes to the development of Matthew's narrative theology by establishing a vital christological node: the same Son of Man who belongs "nowhere" within the prevailing human order (8:20) is also the Son of God who delivers humanity from eschatological evil (8:29), the two categories representing aspects of his person and ministry that can only be properly envisioned in light of one another.

Immediately following this comes a second superimposed triad, 9:2-17, a series of episodes in which Jesus is shown debating with a succession of different religious groups: the scribes (9:2-8), the Pharisees (9:9-13), and the followers of John the Baptist (9:14-17). Formally, the first episode can be categorized as a healing story with elements of a controversy story, while the second and third are similar in that they both represent controversy stories in the proper sense. The first and second episodes are connected by the theme of sin, a theme that carries over into the third pericope insofar as fasting was sometimes interpreted as a penitential practice. The second and third episodes, meanwhile, are related by virtue of having the same narrative setting, namely, Jesus' meal with tax collectors and sinners in "the house" (9:10), a fact reflected in the objections to which he responds, both of which have something to do with food (9:11, 14). Rhetorically, the upshot of the unit is clear and compelling: Jesus' rift with the "old" religious order of Israel (9:16-17) is not only wide-ranging in scope but also "practical" in nature, insofar as it comes to expression in specific religious practices, represented here by forgiveness, table fellowship, and fasting. All this paves the way for the final triad of miracle stories (9:18-34), which, as we have seen, concludes with a report of the Pharisees' condemnation of Jesus (9:34).

Consideration for such superimposed structures, then, provides another vantage point from which to consider the literary composition of chapters 8–9, that is, as a series of interlocking triads: 8:1-17; 8:14-15 + 19-22; 8:18—9:1; 8:23—9:8; 9:2-17; 9:18-34.

A Logic of Limits

Different from but operating concurrently with this narrative structure, it is also possible to discern within chapters 8–9 an implicit or "deep" structure, one that communicates the text's intrinsic logic and lends its diverse contents both coherence and "inclusiveness."[12] If we think of the contents of these chapters as a series of discrete encounters, all featuring Jesus as the central figure, then the basic principle informing this implicit structure can be stated as follows: *Each encounter with Jesus both exposes a limitation to human participation in divine grace and simultaneously reveals a way in which the meaning of that limitation is transcended through a manifestation of the sacred.* The point of departure for the focus on limitations here is the "limits" model of disability, which, as we saw in Chapter One, interprets disability as "an instantiation and reminder" of the fact that the human condition as such is defined by the experience of various kinds of limits, and that it is through reflection on this experience that human beings are led into a deeper and more creative relationship with the divine.[13] In what follows, I unpack certain elements and assumptions at work in this proposition and then provide an

---

12. David B. Howell, *Matthew's Inclusive Story: A Study in the Narrative Rhetoric of the First Gospel*, JSNTSup 42 (Sheffield: JSOT, 1990), 249–59. Also see the discussion of reader-response criticism in Chapter One.
13. Quotation from Deborah Beth Creamer, *Disability and Christian Theology: Embodied Limits and Constructive Possibilities* (Oxford: Oxford University Press, 2009), 31. Cf. Thomas E. Reynolds, *Vulnerable Communion: A Theology of Disability and Hospitality* (Grand Rapids: Brazos, 2008), 180–86, 201–202.

inventory of the different kinds of limitations that one encounters in chapters 8–9.

To begin with, the reference to "participation in divine grace" above encompasses the needs of both human bodies and human communities, that is, everything that might contribute to the participation of the people of God in the reign of God. The term "limitation," meanwhile, is meant to serve as a flexible descriptive category encompassing a variety of different boundaries, obstacles, barriers, and divisions that in one way or another restrict such participation and impede the human experience of divine grace.[14] The imagery of boundaries is of particular value in elucidating the manner in which the text's implicit structure interacts with its narrative structure, insofar as the latter frequently portrays Jesus as crossing (or, in some cases, transgressing) boundaries of various kinds: entering a house, crossing over to "the other side," touching ritually unclean bodies, dining with sinners, and so on. In each instance the person and activity of Jesus occasion a manifestation of the sacred that somehow transcends the boundary and what it represents, not by removing the boundary but by reconfiguring its meaning in light of the impending kingdom.[15] Jesus' revivification of the official's daughter, for instance, does not eliminate the reality of death from human experience but rather subjects this reality to symbolic transformation: "the girl has not died but is asleep" (9:24). In all this Jesus is presented both as a "boundary crossing" character and as a catalyst for reimagining the nature of boundaries themselves, which appear in the narrative not in order to be justified but in order to be contested. The Matthean perspective on limitations, then, can be said

---

14. Cf. John J. Pilch, *Healing in the New Testament: Insights from Medical and Mediterranean Anthropology* (Minneapolis: Fortress Press, 2000), 81–83.
15. Cf. Reynolds, *Vulnerable Communion*, 219.

to manifest a *prophetic* quality—not taking the restrictions on human life for granted but seeing beyond them with a new vision.

As we shall see, there are various kinds of limitations present in chapters 8–9, and no doubt there are various ways of categorizing them. Oftentimes recognition of a boundary will depend on the reader adopting the perspective of a particular character in the narrative (the healer, the one in need of healing, the crowds, etc.) and the nature of such recognition may vary depending on the perspective. In each case the limitation can be shown to reflect a theme of broader theological significance for the Gospel. It is also important to note that the distinctions between the different types are not always sharp; in many cases the types can be seen to complement or overlap with one another. It is also the case that the application of a particular limitation may vary from story to story, depending on the priorities at any given point, which themselves (as we have seen) can vary. Most of the stories expose more than one limitation but no one story encapsulates every limitation. Instead, each story contributes something distinctive to the profile, a fact that reflects the contextual and personal nature of Jesus' healing ministry. Only when the contents of chapters 8–9 are viewed collectively and interdependently does something like a comprehensive picture begin to emerge, and even then we do well to remember that this picture is set within a broader narrative context, one that includes other miracle accounts.

The kinds of limitations outlined below are not presented in any particular order or hierarchy, though in some cases (e.g., spiritual + moral) certain logical pairings suggest themselves.

In many respects the category of *physical* limitations addresses the most fundamental of the boundaries imposed on human existence. By its very nature, the human body is susceptible to disease, disability, and death, the last of these representing the ultimate "limit" on life.

As we have seen, in each of the healing stories of chapters 8–9, the reader encounters one or more human bodies whose restoration conveys some sort of representational meaning, signifying a different aspect or dimension of salvation. By the same token, in each story the reader is also afforded a glimpse into an actual human "drama," one that is as physical as it is personal: for Matthew these are real bodies experiencing real pain and receiving real relief, portrayed in their somatic particularity. Accordingly, the healing stories take the realm of physical existence seriously both as a site of redemption and as a sphere of ministry, constantly mediating between two "landscapes" of meaning: the somatic and the symbolic.[16] Chapters 8–9 are populated by people with an array of different physical disorders, and in each case the problem, even death itself (9:18-26), is transcended through a manifestation of transformative power imparted by a figure who himself participates in physical limitations, who himself will experience physical suffering, brokenness, and death, transcending such limitations through new life. The restored bodies of the healed are thereby "marked" by this transformative power, bearing in themselves the new possibilities that are being made available to people in the midst of their physical pain and constraint.[17]

Human beings are defined not only by physical restrictions, of course, but by perceptual and *cognitive* limitations as well, that is, by limitations in their ability to perceive and comprehend reality.[18] In the context of the Gospel, this pertains especially to the knowledge of sacred realities and the manner in which such realities intrude upon the world of ordinary meaning and experience. Here our attention

---

16. For the language of landscapes and dramas, see Serene Jones, "Graced Practices: Excellence and Freedom in the Christian Life," in *Practicing Theology: Beliefs and Practices in Christian Life*, eds. Miroslav Volf and Dorothy C. Bass (Grand Rapids: Eerdmans, 2002), 51–77.

17. Wainwright, *Women Healing*, 151.

18. Gerd Theissen, *The Miracle Stories of the Early Christian Tradition* (Philadelphia: Fortress Press, 1983), 75–80.

turns to the manner in which the stories of chapters 8–9 constitute events of revelation, events that create a fissure between what is known and what is not known, and the distinction this fissure in turn creates between "insiders" and "outsiders." For instance, Jesus' pronouncement that "the girl has not died but is asleep" (9:24) reveals an eschatological perspective on the nature of death, one that, as such, challenges and disrupts conventional certainties about human existence. Predictably, this is a perspective that meets with incredulity and disdain (9:24), even if there is at least one person in the narrative who seems to anticipate its significance (9:18), as new realizations of what is possible begin to emerge.[19] Similarly, the pair of responses to Jesus' healing of the mute demoniac (9:33-34), as dissimilar as they are, exposes the limitations encountered by those who try to understand Jesus' miracles "from the outside," that is, from outside the circle of faith. Also illustrative is the account in 8:23-27, which, as we have seen, accords with the literary form of an epiphany, specifically, an epiphany of Jesus' divine status. The fact that the witnesses to this event are unable to discern "what kind of man" he is (8:27) brings into relief the cognitive barrier confronting them, one that is subsequently crossed by supernatural beings (8:29) and will eventually be crossed by the witnesses themselves, though only after an additional epiphany (14:33). The story in 9:27-31, meanwhile, highlights human limitations in the arena of sense perception, the blind men demonstrating a capacity to "see" things about Jesus and his miracles that characters without sensory disabilities in the narrative do not.[20] Such narratives expose both human dependence on divine revelation and the manner in which human difficulty in

---

19. Cf. Birger Gerhardsson, *The Mighty Acts of Jesus According to Matthew* (Lund: CWK Gleerup, 1979), 68–81.
20. The secrecy motif of 9:30 draws attention to this problem. Human limitations in "sight" are countered by Jesus' prophetic acuity (e.g., 8:14; 9:2, 4, 9, 22; 12:25).

apprehending the divine is transcended through manifestations of the sacred.[21]

At the same time, and in keeping with the indicia of ancient spirituality, an aura of hiddenness, of the unspoken, surrounds every manifestation of the sacred, a concept that comes to expression both in the private performance of miracles (8:14; 9:25, 28) and in the commands to secrecy (8:4; 9:30; cf. 12:15-21).[22] These narrative motifs draw attention to the cognitive barriers separating insiders and outsiders, even as Jesus' failure to keep his identity private problematizes such barriers, suggesting their fluid and unstable nature.

Characters in the narrative are sometimes represented as experiencing visceral or emotional responses to what is transpiring around them, responses that expose *affective* limitations or barriers to participating in salvation as well.[23] In 8:26, for example, Jesus recognizes that the disciples' plea for help is inspired by fear (cf. 8:34), a byproduct of "little" faith, that is, faith that is deficient or insufficient in character. This is the case despite the fact that they are accompanied by the "Lord," that is, by the one who can "save" (8:25) them not only from the tempest but also from death itself. In 9:27, by contrast, the blind men's plea for mercy (and the mix of hope and despair thereby implied) does not go unanswered but is met by the compassion of the healer, whose mercy extends to those who are both physically (9:29) and morally (9:13) unwell. Similarly, in 9:36, Jesus responds to the dispiritedness he sees around him not with emotional detachment but with shepherdly compassion (cf. 14:14,

---

21. This provides an additional perspective for understanding Jesus as a manifestation of *Sophia*, for which see the discussion in Chapter Nine.
22. Note also how in the story of the Gadarene demoniacs (Matt. 8:28-34) the evangelist drops the material in Mark 5:18-20. Only the twelve are authorized to proclaim the word, and they are to proclaim it only to Israel (10:2-7).
23. Theissen, *Miracle Stories*, 75–80, 287–91.

20:34), even summoning the disciples to assist in his ministry to the people (9:37-38). Yet another kind of affective reaction can be discerned in the crowds' expressions of fear and awe (9:8, 33; cf. 8:27), which are countered by Jesus' experience of amazement in 8:10. The healer's ability to be surprised by those in need of his help can be understood as a further manifestation of the sacred, as well as a manifestation of his humanity.

It is also possible to speak of a *volitional* limitation at work in the narratives of chapters 8–9.[24] It is not unusual for a healing story to begin with someone approaching Jesus and communicating a need for his help, either through words (8:6, 8-9; 9:27) or actions (9:2, 20, 32) or both (8:2; 9:18). However it is conveyed, this initiative embodies a conscious decision to reach out to Jesus for something that lies beyond what is humanly possible. The boundary crossing that this entails can be understood as an act of faith (8:10; 9:2, 22, 29), that is, in the context of the healing stories, faith comes to expression not simply as a matter of belief or assent but as an effort and movement of the will seeking out the sacred.[25] This movement of the will on the part of the one seeking healing does not go unanswered, but is met by a movement of the will on the part of the healer himself, who expresses his willingness to heal (8:3), which in turn expresses the will of his Father in heaven.[26] The extent to which this willingness can also constitute a "barrier" is dramatized most clearly in the story of the centurion, where Jesus initially expresses reluctance about helping him (8:7). The healing of the centurion's

---

24. Ibid., 75–80, 300–302.
25. Heinz Joachim Held, "Matthew as Interpreter of the Miracle Stories," in *Tradition and Interpretation in Matthew*, eds. Günther Bornkamm, Gerhard Barth, and Heinz Joachim Held (Philadelphia: Westminster, 1963), 280–81.
26. Cf. Matt. 7:21; 11:27; 18:14; 26:39, 42; Gerhardsson, *The Mighty Acts of Jesus*, 48–50. Note also how Matthew's redaction of 9:20-22 removes any suggestion that the woman was cured without Jesus' consent (cf. Mark 5:30-32).

slave from a distance accords with the distance that is overcome between the centurion's request and Jesus' willingness to fulfill it.

Even if it is one's intention to seek out Jesus for help, in some instances this is not enough to reach the healer: the cooperation of others is required, a fact that highlights another kind of limitation, one that exposes both the limits of what an individual can do for himself or herself and the extent of his or her dependence on the assistance of others. In 9:2-8, for instance, the paralytic is shown being literally and figuratively supported by the people who bring him to Jesus (cf. 8:16; 9:32). It is "their" faith that Jesus perceives and acknowledges (9:2), the paralytic participating in a collective expression of faith, corresponding to the collective expression of forgiveness that Jesus subsequently authorizes (9:8), a form of forgiveness that is practiced and experienced in community (cf. 18:15-20). Similarly, both the centurion's slave and the official's daughter rely on the faith of others to advocate on their behalf (8:5-9; 9:18-19). The fact that certain individuals in the narrative apparently lack petitioners to advocate on their behalf (8:14-15; 9:20-22) suggests that social assistance is not something to be taken for granted but occurs only within certain limitations.

Such restrictions become pronounced in the story of Peter's mother-in-law. Here the limitation to human thriving that is exposed concerns the woman's isolation from others, her personal options being circumscribed by a symbolic nexus of silence, gender, and domestic seclusion. Unseen, unheard, and with no one to advocate on her behalf, she relies entirely on the perspicacity and initiative of the healer to traverse the "boundaries" of the house and effect healing. A public "servant" (8:17; cf. 20:28) entering private space, Jesus "sees" the woman in her isolation (8:14; cf. 6:6), transforming not only the woman herself, empowering her for disciple-like "service" (8:15; cf. 27:55), but also the space itself, turning it into a venue for communal healing (8:16). The manifestation of the sacred in this case transcends both the *existential* barriers that cut people off from others as well as the *social* barriers that separate the private from the public.

Such considerations also afford an opportunity for pondering the limitations imposed by *gender* in the healing stories. The social status of ancient Mediterranean women, "domesticated" as they were, makes Peter's mother-in-law a logical choice for representing the sense of isolation and powerlessness those in need of healing often experience. The same may be said of the other women who appear in chapters 8–9 (cf. 15:21-28), though the experiences they represent are different, a difference that corresponds in part with the various ways in which the symbolism of the house shapes their respective stories. It is apparent that the options of the three women are socially restricted. In two cases (8:14-15; 9:18-19 + 23-26) the female characters are presented as passively ensconced within a domestic space. Peter's mother-in-law must rely on the initiative of the healer to enter her house. The official's daughter, on the other hand, must rely not only on the healer's willingness to enter her house but also on her father's initiative to venture out and approach the healer in a different house. By contrast, the woman with the flow of blood stands outside the symbolic space of the male household and its attendant systems of power, access, and purity. Accordingly, it is her own initiative that sets the events of the story in motion and, accordingly, her own faith that is said to have "saved" her (9:22). In each case, a manifestation of the sacred transcends the barriers separating the male world of the healer from the female world of those healed.

Within the worldview projected by the Gospel, the human experience of death, disability, and sin can be conceptualized in terms of human susceptibility to the activity of demonic forces. The limitations exposed are properly described as *spiritual* in nature, insofar as they take into consideration the restrictions imposed on human participation in divine grace by the sorts of spirits that Jesus casts out of the demon-possessed (8:16) by the Spirit of God (12:28).[27] Within the context of chapters 8–9, the most debilitating effects of the demonic are illustrated by the experience of the Gadarene demoniacs, individuals who suffer alienation from God, from their neighbors, and even from their own selves. To the extent that they lie beyond human control or comprehension, there are obvious limits to the ability of people to free themselves from such forces and, correspondingly, an obvious need for a manifestation of sacred power to rescue them from the corruption that these forces engender. The Son of God's confrontation with the realm of supra-human evil occurs both on a cosmic scale, anticipating the eschatological *kairos* (8:29; cf. 12:25-29), and on a personal level, not only in the performance of exorcisms but also in the forgiveness of sins (see Chapter Eight).

If physical limitations impose restrictions on human thriving, the same can be said of *moral* limitations. In the symbolic lexicon of the Gospel, then, "sickness" can manifest itself in psychic as well as somatic terms, and the healer is a "physician" of the soul as well as of the body (9:12).

Human beings fall short of the moral perfection modeled by their heavenly Father (5:48). As we have seen, they can also fall victim to demonic forces, including the ruler of the demons (12:24), who actively opposes the kingdom of God not only by sowing evil in the world (13:39) but also by endeavoring to snatch away the good news that has been sown there as well (13:19). The healer therefore seeks out those in need of forgiveness (e.g., 9:9), just as he seeks out those struggling with disease and disability. Indeed, Jesus' entire ministry, his life and his death, amounts to nothing less than the establishment

27. Theissen, *Miracle Stories*, 116–18.

of a sacred covenant whose basis and expression involve saving people from their sins (1:21; 26:28). Within chapters 8–9, the narratives in 9:1-8 and 9:9-13 are of particular importance in exposing the problem of sin as a force that corrupts both human selves and human relations. The power of sin is so insidious and incapacitating that human beings cannot free themselves but must rely for liberation on a manifestation of the sacred, one that both anticipates the eschatological moment (9:6; cf. Dan. 7:13-14) and authorizes a community grounded in practices of forgiveness (9:8; cf. 18:15-35). The narratives in 9:1-8 and 9:9-13 also show how forgiveness can be signaled through acts of hospitality as well as through acts of healing.[28] The boundaries excluding sinners from participating in the joy, bounty, and acceptance symbolized by fellowship at the table are transcended by a manifestation of divine mercy and grace (9:10-13).

Within the context of Matthean Christology it is of particular importance to affirm Jesus' status as the Son of David, the promised Messiah of Israel sent to redeem God's people (e.g., 9:27). Even as this affirmation plays a critical role in shaping the evangelist's perspective on *salvation history* (e.g., 10:1-6; 19:28), the story of the centurion announces something new: because the Messiah is willing to accept faith wherever he finds it, salvation is not limited to Israel but transcends the boundaries that separate people ethnically and culturally (8:5-13). This breakthrough event (and especially the eschatological pronouncement it triggers in 8:10-12) sets the stage for future interactions between Jesus and Gentiles, including the one narrated in 8:28-34. Here Jesus ventures to the "other" side (8:18), traversing a dangerous liminal zone (8:23-27) in order to redeem individuals who from a Jewish perspective would have constituted

---

28. Healing in fact belongs to a set of communal practices that enact the authority to forgive conferred on the church by the Son of Man. See the discussion in Chapter Eight.

the ultimate cultural "other," doing so even in the face of ingratitude and rejection. Such stories draw attention to the complex stance that the First Gospel adopts toward Gentiles and their historical role in the economy of salvation generally.[29]

As we have seen, it is a priority for Matthew to show how the manifestation of the sacred associated with the person of Jesus occurs not as an isolated event but rather within the context of salvation history, that is, within the context of the history and institutions of the people of Israel. One of the ways in which this priority informs the development of the narrative in chapters 8–9 involves dramatizing the mounting tension between Jesus and various religious groups within Israelite society (especially the Pharisees), groups whose authority is predicated upon *other* manifestations of the sacred (especially the Mosaic law). From *their* vantage point, the sort of "boundary crossing" that Jesus represents is seen as illegitimate (9:2), even malevolent (9:34), that is, as a threat to the sacred itself. Disputes over core practices like forgiveness (9:2-9), table fellowship (9:10-13), fasting (9:14-17), and exorcism (12:22-32) solidify sectarian boundaries and intensify sectarian competition. The healer, then, faces a limitation in terms of his own acceptance, that is, in terms of the redemption that he as Israel's Messiah can extend to Israel's people, a limitation that can be described as *religious* in nature. Despite his status as the Messiah, Jesus cannot compel people to abandon their false beliefs and accept the gospel, a fact illustrated by the ignominious conclusion to his ministry in Gadara (8:34), the objections posed by the scribes, Pharisees, and the disciples of John (9:3, 11, 14), and the inconclusive response to his healing of the mute demoniac (9:33-34). The tenacious resistance of the "old" order, then, imposes limitations on Israel's participation in the "new" order of

---

29. Cf. Donald Senior, "Between Two Worlds: Gentiles and Jewish Christians in Matthew's Gospel," *CBQ* 61 (1999): 1–23; and see the discussion in Chapter Three and Chapter Seven.

salvation (9:16-17). Nevertheless, ultimately the new order cannot be contained within the limits of the old: rather, the former "tears away" and "bursts through" the latter (9:16-17). The manifestation of the sacred associated with the new does not abolish the old, however, but transcends it with new meaning, so that "both are preserved" (9:17; cf. 5:17-20; 13:52).

Closely related to this category are what we can refer to as *ritual* limitations. The sacred rituals that were so essential to life in the ancient world were underwritten by codes of purity, codes that stipulated divisions and hierarchies of the holy, separating the clean from the unclean, the latter being associated with social exclusion and stigmatization. In the story of the leper, a manifestation of the sacred transcends the limitations imposed by ritual defilement with Jesus functioning as a conduit of purifying power, facilitating the man's reincorporation into the worshipping community (8:1-4). As a result, the man bears the marks of cleansing power on his body, a body that he offers as a "testimony" and sign for the community, in anticipation of the arrival of the healer himself, who will "cleanse" the holy place with further healing (21:14). Jesus' authority over ritual impurity is further demonstrated in the story of the official's daughter and the woman with the flow of blood (the former being physically dead, the latter—like the leper—socially dead) as well as in the story of the Gadarene demoniacs, where Jesus leads the disciples into a place populated by unclean spirits, people, and animals (8:28-34; 9:18-26). The exorcism that Jesus performs in that space transcends these layers of ritual impurity through a manifestation of the Holy (i.e., sanctifying) Spirit (cf. 12:28-32).[30]

As 8:18-22 reminds us, the "old" order is constituted not only by the sorts of religious groups mentioned above but also by a variety

---

30. Also relevant here is Jesus' sectarian dispute with the Pharisees over table fellowship purity, for which see Chapter Nine.

of social and cultural institutions. The limitation exposed in this instance concerns attachments to family and household and how such attachments can become obstacles to participation in the healer's ministry. Insofar as such attachments would have had an emotional dimension, limitations of a *socio-cultural* nature overlap with those of an affective nature.

The Son of Man belongs "nowhere" within the dominant social order (8:20). Those who would follow him, then, must undertake a symbolic act of departure, separating themselves from the most basic sources of social belonging and security, indeed, separating themselves from the familiar altogether, undergoing a perilous journey to "the other side" (8:18). The mission discourse in particular elaborates on the requirements of such a journey, depicting a life of homelessness, uncertainty, hardship, and rejection.[31] Transcending the bonds of the biological family is the spiritual family created by Jesus' healing ministry, a family of sons (9:2) and daughters (9:22) of the kingdom, outcasts who are now welcomed at the table (8:11; 9:10). Again, however, it should be noted that the manifestation of the sacred associated with the new order does not abolish the old order but infuses it with new meaning. After all, even those who, like Peter, have "left everything" to follow Jesus (19:27) can still have a home and family (8:14).

Matthew's view of salvation history never loses sight of the ultimate horizon, a fact that suggests one final barrier to human participation in divine grace: the *eschatological* barrier. Humanity is currently living in darkness, awaiting the light of a deliverer and the dawn of a new age (4:16). The current era, then, is divided from the eschatological era as the night is divided from the day. The tension between the two is exposed wherever Jesus is manifested

31. For the theme of domestic estrangement, see especially 10:34-36.

as an agent of redemption. With his appearance the eschatological *kairos* is already embodied; with his ministry the reality of final redemption has commenced "before the time" (8:29). Humanity faces a limitation in that the possibilities for participation can be fully realized only in the future kingdom, in all its overwhelming grace, power, and otherness.[32] Yet with each word and act Jesus prefigures the impending advent of the kingdom: healings anticipate liberation and wholeness, exorcisms announce the defeat of evil, meals with sinners provide a foretaste of messianic abundance, and revivifications foreshadow life from death. The miracles as a whole, then, are to be interpreted within the context of a turning point in salvation history, a manifestation of the sacred that opens up understandings and possibilities of existence that transcend the world of the ordinary and anticipate its ultimate transformation.

Boundary Crossings

Capernaum was a border town, situated near the frontier between the tetrarchy of Herod Antipas and the tetrarchy of Philip.[33] As Matthew reminds us in 4:13, it was also situated on the shore, the "boundary" separating the land from the sea, the latter (as we have seen) being rife with symbolic potential. In light of the discussion above, it is not surprising that Jesus would make his home in such a place, the theme of borders having significant implications for understanding both who Jesus is and those whom he serves.

---

32. Vicky Balabanski, *Eschatology in the Making: Mark, Matthew and the Didache*, SNTSMS 97 (Cambridge: Cambridge University Press, 1997), 135–48; Donald A. Hagner, "Matthew's Eschatology," in *To Tell the Mystery: Essays on New Testament Eschatology in Honor of Robert H. Gundry*, JSNTSup 100, eds. Thomas E. Schmidt and Moisés Silva (Sheffield: JSOT, 1994), 49–71.

33. Jonathan L. Reed, *Archaeology and the Galilean Jesus: A Re-examination of the Evidence* (Harrisburg, PA: Trinity Press International, 2000), 146.

To begin with, insofar as each of the limitations just surveyed is transcended by a manifestation of the sacred centered on the person and activity of Jesus, they can be seen as contributing to the development of Matthew's *Christology*. In chapters 8–9, Jesus is shown confronting a host of different threats to human wholeness and overcoming them all, a fact that enhances the general sense of totality informing both the scope and efficacy of his ministry. Through Jesus the sacred is manifested at home and away, on land and sea, in public and in private; for both men and women, adults and children, Jews and Gentiles, free and slave; for representatives of both power and powerlessness; and, moreover, in response to a range of threats: illness, disability, demonic possession, acts of nature, sin, death. Throughout the narrative his authority over all of these situations is shown to be sovereign and absolute, the ministry of healing furnishing the medium through which his identity is revealed in all its dimensions: Messiah, Servant, Wisdom, Son of Man, Son of David, Son of God.

At the same time, these limitations can also be seen as contributing to the development of Matthew's *anthropology*, that is, his understanding of what it means to be human. As they read through the series of short stories in chapters 8–9, the readers can never be sure which limitation it is that Jesus will encounter next, how he will respond, or what repercussions his actions will precipitate. The varied content (not to mention rapid succession) of the stories dramatizes the vagaries and vulnerabilities of the human condition, as the stories' characters are shown coming to terms with one extreme of human life after another. The diversity in the types of extremes presented by chapters 8–9 increases the likelihood that the readers will find characters in the narrative with whom they can identify, both with respect to the different kinds of "diseases"/"illnesses" and with respect to the different kinds of "cures"/"healings" that the characters represent.[34]

Even as the narrative exposes many kinds of human vulnerabilities, however, it also exposes many ways of transcending them, each one tapping into a different vein of human potential. As we have seen, the various "boundary crossings" related in chapters 8–9 have profound implications for the people who encounter Jesus, all of whom experience some kind of empowerment or illumination that sets their lives in a new direction. The categories listed above, then, can be understood not only as identifying obstacles to human wholeness but also as generating opportunities for human thriving, with each opportunity corresponding to a human capacity for transformation. The ministry of Jesus, then, is shown as engaging the human subject in all its complexity and in all its dimensions (physical, spiritual, moral, etc.), dimensions to which any healer following in Jesus' footsteps must attend. Through the ministry of the healer, forces are being unleashed into the world that can shape human subjectivity in imaginative ways, exposing new possibilities of human freedom and opening up new ways for people to reach beyond themselves. The implicit questions generated by the text's implicit structure, then, are these: What might humanity be like if freed from these and indeed all limitations? What sort of human agent would emerge if it were to be shaped by the logic of "boundary crossing" in all its richness?

These questions assume, of course, that people are willing not only to experience the sacred but also to be shaped by it, people like Peter's mother-in-law, who not only recovers from illness but does so in order to "serve" Jesus (8:15), the one sent to serve (8:17; cf. 20:28). These questions also assume that people are willing not only to be

---

34. For these categories, see Pilch, *Healing in the New Testament*, 1–36.

healed but to become healers themselves, people like Matthew the tax collector, who is called by the physician of sinners (9:9-13) to engage in a ministry of healing himself (10:1-3). The logic of boundary crossing, then, entails a clear element of obligation. The human participants in these stories are more than just passive recipients of revelation: they are called upon to make a decision. Accordingly, there is more to the manifestation of the sacred than just the removal of previous limitations. There is also a positive claim being made on each person in terms of identity, commitment, and vocation, a claim that involves being a person whose whole life is oriented toward crossing boundaries and transcending barriers. Christians encounter Jesus in the experience of "healing" that inaugurates this kind of life as well as in the ministry of healing itself, a ministry to which they are all expected to contribute: "I was sick and you visited me" (25:36).

Bibliography

I. PRIMARY SOURCES

Betz, Hans Dieter. *The Greek Magical Papyri in Translation: Including the Demotic Spells*. 2nd ed. Chicago: University of Chicago Press, 1992.

Charlesworth, James H. *The Old Testament Pseudepigrapha*. 2 vols. Garden City, NY: Doubleday, 1983, 1985.

Edelstein, Emma J., and Ludwig Edelstein. *Asclepius: Collection and Interpretation of the Testimonies*. 2 vols. Baltimore: Johns Hopkins University Press, 1945.

García Martínez, Florentino. *The Dead Sea Scrolls Translated: The Qumran Texts in English*. 2nd ed. Leiden: Brill, 1996.

Hooper, William D. *Cato: On Agriculture; Varro: On Agriculture*. Loeb Classical Library. Cambridge, MA: Harvard University Press, 1935.

Jones, Christopher P. *Philostratus: The Life of Apollonius of Tyana*. Loeb Classical Library. Cambridge, MA: Harvard University Press, 2005.

LiDonnici, Lynn R. *The Epidaurian Miracle Inscriptions: Text, Translation and Commentary*. Society of Biblical Literature Texts and Translations 36. Atlanta: Scholars, 1995.

Neusner, Jacob. *The Mishnah: A New Translation*. New Haven, CT: Yale University Press, 1988.

Rackham, H. *Pliny: Natural History*, volume 1. Loeb Classical Library. Cambridge, MA: Harvard University Press, 1938.

Throckmorton, Burton H. *Gospel Parallels: A Comparison of the Synoptic Gospels*. 5th ed. Nashville: Thomas Nelson, 1992.

II. SECONDARY SOURCES

Achtemeier, Paul J. "'And He Followed Him': Miracles and Discipleship in Mark 10:46–52." *Semeia* 11 (1978): 115–45.

———. *Jesus and the Miracle Tradition*. Eugene, OR: Cascade Books, 2008.

Alexander, P. S. "Incantations and Books of Magic." In *The History of the Jewish People in the Age of Jesus Christ*, rev. ed., edited by Emil Schürer, Geza Vermes, Fergus Millar, and Martin Goodman, 3:342–79. Edinburgh: T&T Clark, 1986.

Allison, Dale C. *The New Moses: A Matthean Typology*. Minneapolis: Fortress Press, 1993.

Anderson, Janice Capel. "Double and Triple Stories, the Implied Reader, and Redundancy in Matthew." *Semeia* 31 (1985): 71–89.

Assmann, J. "Isis." In *Dictionary of Deities and Demons in the Bible*, edited by Karel van der Toorn et al., 456–58. Leiden: Brill, 1999.

Aubert, Jean-Jacques. "Threatened Wombs: Aspects of Ancient Uterine Magic." *Greek, Roman, and Byzantine Studies* 30 (1990): 421–49.

Ault, Bradley A. *The Excavations at Ancient Halieis*, Volume 2: *The Houses. The Organization and Use of Domestic Space*. Bloomington: Indiana University Press, 2005.

Avalos, Hector. *Health Care and the Rise of Christianity*. Peabody, MA: Hendrickson, 1999.

———. "Introducing Sensory Criticism in Biblical Studies: Audiocentricity and Visiocentricity." In *This Abled Body: Rethinking Disabilities in Biblical Studies*, edited by Hector Avalos, Sarah J. Melcher, and Jeremy Schipper, 47–59. Atlanta: Society of Biblical Literature, 2007.

Avlamis, Pavlos. "Isis and the People in the *Life of Aesop*." In *Revelation, Literature, and Community in Late Antiquity*, Texte und Studien zum antiken Judentum 146, edited by Philippa Townsend and Moulie Vidas, 65–101. Tübingen: Mohr Siebeck, 2011.

Avrahami, Yael. *The Senses of Scripture: Sensory Perception in the Hebrew Bible*. New York: T&T Clark, 2012.

Baker-Fletcher, Karen. "More than Suffering: The Healing and Resurrecting Spirit of God." In *Womanist Theological Ethics: A Reader*, edited by Katie Geneva Cannon, Emilie M. Townes, and Angela D. Sims, 155–79. Louisville: Westminster John Knox, 2011.

Balabanski, Vicky. *Eschatology in the Making: Mark, Matthew and the Didache*. Society for New Testament Studies Monograph Series 97. Cambridge: Cambridge University Press, 1997.

Barclay, John M. G. *Against Apion: Translation and Commentary*. Leiden: Brill, 2007.

Barton, Stephen C. *Discipleship and Family Ties in Mark and Matthew*. Society for New Testament Studies Monograph Series 80. Cambridge: Cambridge University Press, 1994.

Baskin, Judith R. *Midrashic Women: Formations of the Feminine in Rabbinic Literature*. Hanover, NH: Brandeis University Press, 2002.

Batto, Bernard F. "The Sleeping God: An Ancient Near Eastern Motif of Divine Sovereignty." *Biblica* 68 (1987): 153–77.

Baumgarten, Joseph M. "Messianic Forgiveness of Sin in CD 14:19." In *Provo International Conference on the Dead Sea Scrolls: Technological Innovations, New Texts, and Reformulated Issues*, Studies on the Texts of the Desert of Judah 30, edited by Donald W. Parry and Eugene Charles Ulrich, 537–44. Leiden: Brill, 1999.

Baxter, Wayne. "Healing and the Son of David: Matthew's Warrant." *Novum Testamentum* 48 (2006): 36–50.

Beaton, Richard. *Isaiah's Christ in Matthew's Gospel.* Society for New Testament Studies Monograph Series 123. Cambridge: Cambridge University Press, 2002.

Beavis, Mary Ann. "From the Margin to the Way: A Feminist Reading of the Story of Bartimaeus." *Journal of Feminist Studies in Religion* 14 (1998): 19–39.

Black, Kathy. *A Healing Homiletic: Preaching and Disability.* Nashville: Abingdon, 1996.

Blenkinsopp, Joseph. "Miracles: Elisha and Hanina ben Dosa." In *Miracles in Jewish and Christian Antiquity: Imagining Truth*, edited by John C. Cavadini, 57–81. Notre Dame, IN: University of Notre Dame Press, 1999.

Blickenstaff, Marianne. *'While the Bridegroom is With Them': Marriage, Family, Gender and Violence in the Gospel of Matthew.* Journal for the Study of the New Testament: Supplement Series 292. London: T&T Clark, 2005.

Bohak, Gideon. *Ancient Jewish Magic: A History.* Cambridge: Cambridge University Press, 2008.

———. "Jewish Exorcism Before and After the Destruction of the Second Temple." In *Was 70 CE a Watershed in Jewish History? On Jews and Judaism Before and After the Destruction of the Second Temple*, Ancient Judaism and Early Christianity 78, edited by Daniel R. Schwartz and Zeev Weiss, 277–300. Leiden: Brill, 2012.

Booth, Roger P. *Jesus and the Laws of Purity: Tradition History and Legal History in Mark 7.* Journal for the Study of the New Testament: Supplement Series 13. Sheffield: JSOT, 1986.

Bowie, Ewen L. "Apollonius of Tyana: Tradition and Reality." *Aufstieg und Niedergang der römischen Welt* II.16.2 (1978): 1652–99.

Branden, Robert Charles. *Satanic Conflict and the Plot of Matthew.* New York: Peter Lang, 2006.

Brooks, Stephenson H. *Matthew's Community: The Evidence of His Special Sayings Material.* Journal for the Study of the New Testament: Supplement Series 16. Sheffield: JSOT, 1987.

Brown, Jeannine K. *The Disciples in Narrative Perspective: The Portrayal and Function of the Matthean Disciples.* Society of Biblical Literature Academia Biblica 9. Leiden: Brill, 2002.

———. "The Rhetoric of Hearing: The Use of the Isaianic Hearing Motif in Matthew 11:2–16:20." In *Built Upon The Rock: Studies in the Gospel of Matthew,* edited by Daniel M. Gurtner and John Nolland, 248–69. Grand Rapids: Eerdmans, 2008.

Brown, Michael L. *Israel's Divine Healer.* Grand Rapids: Zondervan, 1995.

Brown, Raymond E. "Jesus and Elisha." *Perspective* 12 (1971): 85–104.

———. *The Death of the Messiah: From Gethsemane to the Grave.* 2 vols. New York: Doubleday, 1994.

Buckley, Thomas W. *Seventy Times Seven: Sin, Judgment, and Forgiveness in Matthew.* Collegeville, MN: Liturgical, 1991.

Busch, Peter. "Solomon as a True Exorcist: The Testament of Solomon in Its Cultural Setting." In *The Figure of Solomon in Jewish, Christian and Islamic Tradition: King, Sage and Architect,* edited by Joseph Verheyden, 183–95. Leiden: Brill, 2013.

Caragounis, Chrys C. *The Son of Man: Vision and Interpretation.* Wissenschaftliche Untersuchungen zum Neuen Testament 38. Tübingen: Mohr Siebeck, 1986.

Carter, Warren. "Jesus' 'I Have Come' Statements in Matthew." *Catholic Biblical Quarterly* 60 (1998): 44–62.

———. *Matthew and the Margins: A Socio-Political and Religious Reading.* Sheffield: Sheffield Academic Press, 2000.

Chae, Young S. *Jesus as the Eschatological Shepherd: Studies in the Old Testament, Second Temple Judaism, and in the Gospel of Matthew.*

Wissenschaftliche Untersuchungen zum Neuen Testament 2.216. Tübingen: Mohr Siebeck, 2006.

Chaniotis, Angelos. "Illness and Cures in the Greek Propitiatory Inscriptions and Dedications of Lydia and Phrygia." In *Ancient Medicine in its Socio-Cultural Context*, edited by Ph. J. van der Eijk et al., 2:323–43. Amsterdam: Rodopi, 1995.

———. "Ritual Performances of Divine Justice: The Epigraphy of Confession, Atonement and Exaltation in Roman Asia Minor." In *From Hellenism to Islam: Cultural and Linguistic Change in the Roman Near East*, edited by Hannah M. Cotton et al., 115–53. Cambridge: Cambridge University Press, 2009.

Charette, Blaine. *Restoring Presence: The Spirit in Matthew's Gospel*. Sheffield: Sheffield Academic Press, 2000.

Christopoulos, Menelaos, Efimia Karakantza, and Olga Levaniou, eds. *Light and Darkness in Ancient Greek Myth and Religion*. Lanham, MD: Lexington, 2010.

Cohen, Shaye J. D. "The Significance of Yavneh: Pharisees, Rabbis, and the End of Jewish Sectarianism." *Hebrew Union College Annual* 55 (1984): 27–53.

Collins, Adela Yarbro. *Mark*. Hermeneia. Minneapolis: Fortress Press, 2007.

Collins, John J. *The Scepter and the Star: The Messiahs of the Dead Sea Scrolls and Other Ancient Literature*. New York: Doubleday, 1995.

Cooper, Ben. *Incorporated Servanthood: Commitment and Discipleship in the Gospel of Matthew*. Library of New Testament Studies. London: Bloomsbury, 2013.

Cope, O. Lamar. *Matthew, A Scribe Trained for the Kingdom of Heaven*. Washington, DC: Catholic Biblical Association, 1976.

Cotter, Wendy. *Miracles in Greco-Roman Antiquity*. London: Routledge, 1999.

Cousland, J. R. C. *The Crowds in the Gospel of Matthew*. Novum Testamentum Supplements 102. Leiden: Brill, 2002.

Craffert, Pieter F. *Illness, Health and Healing in the New Testament World: Perspectives on Health Care*. Pretoria: Biblia, 1999.

Creamer, Deborah Beth. *Disability and Christian Theology: Embodied Limits and Constructive Possibilities*. Oxford: Oxford University Press, 2009.

Crosby, Michael H. *House of Disciples: Church, Economics, and Justice in Matthew*. Maryknoll, NY: Orbis Books, 1988.

Crowe, Brandon D. *The Obedient Son: Deuteronomy and Christology in the Gospel of Matthew*. Beihefte zur Zeitschrift für die neutestamentliche Wissenschaft 188. Berlin: Walter de Gruyter, 2012.

Davies, Margaret. "Stereotyping the Other: The 'Pharisees' in the Gospel According to Matthew." In *Biblical Studies/Cultural Studies: The Third Sheffield Colloquium*, Journal for the Study of the Old Testament: Supplement Series 266, edited by Cheryl J. Exum and Stephen D. Moore, 415–32. Sheffield: Sheffield Academic Press, 1998.

Davies, W. D., and Dale C. Allison. *The Gospel According to Saint Matthew*. International Critical Commentary. 3 vols. London: T&T Clark, 1988, 1991, 1997.

Deissmann, Adolf. *Light from the Ancient East*. Grand Rapids: Baker, 1978.

Deutsch, Celia M. *Lady Wisdom, Jesus, and the Sages: Metaphor and Social Context in Matthew's Gospel*. Valley Forge, PA: Trinity Press International, 1996.

Dewey, Joanna. *Markan Public Debate: Literary Technique, Concentric Structure, and Theology in Mark 2:1–3:6*. Society of Biblical Literature Dissertation Series 48. Chico, CA: Scholars, 1980.

Donahue, John R. "Tax Collector." *Anchor Bible Dictionary* 6 (1992): 337–38.

———. "Tax Collectors and Sinners." *Catholic Biblical Quarterly* 33 (1971): 39–61.

Douglas, Mary. *Leviticus as Literature*. Oxford: Oxford University Press, 2000.

———. *Purity and Danger: An Analysis of the Concepts of Pollution and Taboo*. New York: Praeger, 1966.

Draycott, Jane. *Approaches to Healing in Roman Egypt*. BAR International Series 2416. Oxford: Archaeopress, 2012.

Droge, A. J. "Call Stories." *Anchor Bible Dictionary* 1 (1992): 821–23.

Dunlap, Susan J. *Caring Cultures: How Congregations Respond to the Sick*. Waco, TX: Baylor University Press, 2009.

Elliott, John H. "The Evil Eye and the Sermon on the Mount." *Biblical Interpretation* 2 (1994): 51–84.

Elman, Yaakov. "The World of the 'Sabboraim': Cultural Aspects of Post-Redactional Additions to the Bavli." In *Creation and Composition: The Contribution of the Bavli Redactors (Stammaim) to the Aggada*, Texte und Studien zum antiken Judentum 114, edited by Jeffrey L. Rubenstein, 383–415. Tübingen: Mohr Siebeck, 2005.

Evans, Abigail R. *The Healing Church: Practical Programs for Health Ministries*. Cleveland, OH: United Church Press, 1999.

Eve, Eric. *The Jewish Context of Jesus' Miracles*. Journal for the Study of the New Testament: Supplement Series 231. London: Sheffield, 2002.

———. *The Healer from Nazareth: Jesus' Miracles in Historical Context*. London: SPCK, 2009.

Faraone, Christopher A. "The Agonistic Context of Early Greek Binding Spells." In *Magika Hiera: Ancient Greek Magic and Religion*, edited by Christopher A. Faraone and Dirk Obbink, 3–32. New York: Oxford University Press, 1991.

Fleddermann, Harry T. "The Demands of Discipleship: Matt 8,19-22 par. Luke 9,57-62." In *The Four Gospels: Festschrift Frans Neirynck*, edited by F. Van Segbroek, 541–61. Leuven: Leuven University Press, 1992.

Fonrobert, Charlotte. "The Woman with a Blood-Flow (Mark 5.24-34) Revisited: Menstrual Laws and Jewish Culture in Christian Feminist Hermeneutics." In *Early Christian Interpretation of the Scriptures of Israel*, edited by Craig A. Evans and James A. Sanders, 121–40. Sheffield: Sheffield Academic Press, 1997.

Fontaine, Carole R. "Disabilities and Illness in the Bible: A Feminist Perspective." In *A Feminist Companion to the Hebrew Bible in the New Testament*, edited by Athalya Brenner, 286–300. Sheffield: Sheffield Academic Press, 1996.

Foster, Paul. *Community, Law and Mission in Matthew's Gospel*. Wissenschaftliche Untersuchungen zum Neuen Testament 2.177. Tübingen: Mohr Siebeck, 2004.

———. "Prophets and Prophetism in Matthew." In *Prophets and Prophecy in Jewish and Early Christian Literature*, Wissenschaftliche Untersuchungen zum Neuen Testament 2.286, edited by Joseph Verheyden, Korinna Zamfir, and Tobias Nicklas, 117–38. Tübingen: Mohr Siebeck, 2010.

France, R. T. *The Gospel of Matthew*. New International Commentary on the New Testament. Grand Rapids: Eerdmans, 2007.

Gaiser, Frederick J. *Healing in the Bible: Theological Insight for Christian Ministry*. Grand Rapids: Baker Academic, 2010.

Garrett, Susan R. *The Demise of the Devil: Magic and the Demonic in Luke's Writings*. Minneapolis: Fortress Press, 1989.

Gathercole, Simon J. *The Pre-existent Son: Recovering the Christologies of Matthew, Mark, and Luke*. Grand Rapids: Eerdmans, 2006.

Geller, Stephen A. *Sacred Enigmas: Literary Religion in the Hebrew Bible*. New York: Routledge, 1996.

Gerhardsson, Birger. *The Mighty Acts of Jesus According to Matthew*. Lund: CWK Gleerup, 1979.

Gowler, David B. "Text, Culture, and Ideology in Luke 7:1-10: A Dialogic Reading." In *Fabrics of Discourse: Essays in Honor of Vernon K. Robbins*, edited by David B. Gowler, L. Gregory Bloomquist, and Duane F. Watson, 89–125. Harrisburg, PA: Trinity Press International, 2003.

Grant, Colleen C. "Reinterpreting the Healing Narratives." In *Human Disability and the Service of God: Reassessing Religious Practice*, edited by Nancy L. Eiesland and Don E. Saliers, 72–87. Nashville: Abingdon, 1998.

Green, Joel B. *The Gospel of Luke*. New International Commentary on the New Testament. Grand Rapids: Eerdmans, 1997.

———, ed. *Hearing the New Testament: Strategies for Interpretation*. 2nd ed. Grand Rapids: Eerdmans, 2010.

Grimshaw, James P. *The Matthean Community and the World: An Analysis of Matthew's Food Exchange*. Studies in Biblical Literature 111. New York: Peter Lang, 2008.

Guijarro, Santiago. "The Family in First-Century Galilee." In *Constructing Early Christian Families: Family as Social Reality and Metaphor*, edited by Halvor Moxnes, 42–65. London: Routledge, 1997.

Gundry, Robert H. *Matthew: A Commentary on His Literary and Theological Art*. Grand Rapids: Eerdmans, 1982.

Gurtner, Daniel M. *The Torn Veil: Matthew's Exposition of the Death of Jesus*. Society for New Testament Studies Monograph Series 139. Cambridge: Cambridge University Press, 2007.

Hägerland, Tobias. "Jesus and the Rites of Repentance." *New Testament Studies* 52 (2006): 166–87.

Hagner, Donald A. *Matthew*. Word Biblical Commentary 33. 2 vols. Dallas: Word Books, 1993, 1995.

———. "Matthew's Eschatology." In *To Tell the Mystery: Essays on New Testament Eschatology in Honor of Robert H. Gundry*, Journal for the Study of the New Testament: Supplement Series 100, edited by Thomas E. Schmidt and Moisés Silva, 49–71. Sheffield: JSOT, 1994.

Hamilton, Gordon J. "A New Hebrew-Aramaic Incantation Text from Galilee: Rebuking the Sea." *Journal of Semitic Studies* 41 (1996): 215–49.

Hare, Douglas R. A. *The Son of Man Tradition*. Minneapolis: Fortress Press, 1990.

———. *The Theme of Jewish Persecution of Christians in the Gospel According to Saint Matthew.* Society for New Testament Studies Monograph Series 6. Cambridge: Cambridge University Press, 1967.

Haslam, Molly C. *A Constructive Theology of Intellectual Disability: Human Being as Mutuality and Response.* New York: Fordham University Press, 2012.

Hayes, Christine E. *Gentile Impurities and Jewish Identities: Intermarriage and Conversion from the Bible to the Talmud.* Oxford: Oxford University Press, 2002.

Hays, Richard B. *The Moral Vision of the New Testament: Community, Cross, New Creation.* San Francisco: HarperSanFrancisco, 1996.

Held, Heinz Joachim. "Matthew as Interpreter of the Miracle Stories." In *Tradition and Interpretation in Matthew,* edited by Günther Bornkamm, Gerhard Barth, and Heinz Joachim Held, 165–299. Philadelphia: Westminster, 1963.

Hengel, Martin. *The Charismatic Leader and His Followers.* New York: Crossroad, 1981.

Hiers, Richard H. "'Binding' and 'Loosing': The Matthean Authorizations." *Journal of Biblical Literature* 104 (1985): 233–50.

Hill, David. "On the Use and Meaning of Hosea VI.6 in Matthew's Gospel." *New Testament Studies* 24 (1977): 107–19.

Hogan, Larry P. *Healing in the Second Temple Period.* Novum Testamentum et Orbis Antiquus 21. Göttingen: Vandenhoeck & Ruprecht, 1992.

Holman, Susan R. "Healing the Social Leper in Gregory of Nyssa's and Greogory Nazianzus's *peri philoptōchias.*" *Harvard Theological Review* 92 (1999): 283–309.

Horne, Simon. "Those Who are Blind See: Some New Testament Uses of Impairment, Inability, and Paradox." In *Human Disability and the Service of God: Reassessing Religious Practice,* edited by Nancy L. Eiesland and Don E. Saliers, 88–101. Nashville: Abingdon, 1998.

Horsley, Richard A. *Jesus and the Spiral of Violence: Popular Jewish Resistance in Roman Palestine*. San Francisco: Harper & Row, 1987.

———. "Oral Communication, Oral Performance, and New Testament Interpretation." In *Method and Meaning: Essays on New Testament Interpretation in Honor of Harold W. Attridge*, edited by Andrew B. McGowan and Kent Harold Richards, 125–55. Atlanta: Society of Biblical Literature, 2011.

Howell, David B. *Matthew's Inclusive Story: A Study in the Narrative Rhetoric of the First Gospel*. Journal for the Study of the New Testament: Supplement Series 42. Sheffield: JSOT, 1990.

Huizenga, Leroy A. *The New Isaac: Tradition and Intertextuality in the Gospel of Matthew*. Novum Testamentum Supplements 131. Leiden: Brill, 2009.

Hull, John M. *Hellenistic Magic and the Synoptic Tradition*. Naperville, IL: Allenson, 1974.

Jones, Serene. "Graced Practices: Excellence and Freedom in the Christian Life." In *Practicing Theology: Beliefs and Practices in Christian Life*, edited by Miroslav Volf and Dorothy C. Bass, 51-77. Grand Rapids: Eerdmans, 2002.

Jones, W. H. S. "Ancient Roman Folk Medicine." *Journal of the History of Medicine* 12 (1957): 459–72.

Juel, Donald. *Messianic Exegesis: Christological Interpretation of the Old Testament in Early Christianity*. Philadelphia: Fortress Press, 1987.

Kee, Howard Clark. *Medicine, Miracle and Magic in New Testament Times*. Society for New Testament Studies Monograph Series 55. Cambridge: Cambridge University Press, 1986.

Keener, Craig S. *A Commentary on the Gospel of Matthew*. Grand Rapids: Eerdmans, 1999.

Kelber, Werner H. *The Oral and the Written Gospel: The Hermeneutics of Speaking and Writing in the Synoptic Tradition, Mark, Paul, and Q*. Philadelphia: Fortress Press, 1983.

Kingsbury, Jack D. "Observations on the 'Miracle Chapters' of Matthew 8–9." *Catholic Biblical Quarterly* 40 (1978): 559–73.

———. "On Following Jesus: The 'Eager' Scribe and the 'Reluctant' Disciple (Matthew 8.18-22)." *New Testament Studies* 34 (1988): 45–59.

———. "The Rhetoric of Comprehension in the Gospel of Matthew." *New Testament Studies* 41 (1995): 358–77.

———. "The Verb *akolouthein* ("To Follow") as an Index of Matthew's View of His Community." *Journal of Biblical Literature* 97 (1978): 56–73.

Kittel, Gerhard. "*akouō*." *Theological Dictionary of the New Testament* 1 (1964): 216–25.

Kloppenborg, John S. *Q Parallels: Synopsis, Critical Notes and Concordance.* Sonoma, CA: Polebridge, 1988.

———. *Q, The Earliest Gospel: An Introduction to the Original Stories and Sayings of Jesus.* Louisville: Westminster John Knox, 2008.

Koester, Craig. "Hearing, Seeing, and Believing in the Gospel of John." *Biblica* 70 (1989): 327–48.

Kupp, David D. *Matthew's Emmanuel: Divine Presence and God's People in the First Gospel.* Society for New Testament Studies Monograph Series 90. Cambridge: Cambridge University Press, 1996.

Kvalbein, Hans. "The Wonders of the End-Time: Metaphoric Language in 4Q521 and the Interpretation of Matthew 11.5 par." *Journal for the Study of the Pseudepigrapha* 18 (1998): 87–110.

Laes, Christian. "Silent History? Speech Impairment in Roman Antiquity." In *Disabilities in Roman Antiquity: Disparate Bodies A Capite ad Calcem,* edited by Christian Laes, C. F. Goodey, M. Lynn Rose, 145–80. Leiden: Brill, 2013.

Lambert, David A. "Fast, Fasting." In *New Interpreter's Dictionary of the Bible,* 2:431–34. Nashville: Abingdon, 2007.

Lawrence, Louise J. "Reading Matthew's Gospel with Deaf Culture." In *Matthew*, Texts @ Contexts, edited by Nicole Wilkinson Duran and James P. Grimshaw, 155–71. Minneapolis: Fortress Press, 2013.

———. *Sense and Stigma in the Gospels: Depictions of Sensory-Disabled Characters*. Oxford: Oxford University Press, 2013.

Leske, Adrian M. "The Influence of Isaiah 40–66 on Christology in Matthew and Luke: A Comparison." *Society of Biblical Literature Seminar Papers* 33 (1994): 897–916.

Levine, Amy-Jill. "Discharging Responsibility: Matthean Jesus, Biblical Law, and Hemorrhaging Woman." In *A Feminist Companion to Matthew*, edited by Amy-Jill Levine, 70–87. Cleveland, OH: Pilgrim, 2001.

LiDonnici, Lynn R. *The Epidaurian Miracle Inscriptions: Text, Translation and Commentary*. Society of Biblical Literature Texts and Translations 36. Atlanta: Scholars, 1995.

Lightstone, Jack N. *The Commerce of the Sacred: Mediation of the Divine Among Jews in the Graeco-Roman Diaspora*. Chico, CA: Scholars, 1984.

Lincoln, Andrew T. *The Gospel According to Saint John*. Black's New Testament Commentaries 4. London: Continuum, 2005.

Loader, W. R. G. "Son of David, Blindness, Possession, and Duality in Matthew." *Catholic Biblical Quarterly* 44 (1982): 570–85.

Louw, J. P. "The Structure of Matt 8.1–9.35." *Neotestamentica* 11 (1977): 91–97.

Love, Stuart L. "Jesus Heals the Hemorrhaging Woman." In *The Social Setting of Jesus and the Gospels*, edited by Wolfgang Stegemann, Bruce J. Malina, and Gerd Theissen, 85–101. Minneapolis: Fortress Press, 2002.

Luomanen, Petri. *Entering the Kingdom of Heaven: A Study on the Structure of Matthew's View of Salvation*. Wissenschaftliche Untersuchungen zum Neuen Testament 2.101. Tübingen: Mohr Siebeck, 1998.

Luz, Ulrich. *Matthew: A Commentary*. Hermeneia. 3 vols. Minneapolis: Fortress Press, 2001, 2005, 2007.

————. *Studies in Matthew*. Grand Rapids: Eerdmans, 2005.

————. *The Theology of the Gospel of Matthew*. Cambridge: Cambridge University Press, 1995.

Macaskill, Grant. *Revealed Wisdom and Inaugurated Eschatology in Ancient Judaism and Early Christianity*. Journal for the Study of Judaism: Supplement Series 115. Leiden: Brill, 2007.

Madden, Patrick J. *Jesus' Walking on the Sea: An Investigation of the Origin of the Narrative Account*. Beihefte zur Zeitschrift für die neutestamentliche Wissenschaft 81. Berlin: Walter de Gruyter, 1997.

Malbon, Elizabeth Struthers. *Narrative Space and Mythic Meaning in Mark*. San Francisco: Harper & Row, 1986.

Marcus, Joel. *Mark*. Anchor Bible 27. 2 vols. New Haven, CT: Yale University Press, 2000, 2009.

Mattingly, Cheryl. *Healing Dramas and Clinical Plots: The Narrative Structure of Experience*. Cambridge: Cambridge University Press, 1998.

Mattingly, Cheryl, and Linda C. Garro, eds. *Narrative and the Cultural Construction of Illness and Healing*. Berkeley: University of California Press, 2000.

McCloughry, Roy, and Wayne Morris. *Making a World of Difference: Christian Reflections on Disability*. London: SPCK, 2002.

Meier, John P. *A Marginal Jew: Rethinking the Historical Jesus*. 4 vols. New York: Doubleday, 1991, 1994, 2001, 2009.

Melcher, Sarah J. "With Whom Do the Disabled Associate? Metaphorical Interplay in the Latter Prophets." In *This Abled Body: Rethinking Disabilities in Biblical Studies*, edited by Hector Avalos, Sarah J. Melcher, and Jeremy Schipper, 115–29. Atlanta: Society of Biblical Literature, 2007.

Menken, Maarten J. J. "The Source of the Quotation From Isaiah 53:4 in Matthew 8:17." *Novum Testamentum* 39 (1997): 313–27.

Metzger, James A., and James P. Grimshaw. "Reading Matthew's Healing Narratives from the Perspectives of the Caregiver and the Disabled." In *Matthew*, Texts @ Contexts, edited by Nicole Wilkinson Duran and James P. Grimshaw, 133–54. Minneapolis: Fortress Press, 2013.

Meyers, Eric M. "The Problems of Gendered Space in Syro-Palestinian Domestic Architecture: The Case of Roman-Period Galilee." In *From Antioch to Alexandria: Recent Studies in Domestic Architecture*, edited by Katharina Galor and Tomasz Waliszewski, 107–23. Warsaw: University of Warsaw Press, 2007.

Milgrom, Jacob. *Leviticus*. Anchor Bible 3. 3 vols. New York: Doubleday, 1991, 2000, 2001.

Mitchell, David, and Sharon Snyder. "'Jesus Thrown Everything Off Balance': Disability and Redemption in Biblical Literature." In *This Abled Body: Rethinking Disabilities in Biblical Studies*, edited by Hector Avalos, Sarah J. Melcher, and Jeremy Schipper, 173–83. Atlanta: Society of Biblical Literature, 2007.

———. *Narrative Prosthesis: Disability and the Dependencies of Discourse*. Ann Arbor: University of Michigan Press, 2000.

Moltmann, Jürgen. "Liberate Yourselves by Accepting One Another." In *Human Disability and the Service of God: Reassessing Religious Practice*, edited by Nancy L. Eiesland and Don E. Saliers, 105–22. Nashville: Abingdon, 1998.

Moss, Candida R. "Blurred Vision and Ethical Confusion: The Rhetorical Function of Matthew 6:22-23." *Catholic Biblical Quarterly* 73 (2011): 757–76.

———. "The Man with the Flow of Power: Porous Bodies in Mark 5:25-34." *Journal of Biblical Literature* 129 (2010): 507–19.

Moss, Charlene McAfee. *The Zechariah Tradition and the Gospel of Matthew*. Beihefte zur Zeitschrift für die neutestamentliche Wissenschaft 156. Berlin: Walter de Gruyter, 2008.

Mullen, J. Patrick. *Dining with Pharisees*. Collegeville, MN: Liturgical, 2004.

Neusner, Jacob. *The Idea of Purity in Ancient Judaism*. Studies in Judaism in Late Antiquity 1. Leiden: Brill, 1973.

Nolland, John. *The Gospel of Matthew*. New International Greek Testament Commentary. Grand Rapids: Eerdmans, 2005.

Norris, Frederick W. "Isis, Sarapis and Demeter in Antioch of Syria." *Harvard Theological Review* 75 (1982): 189–207.

Novakovic, Lidija. *Messiah, the Healer of the Sick: A Study of Jesus as the Son of David in the Gospel of Matthew*. Wissenschaftliche Untersuchungen zum Neuen Testament 2.170. Tübingen: Mohr Siebeck, 2003.

Nussbaum, Martha C. *The Therapy of Desire: Theory and Practice in Hellenistic Ethics*. Princeton, NJ: Princeton University Press, 1994.

Nutton, Vivian. "Healers in the Medical Market Place: Towards a Social History of Graeco-Roman Medicine." In *Medicine in Society: Historical Essays*, edited by Andrew Wear, 15–58. Cambridge: Cambridge University Press, 1992.

———. *Ancient Medicine*. London: Routledge, 2004.

Olyan, Saul M. *Disability in the Hebrew Bible: Interpreting Mental and Physical Differences*. Cambridge: Cambridge University Press, 2008.

Orton, David E. *The Understanding Scribe: Matthew and the Apocalyptic Ideal*. Journal for the Study of the New Testament: Supplement Series 25. Sheffield: Sheffield Academic Press, 1989.

Ottenheijm, Eric. "The Shared Meal—A Therapeutic Device: The Function and Meaning of Hos 6:6 in Matt 9:10-13." *Novum Testamentum* 53 (2011): 1–21.

Overman, J. Andrew. *Matthew's Gospel and Formative Judaism: The Social World of the Matthean Community*. Minneapolis: Fortress Press, 1990.

Pesch, Rudolf. "The Markan Version of the Healing of the Gerasene Demoniac." *Ecumenical Review* 23 (1971): 349–76.

Pilch, John J. *Healing in the New Testament: Insights from Medical and Mediterranean Anthropology*. Minneapolis: Fortress Press, 2000.

Plumwood, Val. *Feminism and the Mastery of Nature*. London: Routledge, 1993.

Powell, Mark Allan, ed. *Methods for Matthew*. Cambridge: Cambridge University Press, 2009.

Pregeant, Russell. "The Wisdom Passages in Matthew's Story." In *Treasures New and Old: Recent Contributions to Matthean Studies*, edited by David R. Bauer and Mark Allen Powell, 197–232. Atlanta: Scholars, 1996.

Priest, J. "A Note on the Messianic Banquet." In *The Messiah: Developments in Earliest Judaism and Christianity*, edited by James H. Charlesworth et al., 222–38. Minneapolis: Fortress Press, 1992.

Räisänen, Heikki. *The 'Messianic Secret' in Mark*. Edinburgh: T&T Clark, 1990.

Raphael, Rebecca. *Biblical Corpora: Representations of Disability in Hebrew Biblical Literature*. New York: T&T Clark, 2008.

———. "Whoring after Cripples: On the Intersection of Gender and Disability Imagery in Jeremiah." In *Disability Studies and Biblical Literature*, edited by Candida R. Moss and Jeremy Schipper, 103–16. New York: Palgrave Macmillan, 2011.

Reed, Jonathan L. *Archaeology and the Galilean Jesus: A Re-examination of the Evidence*. Harrisburg, PA: Trinity Press International, 2000.

Regev, Eyal. "Pure Individualism: The Idea of Non-Priestly Purity in Ancient Judaism." *Journal for the Study of Judaism* 31 (2000): 176–202.

Reinders, Hans S. *Receiving the Gift of Friendship: Profound Disability, Theological Anthropology, and Ethics*. Grand Rapids: Eerdmans, 2008.

Repschinski, Boris. "'For He Will Save His People from Their Sins' (Matthew 1:21): A Christology for Christian Jews." *Catholic Biblical Quarterly* 68 (2006): 248–67.

———. "Re-Imagining the Presence of God: The Temple and the Messiah in the Gospel of Matthew." *Australian Biblical Review* 54 (2006): 37–49.

———. *The Controversy Stories in the Gospel of Matthew*. Forschungen zur Religion und Literatur des Alten und Neuen Testaments 189. Göttingen: Vandenhoeck & Ruprecht, 2000.

Rey-Coquais, Jean-Paul. "Decapolis." *Anchor Bible Dictionary* 2 (1992): 116–21.

Reynolds, Thomas E. *Vulnerable Communion: A Theology of Disability and Hospitality*. Grand Rapids: Brazos, 2008.

Riches, John K. *Conflicting Mythologies: Identity Formation in the Gospels of Mark and Matthew*. Studies of the New Testament and Its World. Edinburgh: T&T Clark, 2000.

Ridgway, John K. *"Let Your Peace Come Upon It": Healing and Peace in Matthew 10:1-15*. Studies in Biblical Literature 2. New York: Peter Lang, 1999.

Robbins, Vernon K. *Exploring the Texture of Texts: A Guide to Socio-Rhetorical Interpretation*. Harrisburg, PA: Trinity Press International, 1996.

———. "The Woman Who Touched Jesus' Garment: Socio-Rhetorical Analysis of the Synoptic Account." *New Testament Studies* 33 (1987): 502–15.

Runesson, Anders. "Judging Gentiles in the Gospel of Matthew: Between 'Othering' and Inclusion." In *Jesus, Matthew's Gospel and Early Christianity: Studies in Memory of Graham N. Stanton*, edited by Daniel M. Gurtner, Joel Willitts, and Richard A. Burridge, 133–51. Edinburgh: T&T Clark, 2011.

Saldarini, Anthony J. *Matthew's Christian-Jewish Community*. Chicago: University of Chicago Press, 1994.

———. *Pharisees, Scribes and Sadducees in Palestinian Society: A Sociological Approach*. Grand Rapids: Eerdmans, 2001.

Sanders, E. P. *Jesus and Judaism*. Philadelphia: Fortress Press, 1985.

Sanders, E. P., and Margaret Davies. *Studying the Synoptic Gospels*. London: SCM; Philadelphia: Trinity Press International, 1989.

Savran, George. "Seeing is Believing: On the Relative Priority of Visual and Verbal Perception of the Divine." *Biblical Interpretation* 17 (2009): 320–61.

Sawicki, Marianne. *Crossing Galilee: Architectures of Contact in the Occupied Land of Jesus*. Harrisburg, PA: Trinity Press International, 2000.

Scarborough, John. "Adaptation of Folk Medicines in the Formal Materia Medica of Classical Antiquity." In *Folklore and Folk Medicines*, edited by John Scarborough, 21–32. Madison, WI: American Institute of the History of Pharmacy, 1987.

Schipper, Jeremy. *Disability and Isaiah's Suffering Servant*. Oxford: Oxford University Press, 2011.

———. "Disabling Israelite Leadership: 2 Samuel 6:23 and Other Images of Disability in the Deuteronomistic History." In *This Abled Body: Rethinking Disabilities in Biblical Studies*, edited by Hector Avalos, Sarah J. Melcher, and Jeremy Schipper, 103–13. Atlanta: Society of Biblical Literature, 2007.

Senior, Donald. "Between Two Worlds: Gentiles and Jewish Christians in Matthew's Gospel." *Catholic Biblical Quarterly* 61 (1999): 1–23.

Sheets, Dwight D. "Jesus as Demon-Possessed." In *Who Do My Opponents Say I Am? An Investigation of the Accusations Against Jesus*, edited by Scot McKnight and Joseph B. Modica, 27–49. London: T&T Clark, 2008.

Sim, David C. *The Gospel of Matthew and Christian Judaism: The History and Social Setting of the Matthean Community*. Studies of the New Testament and Its World. Edinburgh: T&T Clark, 1998.

Smit, Peter-Ben. *Fellowship and Food in the Kingdom: Eschatological Meals and Scenes of Utopian Abundance in the New Testament*. Wissenschaftliche Untersuchungen zum Neuen Testament 2.234. Tübingen: Mohr Siebeck, 2008.

Smith, Dennis E. *From Symposium to Eucharist: The Banquet in the Early Christian World*. Minneapolis: Fortress Press, 2003.

Sorensen, Eric. *Possession and Exorcism in the New Testament and Early Christianity*. Wissenschaftliche Untersuchungen zum Neuen Testament 2.157. Tübingen: Mohr Siebeck, 2002.

Stanton, Graham N. *A Gospel for a New People: Studies in Matthew*. Edinburgh: T&T Clark, 1992.

Stendahl, Krister. *The School of St. Matthew and its Use of the Old Testament*. Philadelphia: Fortress Press, 1968.

Stewart, David Tabb. "Sexual Disabilities in the Hebrew Bible." In *Disability Studies and Biblical Literature*, edited by Candida R. Moss and Jeremy Schipper, 67–87. New York: Palgrave Macmillan, 2011.

Stewart-Sykes, Alistair. "Matthew's 'Miracle Chapters': From Composition to Narrative, and Back Again." *Scripture Bulletin* 25 (1995): 55–65.

Strange, James F., and Hershel Shanks. "Has the House Where Jesus Stayed in Capernaum Been Found?" *Biblical Archaeology Review* 8, no. 6 (1982): 26–37.

Suggs, M. Jack. *Wisdom, Christology, and Law in Matthew's Gospel*. Cambridge, MA: Harvard University Press, 1970.

Swinton, John. *Resurrecting the Person: Friendship and the Care of People with Mental Health Problems*. Nashville: Abingdon, 2000.

Talbert, Charles H. *Matthew*. Paideia. Grand Rapids: Baker Academic, 2010.

Taylor, Joan E. *The Essenes, The Scrolls, and the Dead Sea*. Oxford: Oxford University Press, 2012.

Telford, William R. *The Barren Temple and the Withered Tree*. Journal for the Study of the New Testament: Supplement Series 1. Sheffield: JSOT, 1980.

Theissen, Gerd. *The Miracle Stories of the Early Christian Tradition*. Philadelphia: Fortress Press, 1983.

Theophilos, Michael. *Jesus as New Moses in Matthew 8–9: Jewish Typology in First Century Greek Literature*. Piscataway, NJ: Gorgias, 2011.

Thiselton, Anthony C. *Hermeneutics: An Introduction*. Grand Rapids: Eerdmans, 2009.

Thompson, William G. "Reflections on the Composition of Mt 8:1–9:34." *Catholic Biblical Quarterly* 33 (1971): 365–88.

Tilford, Nicole L. "Taste and See: Perceptual Metaphors in Israelite and Early Jewish Sapiential Epistemology." PhD diss., Emory University, 2013.

Twelftree, Graham H. *In the Name of Jesus: Exorcism Among Early Christians*. Grand Rapids: Baker Academic, 2007.

Unschuld, Paul U. "Culture and Pharmaceutics: Some Epistemological Observations on Pharmacological Systems in Ancient Europe and Medieval China." In *The Context of Medicines in Developing Countries: Studies in Pharmaceutical Anthropology*, edited by Sjaak van der Geest and Susan Reynolds Whyte, 179–97. Dordrecht: Kluwer Academic, 1988.

van der Horst, Pieter W., and Judith H. Newman. *Early Jewish Prayers in Greek*. Commentaries on Early Jewish Literature. Berlin: Walter de Gruyter, 2008.

Vanhoozer, Kevin J. "The Reader in New Testament Interpretation." In *Hearing the New Testament: Strategies for Interpretation*, edited by Joel B. Green, 301–28. Grand Rapids: Eerdmans, 1995.

Vermes, Geza. *Jesus the Jew: A Historian's Reading of the Gospels*. Philadelphia: Fortress Press, 1981.

Versnel, H. S. *Coping with the Gods: Wayward Readings in Greek Theology*. Religions in the Graeco-Roman World 173. Leiden: Brill, 2011.

Vledder, Evert-Jan. *Conflict in the Miracle Stories: A Socio-Exegetical Study of Matthew 8 and 9*. Journal for the Study of the New Testament: Supplement Series 152. Sheffield: Sheffield Academic Press, 1997.

Wahlen, Clinton. *Jesus and the Impurity of Spirits in the Synoptic Gospels*. Wissenschaftliche Untersuchungen zum Neuen Testament 2.185. Tübingen: Mohr Siebeck, 2004.

Wainwright, Elaine M. *Towards A Feminist Critical Reading of the Gospel According to Matthew*. Beihefte zur Zeitschrift für die neutestamentliche Wissenschaft 60. Berlin: Walter de Gruyter, 1991.

————. *Women Healing/Healing Women: The Genderization of Healing in Early Christianity*. London: Equinox, 2006.

Weaver, Dorothy Jean. *Matthew's Missionary Discourse: A Literary Critical Analysis*. Journal for the Study of the New Testament: Supplement Series 38. Sheffield: JSOT, 1990.

Wickkiser, Bronwen L. "Asklepios in Greek and Roman Corinth." In *Corinth in Context: Comparative Studies on Religion and Society*, Novum Testamentum Supplements 134, edited by Steven J. Friesen, David N. Schowalter, and James C. Walters, 37–66. Leiden: Brill, 2010.

Willitts, Joel. *Matthew's Messianic Shepherd-King: In Search of 'The Lost Sheep of the House of Israel'*. Beihefte zur Zeitschrift für die neutestamentliche Wissenschaft 147. Berlin: Walter de Gruyter, 2007.

Wilson, Walter T. "A Third Form of Righteousness: The Theme and Contribution of Matthew 6.19–7.12 in the Sermon on the Mount." *New Testament Studies* 53 (2007): 303–24.

————. "Seen in Secret: Inconspicuous Piety and Alternative Subjectivity in Matthew 6:1-6, 16-18." *Catholic Biblical Quarterly* 72 (2010): 475–97.

Wire, Antoinette Clark. "Ancient Miracle Stories." *Forum* 2 (1986): 77–84.

————. "The Structure of the Gospel Miracle Stories." *Semeia* 11 (1978): 83–113.

Witherington, Ben. *Jesus the Sage: The Pilgrimage of Wisdom*. Minneapolis: Fortress Press, 1994.

Witmer, Amanda. *Jesus, the Galilean Exorcist: His Exorcisms in Social and Political Context*. Library of Historical Jesus Studies 10. London: T&T Clark, 2012.

Witt, R. E. *Isis in the Graeco-Roman World*. Ithaca, NY: Cornell University Press, 1971.

Wright, David P., and Richard N. Jones. "Leprosy." *Anchor Bible Dictionary* 4 (1992): 277–82.

Yang, Yong-Eui. *Jesus and the Sabbath in Matthew's Gospel*. Journal for the Study of the New Testament: Supplement Series 139. Sheffield: Sheffield Academic Press, 1997.

Yassif, Eli. *The Hebrew Folktale: History, Genre, Meaning*. Bloomington: Indiana University Press, 1999.

Yong, Amos. *The Bible, Disability, and the Church: A New Vision of the People of God*. Grand Rapids: Eerdmans, 2011.

Young, Allan. "The Anthropologies of Illness and Sickness." *Annual Review of Anthropology* 11 (1982): 257–85.

Index of Authors

Index of Subjects

Index of Biblical and Ancient References